PURĀTATTVA

BULLETIN OF THE INDIAN ARCHAEOLOGICAL SOCIETY

NUMBER 31 2000-2001

Editors

K.N. DIKSHIT AND K.S. RAMACHANDRAN

INDIAN ARCHAEOLOGICAL SOCIETY
NEW DELHI

Purātattva is published annually. The annual subscription – India Rs. 700. Other countries U.S. $ 50

Manuscripts (whether in the form of articles or notes or book reviews) offered for publication, should be sent to the Editor, Purātattva, Indian Archaeological Society, B-17, Qutab Institutional Area, South of IIT, New Delhi - 110 016

Published by: The Indian Archaeological Society, B–17, Qutab Institutional Area, South of IIT, New Delhi- 110 016. Ph: 6960654, 6523728, Tele Fax: 011-6960654

Produced by: AQUARELLE, H-24, Green Park Extension, New Delhi-110 016. Tel: 6166426
Printed at : Multi Colour Services, New Delhi - 110 020

PURĀTATTVA

CONTENTS

ANNOUNCEMENT

CENTRE FOR RESEARCH & TRAINING IN HISTORY,
ARCHAEOLOGY AND PALAEO-ENVIRONEMNT

(Sponsored by Indian Archaeological Society)

The University Grants Commission has given its recognition to the Centre for Research & Training in History, Archaeology and Palaeo-Environment, vide its letter No. F-23-1/2000(ASC/ER) Dt. 3rd November, 2001 to conduct **Refresher Courses in Archaeology**. The lecturers of Universities and Colleges in India desirous of joining these courses may write to the undersigned for details.

Dr. S.P. Gupta
(Course Director)

B-17, Qutab Institutional Area, New Delhi - 110016
Tel: 011-6960654; 6852695 Fax: 011-6960654
e-mail: ias_newdelhi@yahoo.co.uk
iasnewdelhi@redifmail.com

Obituaries

Shri Krishna Deva
(24.08.1914–07.10.2001)

Shri Krishna Deva was born on 24th August 1914 at Biharsharif in a very respected family of businessmen. He studied upto Intermediate in Arts in his hometown, graduated with honours from Patna College in 1935 and secured first class first position in M.A. in Ancient History and Culture in 1937 at Banaras Hindu University. Shri Krishna Deva joined the Banaras Hindu University in 1937 as an Assistant Professor. Later he joined the Archaeological Survey of India and retired as the Director in January 1973.

In the Archaeological Survey of India, Shri Krishna Deva carried out explorations in Sind with N.G. Majumdar in 1938 and with Sir Aurel Stein in 1940-42 in western Rajasthan, Bahawalpur and Baluchistan. He participated in Rao Bahadur, K.N. Dikshit's excavations at Ahichhatra and Sir Mortimer Wheeler's excavations at Taxila, Harappa and Arikamedu and wrote the pottery reports of these sites, which are regarded as models for all subsequent reports on pottery in India. He conducted independent excavations at Nagar, Agroha, Kashipur, Kumrahar (Patliputra) and Vaishali from 1940 to 1950. As Superintendent of various circles of Archaeological Survey of India for nearly sixteen years, he handled antiquities and carried out conservation of the monuments. He held the charge of Temple Survey Project for North India and produced memorable work on Khajuraho temple.

After his retirement, as the Director from Archaeological Survey of India, Shri Krishna Deva was appointed to work as the Archaeological Adviser to his Majesty's Government of Nepal (1973-75), as Director of Birla Academy of Art, Calcutta (1976-77), and as a Research Consultant for the American Institute of Indian Studies, Varanasi (1977-87). The Volume II of Encyclopedia of Indian temple architecture, a research project of International repute, was completed due to his untiring efforts and contributions.

He has contributed nearly one hundred research papers on various aspects of Indian art, architecture, epigraphy, numismatics and archaeology in research journals of India and abroad and chapters in more than a dozen prestigious volumes.

Shri Krishna Deva had widely travelled and delivered lectures in various Indian, American and British Universities on Indian art and architecture. He was the General President of the Indian Archaeological Society at Varanasi in 1986 and had also presided over the International Colloquium of Numismatics Studies at Anjaneri, Nasik in January 1987. Shri Deva was the editor of the Journal of the Indian Society of Oriental Art, started by Abanindranath Tagore and Stella Kramrisch. He was actively associated with Bihar Puravid Parishad, and was a member of its advisory Board.

He died on the 7 th October, 2001 at New Delhi.

S. P. Gupta

Dr. S.C. Ray
(20.12.1924-12.01.2001)

Noted archaeologist and numismatist Dr Sunil C Ray was born on 20th December 1924 at Tamluk, West Bengal. He took his M.A. degree from the Calcutta University and became a James Princep Fellow in Epigraphy and Numismatics in the Asiatic Society in 1948-50. He was the recipient of the Griffith Prizeman of the University of Calcutta. He joined the Archaeological Survey of India in 1950.

His research publication entitled "The Early History and Culture of Kashmir" was widely acclaimed as an outstanding piece of study on a very important region of India. In this work he has not only given a connected narrative of Kashmir's political history based on all available sources, literary, archaeological, numismatic, foreign allusions, etc. but he has also brought out the cultural, religious and social development of the people of the valley. The work was approved for the Doctor of Philosophy degree from the University of Calcutta in 1951.

He received specialized training in archaeology at Paris and Strasbourg. He remained in charge of various circles like Patna, Bhopal, Calcutta and Agra. He joined the Indian Museum, Calcutta in 1977 where he served as the Director from 1977 to 1984. Finally he was invited by the Calcutta University, Department of Archaeology to serve as a Professor from 1984 to 1989.

He also contributed a large number of research papers to various research journals in India and abroad. His last work was on 'Coins and Culture' as a senior research fellow of the ICHR. He was associated as a member of various national and International research bodies and was actively serving till the last moment of his life. He was also the Chairman of Indian National Committee of International Council of Museum and in this capacity he participated in various UNESCO conferences regarding museum development, in the Asia-Pacific Countries. He also attended several International conferences held at Berlin, etc. to present his research papers.

In the later years of his life, he devoted himself off from his professional life and divertedd his interests to Vedantic Philosophy. During this period, he delivered lectures on Vedanta and Vedantic Philosophy.

He passed away on January 12, 2001 at the age of 76 at his residence in Golf Garden, Calcutta. He is survived by his wife and two sons.

S. S. Biswas

Shri R. Sengupta
(7.6.1926-18.5.2001)

Shri R. Sengupta was born at Dhaka (now in Bangladesh) and after his training in Civil Engineering in Assaruly School of Engineering, he joined the Survey in 1947. After initial theoretical and practical training in archaeological conservation in the Archaeological Survey of India, he commenced his professional career with deep interest. He worked in the Archaeological Survey of India for 36 years (1947-1984) and for the last 21 years as the Head of the Conservation Branch with distinction.

During the early career, he left no stone unturned in understanding the methodology of conservation but also studied different problems of architectural monuments and related aspects such as different styles of architectural monuments and materials. Among the notable works mention may he made of his work of conservation of rock-cut caves of Ajanta and Ellora. These caves were taken over by the ASI from the Department of Archaeology, Nizam Government in 1951 on the merger of the States with Indian Union after Independence. The experience gained in conserving these rock-cut monuments helped him in conserving the colossal Buddha images and paintings at Bamiyan, Afghanistan. The work at Bamiyan lasted for nearly eight years (1969-77), which also included repairs to Khwaja Parsa Mosque at Balkh. Later he also prepared a report on Angkor Wat temples in 1980 for their conservation and restoration. He was awarded the honour of Padmashri in appreciation of his work at Bamiyan.

He was a member of the Training Committee of International Council of Monuments and Sites (ICOMOS) and also Indian Representative (1979-84) for the study of the Restoration and Preservation of Cultural Property.

Along with his interest in convservation, he contributed research articles on architecture and iconography, nearing to one hundred in Indian and International Journals.

In the passing away of Padmashri R. Sengupta at the age of 75, the country has lost a very eminent expert in the field of Heritage Conservation. The void caused by his death is difficult to be bridged.

He is survived by his wife and a son and a daughter.

M.N. Deshpande

Professor Ram Chandra Gaur
(1929-2001)

Professor Ram Chandra Gaur (R.C. Gaur) was born in 1929. He did his Post-Graduation in History with specialization in Ancient India from Allahabad University, and started his career from the U.P. State Museum at Lucknow. He joined the Department of History, Aligarh Muslim University as a Lecturer in History in 1958. During the last years of his career he became the Chairman of Department of History of the University (1988-89), and Dean of the Faculty of Social Sciences (1.8.88-3.7.89). He retired from this Department on 3.7.89.

His career as an archaeologist started with exploration of several sites and excavation at Atranjikhera (District Etah) in 1962 as its Director. Later on he took up the excavations at Fatehpur Sikri in collaboration with the Archaeological Survey of India as a National Project.

Professor Gaur learnt the latest techniques of archaeology at the Institute of Archaeology, London, where he was a Visiting Fellow in the year 1971-72.

After his retirement in 1989, he became a Senior Fellow of the Indian Council of Historical Research and completed the report of excavations at Fatehpur Sikri. During his academic career he took active part in several seminars and conferences.

He was a member of several academic bodies, including the Indian Archaaeological Society and the Indian Society for Prehistoric and Quaternary Studies. He was a Life Fellow of the Royal Asiatic Society of Great Britain and Ireland. He had travelled extensively, visited archaeological sites and delivered lecturers in India and abroad. He visited Great Britain, Egypt, some of the European and Middle Eastern countries, former Soviet Union and U.S.A. On behalf of the Government of India, he visited Cyprus to explore the possibility of cooperation in the field of archaeology between the two countries. He delivered Presidential address of the Indian Archaeological Society in the year 1988.

He published sixty research papers and articles, in International and Indian journals and five well known books on excavations. His report on Excavations at Atranjikhera (1983) is a welcome addition to the Indian Archaeology.

He passed away in the morning of 13th August, 2001 at Varanasi. He is survived by two sons and a daughter.

M.D.N. Sahi

Professor B.R. Grover
(10.02.1923-10.05.2001)

Professor B. R. Grover (Baldev Raj Grover) was the Chairman of the Indian Council of Historical Research, New Delhi from 25-10-1999 to 10-05-2001. He was born on 10th February 1923 at Shadiwal, District Gujarat, Punjab. After completing Master's Degree in History and Political Science, he started his teaching career as a lecturer in History in 1946 at S. D. College (Punjab University), Lahore where he continued till August 1947. After Independence, he served in various Universities and Institutions between January 1948 and March 1985 including Camp College, New Delhi and Jamia Milia, Islamia, New Delhi. He was also the Director of ICHR.

At the beginning of his career, he received training at Paris in France under the auspices of a UNESCO seminar, with an objective for promoting history as means of international understanding. Following this, he contributed two volumes on the History of Great Britain and a few books on social studies towards the fulfillment of UNESCO ideals. He worked at Sofia and other places in Bulgaria, and visited Croatia, Canada and USA in connection with International seminars and conferences.

Later for research work in Indian History, he gathered proficiency in Persian language and specialized in Mughal and pre-colonial Agrarian system in India (16th - 19th centuries). Based on contemporary archival materials in India and Europe, he wrote comprehensively on various aspects of Mughal administration, land revenue system and integrated pattern of rural trade in pre-colonial northern India. He has been the last word on the revenue system in Medieval India.

He wrote numerous research papers for well-known journals, such as the Proceedings of the Indian Historical Records Commission, National Archives of India, Indian Economic and Social History Review, Delhi School of Economics, Proceedings of the Indian History Congress, Proceedings of the Punjab History Conference, Punjab Past and Present, as well as in various News papers. He was also member of many Historical organizations and Governmental bodies till his last day.

The death of Prof. Grover has left a vacuum practically impossible to bridge.

R.C. Agarwal

Shri Lakshmi Dutt
(15.08.1924-25.12.2000)

Shri Lakshmi Dutt Khanduri, who passed away on 25th December, 2000 at the age of 76 years, will not only be remembered for many years to come for his distinguished services in the field of archaeology, but for his great humanitarian outlook and affection for all those with whom he worked in the Survey and outside.

Born on 15th August, 1924 at Ratura, a small village in District Chamoli, Garhwal (Uttaranchal) and after completing his secondary education, he went to Lahore for Diploma in Fine Arts and later joined Archaeological Survey of India in 1944 at Taxila (Pakistan). In due course of time he became Head of the Drawing and Graphic section in Survey.

Shri L.D. Khanduri, better known as "Dutt Saheb" in the Archaeological Survey of India, rendered valuable services for 38 years in the Department. He made valuable contribution in archaeological excavations. He had the privilege of working as a technical expert in many excavations. It was his proud privilege to work under Sir Mortimer Wheeler in the excavations at Harappa, Brahmagiri, Taxila, Arikamedu, etc and also in all other major archaeological sites of the country. He was an expert in stratigraphy, section drawing, pottery drawing and other graphic works.

Shri Khanduri took a keen interest in archaeological drawings and achieved par-excellence in the field. During the course of his service he also visited Afghanistan as a member of the archaeological exploration team, headed by Late Shri B.K. Thapar (Director General). Due to his devotion to work, almost all the eminent archaeologists of the country considered him as asset to the organization. He also imparted instructions to the students of the School of Archaeology, New Delhi with great devotion, love and sincerity and attained the affectionate title of "Guruji" from all of them.

After retirement, he settled down at Srinagar, Garhwal situated on the bank of Alaknanda. There also he continued his interest in excavations in the region. Impressed by his contributions and standing in archaeology, the Department of Ancient Indian History, Culture and Archaeology, H.N.B. Garhwal University felicitated him in 1997.

He is survived by two sons.

Lalit Jain

PURĀTATTVA

Number 31 **2000–2001**

Editorial

Now that our own building has been completed, the office of the Indian Archaeological Society is functioning from this building. All academic works—research, publications, etc. are planned and executed from here. The projects sponsored by ICHR, namely—'Atlas of the Indus-Saraswati Civilization', 'Methodology in Archaeological Research' and 'Growth of Cities in Ancient India' are progressing as planned. For these projects, young archaeologists who have passed out from the Institute of Archaeology, New Delhi, Deccan College, Pune and other Institutions have been inducted. Cartographers and Graphic designers are also part of the research team. The collection of books, more than 4300 in our library has been catalogued and fed into computer for easy access.

The country faced a crisis of unprecedented nature on 26th January 2001 with the earthquake in Gujarat. A large number of protected monuments and heritage buildings were destroyed by the severe ground movements. A team of archaeologists from the Indian Archaeological Society, consisting of Prof. B.B. Lal, Sri M.N. Deshpande, Dr. S.P. Gupta and Sri K.N. Dikshit visited the disturbed areas, especially in Kachchh region. Although these natural calamities cannot be averted, it is the bounden duty of every archaeologist and conservationist to conserve what remains in a planned manner and to help the Government to protect built–in heritage for their safe transmission to the future generations. Towards this end, the ICHR has kindly extended financial assistance particularly for the survey of the region and to prepare a status report on the damages of monuments. The Government of Gujarat has come forward to extend cooperation in this work.

There are in all 329 monuments under the State Department of Archaeology, Govt. of Gujarat. The preliminary suveys have shown that most of the large and important monuments have suffered major and minor damages. The tentative estimates are in the region of 30% of all the numbers. In Kachchh the temples at Kera, Kanthkot and Puarogadh (Manjal) stand like ghosts of their formerselves, or are laid up in total devastation. The famous temple of Navalakha at Ghumli in Jamnagar district has developed gaping cracks and its mandapa now lies in an unsightly heap. It is a 12th century Solanki style temple which shares many features with the Sun temple at Modhera, which is also damaged. The pre-Solanki temple of Munibawa, standing on a hillock near Than in the Surendranagar district, has a collapsed Sikhara, while the Siva temple at Dedadra stands forlornly with its tower gone. The Bhujiya Kotha in Jamnagar has been shockingly ravaged with its upper storey in total ruins. The dome on the Naju-Bibi Maqbara at Junagadh has collpased into miniscule pieces. The shaking minarets of Ahmedabad apparently shook so violently that they got dismembered and now look like torn tree trunks. The earth shook but it has put our history in peril. We are giving some photographs of these monuments at the end of the plates.

In the present issue of Purātattva, which is going to be released on 22nd Nov. 2001 at the XXXV Annual Conference of the Society at Vadodara, articles ranging from prehistoric period to medieval times have been included for the publication. Emphasis has been laid on the recent excavations carried out by the different agencies in the country. The archaeological activities carried out in the country are, therefore, well represented in this issue.

Thanks are due to Sri M.N. Deshpande, Dr. Y.D. Sharma, Prof. Ajay Mitra Shastri, Dr. S.P. Gupta and a host of other scholars who extended monetary donations for podium, books, etc.

The publication of this Bulletin was possible due to the generous financial assistance received from the Indian Council of Historical Research and Archaeological Survey of India. We are grateful to both these organizations. However, these organisations are not responsible for the views expressed by contributors of articles to this volume.

We are also thankful to Dr. S.P. Gupta for his help and encouragement for the development of research infrastructure in the Society.

Thanks are also due to Sri Jitu Mishra, our young colleague, who has assisted the editors, in bringing out this issue; Shri Manoj Kumar Harbola for preparing the typed script; Ms. Anuja Geetali, Dr. B.S. Harishankar, Sri Tejas Garge, Ms. Mahua Bhattacharyya, Sri R.P. Sharma, Sri Manoj Kumar, Sri Jassu Ram, Sri M.S. Mani, Sri Himanshu Joshi, Sri Rakesh Dutta, Sri Rakesh Agrawal and Sri B.K. Rajput, all members, of the Indian Archaeological Society, for help in their own way.

Smt. Anita Mehta and her members of the staff also desrve our thanks for bringing out this issue in time.

K.N. Dikshit
K.S. Ramchandran

The Beginning of Agriculture in the Kunderu River Basin: Evidence from Archaeological Survey and Archaeobotany

D.Q. Fuller*, P.C. Venkatasubbaiah**, Ravi Korisettar***

Introduction

The beginning of agriculture in Andhra Pradesh remain obscure. In general terms, it is unclear whether agriculture began through the local domestication of plant species, the introduction of crops by immigrant farming communities, the adoption of crops by indigenous hunter-gatherers, or some combination of these processes. In this paper, we will discuss the available evidence from a small region, spread over two districts of Cuddapah and Kurnool in Andhra Pradesh, including the results of new fieldwork and archaeobotanical studies, which are beginning to shed light on the origins of agriculture. In particular, we focus on the evidence from Neolithic sites in the Kunderu river basin (Nandyal Valley) of the northern Cuddapah and southern Kurnool districts.

This region is geographically and ecologically distinct from the better-studied areas of the Southern Neolithic, such as the Bellary and Raichur districts (see Korisettar *et al.* 2001). The Kunderu River, and its numerous tributary streams and *nalas*, flow generally in a southerly direction and meets the Pennar River. The rock formations consist largely of shales, quartzites and limestones of the Archaean Proterozoic Kurnool Supergroup (Ramam and Murty 1997:122-136). This valley is framed by the Nallamalai Hills on the east and the Erramalai Hills on the west. The region is covered by black cotton soil *(regur)*, in contrast to much sandier soils of the granitic Bellary-Raichur region to the west. Average annual rainfall in this region is also higher than the latter area, and has been classified in bioclimatic terms as 'Tropical Accentuated Dry', with a dry season of some 7-8 months (Meher-Homji 1967). The somewhat wetter conditions than the adjacent region to the west provide for somewhat lush vegetation with the dry deciduous forests of the area being dominated by *Anogeissus latifolia* and *Hardwickia bipinata*, while towards and into the Nallamalai Hills it is even wetter, including a larger amount of teak *(Tectona grandis)* and *Terminalia tomentosa* as well as a number of wet deciduous forest elements (Legris and Meher-Homji 1977; Puri *et al.* 1983). Today, however, much of the region is under cultivation or is covered with degraded *Acacia* scrub and grassland vegetation. Until palaeoenvironmental data are available it will remain unclear to what extent a grassland mosaic was an important part of this environment in Pre-Neolithic times, although we suspect that some Savanna clearings would have been present, in some areas, such as areas well above the *nala*-valleys or those overlying quartzites. The beginnings of agriculture and pastoralism in this region can be expected to have increased the area of

* Institute of Archeology, UCL, 31-34 Gordon Square, London
** Ramakrishna Vidyalayam, M.S. Nagar, Kurnoll, Andhra Pradesh
*** Department of History and Archaeology, Karnataka University, Dharwad, Karnataka

deforested grassland and promoted the spread of thorny shrub vegetation.

Distribution of Sites and Provisional Chronology

When Paddayya (1973) compiled a distribution map of Southern Neolithic sites, relatively few sites were then known from his 'Variant 5'. Subsequent to that various archaeological explorations, including intensive survey in the northern Cuddapah district by Venkatasubbaiah (1988, 1992), have filled in the Neolithic site distribution to a considerable degree (see also Murty 1989). Some 43 sites in the Pennar river region of the Cuddapah district were located and surface collections made by Venkatasubbaiah (1988, 1992). Small test excavations/ surface scrapings were carried out at three of these sites, Hanumantaraopeta, Peddamudiyam and Balijapalle. In addition, Venkatasubbaiah has documented more sites in recent years in the Kurnool district portion of the study area. In archaeological terms, one thing that is notable about this region is the lack of evidence for ashmound sites, which are so distinctive of the adjacent Neolithic region to the west (Paddayya 1973; Korisettar *et al.* 2001). Nevertheless, ceramic forms and general aspects of their style, such as slip and paint colours, are similar to the ceramics from the Neolithic sites of the neighbouring region suggesting broad contemporeneity and cultural contact, although the Kunderu valley is known for its distinctive painted Patpad Ware (see Allchin 1962; Sarma 1967, 1968; Allchin and Allchin 1982; Venkatasubbaiah 1992; Korisettar *et al* 2001).

The known Neolithic sites in the region can be seen to be distributed near the Kunderu river, or its tributaries, including placement on the banks of seasonal *nalas*. As noted in the Cuddapah district, there is a range in the apparent site size, as judged by surface remains: out of 47 sites, 37 are in the size range of 0.25 hectare, 5 are in the size range of 0.25-0.5 hectares, 3 in the range of 0.5 to 1 hectare, 1 in the range of 1-3 hectares and 1 of 3 hectares (Venkatasubbaiah 1992). This pattern of sites can be contrasted with that known in the ashmound tradition region to the west, where the largest settlement sites were located on granitic hilltops away from river or stream valleys, although generally adjacent to other permanent water sources.

While the chronology of this Neolithic region requires further refinement, it is clear that a large proportion of it is equivalent to Phase III of the Southern Neolithic chronology (after Allchin and Allchin 1982). The Patpad Ware, distinctive to the region under consideration, is often related to the more widespread Peninsular 'Jorwe' phenomenon, which is most pronounced in the third phase. According to the calibrated radiocarbon chronology of Watgal (Devaraj *et al* 1995), this phase can be dated back to *Ca.* 1800 B.C., and may continue up to 1200/1000 B.C. The chronological evidence suggests that contrary to the naming of this painted pottery phenomenon, it is earlier in the Southern Neolithic province than further North (Shinde 1994; Devaraj *et al* 1995; Korisettar *et al* 2001). The two available radiocarbon dates from Peddamudiyam and Balijapalle (Venkatasubbaiah and Kajale 1991) when calibrated: 1540 B.C. (BS 811) and 1110 B.C. (BS 785), are in agreement with this periodization.

Stratigraphic Evidence and Site Formation Processes

In February 1997, we visited some 15 sites in the Kurnool and Cuddapah districts, where we conducted surface collection of artefacts, with test pit sampling or scraping of exposed sections at 8 sites. At those eight sites, soil samples were collected and subjected to flotation and wet sieving for the recovery of faunal remains and archaeobotanical evidence. On the basis of these diggings and scrapings, it is possible to propose a basic division amongst the sites in terms of site formation processes, which can be interpreted in terms of different occupational intensity and duration in Prehistory. We would propose that there are two broad divisions amongst sites. First, there are those sites which were inhabited for relatively brief periods of time for any given occupation but were presumably revisited repeatedly, perhaps as seasonal encampments in part of an annual or multi-annual settlement cycle; these sites provide no stratified archaeological deposits and consist of only surface finds. Second, there are sites which have habitational deposits, sometimes with distinct layers and lenses, of varying thickness containing pottery, lithics, bones and generally producing some charred plant remains upon flotation; these sites are presumed to have been long-stay occupations, occupied continuously for much of the year, and perhaps for several years at a stretch.

The basis for making these divisions is certain presuppositions about the nature of soil formation processes in this region and their effects on archaeological evidence. As already noted, this region is covered largely by black cotton soils (Uppal *et al* 1953; Spate and Learmonth 1967). These soils are high in montmorrilonite clays, and prone to extensive argilloturbation, that is wet season expansion and dry season contraction and cracking, leading to a net effect of churning and mixing. As indicated by Waters (1992: 299-300), this will tend to move large inclusions, such as potsherds or other artefacts towards the surface. If we assume that the refuse from short seasonal encampments were subjected to annual argilloturbation the long-term result would be surface scatters without any thickness of archaeological deposit. By contrast, for longer occupations with a greater build-up of refuse and anthropogenic deposits, we might expect that argilloturbation only served to blur the boundaries between layers and destroy fine stratigraphy. In the case of several sites studied, thickness of archaeological soils ranged up to 1.25 m (at Hanumantaraopeta), often with little or no discernible internal stratigraphy within the archaeological deposit. It is therefore presumed that the internal stratigraphy was destroyed by argilloturbation but higher rates of archaeological accumulation in spite of argilloturbation produced continuous and thick archaeological deposits. Argilloturbation is also likely to have obscured chronological ordering of such deposits, although broadly speaking we would expect some modicum of superposition to be preserved.

The Sites and their Archaeobotany

Chintalapalli (CTP): The village is situated east of the Pennar River in Kurnool taluk of Kurnool district. The archaeological finds are restricted to pottery from a ploughed up field dominated by black cotton soil. Stratified deposits are not observed in this area and the pottery collection was made from the plough zone surface. It was not suitable for archaeobotanical sampling.

Hanumantaraopeta (HRP): The village is situated on the Jammalamadugu-Tadapatri road, about 21.5 km north of the Jammalamadugu town, a taluk headquarter in the district of Cuddapah. The Tagileru nala flows in the east-west direction about a km to the north of the village, which is situated at the foot of the sandstone ridge. The Neolithic site is situated about 200 m south of the village. The Neolithic deposit, with an extent of 230 m in the east-west direction and 150 m in the north-south direction, is part of a cultivated field, under cotton in February 1997. The site was recognized by Venkatasubbaiah (1992) as a regional center and therefore one deep test pit to a depth of 1.4 m was dug into the site. Although the cultural deposit of 1.25 m did not reveal clear distinctive stratigraphic layers, seven arbitrary levels were selected for flotation sampling. Artefactual finds included pottery, microliths, lithics and animal bones. Pottery includes black-on-red ware, grey ware, brown ware, red ware, black ware and black-and-red ware. The lithics include pecked and ground stone artefacts and microliths.

Hanumantharaopeta has yielded a wide range of charred seed taxa including at least 30 distinct morphotypes. Most common were small millets, largely caryopses of *Brachiaria ramosa* and *Setaria verticillata* types but with a few probable specimens of *Echinocloa colona*. *Macrotyloma uniflorum* and *Vigna radiata* were also prevalent although a single probable specimen of *V. mungo* was noted from the lowest level. Several fruit/nut types are present, including *Ziziphus* cf. *Mauritania.* Wheat and barley are both present. Additional food plant crops present include one probable *Abelmoschus* type (okra/lady's fingers), which was earlier reported from Peddamudiayam, and a few cucurbitaceae types *(Cucumis cf. prophetarum).*

Injedu (IJD): The village is situated in the Pennar valley in Kurnool district. The archaeological site is situated east of the village of Uyyalavada. The cultural material includes both Neolithic and Early Historic artefacts. About 60 cm of habitational deposit was exposed in a test pit. The cultural material included black-on-red ware, grey ware, burnished ware, brown ware, red ware, terracotta and stone artefacts. Trial samples for flotation were poor, due to small size, low charcoal concentrations and heavy bioturbation. Nevertheless *M. uniflorum* was present.

Mandlem (MDM): The village is situated in Nadikotkur taluk of Kurnool district. The archaeological site is situated east of Mandlem village. The surface scatter yielded lithics and pottery. The lithic debatage found at the site was indicative of a Neolithic factory. Two test pits were dug into the ploughed field. One of the pits yielded fragments of pottery and animal bones at a depth of 26 cm. A lens of wood charcoal but without seeds was encountered at this depth.

Pandipadu (PNP): A suburban village of the town of Kurnool, the district headquarter. Three localities on either side of the Kurnool-Pandipadu road about 5 km south-west of Kurnool yielded Neolithic cultural material including pottery and a stone celt, but no subsurface archaeology was preserved.

Peddamudiyam (PMD): The village is situated on the left bank of the Kunderu River about 21 km northeast of Jammalamadugu. The Neolithic deposits occur at two sites on the left bank of the river: (a) Locality 1, on the east bank very close to the village and (b) Locality 2, a little to the south of the village on the left bank. Locality 1 measures 30 x 30 m and is thoroughly ploughed up. Neolithic stone artefacts, black-on-red ware and black ware are some of the ceramic varieties reported from this locality. Locality 2 measures 65 x 55 m in extent and rises slightly above the surrounding field. Pottery includes back-on-red ware, grey ware, black ware, buff ware and brown ware. The lithics include pecked and ground stone tools, microliths and disc beads. Animal bones were also collected.

The dug up sections in the area revealed a maximum habitational deposit of about 55 cm. Four trenches were dug in the area, two on the perimeter of the area containing the cultural deposit and two in the centre. There was no visible stratification in the cultural material and therefore three arbitrary levels were sampled for flotation. The upper portion in each of these trenches was found to be low in charcoal but five samples floats were collected from lower sediments. The flotation samples have yielded evidence for Setaria *verticillata caryopses*, *Macrotyloma uniflorum*, fruit/nut fragment and parachyma. Locality II yielded a few ancient fragments, including pulse *Vigna* cf. *mungo*, and *M. uniflorum*, chenopodiaceae/amaranthaceae type seeds. (also see Venkatasubbaiah and Kajale 1991)

Tangaturu (TGT): Both Palaeolithic and Neolithic artefacts have been reported from near this village. The Neolithic deposits are located to the northwest of the village. A collection of grey ware, black-on-red ware, burnished ware, red ware, coarse red ware, animal bones, and stone artefacts has been collected from the site. No subsurface deposits were preserved.

Rupanagudi (RPG): The village is situated in Kurnool taluk of Kurnool district, to the east of Uyyalavada, a few kilometers away from Injedu. The Neolithic site is situated on the Erravagu, a tributary stream of the Kunderu River. Three sections in the area revealed stratified cultural material.The cultural material belongs to both Neolithic and Early Historic periods. The cultural remain from this site included black-on-red ware, grey ware, burnished ware, red ware, stone artefacts and animal bones.

Rupanagudi had poor archaeobotanical preservation and low yield generally. One seed from here has been referred to cf. *Abelmoschus sp.*, i.e. okra. Other food crops present in the samples were the ubiquitous small millet caryopses of Setaria *Brachiaria* type, as well as a fragment of *Vigna* sp. and other pulse fragments.

Singanapalle (SGP): The Neolithic site is situated about 2 km north of the village in Kurnool district. The site covers an area of 400 x 350 m (IAR 1967-68:3). This is one of the well developed and stratified sites in the region of our study. The Archaeological Survey of India first studied the site during 1967-68. Four test pits were dug into the deposits at the site. Pottery representing red ware, burnished ware, black-on-red ware, coarse red ware and stone artefacts, steatite and shell beads occur profusely in the sections as well as on the surface. Singanapalle has yielded very few seeds despite reasonable concentrations of charcoal and relatively good stratification for a site in the Kunderu valley. Nevertheless the dominant categories overall were present: *Macrotyloma uniflorum, V. radiata, Setaria/Brachiaria* millet type and parenchyma fragments.

Neolithic Cultivation Practices

Sites of the long-occupation type, with thick archaeological deposits, were successfully sampled for recovery of plant remains. Soil volumes of approximately of 20L were taken for each discernible archaeological layer, and in the case of HRP, where no layers were discernible arbitrary sampling intervals were determined on the basis of depth. By comparison to evidence recovered by the same methods in the Bellary region and at Hallur the samples from these sites were poor (Fuller 1999; Fuller *et al.*

2001) and indeed some sites yielded very few seeds, although charcoal was present on all sites. Nevertheless, the presence of charred seed fragments, including a number of likely crops is significant and greatly augments the existing archaeobotanical dataset from the region, including the evidence of Ramapuram (Kajale 1996), Peddamudiyam and Balijapalle (Venkatasubbaiah and Kajale 1991; Kajale 1996). While there is high density of charcoal at the site of Hanumantaraopeta, the evidence from other sites is low which may be due to preservational conditions and taphnomic processes operating in the area. The somewhat high densities were dominated by wood charcoal. In terms of non-charcoal remains the site of Hanuman-taraopeta again shows larger quantities corresponding with the larger sample sizes. Thus the samples from HRP can be expected to be the most representative available.

The most extensive assemblage comes from HRP and other sites only confirm the presence of selected species from the HRP dataset. The species, which were noted in the largest amounts, include two pulses, horsegram (*Macrotyloma uniflorum* (Lam.) Verdc.) and mungbean (*Vigna radiata* (L.) R. Wilzc.) and two morphotypes of millets, browntop millet (*Brachiaria ramosa* (L.) Stapf.) and bristly foxtail millet-grass (*Setaria verticillata* (L.) P. Beauv.). All of these species were found throughout the arbitrary sampling units at HRP. In addition, charred fragments of parenchyma tissue, suggesting the use of as yet unidentified tubers were also found throughout HRP. In addition, at HRP a few grains of another millet grass, sawa millet (*Echinochloa* cf. *colona* (L.) Link) were identified, and a single *Vigna* cotyledon of probable black gram (*Vigna mungo* (L.) Hepper) was found. *V. Mungo* type was also identified at PDM. No clear evidence of pigeonpea (*Cajanus cajan* (L.) Millsp.) was found at HRP, although this species had been previously reported from PDM (Venkatasubbaiah and Kajale 1991), but a number of large cotyledon fragments, possibly of a leguminous species were noted at HRP. These fragments could be from *C. Cajan*, or *Lablab purpureus* (L.) Sweet, a species well documented from the Bellary region, although other taxa are also possible. From the highest sampling locus only (HRP.1-3), a few wheat and barley grains were recovered, which may represent a later addition to the Neolithic crop repertoire. A number of fragments of probable gathered fruit remains have also been identified, including ber (*Ziziphus* cf. *mauritania* Lam.), probable jamun (cf. *Syzygium cumini* (L.) Skeels), seeds of a wild relative of melons and cucumbers (*Cucumis* cf. *prophetarum* L.) and a few seeds that may be from a wild relative of lady's fingers (cf. *Abelmoschus sp.*), which had previously been reported from PDM (Venkatasubbaiah and Kajale 1991). In terms of assemblage composition at HRP, pulses are generally the most numerous identifiable category followed by the small millets. There appears to be a decrease in the number of parenchyma fragments as one move up through the sequence. While this pattern may reflect declining use of tuberous foods, due perhaps to increasing reliance on millet cultivation, it is also possible that soil processes, including recent ploughing, towards the surface led to differential destruction of parenchyma.

The evidence argues for crop cultivation, and it can be suggested that the crops involved had been introduced from the west although some local domestication cannot be ruled out. The pulses *Vigna radiata* and *Vigna mungo* derive from wild progenitors, which have been reported from the forests of the Western Ghats as well as the Nallamalai hills (Fuller 2001). For horsegram and millets, detailed distributional data on their natural distribution is still needed, but all are probably native to the dry deciduous and/or Savanna zones, and thus could potentially have been domesticated across much of the Peninsula. Nevertheless, given that these species occur together as a crop package across many Southern Neolithic sites, it might be suggested that they were brought into cultivation at roughly the same time and place and we must therefore look to the Malnad region towards the Western Ghats, or perhaps the transition from the Malnad to Maidan for their likely zone of initial cultivation. The available dating evidence from the Kunderu river valley also points to the beginnings of the Neolithic, including ceramics, later than regions to the west.

The evidence discussed above provides a basis for reconstructing in broad terms the nature of subsistence and settlement during the Neolithic in the Kunderu basin. The range of crop species present suggests cultivation largely during the monsoon *(kharif)* season, with probable winter cultivation added on small scale with the adoption of wheat and barley. The millets and pulses could have been readily dry cropped on the rainfall absorbed by the clay-rich soils. It is plausible that some system of shifting cultivation was employed, although further evidence is needed. It is clear from the archaeozoological evidence (Venkatasubbaiah *et al* 1992) that domestic fauna were herded, supplemented by some hunting. As with the rest of the Southern Neolithic, cattle predominated (65% of surface collection from 7 sites; 67% of identifiable fragments from previous test excavations at HRP) and smaller herds of sheep and goat (11.5% of surface collections; 20% of identifiable fragments from previous test excavations at HRP). Chicken bones have also been recovered in small quantities of these sites, including HRP, and might be suggestive of some more sedentary occupation. Pigs, however, a sedentary animal *par excellence*, have not yet been recovered from this region. The presence of long-duration (possibly sedentary) occupations as well as seasonal encampments, might attest to some cyclical process of movement of herds across the landscape over the course of the year, probably following cycles of population concentration and dispersal, with dispersal acting as an effective means of minimizing the stress of the dry season.

Understanding of the Spread of Agricultrue Beyond the Ashmound Tradition

In placing the above evidence into a wider interregional context, we might suggest some of the possible processes involved in the establishment of agro-pastoral way of life in this region. In general terms the spread of agriculture may occur through migration of farmer communities or else the adoption of domesticated plants and livestock by hunter-gatherer groups. Alexander (1977, 1978) has discussed these processes in terms of frontiers, with moving frontiers in the case of immigrant agriculturalists, and static frontiers, often associated with environmental boundaries, at which agriculturalists interact with hunter-gatherers beyond the frontier. The importance of such interactions at the static frontier for understanding the process of agricultural adoption is widely discussed in the context of western and northern European Prehistory (e.g. Alexander 1978; Dennell 1985, 1992; Zvelebil 1986, 1996; Thomas 1996). Static frontiers may be 'closed', in which case there is minimal interaction between agriculturalists and hunter-gatherers or else they are 'open' and a range of inter-relationships develop. Static frontiers may involve a variety of processes, including symbiotic interactions and trade, emulation of one group by another, usually emulation of the agriculturalists by hunter-gatherers (Zvelebil 1986; Fewster 1996), or competition, and may involve intermarriage. In general terms three phases, which may also be somewhat spatially separated, have been proposed for open agricultural frontiers (Zvelebil and Rowley-Conwy 1984): an availability phase, in which domesticates and other technologies are available but not seriously taken up by hunter-gatherers, a substitution phase in which these are adopted on a small scale by some amongst the hunter-gather communities, and a consolidation phase in which agriculture becomes well-established and hunter-gatherer traditions decline or retreat. As discussed by Russell (1998) with regard to situations of marital exchanges, especially in the case of agro-pastoral systems in which cattle or other livestock play an important role as bride wealth, internal social drives within hunter-gatherer communities may be created that to promote the adoption of domestic herds. In such situations, we might expect the adoption of domesticated animals to precede cultivation. Details about the relative timing of these elements in the Kunderu basin, however, are not yet available.

A static frontier situation, perhaps corresponding roughly to the Erramalai hills, i.e. the geographic transition from the granitic peneplain of the Bellary region to the black soils of the Cuddapah and Kurnool regions, can be suggested to have developed between the agro-pastoral culture of the Southern Neolithic ashmound tradition and the Mesolithic hunter-gatherers of the Kunderu basin. Cultivation was present in the ashmound tradition by at least 2200 cal. B.C., and probably earlier, and thus this interaction between the cultivator-pastoralists on the west and the Kunderu hunter-gatherers on the east must have carried on for at least four centuries until *Ca.* 1800 cal. B.C. During this period some trade might be expected, although clear evidence for this is still lacking. However by 1800 cal. B.C. populations in the Kunderu basin had adopted the basic livestock and crops of the ashmound tradition but adapted them to a different settlement system, without the ashmound ritual tradition, and also developed some distinctive aspects of ceramic style. It is hoped that future investigation might focus on the nature of this transition and the extent to which selective adoption and emulation took place across the Erramalai agricultural frontier, and whether or not the European model of availability, substitution and consolidation phases is applicable in southwestern Andhra Pradesh. The persistence of hunter and forager traditions amongst groups such as the Chenchus and Yanandis further east (in the

Nallamalais and Velikondas) would seem to imply that some aspects of the frontier situation have continued until the modern era.

Acknowledgements

Research grants to D.Q. Fuller were provided from the Faculty of Archaeology and Anthropology, St. John's College, and the Smuts Memorial Fund, all of Cambridge University. P.C. Venkatasubbaiah was on a ICHR fellowship while working on this project. A Fulbright Visiting Lecturer grant to R. Korisetter by the United States Educational Foundation in India, New Delhi, enabled him to spend a fortnight in London at the Institute of Archaeology, UCL. Funding for fieldwork was provided by a grant from Karnataka University, Dharwad.

REFERENCES

Alexander, John A. 1977. The 'Frontier' Concept in Prehistory: the End of the Moving Frontier, in *Hunters, Gatherers and First Farmers Beyond Europe* (J. V. S. Megaw Ed.), pp. 25-40. Leicester: Leicester University Press.

Alexander, John A. 1978. Frontier Studies and the Earliest Farmers in Europe, in *Social Organisation and Settlement* (D. Green, C. Haselgrave and M. Spriggs Eds.), pp. 13-29. Oxford: BAR International Series 47.

Allchin, F.R. 1962. Painted Pottery from Patpad, Andhra Pradesh, *Antiquity* 36: 221-224.

Allchin, B. and R. Allchin 1982. *The Rise of Civilization in India and Pakistan.* Cambridge: Cambridge University Press.

Dennell, R.W. 1985. The Hunter-Gatherer/ Agricultural Frontier in Prehistoric Temperate Europe, in *The Archaeology of Frontiers and Boundaries* (S. W. Green and S. M. Perlman Eds.), pp. 113-140. New York: Academic Press.

Dennell, R. W.1992. *The Origins of Crop Agriculture in Europe, in The Origins of Agriculture: an International Perspective* (C. W. Cowan and P. J. Watson Eds.), pp. 71-100. Washington, D.C.: Smithsonian Institution Press.

Devaraj, D. V., J.G. Shaffer, C. S. Patil and Balasubramanya 1995. The Watgal Excavations: an Interim Report, *Man and Environment* 20(2): 57-74.

Fewster, K.J. 1996. Basarwa and Bamangwato Interaction in Botswana: Implications for the Transition to Agriculture in European Prehistory, *Archaeological Review from Cambridge* (for 1994) 13(1): 83-103.

Fuller, D.Q. 1999. *The Emergence of Agricultural Societies in South India: botanical and Archaeological Perspectives.* Ph.D. Thesis. Cambridge: University of Cambridge.

Fuller, D.Q. 2001. Fifity Years of Archaeobotanical Research in India: Laying the Solid Foundation, in *Indian Archaeology in Retrospect: Archaeology and Interactive Disciplines* (Volume 3) (S. Settar and Ravi Korisettar Eds.), pp. 247-263. New Delhi: Manohar in assoication with Indian Council of Historical Research.

Fuller, D.Q., Ravi Korisettar and P.C. Venkatasubbaiah 2001. Southern Neolithic Cultivation Systems: a Reconstruction based on Archaeoloigcal Evidence, *South Asian Studies* 17: 149-167.

IAR Indian *Archaeology a Review.* Annual Bulletin of the Archaeological Survey of India. New Delhi.

Korisettar, R., P.C. Venkatasubbaiah and D.Q. Fuller 2001. Brahmagiri and Beyond: the Archaeology of the Southern Neolithic, in *Indian Archaeology in Retrospect, volume III,* Prehistory (S. Settar and Ravi Korisettar Eds.), pp. 151-236. New Delhi: Manohar in Assoication with Inidian Council of Historical Research.

Kajale, M.D. 1996. Neolithic Plant Economy in Parts of Lower Deccan and South India, in *Abstracts- the Section of the XIII Interational Congress of Prehistoric and Protohistoric Sciences,* Forli (Italy), 8-14 September 1996.

Legris, P. and V. M. Meher-Homji 1977. Phytogeographic Outlines of the Hill Ranges of Peninsular India, *Tropical Ecology* 18: 10-24.

Meher-Homji, V. M. 1967. On Delimiting Arid and Semi-arid Climates in India, *The Indian Geographical Journal* 42(1-2): 1-6.

Murty, M.L.K. 1989. Pre-Iron Age Agricultural Settlements in South India: an Ecological Perspective, *Man and Environment* 14 (1): 65-81.

Paddayya, K. 1973. *Investigations into the Neolithic Culture of the*

Shorapur Doab, South India. Leiden: E.J. Brill.

Puri, G. S., V. M. Meher-Homji, R. K. Gupta, S. Puri 1983. *Forest Ecology* (second edition), *Volume 1. Phytogeography and Forest Conservation*. New Dehli: Oxford and IBH.

Ramam, P. K. and V. N. Murty 1997. *Geology of Andhra Pradesh*. Bangalore: Geological Society of India.

Russell, Nerissa 1998. Cattle as Welath in Neolithic Europe: Where's the Beef?, in *The Archaeology of Value. Essays on Prestige and the Processes of Valuation* (D. Bailey and S. Mills eds.), pp. 42-43. Oxford: BAR International Series 730.

Sarma, I. K. 1967. Painted Pottery from Pusalapadu-Andrah Pradesh and Further Exploitations in the Cuddapah and Kurnool Districts, *Indica* 4:75-94.

Sarma, I.K 1968. Patpadu Revisited: a New Painted Pottery Culture of South India, *Puratattva* 1: 68-83.

Shinde, V. S. 1994. Shinde, V. 1994. The Deccan Chalcolithic: a Recent Perspective, *Man and Environment* 19 (1-2): 169-178.

Spate. O. H. K. and A. T. A. Learmonth 1967. *India and Pakistan: a General and Regional Geography,* 3rd edition. London: Methuen.

Thomas, Julian 1996. The Cultural Context of the First Use of Domesticates in Continental Central and Northwest Europe, in *The Origins and Spread of Agriculture and Pastoralism* in Eurasia (D. R. Harris Ed.), pp. 310-322. London: UCL Press.

Uppal, B. N., J. V. A. Nehemiah and U. N. Chatterji 1953. *Final Report of the All India Soil Survey Scheme*. Indian Council of Agricultural Research. Calcutta: Government of India Press.

Venkatasubbaiah, P.C. 1988. Protohistoric Investigations in the Central Pennar Basin, Cuddapah District, Andhra Pradesh, *Puratattva* 18: 79-84.

Venkatasubbaiah, P.C. 1992. *Protohstoric Investigations in the Central Pennar Basin, Cuddapah, Andhra Pradesh*. Ph.D. Thesis. Pune: University of Poona.

Venkatasubbaiah, P. C and M. D. Kajale. 1991. Biological Remains from Neolithic and Early Historic Sites in Cuddapah District, Andhra Pradesh, *Man and Environment* 16: 85-97.

Venkatasubbaiah, P.C., S.J. Pwankar and P.P. Joglekar 1992. Neolithic Faunal Remains from the Central Pennar Basin, Cuddapah District, Andhra Pradesh, *Man and Environment* 17 (1): 55-59.

Waters, M.R. 1992. Principles of Geoarchaeology.: a North American Perspective. Tocson and London: The University of Arizona Press.

Zvelebil, M. 1986. Mesolithic Prelude and Neolithic Revolution, in Hunters in *Transition* (M. Zvelebil Ed.), pp. 5-16. Cambridge: Cambridge University Press.

Zvelebil, M. 1996. The Agricultural Frontier and the Transition to Farming in the Circum-Baltic Region, in *The Origins and Spread of Agriculture and Pastoralism in Eurasia* (David R. Harris Ed.), pp.323-345.London: UCL Press.

Zvelebil, M. and P. Rowley-Conwy 1984. Transition to Farming in Northern Europe: a Hunter-Gatherer Perspective, *Norwegian Archaeological Review* 17: 104-128.

Further Field Studies at the Lower Palaeolithic Site of Isampur, Karnataka

K. PADDAYYA[1], RICHA JALDIYAL[1] AND MICHAEL D. PETRAGLIA[2]

Introduction

In a previous volume of the journal *Puratattva,* the authors published a comprehensive report on the result of four seasons of field investigations (1997 to 2000) at the Lower Palaeolithic site of Isampur located in the Gulbarga District of Karanataka (Paddayya *et al* 1999-2000); see also Paddayya *et al* 2000 and Petraglia and Paddayya 2001). These field studies comprised both regular excavations and geoarchaeological investigations aimed at a reconstruction of the palaeoenvironmental setting of the site. The above-mentioned paper highlighted the special place, which the site of Isampur occupies in Indian Lower Palaeolithic studies. In particular, attention was called to the following features: a) location of the site on the outer edge of a palaeochannel, probably containing perennial waterpools; b) excellent preservational context of the cultural material; c) the unusually rich nature of the lithic assemblage (almost exclusively based on limestone) enabling one to make valuable additional observations about the techno-typological aspects of the Acheulian culture; d) reconstruction of the site as a localized hub of manufacturing and occupation activities, from where the hominids radiated as a part of their daily foraging activities; and e) the use of the site by a band-like population aggregate, comprising three or four extended families/groups. In this article, the authors would like to place before the readers the results of field studies conducted at the site in March 2001.

The Isampur site (16^0 30'N; 76^0 29'E) lies in a narrow valley forming part of the northwestern portion of the Hunsgi basin and is enclosed by tablelands of shale and limestone. The site covers an area of three-quarters of a hectare and consists of a weathered bed of silicified and limestone which was used by the hominids for both manufacturing and occupation activities. Four seasons of excavations exposed Acheulian cultural material in various preservational contexts ranging from in *situ* to fluvially rearranged positions. A total of over 15000 artefacts were recovered from an excavation along with the Acheulian cultural material has been dated by Electron Spin Resonance (ESR) method. (Blackwell *et al.* 2001).

Palaeoenvironmental Studies

In this season, four geological cuttings (Nos. 6 to 9) were dug in the area to the north of the Stone Age locality (fig.1) in order to understand the nature of sedimentation processes responsible for the deposition of brown/black silts in the area covered by the palaeodrainage tract. About 20 years ago, the Karnataka Irrigation Department quarried away much of the sedimentary fill for preparing the embankment of a major irri-

[1]Department of Archaeology, Deccan College, Pune-62
[2]National Museum of Natural History, Smithsonian Institution, Washington D.C. 20560, U.S.A.

gation canal located just one kilometer away from the Stone Age site. This quarrying was done in an irregular way such that the silt deposit was scooped away almost up to the bottom at some places, while in other places it was left almost untouched.

Two cuttings (Nos. 6 and 7) were excavated in the patches still preserving much of the sedimentary cover in its original context. Cutting 6 (measuring 5x3 m) lay 10 m north of the main Acheulian locality. It was excavated up to a depth of 1.4 m after which bedrock (limestone) was struck pl.1. The various sedimentary levels encountered in the cutting can be grouped into two units:

Unit1: 1.2 m thick deposit comprising four levels of compact, fissured black silt measuring from 12 to 35 cm in thickness and containing angular pieces of limestone (8 to 10 cm across), chert nodules and artefacts; these silt levels are interstratified with five thin lenses (3 to 12 cm) made up of fine sandy/gravelly material comprising small kankar pellets representing lag deposits. The black silt levels of the upper portion produced small chert artefacts of Upper Palaeolithic (?)/ Mesolithic character, while the lower levels yielded some Middle Palaeolithic artefacts of limestone and chert.

Unit 2: 10 to 20 cm thick layer representing a regular Acheulian cultural horizon comprising limestone blocks and fresh Acheulian artefacts (cores, regular tools and debitage). All set in a compact matrix of kankary brown silt and resting on eroded limestone surface.

Cutting 7 measured 5x2 m and lay about 35 m north of the main Acheulian locality. Bedrock (limestone) was struck at a depth of 1.7 m. The following stratigraphy was exposed in this cutting:

Level 1: (1 to 15 cm below surface); plough zone made up of a mixture of kankary brown silt and black silt.

Level 2: (15 to 110 cm below surface); compact brown granular kankary silt containing a clay band (5 cm thick); randomly dispersed chert and quartzite artefacts of Middle Palaeolithic character, especially at a depth of 90 to 100 cm below surface.

Level 3: (110-150 cm below surface); highly compact kankary brown clayer silt yielding Middle Palaeolithic artefacts of chert and quartzite.

Level 4: (150-170 cm below surface); Acheulian culutural horizon overlying eroded limestone surface and yielding artefacts of limestone as well as of quartzite and chert; matrix made up of extremely hard, whitish/brownish silt with a high proportion of carbonate.

Cutting 8 and 9 (each measuring 3x3 m) were laid 100 to 125 m away from the main Acheulian site. These were located in those portions of the quarried area where almost the entire body of silt deposit was dug away by the Irrigation Department. In both the cuttings, immediately below 10 to 20 cm thick brownish silt (yielding a few flakes of chert and limestone), a rubble horizon (20 cm thick) made up of angular limestone blocks, basalt pieces, and chert and quartzite nodules, all set in a hard matrix of kankary brown silt, was encountered. This horizon was free from cultural material and overlay eroded limestone surface.

In this connection, attention may be drawn to cuttings 1, 2, 3 and 5 excavated in previous field seasons. All these cuttings were located in the quarried area north of the main Acheulian site. The results from these cuttings tally very well with the stratigraphical and cultural data obtained from cuttings 6 to 9 excavated in the current season. In all these cuttings, black clayey silt (interspersed with lenses of sand or fine kankar gravel) overlay carbonate-rich, brown silt deposit containing angular to subangular pieces of intertrappean chert, basalt, quartzite and limestone, and Middle Palaeolithic artefacts of chert. The brown silt in turn overlay the Acheulian tool-bearing layer consisting of artefacts and limestone blocks set in a hard matrix of brown silt and carbonate and resting directly over the limestone bedrock (pl. 2). In cuttings 2 and 3 no Acheulian artefacts were found. Here the bedrock was highly weathered and smoothened due to water action and thereby indicated that this part formed a part of the palaeochannel.

The main observations emerging from these dimentary/ stratigraphical features and cultural material exposed by these six cuttings and the mapping work done in the surrounding area is as follows:

1. The palaeochannel is a shallow feature (2 to 2.5 m deep); it is 1.5 km long in a north to south direction and

200 to 300 m wide in a west to east direction. It was carved into the limestone bedrock as result of weathering and erosional processes. The formation of this channel was a part of the larger process of the sculpting of the floors of the Hunsgi and Baichbal basins, which consist of a network of shallow fluves and low interfluves. This valley floor morphology including the palaeochannel at Isampur had already come into existence long before hominid occupation of the area.

2. Limestone blocks with smoothened surfaces found at the base of the cuttings are a clear proof of the erosional origin of the palaeochannel. The thick carbonate matrix of the rubble horizon overlying bedrock clearly resulted from precipitation in stagnant bodies of water, which in fact provided the much-needed sources of water to the hominids. The finding of turtle shell pieces in the main locality once again confirms the palaeochannel area and presence of perennial waterpools were two major attractions to the Acheulian groups. While the main Acheulian site lay on the outer edge of the palaeochannel, the presence of artefacts at the bottom of several cuttings shows that the hominid groups used even the palaeochannel area. The evidence from cutting 6 infact suggests the occurrence of several other regular Acheulian localities in the area.

3. The deposition of brown and black silts in the palaeochannel area in post-Acheulian times was a prolonged process. These sediments were washed down from the surrounding uplands by a combination of colluvial and fluvial processes. The stratigraphical columns exposed in the cuttings prove beyond doubt that the formation of these deposits, far from being one-event phenomenon. Involved many short episodes of sediment deposition and its erosion at the local level, leaving behind thin sandy/kankary gravel lenses. The slow, episodic nature of the depositional history of these sediments entailed no abrupt changes in the valley floor configuration but, on the contrary, provided stable land surfaces for use by the Middle Palaeolithic and later groups.

4. An unexpected but very welcome outcome of the digging of these cuttings confirms the finding of Middle Palaeolithic and later cultural materials in the silt sediments covering the Acheulian level. Many Middle and Upper Palaeolithic and Mesolithic sites had previously been found in the Hunsgi and Baichbal valleys, but all of them of are surface sites lacking stratigraphical context. The Isampur cuttings have for the first time revealed that brown silts form the stratigraphical horizon of the Middle Palaeolithic culture. The overlying black silt forms the stratigraphical unit of the upper and Palaeolithic and Mesolithic materials.

Study of Surface Features

The second major aspect of this season's work concerned detailed mapping and study of cultural features exposed on surface at the main Acheulian site (Isampur II).

Previous studies had led to the recognition of the existence of 4 sub-localities on the site, each covering an area of 500-700 m^2 and separated from each other by diffuse scatters of cultural material. These sub-localities consist of dense patches of cultural material comprising debitage, cores, complete tools and hammerstones. In sub-localities 2 and 3, Trenches 1 and 3 were excavated in previous seasons and yielded *in situ* cultural material is displaced.

This season's work covered sub-locality[1], which forms the southeastern part of the Isampur, site and occupies an area of about 700 m^2. It forms part of the farmland but the shallow water channel flowing on the western side of the site occupies a small portion of it. Like in other parts of the Isampur site, the overlying silt cover of this portion also was quarried away by the Irrigation Department, leaving behind 10 to 20 cm thick sediment. Subsequently, the owner of the farmland took some steps to use this stretch for raising crops.

This involved certain amount of modification of surface features such as leveling, bund making, digging of field channels and dislodging of large limestone blocks. However, because of the uneven nature of the surface and the exposure of large limestone blocks, the patch could not be used for crop raising purposes in any regular way. As a result, much of the area was transformed into a barren patch covered with grasses, shrubs and *acacia* trees.[2]

Quarrying of the silt cover by the Irrigation Department led to the exposure of a tremendous amount of cultural material ranging from large cores to hammerstones to finished tools and debitage including small chips and flakelets. In the previous field seasons two trenches (Trenches 4 and 5, measuring 4x3 m and 5x4 m respectively) were excavated in this sub-locality; similar to that encountered in Trenches 1 and 3. This field season was devoted to a systematic documentation of the various features of the sub-locality exposed to surface Fig 2. This work included:

(1) Gridding of the entire area into 5x5 m units to facilitate detailed recording of the natural and cultural features;

(2) Careful scrutiny of surface features such as patches covered with stone blocks, vegetation and soil sediment;

(3) Knife and brush work to expose artefacts and stone blocks which were already partially brought to the surface due to various land modification activities;

(4) A general study of the nature and distribution pattern of cultural material ranging from large cores to small chips and their preservational contexts including spatial displacement and examination of the physical attributes of the artefacts; and

(5) Plotting of all artefacts and stone blocks exposed to surface in various portions of the locality due to digging of field channels, preparation of field bunds, displacement/quarrying of large stone blocks, erosion by water channel and other land modifacation activities.

The main conclusion arising from these detailed field studies is that the cultural record at this sub-locality is well preserved and is very suitable for behavioral interpretations. While it must be conceded that its level of integrity is not as high as that of the material found in sealed contexts in Trenches 1, 4, 5 and that the individual objects have lost the attribute of point provenance in many cases, still it was very clear that both cultural material and stone blocks did not suffer any large-scale disturbance due to recent land modification activities. Spatial displacement of artefacts ranging from a few centimeters to a couple of metres, smoothening of artefact surfaces, breakage due to trampling, fire and ploughing, and use of stone blocks for bunding were noticed during our field study. But use of stone blocks for bunding was noticed during our field study. But what is to to be emphasized is that though the attribute of point provenance may have been lost in the case of some of the artefacts and it may not be possible to identify activity areas like chipping clusters as revealed in Trench 1, still the cultural record is well preserved in terms of spot provenance. The stone tool assemblage recorded on the surface of this sub-locality proved to be very useful for understanding several aspects of the Acheulian culture including tool typology and reconstruction of tool reduction sequences.

A detailed attribute analysis of 262 artefacts forming the surface assemblage of this sub-locality was undertaken in the field itself. The artefacts were classified on the basis of morphological features and metrical attributes such as length, breadth, thickness and weight. Other features like raw material, flaking angle, planform, cross-section; number of flake scars, platform characteristics and cortex percentage were also recorded. The study brought to light a large variety of shaped tools, cores and flakes. A total of 64 shaped tools were recorded of which 21 were made on flakes, 3 on cobbles and the remaining ones on slabs of limestone. The shaped tools included handaxes (45), chopping tools (9), cleavers (7), scrapers (2) and knife (1). Twelve hammerstones of chert, limestone, basalt and quartzite were also recorded. The surface mapping also brought to light three large discoidal limestone blocks, which had steep flaking around the circumference, and was thus classified as anvils.

Fifty-two cores on limestone blocks were documented, while two were on limestone flakes and another two on chert cobbles. Most of the limestone blocks selected for removal of flakes ranged in thickness from 8 cm to 17.5 cm. Besides shaped tools, cores, hammerstones and anvils, 127 flakes were recorded in the surface assemblage. The large number of flakes exposed to surface facilitated the identification of variability in their forms and types. While many of the flakes were clearly blanks detached for manufacture of artefacts, there were several flakes, which appear to have been used directly for cutting/chopping purposes. This study clearly showed that most of the flakes were removed by the hominids with prior planning so that they could easily be transformed into regular tool types.

Experimental Studies

Experimental flaking of limestone was another

important aspect of this season's work at the Isampur site. Micheal Noll, a post-doctoral fellow at the Smithsonian Institution, Washington D.C., undertook a series of knapping experiments involving the use of locally available limestone blocks and hammerstones of basalt, quartzite and chert. These experiments revealed that the technology of the Acheulian hominids of Isampur, far from being a random process, involved a careful selection of limestone blocks and hammerstones of suitable sizes and shapes. Noll's experiments showed that basalt hammerstones are most effective in detaching large flakes from limestone slabs. Likewise, the use of small, elongated slabs of limestone and initiating flaking along the their lateral edges and tips was found to be the most efficient mode of handaxe manufacture. Production of cleaver flakes was initially found to be somewhat difficult, but Noll soon realized that preparatory steps such as the selection of suitable limestone slabs as cores and trimming off the irregular projections of the platform area, use of hammerstones of speciefic sizes and selection of specific striking angles were the key to the detachment of flakes which with little or no further working could be shaped into cleavers.

Acknowledgements

The authors are grateful to Dr. S.R. Biradar and Shri Prakash Bali of Hunsgi village and Smt. Rangamma (widow of Aminappa Harnal) and Shri Ittappa Hadnur (owners of farmland containing the Isampur Stone Age site) for their valuable cooperation in carrying out this season's field studies at Isampur. They also like to thank Messrs D.D. Phule, Sunil Jadhav, V.S. Bhatawadekar and Candrakant Shendge as well as M.A. and M.Phil students of the Institute for their participation and valuable help in field investigations. Messrs D.D. Phule, B.S. Waghmode, S.D. Rokade, Srikant Pradhan and Sunil Jadhav have prepared the illustrations. Shri S.I. Amin has typed the manuscript.

REFERENCES

Blackwell, B.A.B., Fevrier, S., Blickstein, J.I.B., Paddayya, K., Petragia, M.D., Jhaldiyal, R., and A.R. Skinner 2001. ESR dating of and Acheulean Quarry site at Isampur, India. *Journal of Human Evolution 40* (No. 3)

Further field studies at the Lower Palaeolithic site of Isampur, Karnataka - K. Paddayya, Richa Jhaldiyal and Micheal D. Petraglia.

Paddayya, K., Jhaldiyal, Richa and Petraglia, Michael D. 1999-2000. The significance of the Acheulian Site of Isampur, Karnataka, in the Lower Palaeolithic of India. *Puratattva 30*; 1-27.

Paddayya, K., Jhaldiyal, Richa and Petraglia, Michael D. 2000. Excavation of an Acheulian Workshop at Isampur, Karnataka (India). *Antiquity 74* (2000): 751-2.

Petraglia, Michael D. and Paddayya, K. 2001. Prehistoric Toolmakers of India : An Ancient Quarry Shows the Planning Power of Early Humans. *Discovering Archaeology*. (January-February): 44-51.

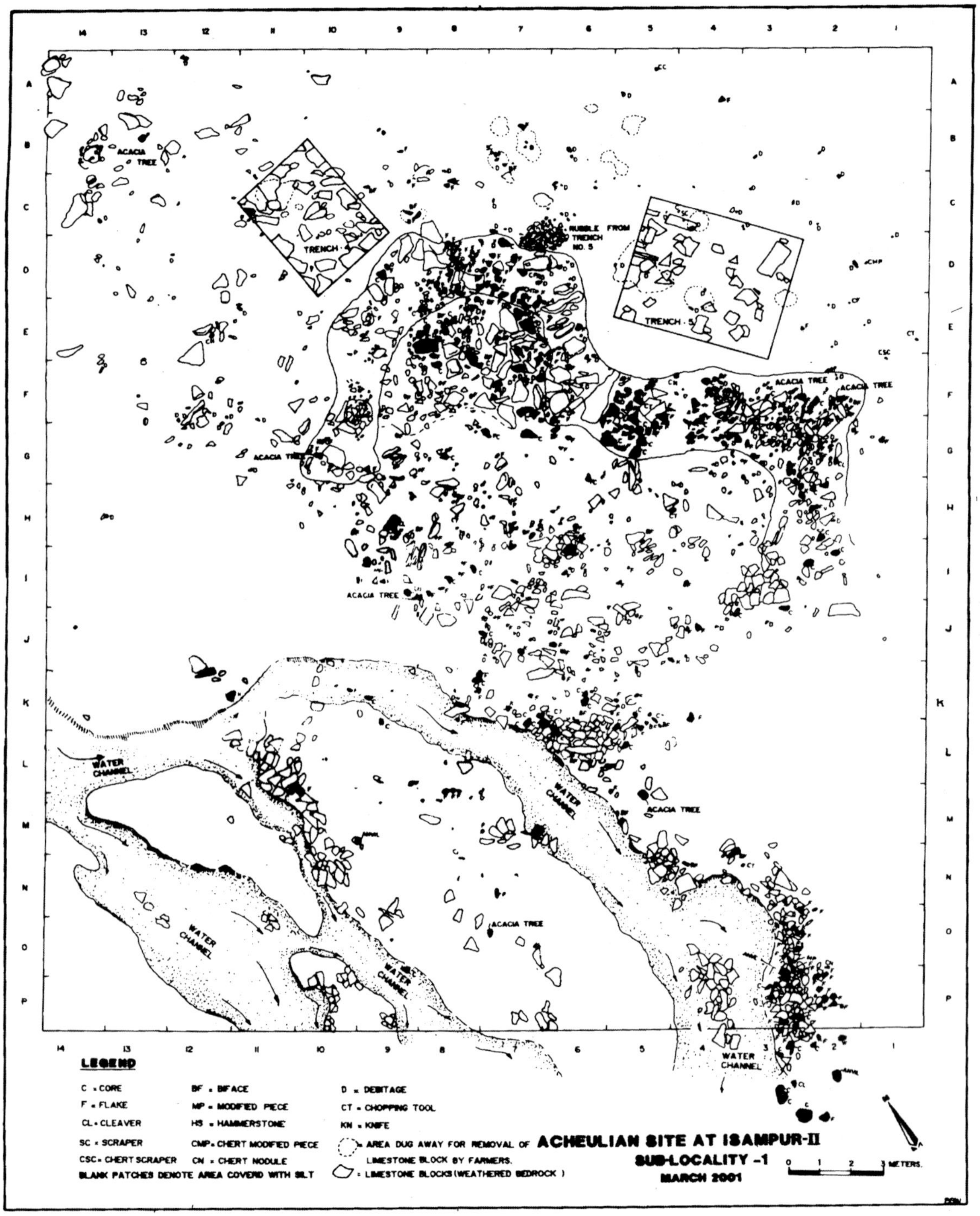

Fig. 1. Map of the Acheulian site of Isampur-II, showing sublocalities (I-IV), excavated trenches (1-5) and geological cuttings (1-9).

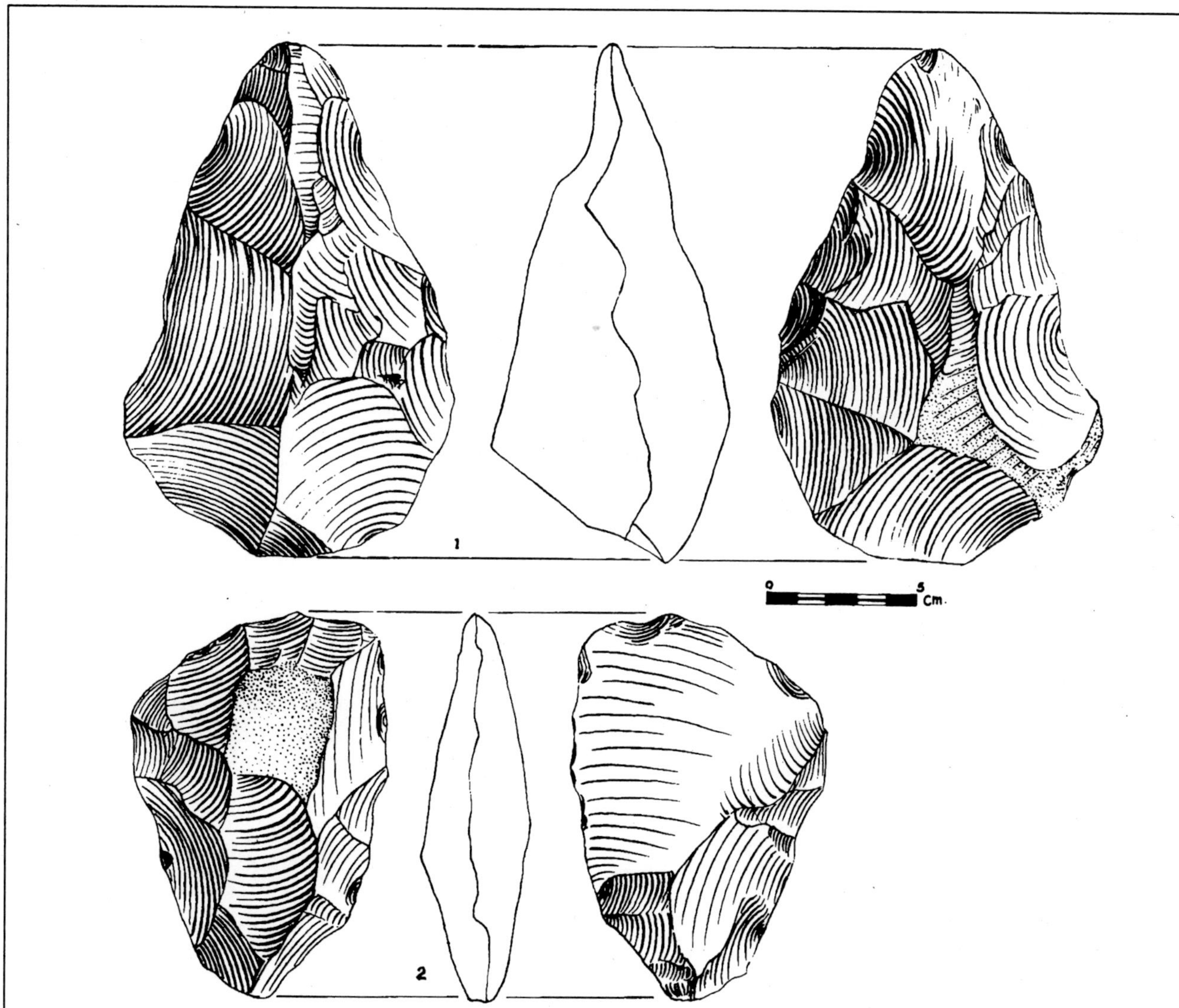

Fig. 2. Artefacts recovered from the Acheulian horizon exposed in geological cutting 6 (1, handaxe; 2, cleaver) at Isampur-II.

Adhwariya: A New Palaeolithic Site from Kharagpur Hills, South Bihar

D.K. Bhattacharya and Manoj Kumar Singh*

Introduction

In an all India context, Lower Palaeolithic is taken to have emerged anywhere between middle of Middle Pleistocene to Late Pleistocene. In South Bihar, however, it seems to have emerged fairly late in time. In fact, looking at the freshness of the tools from many sites from this region it would appear to be, probably, as late as the terminal end of Pleistocene in date. The archaeological potentials of Kharagpur hills was known from as early as 1944-45 when Shri R. N. Tagore and S. N. Kar discovered a fine handaxe from Bhimbandh region. Subsequently R. C. P. Singh (1959) and N. K. Bose, P. Gupta and A. Bose (1960) recorded some fresh finds from this region. P. C. Pant, V. Jayaswal and R. Tiwari (1978), took up an excavation of a new site called Paisra, which was discovered by them. This site lays 18 km northeast of the Bhimbandh region. The present authors undertook an extensive exploration of the entire Kharagpur hills during 1996-99. One of the most conspicuous finds of this exploration was published in 1997 (Bhattacharya & Singh 1997-98).

The present paper reports a site called Adhwariya (ADY) from Kharagpur Hills of Jamui District of South Bihar, where one finds a peculiar mixture of antiquities of form in terms of maintaining pebble cortex on many specimens while showing advanced techniques. It is argued that the evidence shows an older indigenous culture being overpowered by a younger and advanced culture arriving later in date.

The Site

Adhwariya (86°25' E and 25°3' N) is located in the Kharagpur hills, near the east of the village with the same name, in Laxmipur block of Jamui district of South Bihar. It is situated 10 km west from Laxmipur block and 33 km north from Jamui railway station (Fig. 1). The Vall hill is situated in the south direction from the site, where dense vegetation is present. Towards the hill slope, the density of the vegetation is very low. There is a cold spring, which originates from Vall hill and this is named as Bhurahwa. Today the flow of the spring is very low, but one can assume that this may have been more volumnous during the Pleistocene epoch. Consequently early human settlement around these water holes must have been very much sought after.

The site is situated on the pediment of Vall hill and is spread over an area of 1 square kilometer. Thin and hard haematite pellets, overlying decomposed bedrock, cover the pediment surface. The artefacts occur only on this surface in clusters. The selection of this spot for tool making by the Prehistoric people was basically guided by the easy availability of abundant quantity of quartzite blocks of

*Deptt. of Anthropology, University of Delhi-110007

suitable shapes and sizes in this area.

The Adhwariya site is undoubtedly of the primary type. The gentle slope of the pediment surface and absence of any regular drainage tract in the immediate vicinity are the two major factors that explain the remarkably good state of preservation of the site. The pediment surface on which the chipping activity took place was subsequently covered by reddish silt deposit measuring at some places about 4 m in thickness. This was probably derived from the adjacent hill slopes. This has probably helped in the preservation of the site against seasonal desication. It is an altogether different matter that much of this deposit has now been eroded and the tools bearing layer has been exposed, by the channelized watercourses created by the farmers for irrigating their fields. The clayish soil, which covers the lateritic episode in this site, has covered the tool bearing area in general. The site is recorded only from the areas, from where the top clay has been eroded. Therefore, it can naturally be surmised that if the topsoil is exposed by excavation the Adhwariya site would be probably found to be as wide spread as the other sites discovered in this region.

Here it is important to record that the general eroding activity is caused mainly by seasonal hill wash coupled with sustained wind activity. But these agencies can act upon only in those areas, which are free of vegetation growth. Considering the fact that areas of human occupation are rich in organic wastes and hence help in fast vegetation growth, one can surmise that these areas were not actually chosen for occupation. These were used as camps to retrieve raw material and work implements and probably also collecting/cutting wood. These activities continued for several generations have rendered these peneplains prone to seasonal erosion. Hence the site shows the tools buried within a very thin layer of topsoil.

Geo-morpholoy of the Region

The hills of Munger and Jamui districts of South Bihar comprise a number of low ranges and isolated peaks, outliers of the Vindhyan series which entered the districts from south and gradually converge towards Munger town, near Jamalpur, known as Kharagpur hills. This is named after the town, which bears the same name and is situated to the east of the hills. The Kharagpur hills form an irregularly triangular block extending from near Jamalpur to thc Jamui railway station. It measures about 40 km north-south in length and 55 km east west in breadth, and contains within it large number of tribal village settlements of mainly Kora and Santhal tribe (Sherwill 1852). The area consists of a number of steep ridges rising from the low ground on all sides with scarped faces on massive quartzite in places, they are of irregular formation and do not run in any uniform direction. Generally speaking the range is a bold and striking mass of rocks covered for the most part with jungle; but it contains valleys with patches of cultivation and several hot springs, of which the finest and better known ones are Bhimbandh, Sitakund and Rishikund (Waddell 1890). There are several peaks rising to a height of about 1,500 feet and the highest point is called Maruk (1,628 feet above sea level). The central region is a tableland encircled by hills maintaining a thick forest and covered with a deep layer of laterite. The Kharagpur hills form a distinct watershed. The Kiul River draining the western part and the Maan and other streams drain the eastern part of the hills. To the north the hills are having low jungle-cover and this extends within a short distance of Munger urban area. To the southwest is another block of hills, which are known locally as the Gidheswar hills, named after a peak of that name. In geological reports, however, these are referred to as the Gidhour hills range. These hills are a continuation of the hill in the Nawada district and cover an area of about 80 square kilometers, forming a compact cluster between Khaira and the western boundary of the Munger town. They rise sharply from the plain, but in most places, there is a belt of jungle along their northern face before the actual ascent begins. To the east, there is a fine cliff overlooking Khaira and the Kiul River, and the range falls away to the south into the rocky valley of the Kiul. On the south in the village of Sakdari, there is a spring called Panchbhur, which is surrounded by precipitous walls of rock. The highest point of the range is at Ekgora (1,813 feet). The co-existence of the mature and immature drainage systems in the Kharagpur hill tract signifies that the hill and adjoining valley areas have undergone neo-tectonic movement in Early Quaternary period. This also explains the presence of only Quaternary sediments (Middle Pleistocene and younger) in the valley areas adjoining the Kharagpur hill tract (O'Malley 1926).

The Quaternary sediments covering the Kharagpur hills are known as Jamui formation. The multiple alluvial fill of Jamui terrace, which is described as the 'Jamui formation' constitutes the oldest continental Quaternary deposits in this region, which is known as 'older alluvium' in Indian geology (Passoe 1964).

The laterite occurrences on the top of the Kharagpur hills and the ferruginous residual soil over the bedrock below the alluvial fill of Jamui terrace is indicative of a tropical climate at the beginning of the Quaternary period. This was gradually replaced by a relatively cold and dry climate during the aggradation of the basal boulder sand member of Jamui formation.

The thickness of colluvium and residual deposit in the Kharagpur hills increases upto 4 m in the narrow pediment zone, bordering the Kharagpur and Gidheshwar hills, within the Jamui terrace has a 0.5 m to 2 m thick cover of colluvium and residual deposits. In the pediplain area bordering the Kharagpur hills, the thickness of the residual soil is much less than the colluvium deposit and the material is mainly reddish brown silt and clay.

The lithological and sequential equivalent of upper Jamui formation has been considered to be of Upper Pleistocene to early Holocene in age, on the basis of the palaeontological finds (Dassarma *et al* 1976, 1977). Since no fossil has been found in Quaternary sediments from this region till now, therefore, estimation of the age can be inferred only on the basis of sequential lithological, pedological and climatological analysis. In Narmada Valley, the oldest continental Quaternary sediments, which is lithologially similar to lower Jamui formation, has been dated as Middle Pleistocene, on the basis of vertebrate fauna (Dassarma *et al* 1977). Hence the Jamui formation of the Kharagpur hill region is provisionally considered to be of Middle to Upper Pleistocene, extending upto Early Holocene in age (Roy *et al* 1987).

The Industry

This is another rich site of Palaeolithic occurrence recorded from the Kharagpur Hills. A total of 1160 specimens could be collected from the site. Of these 39.4 percent are cores while the rest 59.7 per cent are flakes. Table 1 shows the break up of the various components of the industry with their relative frequency. Of the total number of cores (462) collected from this site, almost 68 or 14.7 percent have been identified as types. In the group of unfinished specimens flake cores constitutes the maximum frequency (42.6 percent). The next higher in frequency are found to be nucleates (16.4 percent) and blade cores (14.7 percent). Besides these discoid core (4.7 percent), retouched cores (3.4 per cent) and levalloisian core (2.5 percent) are the other core varieties recorded at Adhwariya Fig 2.

The flake cores are generally spherical in shape and range between 13 cm to 8 cm in length. Many of these maintain a large amount of original cortex on them. Obviously these have not been used till exhausted. The nucleate, on the other hand are totally exhausted and round shaped specimens. The blade cores are also large and chunky with few blade beds visible in each of them. The discoid cores, as against the above are much more regular in shape and show regular bifacial flakings done from all around a circular border so that the maximum thickness remains in the centre. These measure between 10.5 cm to 5.5 cm in diameter.

The unfinished flakes and blades constitute the largest chunk of the total debitage. The flakes measure 14.5 cm to 7.0 cm in length while the blades are found to be equally big in shape. These range from 11.5 cm to 5.2 cm in length. Levalloisian flakes like in earlier sites occur in reasonably good frequency. Being reasonably thick this was given some controlled retouching towards the butt-end as also the proximal end of the two lateral borders. A very significant occurrence at this site is chipped pebbles, which were earlier recorded in other sites of the region and named as elongated pebble with chisel edge. At Adhwariya, 7 such specimens have been recorded. These are heavy cylindrical pebbles measuring between 20.5 cm to 15.5 cm in length.

Table 2 shows the frequency of the tool types. Of the finished pebble based tools 2 chopping tools and one chopper has been recorded. Large patches of original cortex are visible on both the surfaces. Unlike almost all the other sites discovered in the Kharagpur Hills, Adhwariya does not show either handaxes or cleavers forming the highest percentage of finished types. Here side scrapers form the highest frequency (30.3 percent). These are prepared on rather large simple flakes measuring 14 cm-6 cm in length. The next higher frequency of type is end scrapers (11.7 percent). These are also prepared on rather large and broad rectangular flakes and measure between 12 cm

Jamui Table: 1. Palaeolithic Industry of Adhwariya

Total Industry : 1160

Cores	Absolute Number	Percentage: Out of Total Cores	Percentage: Out of Total Industry
Flake Core	197	42.6	17
Retouched Flake Core	03	0.6	0.2
Nucleate	76	16.4	6.5
Blade Core	68	14.7	5.8
Retouched Core	16	3.4	1.3
Discoid Core	22	4.7	1.8
Levalloisian Core	12	2.5	1.0
Finished Types	68	14.7	5.8
Total	**462**	**99.6**	**39.4**

Flakes	Absolute Number	Percentage: Out of Total Flakes	Percentage: Out of Total Industry
Simple Flake	178	25.5	15.3
Retouched Flake	91	13.0	7.8
Simple Side Flake	72	10.3	6.2
Simple Retouched Side Flake	28	4.0	2.4
Un-Retouched Bifacial Flake	04	0.5	0.3
Blade	79	11.3	6.8
Core Trimming Blade	21	3.0	1.8
Core Trimming Flake	19	2.7	1.6
Levalloisian Flake	48	6.8	4.1
Levalloisian Point	03	0.4	0.2
Pseudo Levalloisian Point	02	0.2	0.1
Finished Types	153	22	13.1
Total	**698**	**99.7**	**59.7**

to 4.5 cm in length. Retouched blades have been also recorded from this industry (4.9 percent). This has been retouched boldly along one of the lateral borders as also across the terminal end. This specimen again points towards a large involvement of pebble-based workmanship at this site. Handaxes occur in 15.7 percent proportion among the finished types of this industry. These are large measuring almost 18 cm in length in some instances while in others these can measure as little as 7 cm in length. The larger ones show a greater degree of weathering and also often maintain big patches of original cortex. In the flaking tchnique, however, there is no archaic feature visible. All these are finished with advanced cylinder hammer flaking and also a final series of retouchings. This is a real big specimen measuring 19.5 cm in length and 10.5 cm in breadth. The thickness of the specimen uniformly slender in measurement, however never exceeds 3 cm in thickness. The flakings evidenced on both surfaces are large but extremely shallow and this certainly demonstrates an advanced expertise of the people in their tool manufacturing technology. Incidentally this forms one of the rarest types from this industry. It is

Table: 2. ToolTypes of Adhwariya, Jamui

Total Industry: 1160

		Percentage	
Types	**Absolute Number**	**Out of Total Types**	**Out of Total Industry**
Handaxe	15	6.7	1.2
Flake Handaxe	02	1.0	0.1
Vaal Handaxe	01	0.4	0.08
Unfinished Handaxe	05	2.2	0.4
Diminutive Handaxe	11	5.0	1.0
Proto Handaxe	01	0.4	0.08
Diminutive Flake Handaxe	02	1.0	0.1
Cleaver	01	0.4	0.08
Diminutive Cleaver	01	0.4	0.08
Flake Cleaver	03	1.3	0.2
Ovate	02	1.0	0.1
Core Scraper	05	2.2	0.4
Chopper	01	0.4	0.08
Chopping	02	1.0	0.1
Handaxe Fragment	04	1.8	0.3
Cleaver Fragment	02	1.0	0.1
Rabot	01	0.4	0.08
Elongated Pebble With Chisel Edged	07	3.1	0.6
Backed Knife	09	4.0	0.7
Naturally Backed Knife	01	0.4	0.08
Notch	03	1.3	0.2
Notch On Levalloisian Flake	01	0.4	0.08
Single Side Scraper	67	30.3	5.6
Bifacial Side Scraper	03	1.3	0.2
Transverse Scraper	02	1.0	0.1
S.S.S. On Pebble	01	0.4	0.08
Convergent Side Scraper	11	5.0	1.0
Double Side Scraper	03	1.3	0.2
Alternate Side Scraper	01	0.4	0.08
End-Scraper	26	11.7	2.2
Retouched Blade	08	3.6	0.6
Notched Blade	03	1.3	0.2
Burin	02	1.0	0.1
Point	07	3.1	0.6
Disc	06	2.7	0.5
Atypical Borer	01	0.4	0.08
Total	**221**	**99.3**	**17.6**

a medium sized specimen measuring 12.2 cm in length, 6.8 cm in breadth and 1.9 cm in thickness. It is prepared on a side flake with alternate borders flaked from alternate directions. This has given it a typical parallelogram section. One of the most significant features of this cleaver is that it has a specially prepared narrowed butt-end. But the working border is formed by the intersection of a flat pebble cortex from the dorsal surface with the scar of detachment of the ventral surface plate 1 and 2.

Discussion

Compared on a Pan-Indian scale it would seem that the Adhwariya evidence represent, a very late intrusion of Acheulians in this area. Since there is no such cultural evidence known from the area lying immediately north of the region, one would have no other alternative but to surmise that these represent colonies of migrations, which must have originated in the south. Rich Palaeolithic evidences are known from Singhbhum district (Ghosh 1970) and from further south in Mayurbhanj district (Bose and Sen 1948) of Orissa. One can naturally assume that the Adhwariya population must be derived from these southern sources. But a close examination of the tools would indicate that Palaeolithic evidences from most of the Kharagpur hill region is much more advanced in technology. Adhwariya would seem to be representing an autochthonous group which might be showing an earlier migration from Santhal Pargana in Bihar and Bankura and Midnapur in West Bengal, where Acheulian tools with pebble base is known.

The Kharagpur Hills constitute almost the northern most extension of the Chotanagpur region, although it is not included within the administrative boundary of the newly formed Jharkhand state. The latter includes large expanses of a plateau type physiography with occasional intrusion of small hillocks. The Kharagpur Hills in contrast forms an extension of the Mahadeo hills and is densely forested. Sankalia (1974) summarizes this difference very succinctly. "There are two different environments of habitation of early man in South Bihar. The one is the rolling, undulating, lateritic plains of Chotanagpur plateau with occasional grooves of bamboo and Sal forests, while the other is the hill-girt valleys in the southern plain which are heavily forested at places like Rajgir, Jethian, Bhimbandh, Chormara and Paisra" (page 43). It has been argued earlier that this hill-girt region drained by small water sources form a distinct eco-zone, which is worth considering for understanding differential adaptational imperative as an explanation of culture (Jacobson 1975). This becomes a strong possibility mainly because the kind of geographic specialization of prehistoric colonization evidenced in Bihar is possibly nowhere else so strongly marked. To quote Basudev Narayan (1996), "The north Bihar plain represents a complete blank as far as Palaeolithic and Mesolithic tool types are concerned..." (Page 548). Yet as one enters the region south of the course of Ganga (approximately south of 25°10' N latitude) evidences of Stone Age prehistory starts emerging. If one can take a survey of all Prehistoric evidences known from entire Chotanagpur, as also from the hilly regions lying further east in West Bengal, it will be seen that the Kharagpur Hills yield the richest and also the most prolific evidences of Stone Age colonization.

Conclusion

The evidences from Adhwariya show that probably Lower Palaeolithic tools types continue to occur till very late in Pleistocene in this area. This is a special feature, which has been earlier suspected from many other sites, like Damin area in Santhal Pargana, but no one has been very positive about this (Chakrabarti 1986). The main contention of this paper is to demonstrate that there is no evidence of a three fold Palaeolithic succession demonstrable in this region.

Human population come here in Upper Pleistocene and proliferates over a large zone. But does not change its culture demonstrably until about later Pleistocene, when an epi-Palaeolithic culture develops. The site Jurpaniya (Bhattacharya and Singh 1998) shows this feature in a very marked way. Subsequently there must have been marked population depletion. This is believed because the number of early Holocene sites known from the entire Kharagpur hills is almost negligible, when compared with the evidences from the preceding period. Man does return here, although in much lesser number but by this time a rudimentry farming is already demonstrable from at least the archaeological material.

The mixed nature of the industry can raise many theoretical as well as semantic issues in Indian Archaeology, which has not received adequate attention. The present study indicates that the usual approach of looking at

Palaeolithic cultures as constituting discrete water tight compartments of Lower, Middle and Upper Palaeolithic may not always be reflecting the reality as it might have been happening in the prehistoric period. Culture progresses on its own imperatives which in turn may be influenced by such a large number of factors as ecology, technology, demography, social structure, as well as ideology and cognition. This kind of overlapping would appear to be more clearly demonstrated in the Kharagpur hills. It is likely that this is caused by a comparatively late arrival of human beings in this region.

Acknowledgements

We are very grateful to Mr. Ajay Teotiya, D.F.O. Munger and Anil Jha, Ranger of Kharagpur Hills Range, for providing forest rest house for accommodation and Nathu ji, Suresh and Binod of Bhimbandh village for their kind cooperation during the fieldwork. Dr. S.N. Rajguru, retired Professor of Department of Archaeology, Deccan College, Pune had been very kind in helping us with all the intricate problems of geo-morphology and hence chronological status of our sites in Kharagpur Hills. We thank him most respectfully for all his helps.

REFERENCES

Bhattacharya, D.K. and Manoj Kumar Singh 1997-98. The Palaeolithic evidences from Pathalgarwa in Bihar. *Puratattva* 28: 12-25.

Bhattacharya; D.K. and Manoj Kumar Singh 1998. Jurpaniya: The Epl-Palaeolithic Tradition of Kharagpur Valley in Chotanagpur Plateau. *Man in India* 78 (3&4) : 189-204.

Bose, N.K. and D. Sen 1948. *Excavations in Mayurbhanj*. Calcutta: Calcutta University.

Bose, N.K., P. Gupta and A. Bose 1960. Palaeoliths from Monghyr District Bihar. *Man in India* 40 (1): 68-75.

Chakrabarti, D.K. 1986. Lithic Industries of the Santhal Parganas with Notes on the Damin Industry. *Man and Environment* 10: 141-149.

Dassarma, D.C. and S. Biswas 1976. Quaternary Deposits of Belan-Seoi Valleys, Allahabad District, Uttar Pradesh. *Proceedings VI, Indian Geological Micropaleontology Stratigraphy*, India.

Dassarma, D.C. and S. Biswas 1977. Newly Discovered Late Quaternary Vertebrates from the Terraced Alluvial Fills of Son Valley. *Indian Journal of earth science* Vol. 2 Part 2.

Ghosh, A.K. 1970. The Palaeolithic Culture of Singhbhum. Philadelphia: *Transactions of the American Philosophical Society*. New Series-Vol.60, Part I.

Jacobson, Jerome 1975. Early Stone Age Habitation Sites in Eastern Malwa. *Proceedings of the American Philosophical Society* 119 (4): 280-297.

Narayan, Basudev 1996. *Prehistoric Archaeology of Bihar*. Patna : K.P. Jayaswal Research Institute.

O'Malley, L.S.S. 1926. *Bihar and Orissa District Gazetteers: Munghyr*. Superintendent Government Printing, Bihar and Orissa.

Pant, P.C.; V. Jayaswal and R. Tiwari 1978. Paisra : An Acheulian Site in Bihar. *Man and Environment* 2: 21-31.

Passoe, E. 1964. Manual of Geology of India and Burma, Vol. III. ***Miscellaneous publication, Geological Survey of India.***

Roy, R.K.; G.S. Chattopadhayay and B.K. Bisaria 1987. *Project Munger*. Bulletin Series B, No. 49. Calcutta : Geological Survey of India.

Sankalia, H.D. 1974. *Prehistory and Protohistory of India and Pakistan*. Pune : Deccan College.

Sherwill, S.R. 1852. The Kurrukpoor Hills. *Journal of the Asiatic Society of Bengal* 21 (3) : 195-206.

Singh, R.C.P. 1959. Palaeoliths from Bhimbandh. *Journal of the Bihar Research Society* 45 (Part 1-4) : 195-203.

Tagore, R.N. and S.N. Kar. 1944. Referred by N.K. Bose; P. Gupta and A. Bose 1960. Palaeoliths from Monghyr. *Man in India* 40 (1): 68-75.

Waddell, L.A. 1890. On Some New and Little Known Hot Springs in South Bihar. *Journal of The Asiatic Society of Bengal* 59 (3) : 224-235.

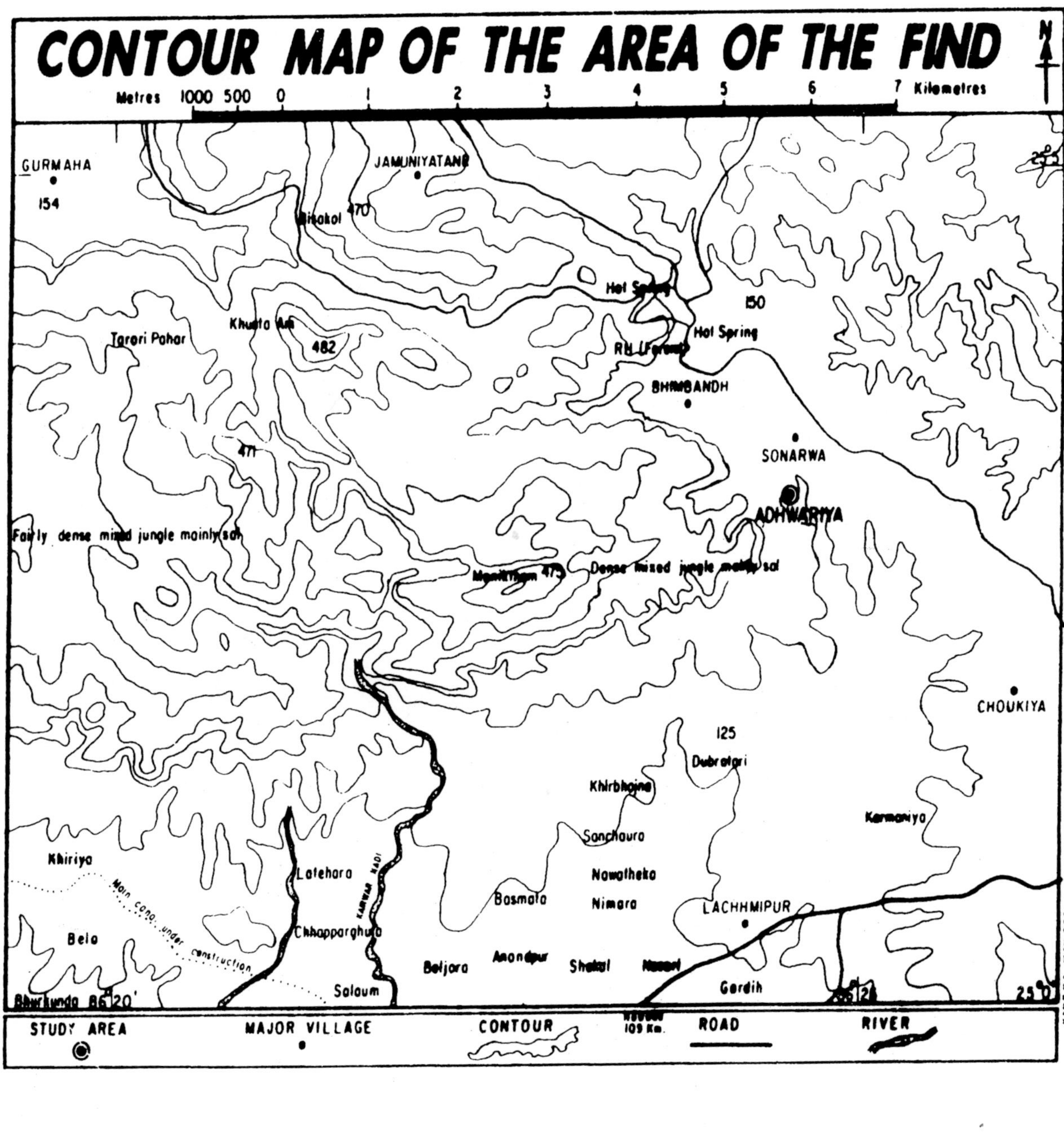

Fig. 1. Physiographic Regionand Contour of the Kharagpur Hills.

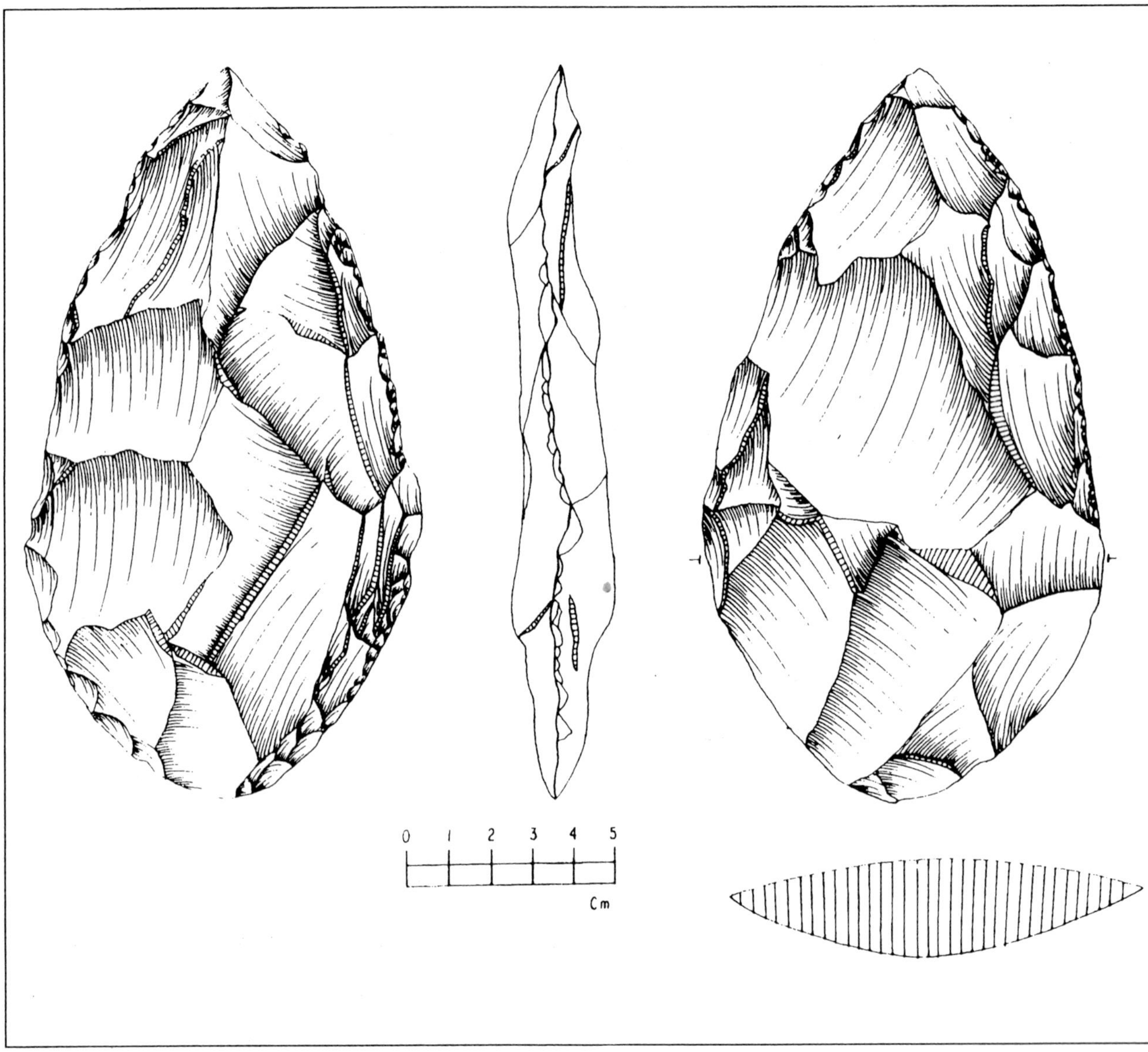

Fig. 2. A Laminar and Massive Handaxe from Ady.

Mesolithic Industry from Bankura: A Preliminary Study

SUBRATA CHAKRABARTI AND BANANI BHATTACHARYYA*

Introduction

The exploratory journeys undertaken by a geologist in the northwestern portion of the district of Bankura in the first half of the last quarter of the 19th century resulted in the discovery of the first Acheulian artefacts, in the vicinity of the Biharinath hill complex, about 17.5 km southwest of Govindapur (Ball, 1865) and Gopinathpur (Ball 1867, 1880) from the upland region of South Bengal. Neither Ball nor any other workers took up further research in pursuit of the significant discovery that Valentine Ball made from this region. In 1960s, nearly after a century, scholars such as V. D. Krishnaswami *et al* (1960), P. C. Dasgupta (1960) and D. Sen *et al* (1963) made new beginning of research into the archaeological, notably Palaeolithic and Mesolithic past of the Bankura region in particular and the Eastern Plateau of India in general. The aims of these works were limited, even though, mostly exploratory in nature, the researches have shown that cultural developments did not remain restricted to one specific area in Bankura. On the contrary, at least three geo-cultural zones could be recognized from Bankura, the hilly regions lying between the Susunia hills and the Gandheswari river valley, the valley of the Dwarakeswar River in the rolling upland areas in southwest portion of the district of Bankura. It should be emphasized that cultural development varied from region to region in Bankura and more importantly, the lands in the northeastern portion of the district still remained largely *terra incognitae* so far as Paleolithic or Mesolithic archaeology is concerned.

In 1992, the first author discovered two sites, one at Chak Dhoyakure, about 4 km southwest and the other at Manipur, about 2 km south from Dhansimla in northeastern Bankura. In 1999, an extensive exploration was carried out in these two sites resulting in the discovery of the Upper Paleolithic-Mesolithic transitional industry and microlithic industry.

This paper presents a preliminary account of the last seasons (1999-2000) fieldwork and field-data obtained from the northeastern region of Bankura.

General Background

The Bankura region, lying between 22° 38` and 23° 38` north latitude and 86° 36` and 87° 46` east longitude, is the western most district of the Burdwan division in South Bengal (Fig.1). It is a region where the plains of Bengal meet the plateaus of Bihar and Chota Nagpur. From physiographical point of view it consists of two distinct landscapes: the tracts of tableland in the western portion of Bankura and the deltoid lands in the east of the region. As a whole, the Bankura region is a Precambrian landmass of rugged beauty with its wide expanse of gen-

*Department of Ancient Indian History, Culture and Archaeology, Visva Bharti, Shantiniketan (West Bengal)

tly undulating grounds, intersected by rivers and streams flowing from northeast to southeast which divide it into a number of parallel strips (O' Mallry 1908). In Bankura, as described by Sir William Hunter (1876) the alluvial flats end in undulations, isolated peaks, and short-low ranges, which form the advanced guard of the hill system of the central Indian Plateau.

The geomorphological setting between west and east Bankura are not only different, but even there is a noticeable difference in the demographic pattern between these two units of Bankura. Whereas the Santals and other tribal groups predominate in west Bankura, the cast Hindus are found in east Bankura in greatest strength.

The northeastern portion of Bankura, the area of our present investigation, is one such area where alluviums end in undulations can be described as a meeting point of two dissimilar morphological regions and two distinct climatic zones. This portion of Bankura though geographically falls under the Damodar Valley; the western part of the valley is formed of the ancient crystalline complex of Peninsular India, whereas the eastern portion falls within the recent alluvial formations of Bengal Basin (Betal 1970). The undulated regions of the Damodar river valley is covered with open and dense Sal forests whereas the rest of the region has Sal and mixed forests. The open and mixed forests from this region have a number of edible flora and fauna with their wild varieties, which must have attracted the hunter-gatherers in the past as it does to the present day tribal population. It is in the light of these background rests the importance of the discovery of the Mesolithic sites from this region of Bankura.

Geographical Setting

(a) The Chak Dhoyakure Site

The village of Chak Dhoyakure (23 degree 15`N and 87 degree 27`E) is a small hamlet situated about 4 km southwest of Dhansimla, a village in the district of Bankura (Fig.1). The Chak Dhoyakure site is situated about a km upstream from the north of the village on the south bank of the Kuasuta river, a feeder channel of the Sali river which is a right bank tributary of the Damodar.

Geomorphologically the region is of a great interest as here the fringe of the eastern plateau of India meets the deltaic region of Bengal built up by the Damodar and its tributaries.

The soil of the area is characteristically red in colour, older alluvium, its thickness varies from 0 to 3 m. Below it, laterite capping is seen which has an approximate thickness of 60 cm-1 m. This rests at places over quartz pebbles and gravel beds deposited by the tributaries of the Damodar. The isolated exposures of Tertiary formations can also be seen here and there in this area. Hundey (1954) has reported *in situ* occurrence of dicotyledonous fossil wood in some Tertiary formations from this region.

At Chak Dhoyakure area, a type section exposed by the Kuasuta river on its south bank, shows four beds. The total thickness of the section is 4.5 m and comprises of the following four members:

Bed IV	pebble conglomerate member
Bed III	sandstone member
Bed II	cobble conglomerate member
Bed I	horizontally bedded claystone member

From archaeological point of view, the pebble conglomerate member is important as a pebble chopper was found embedded in the upper half of the gravel with a ferruginous matrix and lower half of the lateritic capping. A few tools (burins, waste flakes etc.) were also found in the gully erosion from this locality.

In another gully, about a quarter km north from the Locality I, on the south bank of the Kuasuta, a scatter of artefacts, measuring 5 m x 2 m, had been recorded. The geological context of their archaeological horizon here is yet to be ascertained. However, the matrix in which these artefacts are found to lie consists of rounded to sub-rounded pellets of laterite and granular quartz pieces of various sizes. The artefacts do show signs of weathering but some specimens are quite fresh.

(b) The Manipur Site

The village of Manipur (23° 05`N and 87° `E) is situated about 2 km south of Dhansimla. Its population, some time in the past has abandoned this village. Aside from the ruins of a Saiva temple, of *nagara* style built on laterite blocks, there is no trace of any other remains of the past settlement here. The Mesolithic site of Manipur is a wide expanse of lateritic outcrop. Mesolithic artefacts were found *in situ* in clusters or as scatter objects on the surface of this lateritic outcrop. Geographically the area presents a badland topography. A dense Sal forest covers the area.

The Artefact Assembladsge

The artefacts were collected from four different localities of the two sites described above. The context of occurrence of artefacts between the localities differ, for example at Locality I of Chak Dhoyakure a small pebble chopper was found upon a ferruginous matrix sealed in by laterite and pebble conglomerate bed. Some tools were also found in the gully erosion. This suggests that tools found from the erosional gullies are not in their actual archaeological horizon. About a quarter kilometer north from the Locality-I is another gully on the south bank of the Kuasuta River where the Locality II is situated. From this locality a scatter of artefacts, measuring 5 m x 2 m in diameter, has been recorded. The matrix in which these artefacts are found to lay, consists of rounded to sub-rounded pallets of laterite and granular quartz pieces of various sizes. The artefacts are quite fresh; some however show signs of weathering due to long exposure. The context of their occurrence suggests that these have undergone minimal dislocation from their original locale of manufacture but as the collection includes more finished tools than rough out it should be regarded that some displacement of the tools have taken place at this locality because of water action or erosion.

At Manipur, the artefacts occur as loose finds, as scattered objects embedded in lateritic matrix or in loosely cemented clusters upon the lateritic outcrop. It does seem from the nature of occurrence of artefacts from this site that they are subjected to some displacements but since majority of them are remarkably fresh, it would suggest that these have not been subjected to long distance transportation.

However, the geological context and the true archaeological horizon or horizons of the two sites from this region could be known only when excavation is carried out at these two sites.

The Chak Dhoyakure collection shows that quartz is the most predominating raw material followed by chert, quartzite and fossil wood. Whereas, at Manipur chert is the most predominating raw material followed by quartz quartzite, agate, chalcedony and sandstone. A comparative statement of distribution of raw material by rocks employed at Chak Dhoyakure and Manipur is given in Table-1. For raw material, the tool makers need not have to travel long distance because these material form part and parcel of the lateritic formation spreading over the region all around.

The assemblages also show that finished tools dominate over the waste material. At Chak Dhoyakure, blade tool group predominates over the other tool group. The representation of tools in Chak Dhoyakure collection is in the descending order: borers/awls (36.68%), blades (17.91%), scrapers (14.92%), burins (10.44%), lunates (7.46%), points (2.98%), knives (2.98%) and triangle (1.49%). Whereas the Manipur collection shows that blades (15.73%) predominate over the rest of the types in the following order: scrapers (11.23%), borers/awl (10.10%), triangles (7.86%), lunates (4.49%), points (4.49%), beak points (2.24%), combined tool (1.12%), burin (1.12%), micro burin (1.12%) and arrow heads (2.24%).

The debitage includes only one specimen of flake in the Chak Dhoyakure collection, but the Manipur collection has 38.20% of waste material compared to its 61.79% finished tools.

Microlithic industries found from Chak Dhoyakure and Manipur do show similarities and differences in their character and composition. They have been found in iso-

Table : 1 Raw Materialwise Disribution of Artefacts at Chak Dhoyakure and Manipur

Site	Raw Material						
	Quartz	Chert	Quartzite	Fossil Wood	Agate	Chalcedony	Sandstone
Chak Dhoyakure	57.71%	22.38%	20.89%	5.97%	0%	0%	0%
Manipur	24.71%	31.46%	13.48%	0%	6.74%	2.24%	2.24%

lation from pottery and other signs of settled life. However microliths with scrapers and burins found from Chak Dhobakure show that Upper Paleolithic technology was carried forward in the manufacture of the Mesolithic artefacts. On the other hand, Manipur is an industry of lunate microliths with a few triangular variants and scrapers on burins.

Observation

At the present state of our knowledge relating to the Mesolithic assemblages from north-eastern Bankura, it would be difficult to arrive at any definitive conclusion regarding their cultural or chronological status. Nevertheless, the significance of the occurrence of microlithic industries from a region where the lateritic Bengal meets the deltaic Bengal could not be over looked. It suggests that the hunting gathering populations were taking adventurous journeys to look forward to new avenues for cultural colonization.

Secondly, though the collection is small, it shows that microlithic industries of Mesolithic tradition cannot be seen as belonging to one single industrial complex. For example, the evidence of a transitional phase between Upper Paleolithic and Mesolithic is beginning to reveal the process of cultural development step by step.

Thirdly, lunate microliths in West Bengal have been seen largely as industry without triangular and trapezoid variants, or wherein microlithic collection includes geometric tools is considered to be chronologically younger than those from which they are absent. The collections from the area of our present investigation suggest that careful sampling of cultural material from Mesolithic sites would likely to change the idea that lunate mocroliths are devoid of triangular variants.

Finally, as a meeting point of two dissimilar morphological regions and two climatic zones with the presence of the tribal population, the region provides a unique opportunity to approach the cultural development during the Holocene from a multi-disciplinary perspective.

REFERENCES

Ball, V. 1865. Stone implements in Bengal, *Proceeding of the Asiatic Society of Bengal Calcutta*. pp. 127-128

Ball, V. 1867. Stone implements found in Bengal. *Proceeding of the Asiatic Society of Bengal Calcutta*. pp. 136-153.

Ball, V. 1870. Stone implements discovered in Singhbhum, *Proceeding of the Asiatic Society of Bengal*. p. 268.

Ball, V. 1880. Jungle Life in India. *The Journal and Journeys of an Indian Geologist*. London : Thos. De. La. Rue & Co.

Dasgupta, P.C. 1962. *Indian Archaeology-A Review* 1961-62. p. 59.

Deb, Urmila 1995. A new Lithostratigraphic unit at the western fringe of West Bengal, India. *Indian Journal of Geology*, 67(4) : 282-288.

Hundey, A. 1954. On the newly found Tertiary Patches in Bankura Burdwan and Birbhum districts in West Bengal. *Science and Culture* 20:245-246.

Hunter, W.H. 1877. *A Statistical Account of Bengal*, London.

Krishnaswami, V.D. 1960. *Indian Archaeology-A Review* 1959-60. p. 48.

O'Malley, L.S.S. 1908. *Bengal District Gazetteers Bankura*, Calcutta : The Bengal Secretariat Book Depot.

Sen, D., A.K. Ghosh and Meera Chatterjee. 1963. Palaeolithic industry of Bankura, West Bengal. *Man in India* 40 (2) : 100-113.

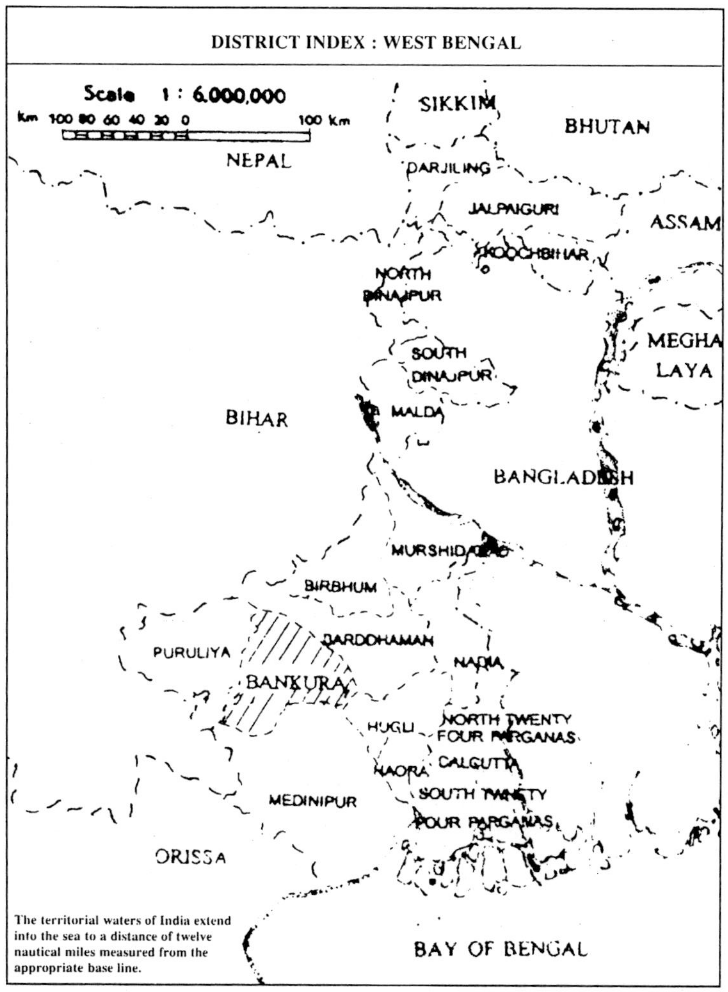

Fig. 1. The location Map of Bankura in West Bengal.

River Saraswati in History, Archaeology and Geology

S.P. GUPTA*

Introduction

It has now being increasingly realized that in the making of the Harappan Civilization both the Indus and the Saraswati played important roles. Of late, there has been a lot of controversy with regard to the origin and flow of the Saraswati. The controversy emerged out of the present-day flow of the river, which is very meager, and the references in the Vedic literature which describe the flow of the Saraswati in terms of a 'gigantic river' emerging 'from the mountains and flowing towards the seas', there are; are apparently contradictory situations. The situation has become more complicated since the discovery in India and Pakistan of 1041 Harappan sites (648 in India and 393 in Pakistan) in the basin of the Saraswati since it pre-supposes the perennial nature of the river in the 4th and 3rd millennia B.C., a fact which in a way supports the Rigvedic references but creates doubt if the present-day scenario of the Saraswati represents the ancient scenario of this river.

Unfortunately, till recently the research was confined to the history and archaeology of the Saraswati covering the ancient and modern drainage from Adi Badri in the Siwaliks to Sindh. Of late, Indian geologists have explored the area beyond Adi Badri, in the central Himalayas, and have shown to us that in ancient times the Saraswati was fed by the waters of glaciers, like the Indus, which was fed by the glaciers. This fact, according to them, insured that the river Saraswati received enormous water round the year. In other words, although the Saraswati today is only an ephemeral river because it is only rain-fed, yet anciently it was a perennial river because it was glacier fed.

The river Saraswati appears to be as old as the last phase of the Upper Pleistocene period, if not earlier. This fact is based upon the geological terraces, which have been located by geologists between the Shimla hills, and Yamuna River, some of which, located on the river Markanda, have produced Paleolithic tools.

Saraswati in History

Period I, Rigvedic

The Saraswati is described in the Rigveda as a great river, rushing down from the mountains towards the ocean VII Mandala, 95th Sukta, 2 verse (VII.95.2) with tempestuous roar (VI.61.8) breaking, and carrying down ridges of hills like lotus stems (VI.61.2), filling the realism of earth and the wide tracts of the firmament (VI.61.11). She is far superior to her companions (VII.95.4) and surpasses all other streams by her sheer majesty (VII.95.1) and glory (VI.61.13). This is fierce (VI.61.13), swiftest of the swifts (VI.61.13), mightiest of

*Chairman, Indian Archaeological Society, New Delhi-110016

her class (VII.96.1). She is the best of the rivers (II.41.16), best of mothers (II, 41, 16) and even best of goddesses (II, 41, 16).

Period II, Brahmana Period

The later Vedic literature, however, gives a very pathetic condition of this river. During this period it shrank. It shrunk enormously. It had now very little water to flow perennially and over long distances. It could no more reach the ocean. It got fanned out in the deserts of Cholistan. The *Aitareya* and the *Satapatha Brahmana* repeatedly mention this fact.

Period III, Mahabharat Period

In the Mahabharat we get many references to prove that by then the Saraswati, which was, joining the Arabian Sea, had fanned out, or lost, so to say in the deserts. It is the region of Vinasana (Salya 35.53). Archaeological and geomorphological evidence place the Vinasana in the deserts near the Derawar Fort in Bahawalpur region of Pakistan. Presently, there is a shallow depression, almost parallel to the Indus, through which a canal, called 'Nara', is flowing. This was the ancient channel of the Saraswati as is held by most of the scholars in the world, including M.R. Mughal and Louis Falm, two distinguished scholars working in Pakistan. The Saraswati, called (Hakra) in the local language of Cholistan, had reached the region just east of Rohri near a place called 'Thar' from where Eastern Nara emerges.

Period IV: 19th Century

In the 19th century the British explorers worked on this river and noted that the Saraswati river which flows near Thanesar or Kurukshetra rises in the hills of Sirmur State, then debouches on the plains at Adi Badri, then disappears in the sands a few miles farther and comes up again about three miles to the south of Bhawanipur. The study mentions that, it once again vanishes at Balchhar for a short distance to emerge once again and flows on in the south-westerly direction across Karnal, until the Ghaggar in Patiala territory joins it after a course of about 110 miles. Running along the towns of Tohana and Sirsa it turns southward to enter Rajasthan in Ganganagar Distt. A little further it vanishes in the deserts of Bahawalpur. R. D. Oldham (1886) and C. F. Oldham (1893) were in fact the pioneers who worked on the Saraswati extensively both in the light of ancient and medieval literature and geology. However, some scholars have been calling the Saraswati river as 'Ghaggar', a river which starts near Kalka in the Shimla hills as a rain-fed small river and meets the Saraswati in Patiala. To impose this name on the entire course of the Saraswati is hardly justified, since Ghaggar is nowhere mentioned in the ancient literature of India. It may also be noted that, since for thousands of years, the Saraswati was seen by different people at different parts of the river in fragmentary condition, each group gave a separate name for the stream they were seeing and experiencing. Hence, we have such names as Nara, Wahind, Hakra, Sotar, Ghaggar and Sarsuti, starting from Sindh, Thar, Cholistan, Punjab and Haryana.

In recent years although several scholars and scientists worked on this subject two groups of scholars worked extensively and intensively on the geographic history of the Saraswati river: Yash Pal, Baldev Sahai and others, and V.M.K. Puri and B.C. Verma. Lately D.P. Rao, Yash Pal and others, has also used Remote Sensing methods to work out the drainage of the Saraswati systems, present and the past.

Saraswati and Glaciers

Geologically speaking, only glaciers could provide water to Saraswati on perennial basis and glaciers were always confined to the Himalayas, they never came down to the Siwaliks. Thus, a search was made in the central Himalayas in the north-east of Patna Saheb across the Siwaliks (Fig. 1). The method adopted was as follows:

First, the area-of-search in the Siwaliks was narrowed down on the basis of literary references and geological formations. It was located between Satluj in the west and Yamuna in the east.

Second, openings in between these two rivers in the Siwaliks were then located. One is the site of Adi Badri near Markanda and the other is Kalesar near Yamuna. Tradition upholds Adi Badri as the source of Saraswati in the plains, and Kalesar as the entry-point for the Yamuna in the plains; above these points are the highlands of the Siwaliks.

Explorers in the past had already worked out the

courses of the Saraswati and Yamuna in the plains. In recent years Satellite imageries of these regions were taken, palaeo-channels of the Satluj and the Yamuna were identified, and their relation with the Saraswati worked out by scholars like Yash Pal, Puri, Rao and others. It was found that Satluj was once a tributary of the Saraswati; it is only in recent times of historical period that Satluj shifted westward and joined Beas, a tributary of the Indus. Archaeological, geological and geographical explorations and their combined studies also establish the process of shifting of the Satluj from the southwest to extreme west.

Third, Yamuna was already studied by geologists, geographers, archaeologists and historians from its origins in the Yamnotri glaciers to its merger in the Ganga at Allahabad. In recent years Yash Pal and his colleagues have worked on this river also, through the Landsat imagery of the palaeo-channels in the plains.

In other words, the study of Palaeo-channels of the Satluj and the Yamuna prove that anciently both the Satluj and the Yamuna, the two perennial rivers, were the tributaries of the Saraswati, the former was then called Shatudri and the latter was called Drishadvati, both are mentioned in the Vedic literature.

With this knowledge about the Saraswati and its tributaries, Puri and his associates moved in the mid-Himalayas to locate the signatures of the old channels of the Saraswati. Puri, therefore, concentrated on the glaciers and rivers emerging from them, and Verma concentrated on the terraces of these rivers. They hold a particular channel as 'Vedic Saraswati' or Palaeo-Saraswati. Puri and Verma worked out its geological history. Their findings are as follows:

A. There is a large watershed area in the Siwalik belt north of Kalesar, which is called 'Paonta Doon'. It came into existence between 0.6 and 0.1 million years, i.e. in the late Upper Pleistocene period. There are five present-day rivers, which converge here—the Algar, the Yamuna, the Tons, the Giri and the Bata. Paonta Doon area is 'situated over a thick pile of sediments and the drainage here acquires a considerable width. The elevation difference between Paonta and Kalesar, a stretch of nearly 10 km, is hardly 12 m (40 ft.). Obviously, since 'the valley sediment is very thick... probably a larger drainage was occupying this valley in the past', they surmised.

In order to study the drainage pattern of the five above mentioned rivers and the Paonta Doon area, both of which hold the key to our understanding of the Vedic or Palaeo-Saraswati, Verma did geological mapping of the region between the Yamuna and the Markanda rivers in the Siwaliks and beyond. He identified four terraces, numbered T, T1, T2 and T3, T being the highest, hence oldest, and T3 being the lowest, hence youngest. These are respectively (Plate 1):

(i)	Sudanwala Terrace	:	T
(ii)	Bata Terrace	:	T1
(iii)	Garibnath Terrace	:	T2
(iv)	Markanda Terrace	:	T3

'The discovery of Sudanwala Terrace (T) constitutes a major break-through in delineating the course of Vedic Saraswati. It contains a signature of this river that is completely masked now'. This terrace is located nearly 2 km S, 10^0E of Sudanwala, and nearly caps the top Siwalik Hills. The average elevation of this terrace is 660 m (2178 ft.) above MSL. Contituent pebbles of this terrace consists of different lithological compositions but quartzite and metamorphic materials are prevalent'.

The Bata terrace (T1) is 'located almost linear in shape on the southern slope of Bata valley and occupies its higher portion'. Like the Sudanwala terrace, it is also composed of pebbles and boulders of quartzite and other metamorphic rocks.

The Garibnath terrace (T2) is located in the most strategic position in Paonta Doon and lays North-North-East of Paonta- in N 15^0 E - S 15^0 W direction. The elevation difference from Terrace top (594 m) to the present riverbed (408 m) is nearly 180 m (600 ft.). Here also the pebbles, etc. are of quartzitic and other metamorphic rocks.

The Markanda terrace (T3) is 'located almost in linear disposition on the southern slope of Markanda valley, ESE of Nahan'. The pebbles of quartzite are in abundance here also. Archaeology and geology place the terrace in the Upper Pleistocene period. Rajguru and Badam have worked on the geology and prehistory of the Markanda valley terraces.

It is extremely significant to note that 'the present day provenance of the Bata and Markanda terraces consists of Siwalik rocks only; they do not contain any metamorphic rock and quartzite. The presence of these (metamorphic and quartzite) rocks as pebbles in T and T1 terraces points towards the conclusion that another river that occupied these valleys had traversed a region where quartzite and other metamorphic rocks were found in abundance'.'It is also significant to note that younger terraces (T2 and T3) in these valleys do not contain even a single pebble of quartzite and other metamorphosed rocks, except along the present Yamuna course. This scenario indicates that provenance of the terrace material got restricted to Siwalik belt only. Moreover, Bata-Markand divide is only 30 m (100ft.) high at present, which separates these rivers flowing in opposite directions'.

Thus, there is the clinching evidence 'of a huge river, flowing from the east to the west in the Paonta valley at a much higher level, prior to the birth of the present day Yamuna river, whose terraces are still observed along Adh Badri- Markanda link in the plains immediately to the south of the Siwalik belt'.

The Drainage of Palaeo-Saraswati and Saraswati Glacier in the Himalayas

The most crucial area for the drainage study of the Palaeo-Saraswati in the Himalayas is the Tons fifth order basin, where lie thick strata of formations of quartzite and other metamorphic rocks at several places, the pebbles of which are found in the river terraces mentioned earlier. It may be noted that 'Tons river passes a very high average discharge, which almost exceeds the combined discharge of Aglar, Yamuna, Giri, Bata and also Markanda rivers. Further, the most significant criterion is the presence of a number of glaciers in this basin.'

The Saraswati seems to have originated in the geological times and passed through the prehistoric times of early to late Stone Ages. Puri and Verma feel that, *'All the evidences [geomorphological, glaciological and geological] point to only one coclusion that the present day Tons was in fact the Vedic Saraswati in its upper reaches. This river was in existence during Upper Pleistocene period as it was fed by glaciers that had descended to much lower limits in Garhwal Himalaya than the present day level due to the influence of Pleistocene Ice Age'*. Presently the Snowline is farther and on higher altitudes than what it was during the Pleistocene. In fact the glaciers in this region, including Gangotri, have been and are being fast receding.

The origin of the Palaeo-Saraswati lies at 5 km southwest of Naitwar. Situated on the confluence of the Rupin and the Tons rivers, the former emerging out of the Rupin Glacier and the latter emerging out of the Glacier named 'Saraswati Glacier' by Puri. 'The Saraswati Glacier was 58.8 km in length that possessed an average width of 3.5 km, covering an area of 205.8 km.'

From Naitwar, the Palaeo-Saraswati, same as modern Tons flowed for 40 km in southwesterly direction where it met another glacier-fed river called 'Pabbar', after the name of the glacier. From here, the Palaeo-Saraswati took a southerly route and travelled for 100 km before entering the region of Paonta Doon. It is here that the Palaeo-Saraswati joined the Algar, the Yamuna and the Giri rivers coming to Paonta Doon from northwesterly region. From here 'it took a course that is aligned along south of Kalsi, Garibnath, Paonta and Bata valley, i.e, west to south-westerly direction and flowed over the raised and filled platform of the Siwaliks.' In the third and last stage, when the Palaeo-Saraswati reached the Bata valley, it took the southwesterly swing and 'entered the plains through Adh Badri'. In other words, at this point of time, there did not exist the so-called 'Yamuna Tear' near Kalesar for the Palaeo-Saraswati to escape into the plains, Adi-Badri was the only first available gap in the Siwaliks for the Palaeo-Saraswati to descend into the plains (Fig. 2).

Here, it may be noted, that next and close to it is the Markanda valley. 'The field evidences suggest that the area between Garibnath-Kalesar and Markanda valley was once filled with a huge pile of fluvial sediments. The main drainage of Vedic Saraswati followed this terrain and oscillated between present-day Adh Badri and Markanda valley due to tectonic activity, whereby the Siwalik belt was uplifted. In due course of time, it is possible that it was entering plains from Adh Badri as well through Markanda conduit'. Here it may be kept in mind that the Kalesar gap with 'Proto-Yamuna', which was a tributary of the Palaeo-Saraswati, was not at all active at this point of time, here there was no flow which could give rise to the present-day Yamuna.'

'From Adh Badri region, the Palaeo-Saraswati took the south-westerly course and reached Kurukshetra. From here it turned to slightly westerly direction and met the monsoon-fed Ghaggar, which emerged from the hills near Shimla. Around 25 km south of Patiala, the Tibetan glacier fed Perennial River Satluj joined this course of the Saraswati and made it the mightier of the mightiest river with enormous quantity of water flowing through a very wide channel. It was certainly the case from 4000 B.C. through 2000 B.C.'

Puri feels that 'consequent to erosion and tectonic activity, the Vedic Saraswati shifted its course finally from Adh Badri conduit and occupied the present-day Markanda valley' which is close to Adi-Badri.

The Yamuna Tear: Its Role in the Saraswati's Disappearance

It brings us to the question of desiccation of the Saraswati, and the role that the Kalesar Gap and Yamuna tear played.

In course of time, Neo-tectonic movements and climatic changes gripped the catchment area of the Palaeo-Saraswati. According to Puri, six major episodes took place.

Around Kalesar there is what is called 'Yamuna tear fault' which has always been prone to tectonic movements and great disasters. This tear 'got activated after Vedic Saraswati came into existence' due to which the Proto-Yamuna left the Saraswati and started flowing through the Kalesar conduit and became the Drishadvati of the Rigveda fame. It soon became a tributary of the Saraswati (Yash Pal's Y2 channel) after flowing past Hissar, Bhadra, Nohar, etc. and joining the Saraswati near Suratgarh in Rajasthan.

Episode II is marked by the upliftment of the Bata-Markanda divide by about 30 m (100 ft.). It created such a critical situation in which the rivers like Bata had to change their direction of flow, almost in the reverse direction.

Episode III is the result of the Episode II which changed the slope and 'reversed the drainage of Bata from west to southeast and south' resulting in the change of Saraswati water flow, most of it now joined the Palaeo-Yamuna or Drishadvati and made it a perennial river. The Saraswati was now completely depended on the monsoon precipitation and the Satluj water. This was the beginning of the end.

In Episode IV new tectonic activities shifted the Palaeo-Yamuna or Drishadvati (Y2 channel of Yash Pal) in the plains further to the east, making it an independent river now called Yamuna (around 1500 B.C.-1000 B.C. period of Painted Grey Ware), which are Y3 channel of Yash Pal, flowing past Bharatpur and merging into Chambal (Fig. 3).

Soon new shifts took place due to fresh tectonic movements and the Yamuna changed its course to present-day Yamuna flowing past Mathura and joining the Ganga at Triveni in Allahabad.

The Episode V is marked by the change of the course of river Satluj. Around Ropar (Modern Roopnagar) it took the 90^0 westerly swings, and slowly and gradually met the Beas in 12th century A.D. at Bhao-ka-Pattan (between Kasur and Ferozpur). Later on, the confluence shifted to Hari-ka-Pattan in the 16th century. It is interesting to note that during the last 100 years, the Satluj has shifted its course westward by almost 16 km from Budha Nala near Ludhiana. Satluj has been a most unfaithful river whose history can be compared in Asia only with the Oxus, which also shifted its course drastically, first it discharged its waters in the Caspian Sea then took a sharp turn and started emptying itself in the Aral Sea.

Episode VI is marked by the disorientation of the Vedic Saraswati. It was the 'cumulative effect of all the five episodes viz. reactivation of the Yamuna tear, constriction of the catchment area of the Palaeo-Saraswati by 94.05%, emergence and migration of river Drishadvati towards south-east acquiring the present day Yamuna course and finally shifting of Shatudri (Satluj).'

Sum Up

It is now clear as to why the *Rigveda* described the Saraswati as a 'mighty river flowing from the mountains'; at one point of time it did emerge from the waters of the glaciers and it had also the water of the perennial river Satluj emerging from the waters of the Tibetan glaciers.

It is now also clear as to why the *Mahabharat* mentions it as getting lost in the deserts; at a later date the perennial Saraswati lost the waters of the glaciers and also of the Satluj. Now it is only a monsoon-fed disjointed river of a series of dried up lakes. Even the *tirthas* such as Kurukshetra and Pehowa on its bank in Haryana, have been abandoned by the Saraswati, these are fed with waters brought from man-made canals.

BIBLIOGRAPHY

Bakliwal, P.C. And Grover, A.K. 1998. Signature and migration of Saraswati River in Thar Desert, Western India, *Rec. Geol. Surv. India,* 116(3-8) pp. 77-86.

Flam, Louis 1984. The Palaeography and Prehistoric Settlement Patterns of the Lower Indus Valley, in *Studies in the Archaeology and Palaeoanthropology of South Asia* (Eds. K.A.R. Kennedy and G.L.Possehl) pp.65-89.

Gupta, S.P. 1996. *The Indus-Saraswati Civilization,* (Pratibha Prakashan, New Delhi).

Misra, V.N. 1994. Indus Civilization and the Rigvedic Saraswati, in *South Asian Archaeology,* 1993, Vol. II, pp.511-525.

Mughal, M.R. *Cholistan,* (Karachi, 1977).

Puri, V.M.K. and Verma, B.C. 1998. Glaciological and Geological Source of Vedic Saraswati in the Himalayas, *Itihas Darpan,* vol. IV, No. 2, pp. 7-21. References in the text against Puri and Verma are from this article.

Puri, V.M.K. and Siddiqui, M.A. 1996. Glacial Deformation and Strain Rate Tensor Analysis of Gangotri Glacier, Uttarkashi Distt. U.P., *Proc. Symp. North-West Himalaya and Foredeep*, Geol. Survey of India, Spl. Pub. 21(2) pp. 307-310.

Radhakrishna, B.P. and Merh, S.S., *Vedic Saraswati*, Memoir 42, Geological Society of India, Banglore, 1999. It contains several articles by archaeologists and geologists including those of R.D. Oldham (1886) and C.F. Oldham (1893).

Rajguru, S.N. and Badam, G.L. 1999. Late Quaternary Geomorphology and Environment of the Markanda Valley, Himachal Pradesh, *Vedic Saraswati*, Memoir 42, Eds. B.P. Radhakrishna and S.S. Merh, *Geological Society of India*, Bangalore, pp.143-152.

Rao, D.P. 1999. Role of Remote Sensing in understanding of Palaeo-drainage Evolution in *Vedic Saraswati*, (Eds. B.P. Radhakrishna and S.S. Merh), pp.39-44.

Ravi Shanker, Kumar G. and Saxena, S.P. 1989. Stratigraphy and Sedimentation in Himalaya- A Reappraisal, Geology and Tectonics of Himalaya, *Geol. Survey of India*, Spl. Pub. 26, pp. 1-6.

Shome, S.K. and Mandwal, N.K. 1979. Yamuna Tear- its implications on Project Planning in the Area, *Jr. Engg. Geol.*(Ind. Soc.Engg.Geol.) 9(1) pp. 25-30.

Yash Pal; Sahai, Baldev; Sood, R.K., and Agrawal, D.P. 1980. Remote Sensing of the 'Lost' Saraswati River, Proc. *Indian Academy of Science* (Earth Planetry Science) 89(3), pp. 317-331.

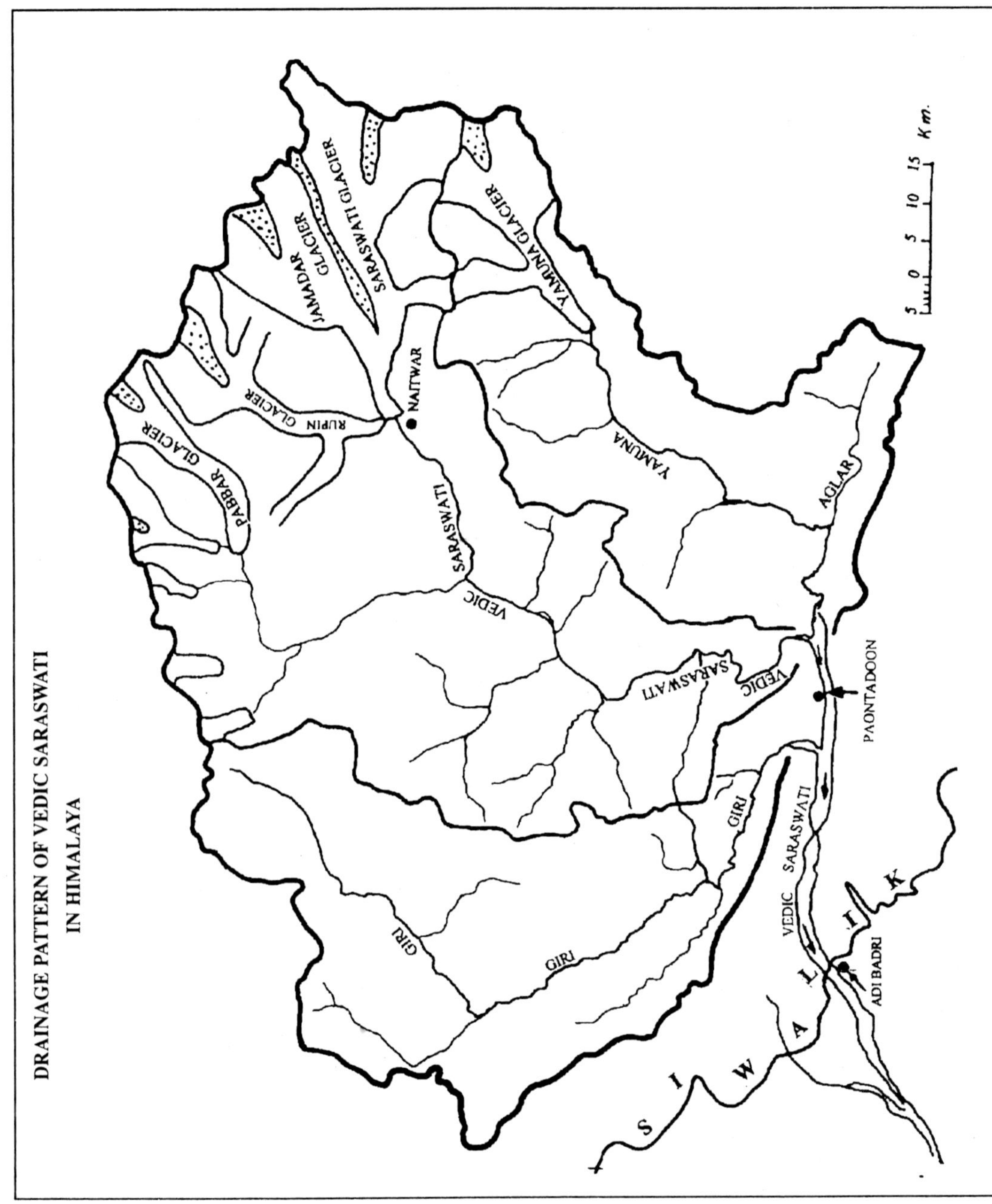

Fig. 1. Vedic or Palaeo-Saraswati emerging from the Rupin Glacier (after Puri and Verma).

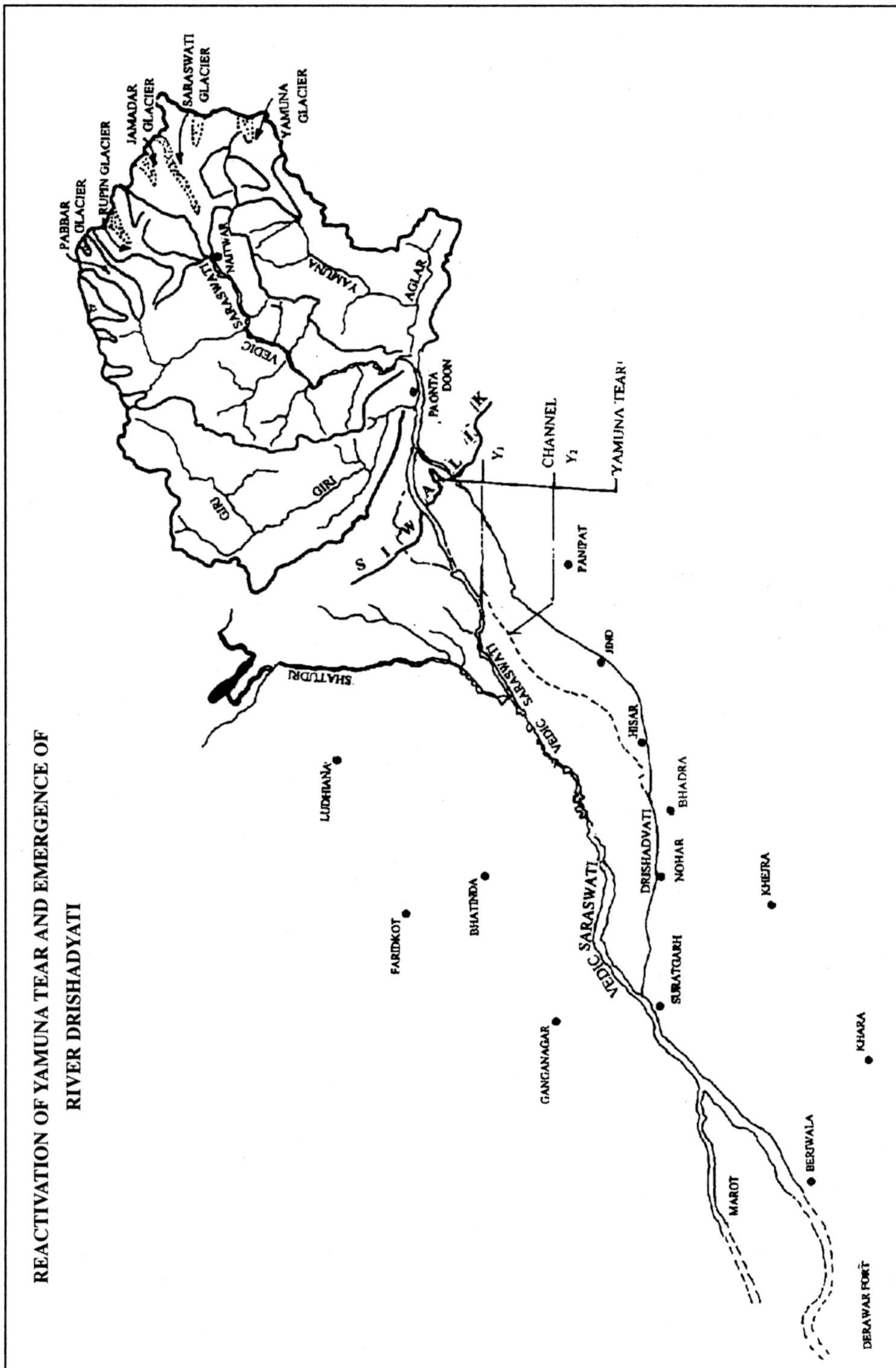

Fig. 2. After Puri, Verma and Yash Pal.

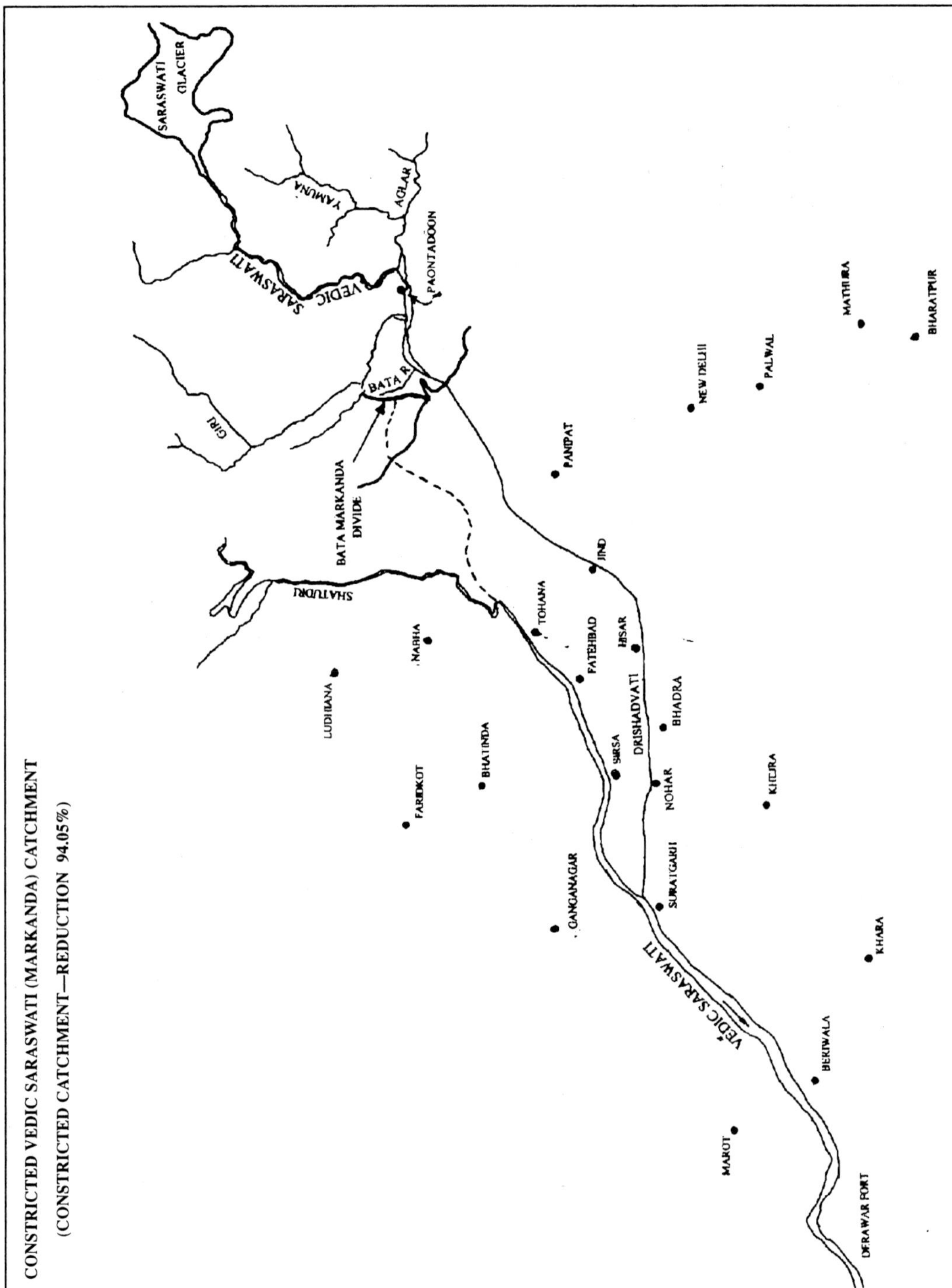

Fig. 3. After Puri and Verma.

Harappan Remains at Ropar

Y.D. SHARMA*

Situation

In 1952, when excavations were undertaken, Ropar was the headquarter of a Tehsil in Ambala district. Later with the partitioning of Punjab into Punjab and Haryana, it became a district and its English spelling Ropar was modified to Ropar ('o' in place of 'u') in order to bring it nearer to the local prounciation of the name. Later, the town was renamed as Rupnagar, in recognition of a prevalent local tradition that this was its ancient name. I shall, however, continue to call it Ropar.

Situated at the point where the Sutlaj rushes into the plains, Ropar occupies an exceptionally strategic position, which accounts for its almost continuous occupation. Its fertile alluvium produced ample food, and the river/and the Siwaliks-opposite the town, not only gave it a unique setting of picturesqueness, they also afforded it protection from likely raiders.

Mainly there are three mounds at Ropar, northern, southern and a smaller one to the west of the former. The northern mound is presently free form building, the southern one is occupied by the present town, while the western one is also uninhabited, but conceals the Harappan cemetery.

While I excavated at Ropar, I also explored its neighbourhood and discovered other ancient sites, I sank some trenches at two other sites. These are Kotla Nihang Khan, 3 km, south-east of Ropar, and Bara, 8 km south. The three sites form a triangle, and since each represents a different 'brand' of Harappa or pre-Harappa culture, it is very essential to understand their inter-relationship.

Periods

The past of Ropar may be devided into six main periods:

Period I	Pre-Harappa, Harappa and cognate cultures divided into three sub-periods, A, B and C.
Period II	Painted Grey Ware Period, *C* 1100-600 B.C.
Period III	Northern Black Polished Ware Period, *C* 600-200 B.C.
Period IV	Early Historical-to-Historical Period, *C* 600-200 B.C.-A.D. 700.
Period V	Early Medieval Period, *C* A.D. 700-1200.
Period VI	Middle Medieval Period, *C* A.D. 1200-1700.

Like period I, each of the subsequent periods is also

*B-16, Kailash Colony, New Delhi-110048

divided into sub-periods, but these sub-periods have been omitted here.

Ropar-I

When I excavated Ropar, the division of Period I into sub-periods was not very clear, but with detailed analysis of finds, and in view of fresh information from other sites excavated subsequently, this sub-division has became distinct. It is essential here to say something also of the excavations at Kotla Nihang Khan and Bara, in order to understand the lowest levels of Ropar. Originally, I visualized three phases of Harappa culture on the upper Sutlej, sequentially represented by Kotla Nihang Khan, following by Ropar, which in turn was followed by Bara, so that Bara represented the latest phase and was thus described as late Harappan.

The assemblages are now interpreted a little differently. Kotla Nihang Khan represents largely the classical phase of Harappan culture, although the site is comparatively small. Apparently Bara represents a pre-Harappan tradition. The base originates perhaps from a culture, which is essentially pre-Harappan. There are common pottery types in pre-Harappan Kalibangan from each other. Plian pottery is scanty at Bara; it is decorated either with paintings or with incised designs. Out of the six varities of pre-Harappan Kalibangan fabrics, it is only the roughened surface of Fabric B and Fabric D and F that occur also at Bara. In the matter of painted designs Bara is closer to northern Baluchistan than pre-Harappan Kalibangan. Apart from pottery, faience bangles show a unique richness, otherwise Bara is only a village settlement. What is more, it has little to offer in the matter of architecture. Bara may possess an urban impulse, but nothing more.

Over twenty trenches were laid at Ropar, among which three are important for period I: RPR-1, north-south, RPR-2, east-west, on the east of the mound, and RPR-7, being the southern extension of RPR-1 with a long unexcavated gap between the two. In RPR-1, in a representative section, the lowest two layers, (35-B) and (35-A), have some pre-defence Harappan material, with a few likely Bara and Harappan sherds. Other parallels of (35-B) and (35-A), pottery of RPR-1 are found in Kalibangan I, Siswal B and Kot-diji. Above (35-A), pre-defence material abruptly comes to an end, and in layer (35), after a sprinkling of Bara pottery, mature Harappan forms appear in good strength, and continue in the same measure in the upper levels, along with some Bara wares. In RPR-2, the habitation begins in layer (44) with Bara ware. There is no trace of pre-defence Harappan here. It is only in layer (41) that some unmistakable frangments of Harappan ware occur for the first time, and they are not plentiful even in there upper levels. There are thus three sub-periods of Period I. Period I A, covering layers (35B) and (35A) of RPR-1, represents pre-defence Harappan. In RPR-2, layers (44) to (42) represent Bara and may be called Period IB. The remains of Period I C, which cover the arrival of Harappans and their overlap with Barans, are seen in layers (34A), (34), (33A) and (33) of RPR-1 and in layers (41), (40), (39), (38) and (37) of RPR-2. In the overlap sub-period while Bara predominates at RPR-2, Harappan does so at RPR-1. Once the Barans and the Harappans occupied the same site, both lived together, apparently harmoniously. They influenced each other, yet maintained their independent identities. At Ropar, with Barans at the eastern end and the Harappans occupying the remaining site, the two groups lived in separate *mohallas* as it were. This may have even far-reaching sociological implications, and may be somewhat to the caste system. For, a number of towns and villages in India are divided into *mohallas* for different castes even to this day. Significantly the graves at Ropar represent the R-37, pattern of burials at Harappa, and contain little Bara pottery. The cemetery of the Barans, if they practised burials, is yet to be discovered.

The characteristic type of Ropar I A pottery is a vase of matt brown-red ware, having a wide black band at its concave neck, with an almost featureless rim. The rim and the body of the vessel are potted separately and then luted. This characteristic obtains also in Kalibangan I, but I am not aware of its occurrence in pre-defence Harappa, Siswal B or Kot-Diji. Ropar I B, Bara types have parallels in Harappan wares, but the two assemblages are quite distinct. The Harappan types of Ropar I C include the long-stemmed and wide based dish-on-stand or bowl-on-stand, disc-based goblet, flat-based or disc-based globular or barrel-shaped jar, cylindrical beaker, elliptical vase, graceful elliptical vase with hollow pedestal base, wide and deep bowl with ring base, perforated jar and internally knobbed lid. Among typical vessels of classical Harappan assemblage, which are absent at Ropar, are goblets with pointed base and flat-based dishes *(thalis)*.

These types are absent in Ropar I B and Ropar I C. The Bara pottery is brownish, as distinct from Harappan pottery, which is matt red. The Bara dish-on-stand is short-stemmed. Small globular painted jars, cylindrical beakers, barrel-shaped vases, deep, wide bowls and internally knobbed lids are some of the other chracteristic types at Bara. Intersecting circles, fish-scales, *Peepal* leaves and fish are the prominent painted designs on Harappan pottery. Fish occurs, also in Bara pottery, but not the other designs. Wavy bands between horizontal bands is a recurring painted pattern on Bara wares. Other motifs include a hornlike representation, opposed triangles or 'butterfly', vertical or horizontal willow leaves in series, 'fishing net', hatched triangles, squares or rectangles, solid dots in series, tree with needle like leaves, rosette and chequer decorations on the shoulders of cooking vessels or storage jars. The incised designs have a rich combination of simple lines, horizontal, wavy, looped or criss-crossed. The bases of cooking vessels or storage jars are generally rusticated with honeycombed pinches, brush-executed spirals or fingered patchwork.

Among other articles of everyday use of the Harappans are bronze implements and utensils, beads and bangles of faience, terracotta cakes, chert weights and blades.

Structures are not plenty in Ropar I A levels. Ropar I B revealed a wall of river pebbles, while the sun-baked and kiln-burnt bricks and cut kankar stones formed the building material in Ropar IC levels.

Evidence on streets, size and layout of houses, public drains etc. could not be expected in a limited area, which had shrunk to a very small size when we reached the Ropar I A levels at a depth of 12-15 meters after part removal of upper levels.

A single Harappan seal found in RPR-1 is manufactured with steatite and bears three familiar symbols on the obverse and concentric circles on the reverse, much as the seals found at Harappa and Mohenjodaro but its thinness and small size, without any perforated base, place it in a class by itself. Another burnt clay lump bears impressions of three typical seals with bull motif and inscriptions in the familiar Indus script. Graffiti on pottery included Indus script.

A cemetery of the Harappans, recalling Cemetery R-37 of Harappa, was also located at Ropar to the west of the northern mound. It was found considerably disturbed by later occupants, mainly by the users of the P.G.W. but some of the burials were sufficiently intact to give an adequate idea of the method of burrial. The body was laid in grave pit, measuring 2.45 cm x 91.50 cm x 60 cm deep on an average. The head was usually placed on the north-west. Most of the burials contained as assemblage of typical pots and some of them also revealed personal ornaments, such as bangles of shell or faience and beads of faience and semi-preceious stones. A faience bangle was still on the left wrist of the wearer, while in another skeleton the middle finger of the right hand had a copper ring.

The entire range of objects discovered at Harappa and Mohenjodaro is certainly not present at Ropar. Several factors may, however, be responsible for this. Ropar was no doubt an important settlement, but it could by no means compete with the likely metropolitan status of Harappa and Mohenjodaro. Allowance must also be made for the fact that Ropar has so far been excavated on an extremely limited scale. Finally, and this is the most important reason, by the time the Harappans reached Ropar, their civilization had undergone substantial transformation.

The date of Ropar I levels is a matter of estimating at present. The fact that a sherd of typical Kalibangan I type occurs at the lowest levels of Ropar I A and another in the upper levels of Ropar I C shows that its date cannot be very late. On the other hand we must take into consideration the evidence of Bhagvanpura in Harayana, where a late phase of Bara everlaps with the P.G.W. The Ropar I levels, therefore probably date from about 2100 B.C. to 1400 B.C. But these dates may have to be revised in the light of further evidence.

The Barans and Harappans, who appear to have lived together in sub-period Ropar I C, left the site finally, perhaps in search of 'new pastures '. There might have been other considerations and circumstances, which are at present matters of debate among scholars. There is no doubt that from Ropar serving as the spring-board, the integrated Bara-Harappa people jumped on to the Ganga-Yamuna *Doab*, where they are met with at several sites, but which still await detailed investigation. This much, however, is certain that the character of Bara-Harappa culture in the

Ganga-Yamuna *Doab* had undergone further transformation beyond tht of the upper Sutlej.

The site of Ropar appears to have remained uninhabited for some time after the departure of Bara-Harappa folks, till before the end of the second millennium B.C. The users of the P.G.W. came and settled there.

Rakhigarhi: 1999–2000

AMARENDRA NATH*

During the third field-season[1], the excavations at Rakhigarhi were resumed with five principal objectives. Three were related to the objectives based on the findings obtained during the preceding field seasons while two remain outstanding since the project was initiated. Firstly, to expose the outline of Hapappan fortification (Period II) in the western half of the citadel mound (RGR-2), the trenches subjected to excavation were: A -15, A - 16, B-13, B-14, B-15, B-16 and C-15. Secondly, to further ascertain the nature of structures (Period II) in some desirous parts of the citadel, the trenches subjected to excavation were- G-25, H-25, T-28, U-19, V-17, V-18, W-14, W-16, X-16, X-17 and Y-17. Likewise on the southern slope of RGR-4, the trenches opened were: A-2, L-4, B-1, C-1, D-1, D-2, XA-2, XA-3 and ZC-1. Similarly at RGR-1, the trenches subjected to excavation for structural remains of Period II were: H-6, H-7, J-6, J-7, K-3, K-4, L-4, L-5, L-6, M-6, M-7, and R-3, while for the structural remains of Period I, the trenches, located on the southern slope, opened were M-10, M-11 and P-11. Thirdly, to ascertain the southeastern extent of habitation (RGR-5) of Period II, U-19 was opened. Fourthly in order to ascertain the lay out of Early Harappan settlement at RGR-6, the trenches subjected to excavation were: M-11, M-12, and M-13 and fifthly, to realize the most significant objective of identification of the Cemetery area (RGR-7), R-20 was opened (Fig. 1).

The sequence of culture as noted during the last field season was reconfirmed. Besides RGR-1, the occupation of Early Harappan period was noticed in the northern half of citadel mound (RGR-2), overlain by occupation of Mature Harappan period. However, the cuttings at RGR-6 reported deposit of over 5 meters attributed to the different phases of Early Harappan period.

Period-I (Early Harappan): The occupation of Early Harappan period was further sub-divided into two broad sub-periods, namely, Period-I (a) pre-formative urbanism and Period-I (b) formative urbanism.

Period I

Period-I (a) of pre-formative urbanism at RGR-6 reported circular structure (dia-2 m) with an entrance (90 cm wide) towards south, was made out of wedged shaped sun dried mud bricks. Contemporary to the circular structure was noticed, a rectangular structure (2.20 m x 1.60 m) made of sun-dried mud bricks (33 x 24 x 9 cm). Both the structures had mud floors. At RGR-1, also a circular structure (dia 1.90 m) with an entrance (90 cm) towards east was noticed. Here, the structure was outlined by four courses of mud brick wall with post-holes at intervals to hold enclosure wall of wattle and daub, possibly supporting a conical thatched super structure. The inner floor of the structure was of mud while the courtyard was paved

*Director, Institute of Archaeology, Archaeological Survey of India, New Delhi

with burnt brickbats.

Period-1 (b) of formative urbanism was characterized by planned settlement and emergence of other cultural traits namely un-inscribed seals, inscribed pottery, terracotta bull figurines, chert blades and weights etc. The cuttings at RGR-1 and RGR-6 had revealed these evidences.

At RGR-6, in trench M 12, houses were built on either side of 1.92 m wide-east west running street. The cutting of street exposed three successive structural phases, overlying one above the other. In phase-I (b) (i), a rectangular structure (3 m x 2.45 m) built of sun-dried bricks of 3:2:1 ratio was noticed, sealed by layer (6). In side this structure, two oblong pits were noticed showing fire activity, filled with ash and bits of charcoal. In successive phase-I (b) (ii), a house consisting of two rectangular rooms (4.35 x 1.78 m; 4.35 x 2.62 m) with a courtyard was planned on the southern side of above-mentioned street, intersected by a north-south lane. On the other side of the lane, a similar layout of the house could be traced partially. A circular brick lined hearth (dia-1 m) was noticed in one of the cells (2.20 m x 2.40 m). Similar hearth was also exposed within a cell located on the northern side of the street. This type of hearth, locally known as '*arha*' is still being in vogue for boiling milk. In the last structural phase-I (b) (iii), a square room (3.20 m x 3.20 m) with an entrance (1 m) towards south was exposed.

The Early Harappan ceramic industry included all the six Kalibangan fabrics, besides a few examples of hand made pottery. Apart from these pottery types, some shreds reminiscent to *Hakra* ware, were also reported which included (i) incised (ii) applique, (iii) dendritic (iv) ribbed or striated varieties. The incised ware were the characterized by thick and thin medium six vases which was decorated externally with groups of multiple incised lines drawn horizontally, diagonally and in wavy compositions. Applique ware was basically red, characterized by thick applique zigzag bands occurring over big jars having pronounced out curved rim. The dendritic ware was of medium fabric and the shape met with was vases of medium size. It was first painted from neck to shoulder and the shape met with was vases of medium size. It was first painted from neck to shoulder and subsequently treated with secondary coating of mud mixed with coarse particles. The paste has generally been overlapping the chocolate slip applied over the out turned rim, neck and shoulder portion of a pot. The ribbed ware was both in thick and thin fabrics; the shape however, could not be determined. Among the typical grey ware shapes of Rakhigarhi, mention may be made of legged basin, dish and dish on stand, while a considerable number of bowls found in *bichrome* ware also deserve mention. Other noteworthy shapes in red ware were vase, *lota*, storage jar, *handi*, dish-on-stand, bowl, trough etc. Painting horizontal bands generally found around the neck of the pot and triangles in a row, and other restricted varieties include sun, *peepal* leaf, floral and geometric motifs, besides typical horn motif. Large number of animal bones found during the excavation throw important light on animal husbandry pattern of the Early Harappan people.

Important antiquities reported were terracotta rattles and bull figurines, segmented bangles, stone bead polisher and sling balls, graffiti marked potsherds, hopscotch, wheel and toy cart frame, bone point, quern and Muller a set of stacked hopscotch found *in-situ* takes back the antiquity to the Early Harappan period of playing the game of *pitto* of modern times. This could be one of the earliest survivals of the game of its kind, found in an open area behind the structural complex[2].

Period II

Period-II reconfirmed the cultural traits of Mature Harappan period reported during the last two field seasons. At RGR-1, important structure was found aligned along the main street running north-south to which another street was joining from the western side. The lapidary workshop was identified in the cuttings of J-6 (RGR-1). Roughly three thousand unfinished beads and rough outs in various stages of manufacturing, together with finished ones mostly in carnelian, chalcedony, agate and jasper, along with bead polishers for grounding and hearth for heating the stones at different stages of chipping were reported from the floor levels of this complex. In the western cuttings (A16, B13 & B14) of RGR-2, an enclosure wall (25 m in length and 12 m in width) to citadel mound was exposed with an entrance towards southwestern slope. It had 15 to 18 mud bricks courses in tapering order; the wall is internally plastered while externally the bricks are arranged in recessed order. The entrance had burnt brick construction with steps externally while the pathway attach to it was 1.10 m wide. In the core area of citadel mound further evidence of platforms and brick well adjoining the former was reported. Likewise in RGR-4, structural evidence of platforms and streets running north-south was noticed. However in the limited cuttings of RGR-5, clear evidence of bone and ivory craft activities were noticed in the form of finished and unfinished bone points, comb, needle, engraver etc. Long bones, antlers and ivory pieces used as raw material were reported from the cuttings.

Cemetery Area

The cuttings at RGR-7 (R20) identified the mound as cemetery area of the Mature Harappan period. It was located say 200 m north of RGR-1, RGR-2 and RGR-3. Eleven extended burials of primary inhumation type were found buried individually in oblong pits with head kept towards north, slightly raised and titled towards east (with a few exceptions of west-ward tilt). There were disturbance due to contemporary later burial pit activities, denoting three phases of burials. In majority of cases, grave goods generally consisting of pots and pans were kept behind head of the deceased. Three female skeletons were exposed showing the evidence of shell bangles in their left wrists. A miniature gold armlet was also found near the elbow of a female skeleton. Apart from this, steatite beads were also noticed around the skull, worn as necklace.

The antiquities reported were of usual variety in terracotta, metal and stone. The pottery types were of similar nature what had been reported during the last two field seasons.

It is proposed to continue further excavations of the site in order to understand the nature of beginning of settlement and various phases of development in period I.

REFERENCES

1. Amarendra Nath (1998), "Rakhigarhi: A Harappan Metropolities in the Saraswati-Drishadwati Divide" in *Puratattva* No. 28. Indian Archaeological Society, New Delhi, pp. 39-45.

2. Amarendra Nath (1999), "Further Excavations at Rakhigarhi" in *Puratattva* No. 29. Indian Archaeological Society, New Delhi, pp.46-49.

3. B.B. Lal (2002) in "Saraswati flows on - The Continuity of the Indian Culture" Delhi: Aryan Book mentions about the stack of hopscotches (Fig. 4-15), belonging to Mature Harappan period; which actually comes soon after the early Harappan on period I (b).

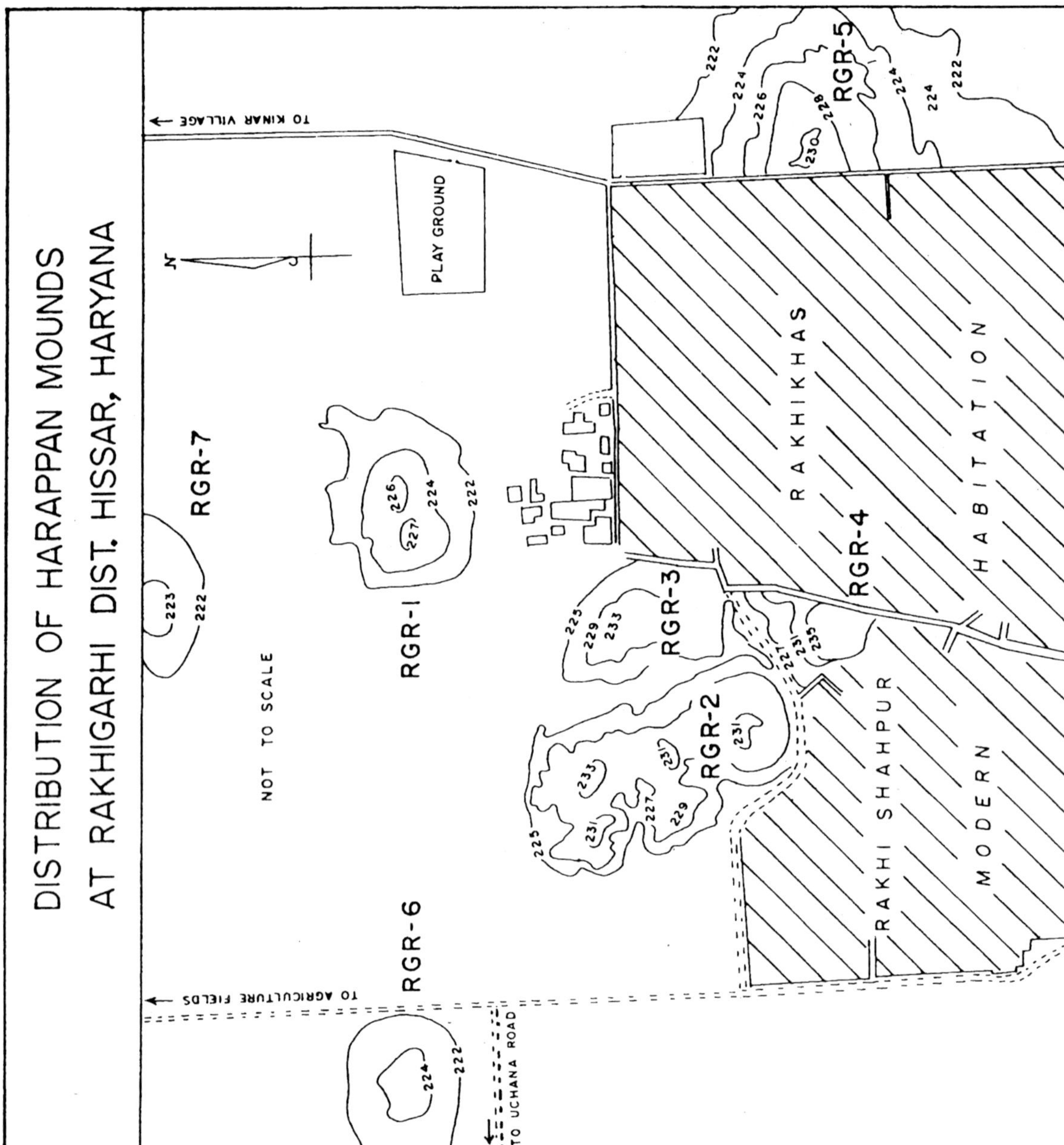
DISTRIBUTION OF HARAPPAN MOUNDS
AT RAKHIGARHI DIST. HISSAR, HARYANA
TO KINAR VILLAGE
PLAY GROUND
RGR-7
RGR-1
RGR-2
RGR-3
RGR-4
RGR-5
RGR-6
NOT TO SCALE
RAKHIKHAS
RAKHI SHAHPUR
MODERN HABITATION
TO AGRICULTURE FIELDS
TO UCHANA ROAD

Fig. 1.

Post-urban Harappan Phase Settlements in North-Eastern Saurashtra

KIRAN DIMRI*

The causes for the decline of Harappan culture and the characteristics of the Post-Urban phase have been a subject of great interest among scholars. Much research has been carried out in various regions of Harappan domain to understand these aspects. Though various views have been put forward regarding the factors that led to the end of the Harappan Civilization, there is no unanimity among scholars (Possehl and Raval 1989:20-21; Allchin 1995:27-28). This was perhaps due to the play of numerous variables like change in climate, tectonic activity, hydrological changes, shift in subsistence system, trade and economy, invasion, which resulted in the collapse of urban centers, although no single cause can be considered to have lead to the degeneration of the Mature/Urban phase. However, the characteristics of the Post-Urban phase in various regions are fairly well known though the understanding is far from complete. Nevertheless the decline of the Harappan culture was not uniform and simultaneous in the entire-region. Like the Pre-Urban or Early Harappan phase, the Post-Urban phase has a number of regional cultural variations. Wherein in Punjab and Cholistan region this phase is represented by Cemetery H culture, in eastern Punjab and Haryana it is the late Sothi and Bara culture, in Sind the Jukhar culture and in Gujarat by Rangpur IIC and III occupation. This was the time when the local cultures were coming into prominence and the Pan-Harappan phenomena were on a decline.

The excavations at Rangpur (Rao 1963), for the first time brought up the manifestation of the Post-Urban Harappan occupation in Gujarat. Subsequently, a number of sites belonging to this phase of occupation were explored and excavated in Gujarat. At present there are more than three hundred settlements belonging to the Post-Urban phase occupation (Ajithprasad and Sonawane 1993; Possehl 1997). Till now Rangpur III was thought to be representative of the Post-Urban phase in Gujarat, which is marked by the introduction of the characteristic Lustrous Red ware ceramic. Though Rangpur II C phase has been variously designated as the initial phase of Post-Urban or early Post-Urban (Rissman 1985; Bhan 1989; Dhavalikar *et al* 1996), it was not properly understood and so was never accounted for as belonging to the Post-Urban phase. This was mainly due to the presence of fairly little quantity, or most of the time total absence of Lustrous Red ware during this phase as well as due the characterization of settlements as belonging to Rangpur II B-C category, when these two phases of Rangpur had quite different characteristics. The present effort is directed primarily to recognize such aspects and to try and analyze them.

The present village-to-village survey was carried out as part of the Doctoral thesis of the author for three field seasons covering about one hundred and twenty three villages (Kiran Dimri 1999). The area covered under the

*Department of Archaeology, Faculty of Arts, M.S. University, Vadodara-390 002

present study is confined to the Bhogava, Sukha Bhadar and Lilka rivers basins between 22^0 14`N to $22^0$ 42`N latitude and 71^0 34`E to $71^0$ 17`E longitude. It comprises of Dhandhuka and Dholka Talukas of Ahmedabad District, and Limbdi and Wadwan Talukas of Surendranagar District in Saurashtra, Gujarat. The area under study extends into the *Bhal* plains drained by the Bhogava and the Sukha Bhadar rivers in the north to the outskirts of Bhavnagar in the south, drained by Sukha Bhadar and Lilka rivers. The Nal region, also known as *Nalkantha*, is located on the north-west of the survey region and remains under water for some part of the year, that is, after the monsoons. The Nal is currently a large brackish water lake (though the water remains sweet at least for a few months after the monsoons) located almost in the center of a low-lying belt linking the Little Rann of Kutch to the Gulf of Khambhat. The western extent of the present survey region is marked by Deccan Trap formation while other is forming a range of hills, such as Chotila, Gir and the Barda, reaching a height of 650 to 1100 meters. The eastern margin is determined by the marshy land and mud flats of the Gulf of Khambhat.

The soil in the vicinity of Bhogava, Sukha Bhadar and Lilka rivers is rich and deep, due to the annual flooding. The soil matrix in the survey region consists of *goradu Mitti and kali mitti (karal).* The black soil of this area is known to be excellent for dry cropping and yields maximum amount of wheat and cotton. The other important crops grown in this region are *jowar (Sorghum bicolour), bajri (Pennisetum typhoideum)* and pulses like black gram and mug.

Periodization of Settlements

Different nomenclatures have been used by scholars since the last century to describe the various phases of Harappan occupation (Rao 1963; Mughal 1970; Possehl 1974; 1997; Chitalwala 1985; Herman 1997; Dhavalikar 1995). Though gradual development of any culture cannot be placed into watertight compartments, but to follow the development and understand the changes at various stages proper periodization is felt necessary. The terminology used in the present study are Mature/Urban Harappan (Early Mature and Late Mature), Mature Harappan Transitional phase or early Post-Urban phase and late Post-Urban Harappan phase. On the basis of radiocarbon dates as well as relative dating the early Mature/Urban settlements can be dated to 2500-2200 B.C., the late Mature/Urban Harappan occupation to 2200-1900 B.C., the early Post-Urban phase settlement to 1900-1700 B.C. and the late Post-Urban phase can be tentatively dated to 1700-1400 B.C. The first two dates fall within the Mature/Urban Harappan time bracket while the latter two forms part of the Post-Urban phase occupation in Gujarat. This periodization was all the more facilitated by the Rangpur sequence, where a four-fold division of the Chalcolithic occupation can be clearly seen. Though much debate has been generated on the fallacies of the Rangpur sequence, it was found to be consistent after excavations at various other sites in the region (Ajithprasad *et al* 1999). Thus, the Early Mature Harappan can be correlated with Rangpur II A, (RGP) Late Mature Harappan with RGP II B, early Post-Urban phase with RGP II C and the late Post-Urban with RGP III.

These phases are indicated by a technological, economic and socio-cultural evolution, progression, disintegration and finally transformation. The Post-Urban phase indicates the culmination of the Chalcolithic occupation. This phase is identified with the archaeological assemblage, which follows the late Mature Harappan phase traits and further leads to the process of de-urbanization. Post-Urban phase indicates the end of the Mature/Urban phase and the beginning of the localization era. It also represents end of the first urbanized society. However, the process of this change was gradual and might have taken a few centuries. This is the period when the characteristic features of the Mature/Urban Harappan phase had disappeared and the decline had set it.

The Post-Urban phase is centrally less systematized and specialized although more differentiated than the Mature/Urban phase. The socio-cultural attainment, which existed throughout the Mature Harappan phase, had slowed down in this stage. This phase is also marked by change in civic standard, economy, material culture and socio-cultural process. This is very clear from the material inventory found associated with this phase. However, in spite of all this the Post-Urban phase does show an affinity with its preceding phases, though in its degenerated form. It can also be said with some certainity that this phase positively shows the evidence of much pronounced local cultures.

Here the emphasis would mainly be on the characteristic features of the Post-Urban phase settlements discovered during the exploration carried out in Bhogava, Sukha Bhadar and Lilka river basins in northeastern Sourashtra. A separate discussion on this phase was deemed necessary so as to understand the nature of these settlements and factors and circumstance involved in bringing a cultural change. Here emphasis is also given to the frequency of sites during different phases of occupation. The increase in the number of settlements in this period is contrary to the earlier evidence of a decrease in there number (Possehl 1980, Bhan 1992). Hence, an attempt has been made to understand the Post-Urban phase occupation in its definite perspective.

During the present survey forty-eight settlements belonging to the different phases of Harappan occupation has been brought to light in the survey region. Of these, eight belong to the Early Mature Harappan phase, twenty-one belong to the late Mature-Harappan phase, thirty-four to the early Post-Urban Harappan phase and twenty-two to the late Post-Urban Harappan phase.

Characteristics of Post-urban Harappan Phase

The Post-Urban phase in Gujarat is represented by Rangpur II C and III (Rao 1963), Rajdi C (Possehl and Raval 1989), Vagad I C (Sonawane and Mehta 1985), Kanewal (Mehta *et al* 1980), Kuntasi II (Dhavalikar *et al* 1995), Vallabhi (Nasadi) (Mehta 1984), Ratanpura (Sonawane 1994-95, 8-9), Oriyo Timbo (Rissman and Chitalwala 1990), Malwan (Allchin and Joshi 1995), Jokha (Mehta *et al* 1971), Dhatva (Mehta and Chowdhary 1975) and Dholavira Stage VI and VII (Bisht 1997). Various parameters have been used for understanding the diagnostic character of the Post-Urban phase settlements that makes it distinct from the preceding phase. These parameters include size of the settlements, site scatter, architectural features if any and diagnostic artefacts pertaining to this particular phase. The main attributes in this phase from the preceding phases of occupation. This is due to appearance of new ceramic types like Lustrous Red ware, fine Black-and-Red ware and other burnished variety and forms like corrugated stem, carinated bowl, bowl on stands etc. Disappearance of a few ceramic types like Buff ware and Micaceous Red Ware is also observed. This phase is moreover marked by the absence of many of the earlier forms of ceramics like 'S' profile jar, perforated jar, convex sided bowls, goblet etc. The fabric in general becomes coarser, though fine fabric is not totally absent. Painting becomes a prominent feature in the Post-Urban phase in comparison to the simple bands and loops of the preceding Mature/Urban phase. Other artefacts related to Mature/Urban phase are also absent in this period. Although, Micaceous Red ware is very prominent in the early Mature/Urban phase in the survey region, its quantity gradually decreases during the subsequent phase of occupation and is totally absent during the late Post-Urban phase.

However, the Post-Urban phase in Gujarat does not commence with the appearance of Lustrous Red ware. This has led to some misconception that the Post-Urban phase begins with RGP III occupation, which is marked by the presence of substantial quantity of Lustrous Red ware. Though from Rangpur, Lustrous Red ware is found within the early Post-Urban RGP II C occupation, no other excavated settlements in the region of Gujarat, belonging to early Post-Urban phase, has given evidence of this ware. Even in Rangpur, the II C occupation has been heavily disturbed by the later occupation, where a large number of pits have been dug cutting through II C deposits, which could have been one of the reasons for the presence of Lustrous Red ware in this deposit. At Lothal (Rao 1979; 1985), Rojdi (Possehl and Raval 1989) and Bagasra (Sonawane *et al* 1999), where the occupation terminates with the early Post-Urban Phase, the Lustrous Red ware is totally absent from the regular habitation deposit. This characteristic ceramics makes its appearance and becomes fairly common only in the deposit related to late Post-Urban phase occupation. Therefore, this should not be taken as criteria to ascertain the beginning of the Post-Urban phase in Gujarat.

The archaeological assemblage associated with Post-Urban phase includes both fine and coarse ceramics and lithic assemblage. However, ceramics constituted a major portion of the assemblage as only few other artefacts have been found. The ceramic assemblage comprises of Red ware, Lustrous Red ware, fine Black-and-Red ware, coarse Red ware, coarse Black-and-Red ware and coarse Grey ware and a few sherds of Gritty Red ware. The striking feature of this period-is the presence of Lustrous Red ware and fine Black-and Red ware and the total absence of Micaceous Red ware and Buff ware. This period is also marked by the presence of burnished variety of Red ware with intricate designs and shapes similar to Lustrous Red ware. A number of sherds of Red ware are burnished and this feature makes it very difficult to differentiate this ware with the Lustrous Red ware. The presence of Lustrous Red ware seems to have been the hallmark of this period, a type ceramic found mainly in Gujarat in the Post-Urban context. However, Lustrous Red ware is found in association with other ceramic types and is not predominant when compared to the other wares, mainly Red Ware of the burnished variety. Lustrous Red ware is only 20% of the total ceramic found is association with the Post-Urban phase in the survey region.

In the Bhogava-Sukha Bhadar region only limited quantity of fine Black-and-Red ware is found in association with the Post-Urban Phase. Rao (1963:122) observes that at Rangpur the quantity of the Black-and-Red ware increases during the Post-Urban phase, which however is not evident in the survey region. The fine Black-and-Red ware of medium fabric found in the survey region are generally devoid of white painting though a few sherds do have the remains of painting on them. Bowl with carinated body and everted rim is the predominant shape of Black-and -Red ware in this phase.

The disappearance of few vessel forms and appearance of new ones is observed in this period, which can also be clearly seen at Rangpur. The shapes of the ceramics include bowls with concavo-convex sides, with both sharp and blunt carination; dishes with beaded, rounded and drooping rim with a prominent groove below the rim; long necked globular jars sometimes the neck being concave having a triangular and rounded rim; basins and lamps with incurved and pinched lip. Grooves below the rim in case of dishes become a prominent feature in this period. The decorative motifs include intersecting loops, zigzag lines, thin bands confined to the rim, neck and shoulder portion of the vessels, cross-hatched lines, cord-impression, fish-net design, vertical and horizontal lines and fronds design. It is observed that dishes and bowls in this period are intricately decorated both on the exterior and the interior. Fishnet designs on bowls appear during this phase and become very common.

The texture of ceramics from these sites were of medium fabric in most cases though very fine and sturdy pottery with shapes similar to that found from Period II C and III of Rangpur were also present. The surface pottery in comparison to preceding periods was coarser and a thick bright slip was applied so as to hide the coarse surface of the fabric. From the macroscopic observation it appears that the clay used for making these vessels was not well levigated. Fine and medium sand particles are present throughout the core of the vessel and its colour suggests that they were inadequately baked. All this on one hand indicates a poor technology of pottery production, while on the other hand its surface features such as burnishing and decoration indicates tendencies to achieve a high quality appearance.

Graffiti on sherds are commonly found in the survey region within the settlements belonging to the Post-Urban phase, though in the early Post-Urban phase it is more frequent. Most commonly found designs are simple strokes or geometric patterns, while in some cases naturalistic designs like floral and faunal motifs are also found.

The present survey has revealed a large number of Post-Urban settlements associated with lithic assemblage. The lithic assemblage mainly consisted of flakes and cores made predominantly on chert, jasper, agate and rhyolite. Compared to the earlier phases, the amount of lithic debitage is greater in this period. The use of asymmetrical flakes appeared to be very common during the Post-Urban phase. This has been observed at Rangpur (Rao 1963:52) Oriyo Timbo phase II (Rissman and Chitalwala 1990: 87-104), Kenewal (Mehta *et al* 1980:57) and Vagad I C. The collection of lithic tools from the present survey resembles with those found from the above sites. These tools are mainly flakes, which are crudely worked into side scrappers. Rao (1963:52) has also suggested that the availability of small pebbles in the vicinity led to the use of asymmetrical flakes, which could be worked into scrapers of various types.

The Post-Urban phase "seems to represent some form of "deurbanization" and a redistribution of the population over the landscape. Both these process imply substantial changes in the system of settlement and subsistence, as well as important alterations of the political and economical institution." (Possehl 1997: 429). This is clearly seen in the survey region as well, where a shift in settlements from Black Cotton soil during the Mature/Urban phase to the marshes of the Bhal and the Nal in the Post-Urban phase is noticed. These marshy lands and mud flats around the alluvial tracts of Bhal and

Nal have excellent grasslands favoring pastoralism in this region.

Distribution of Settlements

The issue regarding the frequency of settlements during different phases of Harappan occupation in Gujarat has been a subject of scholarly debate for many years now. There has been a marked change in the number of settlements belonging to the Mature Harappan and Post-Urban phase occupation over the year mainly due to the perception of scholars working on this subject. Earlier it was believed that the number of settlements belonging to Mature Harappan phase was very less in comparison to the frequency of sites during the Post-Urban phase. Further work carried out with new set of data available changed the whole proportion dramatically, with Mature Harappan occupation far outnumbering the Post-Urban settlements. This was basically due to the settlements belonging to RGP II B-C category, which numbered about 150 (Bhan 1992:174). Earlier it was thought that II B-C sites fall within the Post-Urban category, hence the ratio titled towards the Post-Urban phase (Possehl 1980; Bhan 1989). After the excavations at Rojdi the whole thought process changed with new set of radiocarbon dates, where IIB-C phase was brought within the Mature Harappan time bracket, suddenly increasing the number of sites belonging to the Mature/Urban phase (Possehl 1992; Bhan 1992). This sharply decreased the number of Post-Urban phase settlements.

However, the basic flaw with this periodization was that the two very different phases of Rangpur, II B and II C, were taken as a single phase. The difficulty was that the former is part of the Mature Harappan complex while the latter belongs to the Post-Urban phase. This was clearly demonstrated from the excavations at Rojdi. The habitation deposit at the site was divided into three phases, viz. Rojdi A, Rojdi B and Rojdi C. This tripartite division of the occupation was not based on the Rangpur formula, although Herman, while classifying the ceramic at the site, notes that though unintentional the periodiazation quite closely matches with the first three phases of Rangpur sequence (Herman 1989: 56). He further notes that the ceramic of Rojdi B closer to Rojdi A than to Rojdi C and that there are clear marker of a separate Rojdi C phase as proposed by Rao (1963) at Rangpur. There is also clear demarcation in stratigraphy as well as material remains between II B and II C phases at Rangpur. Clubbing these two phases together has wrongly inflated the number of settlements either during the Mature Harappan or the Post-Urban phase occupation in course of time.

Hence, during the present study, the newly explored settlements were classified into four-fold division as applicable to Rangpur, classifying Rangpur II B and II C as separate phases. This has helped in placing the date in proper perspective. The present data indicate that there is a substantial addition in the frequency of settlement during the Post-Urban phase, which increases from 29 settlements during the Mature Harappan phase to 56 during the Post-Urban occupation (Table 1).

The settlements in the Post-Urban phase are generally large in size but the artefacts are distributed superficially, often in clusters. These clusters of artefacts may represent occupation of the Post-Urban phase community well separated in space and time. These sites are sparsely distributed mainly north of Sukha Bhandar River, that is, in the Nalkantha and Bhal plains, towards the marshy region surrounding the catchment area between the Nal and Gulf of Khambhat.

Most of the settlements in this phase are away from the river, which can be sometimes more than 2 km from the river. A shift towards the interior (hinterland) is also noticed during the Post-Urban phase, which is in contrast to settlements in the preceding phase Mature/Urban Harappan phase. All this possibly indicates a shift in the subsistence strategies during the Post-Urban phase. However, some of these sites are situated near depres-

Cultural Phase		**Number of "Fresh sites"**	**Total Number of Sites**
Mature/Urban phase	Early Mature/Urban Phase	08	08
	Late Mature/Urban Phase	21	29
Post-Urban phase	Early Post-Urban Phase	18	34
	Late Post-Urban Phase	01	22

sions, which might have retained monsoon water and would have served as water reservoirs or ponds in the past.

This is also suggested by the shift in the settlements closer to the marshes during this phase. Also the settlements were shifting more often before, indicated by a number of Post-Urban sites with only superficial occupational deposit. The settlements tend to get more dispersed during the early Post-Urban phase itself in contrast to the dense clusters of settlements in Mature/Urban phase. A much wider area seems to have been chosen by this community, mainly due to the proliferation in the number of settlements in the early Post-Urban phase occupation is related with the shift in the land use pattern as a result of increased emphasis on pastoral and animal husbandry (Rissman 1985; Bhan 1982). Rissman has also proposed a decrease in farming and an increase in pastoral during the Post-Urban phase.

In the late Post-Urban phase, twenty-one of the twenty-two sites were preceded by the early Post-Urban phase or the initial phase of Post-Urban occupation. Only one "fresh site" belonging to the late Post-Urban phase has been identified indicating that the need to acquire new areas might have diminished during this phase. This is contrary to the evidence received from the urban (bigger) settlements in Saurashtra, where the sites are found abandoned after the Initial phase of the Post-Urban occupation, that is before the appearance of the Lustrous Red ware into the Harappan assemblage corpus. This suggests that at least the rural settlements the occupation continue to the Post-Urban phase instead getting terminated after the early Post-Urban phase. This directs towards the possibility of these settlements being more regional as by now the Harappan story had come to an end.

Summary

As has been suggested earlier, the transformation of the urban phenomena of the Harappan culture was not simultaneous or evenly paced within the Harappan domain in the Indian subcontinent. Nor the changes show any uniformity in all the regions of the Civilization. As Possehl puts it "The timing of change, its pace and outcome are all features of marked cultural diversity with the emergence of the Post-Urban Harappan" (Possehl and Raval 1989:19). It has been suggested that the effect of decline was more pronounced and might have started earlier in the core region and have trickled down to the peripheral region at a later date. Gujarat being the peripheral region of the Harappan domain and hence not heavily dependent on the core region for survival, felt the effect only by around 1900 B.C., when the redistribution of population within the landscape can be seen. This phase has been termed here as initial phase of the Post-Urban or early Post-Urban phase.

This phase gives evidence of change in the policies of settlement pattern and subsistence economy adapted by the community. This being evident by the expansion of the settlement into hitherto unoccupied region, away from the rivers and closer to the marshes. These sites are occupied for a smaller duration, with the population shifting at a more regular interval. These evidences suggest a change in the subsistence pattern of the community. This can be seen from the proliferation of settlements during the early Post-Urban phase in the survey region. The importance of an agricultural based economy was on a decline and the population was dependent more on a pastoral-cum-farming economy. This phase was therefore considered as the initial phase of the Post-Urban occupation.

By the late Post-Urban phase occupation, the population seems to have settled down with the newly adopted economic policies. Thus the need for exploring fresh region has declined by this phase as evident from only one freshly occupied site during the late Post-Urban phase. This newly found stability gave rise to a new set of ceramic called Lustrous Red ware. This ceramic group becomes the hallmark of the Post-Urban phase, though this is not the predominant pottery of this phase nor it should be taken as the focal point in describing the Post-Urban phase in Gujarat.

The present data suggests that there is a significant increase in the site counts during the Post-Urban phase considering the Rangpur II C settlement as initial phase of Post-Urban occupation. Therefore the settlements earlier put into the II B-C category should be re-analyzed which would help in putting the site count in proper perspective. Hence, the present effort has been directed in clearing certain misconception regarding the Post-Urban phase in Gujarat and to bring forth a new framework for further research in this direction.

REFERENCES

Ajithprasad, P. and V.H. Sonawane. 1993. Harappa Culture in North Gujarat: A Regional Paradigm Paper presented at the workshop on "The Harappans in Gujarat: Problems and Prospects", Pune: Deccan College.

Ajithprasad, P., V.H. Sonawane, A. Majumdar and Kiran Dimri, 1999. The Chalcolithic Cultural Sequence at Rangpur and New Data from Bagasra. Paper presented at the Annual Conference of the ISPQS, IAS and IHCS, Pune: Deccan College.

Allchin, F.R. 1995. *The End of Harappan Urbanism and its Legacy.* Cambridge University Press.

Allchin, F.R. and J.P. Joshi, 1995. *Excavation at Malvan.* Report of the Collaboration of the Archaeological Survey of India and Cambridge University in 1970 on the Gujarat Plain, New Delhi: Archaeological survey of India.

Bhan, K.K. 1989. Late Harappan Settlements of Western India with Specific Reference to Gujarat. In *Old Problems and New Perspective in the Archaeology of South Asia*, Ed. J.M. Kenoyer, Madison: Wisconsin Archaeological Reports, 2:219-243.

Bhan, K.K. 1992. Late Harappan Gujarat. *The Eastern Anthropologist* 45 (1-2), Ed. V.N. Misra: 173-192.

Bisht, R.S. 1997. Dholavira Excavations: 1990-94. In *Facets of Indian Civilization: Recent Perspectices* (Essays in Honour of Prof B.B. Lal), Ed. J.P. Joshi, Vol. I, New Delhi: Aryan Book Depot: 107-120.

Chitalwala, Y.M. 1985. Late Harappan Culture. In Recent Advancements in Indian Archaeology (S.B.Deo and K. Paddayya Eds.), Poona: Deccan College: 57-64.

Dhavalikar, M.K., M.R. Raval and Y.M. Chitlwala. 1996. *Kuntasi: A Harappan Emporium on West Coast.* Pune: Deccan College.

Herman, C.F. 1989. Rojdi Material Culture: The Sorath Harappan Ceramic. In *Harappan Civilization and Rojdi*, Ed. Possehl G.L. and M.H. Raval, New Delhi: Oxford and IBH: 53-140.

Herman, C.F. 1997. The Rangpur Sequence of 'Harappan' Gujarat (India) : A Reassessment, *South Asian Archaeology* 1995:187-198.

Kiran Dimri 1999, *Chalcolithic Settlements in Bhogava and Sukha Bhandar Valley*, Ph.D. Dissertation, M.S. University of Baroda, Vadodara.

Mehta, R.N. 1984. *Vallabhi-A Station of Harappan Cattle Breeders. Frontiers of the Indus Civilization,* Eds. B.B. Lal and S.P. Gupta.

Mehta, R.N. and S.N. Chowdhery, K.T.M. Hegde and D.R.Shah, 1971. *Excavation at Jokha.* Baroda : Maharaja Sivajirao University, Archaeology Series 11.

Mehta, R.N. and S.N. Chowdhery, 1975. *Excavation at Dhatva Baroda:* Maharaja Sivajirao University Archaeology Series 12.

Mehta, R.N., K.N. Momin and D.R. Shah, 1980. *Excavation at Kanewal Baroda:* Maharaja Sivajirao University Archaeology series 17.

Mughal, M.R. 1970. *The Early Harppan Period in the Greater Indus Valley and Baluchistan*, Ph.D. Dissertation, University of Pennsylvania, Philadelphia.

Possehl, G.L. 1974. *Variation and Changes in the Indus Civilization:* A Study of Prehistoric Gujarat with Special reference to the Post-Urban Harappan. Ph.D. Disseratation, University of Chicago.

Possehl, G.L. 1980. *Indus Civilization in Saurashtra. New Delhi:* B.R. Publication.

Possehl, G.L. 1992. *The Harappan Civilization in Gujarat: The Sorath and Sindhi Harappans.* The Eastern Anthropologist 45 (1-2), Ed. V.N. Misra: 117-154.

Possehl, G.L. 1997. The Transformation of the Indus Civilization Journal of World Prehistory. Vol. 11, Number 4: 425-472.

Possehl, G.L. and M.H. Raval, 1989. *Harappan Civilization, and Rojdi,* New Delhi: Oxford and IBH.

Rao, S.R. 1963. Excavation at Rangpur and other Explorations. *Ancient India,* 18-19. 5-207.

Rao, S.R. 1979. Lothal: A Harappan Port Town 1955-62. In *Memoirs of Archaeological Survey of India,* 78. Volume I, New Delhi: Archaeological Survey of India.

Rao, S.R. 1985. Lothal: A Harappan Port Town 1955-62. In *Memoirs of Archaeological Survey of India,* 78. Volume II. New Delhi: Archaeological Survey of India.

Rissman, Paul C. 1985. *Migratory Pastoralism in Western Indian in the*

Second Millennium BC: The Evidence from Oriyo Timbo. Ph.D. Dissertation, University of Pennsylvania.

Rissman, Paul C. and Y.M. Chitalwala, 1990. *Harappan Civilization and Oriyo Timbo*. New Delhi: Oxford and IBH.

Sonawane, V.H. 1994-95. Harappan Settlements in Rupen Estuary, Gujarat, *Pragdhara*, 5:1-11.

Sonawane, V.H. and R.N. Mehta, 1985. Vagad-A Rural Harappan Settlement in Gujarat. *Man and Environment* 9:38-44.

Sonawane, V.H., P. Ajithprasad, K.K. Bhan, S. Prathapachandran, K. Krishnan and A. Majumdar, 1999. Excavation at Bagasra-1998-99: A Preliminary Report. Paper presented at the Annual Conference of IAS, ISPQS and IHCS, Pune: Deccan College.

Excavation at Birchhabili Tila, Sikri

D.V. SHARMA, V.N. PRABHAKAR, A. PRADHAN, K.A. KABUI*

Sikri is situated on an extension of the upper Vindhyan ranges on the bank of a natural lake, which has now mostly dried up and under cultivation. The ridge is composed of red sandstone formations. Rock shelters with paintings exist on the periphery of the lake. Stone Age tools, Ochre Coloured Pottery and Painted Grey Ware have also been found here. The excavation carried out by the Agra Circle of the Archaeological Survey of India at Birchhabilli Tila in Sikri village has brought to light the remains of a Jaina temple and sculptures. The total period of occupation at the site is around 1000 years, beginning from the Post-Gupta period up to Mughal period. The excavation has revealed a hitherto unknown phase at Fatehpur Sikri. This paper discusses important finds from this excavation and their historical importance.

The archaeological potential of Fatehpur Sikri region is well established in previous work that have been carried out since the times of Edward W. Smith. The Archaeological Survey of India carried out the excavation at eight different sites at Fatehpur Sikri under a joint national project with the Aligarh Muslim University; mainly concentrated on the problems relatievely to town planning under the Mughals. The Archaeological Survey of India during the final two field seasons of this project (IAR 1987-88 and 1988-89) excavated a site near Hada Mahal which revealed a cultural sequence from Ochre Coloured Pottery and Painted Grey Ware (Plate 1) period to the Medieval times. The cultural sequence revealed by this excavation suggests that there was a continuous human habitation in this region since Protohistoric period. The existence of rock-shelters with Prehistoric paintings in villages Rasulpur, Patsal, Bandrauli, Sonauti and Madanpura on the periphery of the ancient lake indicate the presence of Prehistoric men in this area. The microliths have been reported during exploration in the vicinity of these rock-shelters. At Rasulpur, the Agra Circle also discovered microliths recently. These discoveries pushed back the antiquity of this region to the Mesolithic period.

TOPOGRAPHY

Sikri has been mentioned in the *Mahabharata* as Saik in connection with Sahadeva's southern campaigns on the eve of the Pandava's *Rajasuya yajna*. Lexicons define Saik as a region surrounded by water. This denotes its original topography which included several lakes, reservoirs and low lying areas, including the Keola-Dev lake in the north-west and Goverdhana and Asta-Sakhi Kundas (Radha-Kunda and others) in the north, covering the entire western and southern Braja-*Ksetra* and connecting it with the legend of Krishna lifting the Goverdhana, which denotes his water-management system to save the region from Ativrsti (excessive rainfall). Abundance of water and greennry supported large-scale agriculture and

*Archaeological Survey of India, Agra Circle, 22, Mall Road (AGRA)

dairy farming that is why it was named 'Goverdhana' (the region where cows abounded). In fact, a few events of the *Mahabharata* were enacted in this region, on the banks of the Jamuna, which has been changing its course since ancient times. As of this reason, Painted Grey Ware sites are found here. Sikri is derived from this root Saik. The inscription on the sculpture of Jaina Saraswati dated in V.S.1067/1010 A.D. mentions the place as 'Sekrikya', which is also a similar derivative. Babur, who visited it on the eve of the Khanwah battle in 1527 A.D. mentioned as Sikri in his *Memoirs* and the lake as 'ocean like'.

LOCAL TRADITIONS

Ethno-archaeology, traditions and customs of the region were carefully studied. The site is highly venerated among the Sikarwar Rajput clan of this region. They definitely come to this place for mundane ceremony of their newborn children. This tradition carries the antiquity in Sruti also. Bir-Chhabbili is a corrupt form of the probable name attributed to their Goddess (Devi).

EXPLORATION

The Fatehpur Sikri region is full of sculptures datable to the 9th century A.D. These have been discovered during the course of scientific exploration at sites like Chichana, Nadbai, Chauma Shahpur, Imlaoda, Patsal, Churiyari, Sikri, Dura, Kagarol, Mathura and Bateshwar. The exploration has yielded enough archaeological material to establish that not only Jaina temples were erected in this region but a large number of Saiva, Vaisnava and Sakta temples were also built and patronized by the contemporary rulers, who professed the *Chakravartin* concept and provided ample opportunity and protection to the believers of all sects and religions. The divine theory of kingship and *Chakravartin* concept of Medieval Age inspired the rulers of this region for such activities. Toleration and co-existence was a way of life in Medieval India, as it is evident from the cluster of temples of different faiths, e.g., in Khajuraho under the Chandellas, Gwalior under the Tomars, Sikri under the Kachchhapagatas, Delhi under the Chauhanas.

The village Sikri has remains of three/four temple sites where architectural remains, sculptures and ancient relics are found, scattered in large number. Sculptures discovered during exploration suggest the existence of Vaisnava, Saiva, Sakta and Jaina Temples at Sikri during 9th-11th centuries A.D. Before carrying out horizontal excavation at the site, the area within a radius of 25 km in and around Fatehpur Sikri was scientifically explored to ascertain settlement pattern, topography, water management system and archaeological remains. The villages such as Chauma Shahpur, Imlaoda, Chichana, Churiyari, Jainpura, Jotana, Dura, Kagarol and Kiraoli were systematically explored. Those villages yielded architectural remains of temples, sculptures and other antiquities datable between 2nd century A.D. and 11th century A.D. The settlement pattern of this region also indicated existence of Vaisnava, Saiva, Sakta and Jaina temples during this period. To ascertain results of exploration and to throw more light on settlement pattern and cultural sequence, it became essential to excavate a site scientifically and the Birchhabili-Tila was selected for horizontal excavation due to its location on the bank of the lake and existence of architectural remains in *situ*. It is situated on the south-eastern bank of an ancient lake (mentioned as 'Moti Jheel' and 'Dabar Jheel' in Jaina literature) (Plate II). It was approximately 35 km in circumference and was formed (naturally between two branches of Upper Vindhyan ranges) by river Uttangan flowing in a south-westerly direction. Now it has almost dried up and is under cultivation.

During the field season of 1982-83, Birchhabili Tila was undertaken for excavation and a few Jaina sculptures and architectural remains were discovered. The *adhisthana* of a temple was also partly exposed at its southern portion along with walls constructed of random rubble masonry. The tilla was deserted and was being used as a graveyard.

EXCAVATION

Excavation was resumed here during 1999-2000 to ascertain cultural sequence and settlement pattern of the site (Fig 1). The total area of the mound measures 2000 sqm and 44 quadrants were undertaken for excavation. Six quadrants were excavated up to the natural soil and the remaining was left due to occurrence of structures and habitational deposits of subsequent period.

(A) CULTURAL SQUENCE

The excavation at Birchhabili Tila revealed a total habitational deposit of 6.5 m which has been divided into following cultural periods (Figure 2).

I)	Period-I	-	*Circa.* 6th to 9th century A.D.
II)	Period-II	-	*Circa.* 9th to 12th century A.D.
III)	Period-III	-	*Circa.* 12th to 16th century A.D.
IV)	Period-IV	-	*Circa.* 16th to 18th century A.D.

The periodization/classification of cultural deposits was determined on the basis of finds, dated inscriptions, pottery types, coins, structure, antiquities and other associated materials unearthed during excavation. The co-relation of structures of different phases/period was done to study house plan, orientation and their probable use. Accordingly, different structural phases were identified on the basis of stratigraphy and material culture.

I) Period-I *(Circa.* 6th century A.D. to 8th century A.D.)

The cultural deposit of this period is 2.69 m. Interestingly, an isolated discovery of a partly broken neolithic celt of buff sandstone was an important find from this level. This is a stray find and it indicates the existance of a Neolithic site in the vicinity of Sikri. The neolithic celt has clearly visible working edge, fine finishing and polishing.

The structures of this period were revealed in trenches G-9, E-8, F-8, and F-9. These structures are made of random rubble masonry and mud bricks measuring 30x15x4 cm. Two mud brick walls visible in sections facing north and south of G-9 were unearthed below random rubble masonry structures of Period-II. These mud brick walls measure 1.15 m in length and run in east-west orientation, parallel to each other. The distance between these two walls is 3 m. In between these walls, another wall of random rubble masonry/brick bats was exposed in the same orientation. Besides this, a burnt brick wall (measuring 40x35 cm.) having four courses, was also exposed near northern mud brick wall. The size of the bricks is 31x16x5 cm. The complete plan of structures in this period could not be ascertained due to limited working space in the trench.

Two structural phases of Period-I were identified in F-8. The structure in early phase comprises of two rooms. The larger one measuring 3.05x2.26 m and the smaller 2.3x1.8 m. The thickness of walls ranges from 45 cm to 50 cm. The complete plan of this structure could not be exposed because it runs below the structure of Period-II. In this phase one dressed red sandstone piller was found lying on floor level to the east of above-mentioned structure. The piller measuring 1.72x0.29x0.23 m (l x b x t) in dimensions, is plain and lies in a north-south direction. The area to the west of two-room structure was excavated up to the natural soil at the depth of 4.04 m. The structure of late phase in Period-I is comprised of one room measuring 2.68x0.7 m with 0.54 m width walls. The walls have random rubble masonry foundation and burnt bricks were used for superstructure. Two courses of burnt bricks (31x16x5 cm) were exposed. A hearth with brickbat lining was excavated towards the west of above-mentioned room. The dimension of the hearth is 45x25 cm and ash was found in *situ.*

Another mud brick wall running in east-west direction was also exposed in E 10. The length of this wall is 1.4 m and width 0.4 m.

In F-9, habitational deposit of Period-I was excavated below man-made pit of red sandstone slabs. An area measuring 95x65 cm was excavated up to a certain depth near the pit but natural soil could not be reached. The excavation in this area revealed successive floor levels with a thin habitational deposit on each level. The thickness of floors ranges between 2 cm and 7 cm. A rectangular shaped trough of mud was exposed in the section facing south resting on a floor level at the depth of 5.95 m. The colour of the floor was pinkish. An earthen vase partly buried in floor was found at this level. A thick deposition of ash was found south of this vase. The floor, even in nature, is made of lime, mixed with *kankar* and mud nodules.

In E-8, structures of two phases of Period-I were found running underneath the outer enclosure wall of Period-II. A mud deposit of 65 cm thickness was found below the enclosure wall of the temple of Period-II. This indicates that the temple of Period-II was constructed over the habitational deposit of Period-I after leveling the ground properly. The structure of early phase consists of two rooms, walls whereof were found partly continuing in the sections. The structure of the late phase of Period-I runs in north-south orientation.The wall is made of random rubble masonry with a length of 2.55 m and thickness 60 cm.

Two stone-walls running in east-west and north-south orienatation in Quadrant III of F-9, probably a room, were found below foundation of the temple of Period-II. One metre habitational deposit was found in this trench below the foundation of temple of Period-II. These walls are constructed of random rubble masonry. The length of wall, running east-west, is 1.45 m, while its width is 0.9 m. The length of wall running north-south is 0.85 m, while its width is 0.40 m.

The occurrence of above-mentioned structural remains and cultural deposits are datable between *Circa* 6th-8th century A.D. The structures exposed in E-8, F-8, F-9, and G-9 are contemporary and belong to the Period-I while structures found in trenches G-9 and F-9 are part of one structural complex.

(1) POTTERY

The pottery from Period-I is plain red ware, and black ware. Some sherds of red ware have decorations in applique technique. Mica dust has been used on this pottery for decoration. A few sherds of red ware were treated with golden colour slip and a band in black colour. The main shapes of pottery are vases & miniature pots (Figure 3), bowls &*'handi'* (Figure 4), basins, dishes, *'lotas'* storage jars, etc. A variety of designs were produced on the pottery by use of applique technique and nail-impressed designs. Adequately fired (Figure 5-nos. 3 & 4) sherds of red ware with fine texture were found with stamped decoration (Figure 5-nos. 1 & 2). An interesting potsherd displaying a horse figure in motion executed in low relief was also found (Figure 5, no. 7). A few pottery types such as sprinklers and extremely ornamented designs as found on Gupta pottery assemblage are absent from this period. This suggests occupation of this site during the late Gupta period.

(2) ANTIQUITIES

The discovery of a broken Ambika sculpture in red sandstone datable to *Circa* 6th-7th century A.D. is of immense archaeological importance. The ornaments and drapery of the Devi is comparatively simple and in low relief. This suggests existence of a Jaina shrine at Sikri during the late Gupta period. Similar type of sculpture of Ambika was discovered from Kankali Tila, Mathura. The discovery of Ambika sculpture, red sandstone pillar and a two-letter Brahmi inscription on a piece of stone suggest existence of a Jaina shrine at the site during this period. The other noteworthy antiquities of this period are terracotta beads, tablets, moulds, slings balls, gamesmen, hopscotch, glass beads, glass and iron bangles, chisel and spearhead.

II) Period-II (*Circa* 9th century A.D. to 11th century A.D.)

This period is represented by remains of a Jain temple, sculptures, antiquies and other archeological findings. The entire area was properly levelled and rammed before construction of a shrine over it. The area on south -western side of the mound indicates that rectangular stonewalls were constructed parallel to each other by providing cells like chamber below the platform. Similar type of structures was traced in some area exposed in south-eastern portion of the mound. The walls of these cells, like structures, run parallel to temple plateform and perhaps were filled with earth to make the ground firm and stable to bear load of massive superstructure upon it. The evidence of such type of cells was not found on north-east and north-west portion of the mound.

(B) THE TEMPLE REMAINS (Figure 6)

1. The platform (base of *adhisthana*) of the temple is constructed of massive undressed stone blocks of sandstone regularly placed on each other towards north-east to south-west direction and measures 18 m in length and 4.5 m at rear and front side.

The platform of the temple is constructed with massive stone blocks of red sandstone locally available around Sikri. These undressed sandstone blocks were arranged for construction according to available size and shape. The height of platform on south is 2.8 m, on east 2.85 m, on west 2.8 m and on north is 2.71 m, above the foundation. The temple platform measures 4.5 m on south, 9 m on north. The length of the temple platform is

18 m. A projection has been provided on southern portion of the temple platform thus reducing its width from 9 m to 4.5 m. The platform is further covered with flat and massive sandstone blocks to provide smooth surface for the superstructure. The average size of these stone blocks is 2 mx 0.5 mx0.2 m (lxbxt). These massive block/slabs of sandstone served as a firm and stable base over the platform. In later period, a large number of such slabs from the platform were found disturbed and reused at the site. The excavation revealed projections in east, west directions to provide space for steps to approach the shrine from lower platform. The northern projection on eastern side has a flight of steps. Another flight of steps was discovered near the lower step of the southern projection. A broken head of Parsvanatha sculpture was discovered near the lower step of this projection. The discovery of moulded and carved sandstone architectural parts from the site indicates the form and shape of the temple. Such remains as *kumbha, amalaka, piller base, beki* were found in large quantity and are datable to 9th-11th centuries A.D.

2. Random rubble masonry wall was provided in between the exterior wall of the temple and base of adhisthana probably to provide steps to reach main shrine.

A random rubble masonry wall was found running all around the *adhisthana* parallel to the respective side. The length of this wall is 25 m and width is 16 m while its thickness is 65 cm. The purpose of this wall appears to provide structural stability to the shrine and space all around the temple.

3. Massive peripheral wall of shrine was found measuring 20 m in width (east to west) and 33 m in length (north to south). The thickness of the wall is 1.8 m.

The main shrine is enclosed by a massive random rubble masonry wall constructed with mud mortar and strengthened by well-dressed veneering stone. The average thickness of this wall is 1.8 m and extant height 1.66 m from the base level. A solid and well-rammed ground was prepared before construction of this wall below foundation. Massive undressed stone slabs were placed flat over rammed ground as base for superstructure. These slabs were found uniformly laid all around as a protection against sub-soil water and to prevent capillary action. This technique was used because of constant stagnation of water in the lake close to the foundation. This arrangement was essential as a protection against sub-soil water and salt, two prime enemies of structure. The well-dressed veneering stones were fixed on the exterior of wall for strength as well as for effect. Some veneering stones still have evidence of rusted iron dowels in *situ* with grooves.

A projection measuring 5x3.8 m was found in the centre of northern wall, which was probably an entrance to the shrine. The whole construction of this projection is similar and utmost care was taken to place massive stone slabs before raising the superstructure. A flight of steps was also provided over this structure. A chamber adjoining this projection measuring 4.3x1.6m was also discovered. The exterior wall of this chamber has veneering stones. The floor of this chamber was laid by well-remmed brickbats.

4. The man-made pit of red sandstone slabs are covered with two massive stone slabs. Similar slabs were found, used as basal slab of walls and superstructure.

The important archaeological evidence of religious disposal of damaged mutilated sculptures was excavated here in the form of a man-made pit built of stone slabs (one of which being an architectural remains of the shrine). This pit was encountered at a depth of 3.52 m from the reference peg and with dimensions 1.33x0.72x1.12 m (lxbxh). The pit is constructed with red sandstone slabs, which are well dressed and seems to have been part of some structure. The stratigraphy indicates that a foundation trench was dug out before the construction of the pit. The pit is covered in two levels with massive stone slabs, which are generally used as basal slabs of temple boundary wall and temple *adhisthana*. Only one prominent sculpture was excavated from this pit, which is the red sandstone sculpture of Ambika, the Yaksini of Neminatha (Plate 2). The sculpture was found in two pieces and in upside down position with the portion above neck broken. The deposit corresponding to the sculpture is 1.12 m and consisted of stone chips, broken sculptures and fragmentary potsherds. The broken sculptural fragments and fragmentary potsherds correspond to Period II, which indicates that the Ambika sculpture was buried in Period II. Although the sculpture was buried in Period II, it is stylistically of early period, as mentioned above.

The stratum immediately above the covering of this pit consists of various kind of broken sculptures buried in a haphazard manner. This activity corresponds to layers 4 & 5 of the corresponding trench and the sculptures found include, seated Jaina Tirthankaras, Kuntunatha, other fragmentary sculptures, portion of a *prabhavali*, etc. After this activity, the Period II people constructed a random rubble wall forming an enclosure above the buried sculptures. Then again the remaining sculptures were placed inside this inclosure. The sculptures were found placed in a haphazard manner right up to the top of this enclosure. It seems there were some more sculptures to be buried, as this is very well supported by the discovery of an Adinatha sculpture nearly 4 m to the east of this enclosure and outside it. The sculptures found above the red sandstone pit included images of Sambhavanath, Risabanatha, Santinatha and Kuntunatha with inscriptions on pedestals *(padapitha)* in *kayotsarga* posture, 7 Tirthankaras (without lanchana) in *padmasana*, Yaksini images of Prachindi and Ambika with inscription, two broken Tirthankara heads, and fragments of other sculptures. Some Tirthankar images were placed in perfectly seated and upright position; many others were lying in haphazard manner. One seated Tirthankara image was found reused in a Period-III structure as part of masonry. A broken piece of this sculpture was found lying nearby which was joined together with the original one.

Thus the evidence indicates that the people of Period II after arriving at the site, immediately or little later of the demolition that took place at the site, might have considered disposing of the broken and mutilated sculptures for religious reasons. They dug a pit and constructed a small chamber of red sandstone slabs and placed the Ambika sculpture first and then covered it. The exact purpose of placing the Ambika sculptures only and covering it with massive stone slabs is not known. The reasons and causes for this act could only be speculated. After covering this pit, the Period II people started to place the remaining sculptures above this pit. It is important to note that they had dug out the earth for the construction of this red sandstone chamber only. The top portion of this pit could have been the working level of Period II. This could be deduced by the absence of foundation pit above this pit for the remaining sculptures. It seems the space in between the eastern arm and temple *adhisthana* had been used effectively for placing these sculptures in an order and at one place.

(1) POTTERY

The ceramic types excavated from his period include red ware and black ware. The shapes of pottery are vases of medium and large size, jars, knife edged bowls, dishes, basins, miniature pots, terracotta lamps, spouted vases. The applique and stamped decoration on red ware continued in this period too, comparatively less in number (Figure 7).

(2) ANTIQUITIES

The antiquities of this period include large number of Jaina Tirthankara sculptures and subsidiary deities. The Jaina Tirthankara images discovered are Adinatha or Risabhanatha (Plate 3), Sambhavanatha, Kuntunatha, Santinatha, (Plate 4), Parsvanatha. The Yaksini images of Chandi or Pracandi, Yakshini of Vasupujya, Ambika, Yakshini of Neminatha, Chakresh-wari, Yakshini of Adinatha were also discovered. These Tirthankara have *lanchanas* and *astapratiharyas* according to the Jaina *sastras* and ancient literature like *Pratishthaasarangraha, Pratishthasaroddhara, Pratishthatilakam, Acaradinakara, Vividhatirtakalp, Chaturvimsatika, Chaturvimsatistotra, Samaranganasut-radhara, Aparajithaprichha, Rupamandana, Manasara, Adipurana, Uttarapurana, Harivanspurana and Diparnava-Jinadarshan* (Plate 5). The discovery of Jain Srutidevi Saraswati is important owing to its uniqueness (Plate6). It is different from the Hindu Saraswati and its iconography has been precisely laid down in Jain texts as *'Vastu'* and *'Pratima'*. Twenty-four Jinas (Tirthankaras) are consecrated with respective 'Yaksas' and 'Yaksini' with their identifying symbols, weapons and vehicles in a fairly large Jaina temple *(Chaityalaya)*. Ten *Dikpalas*, nine *grahas*, eight *Pratiharas* and four *Pratiharis* are installed in larger Jain temples. Some Sakta icons like Kshetrapala, Manibhadra and Ghantakarna-Mahavira are used in still in larger temples, perhaps as a matter of compromise, and, in addition to them, Stutidevi Saraswati is also prescribed to be worshipped in such temples.

Her icon is prescribed that, she is youthful and fair complexioned, she has a halo and all ornaments from head to toe, she is four-armed and has *'varada'* and *'kamal'* in two right hands, and *'pustaka'* and *'mala'* in the other two hands. *'Hamsa'* is her vehicle. This sculpture fully and precisely responds to the textual prescription and in addition, it also has images of *'jinas'* on its side panels, confirming, unequivocally, that it is the image of Jaina Saraswati, different from the Hindu Saraswati. It bears an inscription dated in Vikram Samvat 1067/1010 and (Figure 8). It is a unique sculpture discovered here for the first time and the like of which has not been found any where else, and it suggests, as the texts lay down, that it was consecrated for worship in a large Jaina temple at Fatehpur Sikri. The Srutidevi Saraswati in standing *tribhanga* posture, was fixed on a pedestal, placed against the wall (as is evident from its rough back side). The sculpture was found damaged at its foot and placed with face downward near a wall. The circumstantial archaeological evidence supported by the marks near foot suggests that the believers tried to remove the sculpture from its original position. The sculpture was placed carefully with its rough back to avoid visibility and hence remained little damaged. The image is unique when compared with the images of Saraswati so far discovered. The image *(chhavi)* is also unmatched (*adbhud;* wonderful). The *jatamukuta* of the devi embedded with lotus buds, decorated with *kirtimukhas*, *sankuchit-lat* on forehead, *kundala* in ear, *grevika* (ornament in neck), *kanthsri* (*shobha* of *kantha*), *vyjayantihara*, eyebrows stretched like bow, *ratnare nayan*, sharp and long nose, round chin, prominent cheek, thin lips are certain marvelous iconographic features of the devi.

A large number of headless Tirthankara images, seated in *padmasana* posture were found in black, white, and buff coloured stone. A fragment of an arm of a Tirthankara in marble and other sculptures such as *Yonipitha*, broken bull, *Yaksini* Ambika with her consort holding Priyankara were also found (Plate 7). Some noteworthy antiquities of this Period include terracotta moulds of human face and ornamental jewellery.

III) Period-III (*Circa* 12th century A.D. to 16th century A.D.)

The habitational deposit of Period-III was excavated in east, south and north of the shrine. The circumstantial archaeological evidence indicates that the site was deserted for some time and was subsequently re-occupied. The original material was lavishly re-used for constructional activities by the inhabitants. The walls constructed of random rubble masonry with mud mortar and pucca lime floors were provided in this period. The burnt bricks measuring 21x16x5 cm were found used in constructions. Some structures in this period were found raised right over temple remains. The concentration of constructional activities during this period took place over outer periphery wall on the east and near boundary towards north. It is evident that residential complexes were constructed after temple fell into disuse.

Two noteworthy structures in east-west orientation located on eastern side deserve mention. One chamber having lime floor over brick pavement was exposed. The second structure appears to be a portion of a room with entrance on north. The remains of brick paved floor were exposed in this room. A small niche pierced on exterior wall was also found. The complete plan of these structures could not be ascertained because the remaining portion of original mound had been disturbed due to cultivation and human vandalism. A one roomed structure in southern direction was found having entrance from north. Dressed stones were re-used for construction near entrance.

(1) POTTERY

The main pottery types in Period-IV include red ware, grey ware and glazed ware. The shapes include vases, bowls, dishes, storage jars, *surahi* with long neck and lids (Figure 9).

(2) ANTIQUITIES

The noteworthy antiquities found from Period-IV are two circular copper coins, highly corroded and unidentifiable. Iron nails, knives, arrow-head, terracotta hopscotch, gamesmen, animal figurines, beads, sling balls, spindle whorls, copper bells, miniature pot, stone pestle and rotator quern were also found from this level.

IV) Period-IV (*Circa* 16th - 18th century A.D.)

The site was deserted during this period. This is evident due to absence of constructional activities and human habitation. A few sherds of Chinese porcelain ware were found from this level. Typical Chinese clouds were found depicted on a sherd boldly.

The site was deserted for a long period and was used as a burial ground. Some burials have platform, while some are plain. One burial has an inscribed cenotaph.

(1) POTTERY

On the basis of discovery of a few Chinese porcelain sherds with typical design and decoration, it is ascertained that such ceramic was in use during this period.

(C) INSCRIPTIONS

The excavation at Birchhabili Tila revealed a large number of Jaina sculptures. Some sculptures have inscriptions (mostly on pedestals). The contents of these inscriptions are donatory and these form a good source of history of the period. The inscriptions are of following categories:

1) Donatory inscriptions mentioning date, name of the deity, name of the donor, locality and place.

2) Donatory inscriptions mentioning date and name of the donor.

Besides these, a fragmentary red sandstone piece bears two letters in Brahmi script. Palaeographically the script is datable to 2nd -3rd centuries A.D. This inscription probably is a broken piece from a bigger one.

The inscriptions found on pedestal of sculptures can be divided into following categories:-

1) Inscriptions found on pedestals of deities in standing postures, namely on the sculptures of Sambhavanatha, Risabhanatha (two in number), Santinatha, Kuntunatha and Saraswati.

2) Inscriptions found on pedestals of deities in *padmasana* posture, wherein names of deities are unknown, as their names are not mentioned in the inscriptions. One seated Jaina Tirthankara depicting long hair on the shoulder is definitely of Adinatha or Risabhanatha as generally depicted iconographically.

3) Inscriptions found on pedestals of subsidiary deities or Yaksinis found seated on their respective vehicles, namely Ambika and Chandi or Prachandi.

SCRIPT AND LANGUAGE

These inscriptions were sent to the Epigraphy branch of the Archeological Society of India at Mysore. According to the report received from them, two types of script were used in inscriptions, viz., Brahmi and Nagari. The lone fragmentary inscription is in Brahmi script while rest of the inscriptions is in Nagari script of 10th - 11th century A.D. The language of the inscription is Sanskrit and the local dialect.

Content and subject matter of the inscriptions (Annexure I)

The majority of these inscriptions are donatory in nature and records donor's name, date, *gotra* or family *(vamsa)* which they belonged to and name of the deity. The *'santi Vimalacharya vasatau'* and *'Saikrikya'*. *'Saikrikya'* obviousely denotes Sikri and *'Vajrama'* has been identified as Kachhchhapaghata ruler, Vajradamana. This shows that king Vajrama (Vajradamana) was ruling at Gwalior in 1010 A.D.

Inscriptions of the Kachchhapaghata dynasty found so far :

The inscriptions of three branches or three families of Kachchapaghata family have been discovered so far. These are–

(a) Dubkund stone inscription of the time of Vikramasimha [3].

(b) Gwalior stone inscription of Mahipala[4].

(c) Narwar copper plate inscription of Virasimhadeva[5].

The Gwalior Branch: circa. 950-1100 A.D.

Lakshmana (*C*.950-75)-Vajradaman (*C*.975-95)-Mangalaraja (*C*.995-1015)-Kirttiraja (*C*.1015-35) - Muladeva alias Bhuvanapala and Trailokymalla (*C*. 1035-55) - Devapala (*C*.1055-75) - Padmapala (*C*.1075-80) - Mahipala alias Bhuvanaikamalla (*C*.1080-1100).

The Dubkund Branch (*Circa.* 1000-1100)

Yuvaraja (*C*.1000) - Arjuna (*C*.1015-35) - Abhimanyu (*C*.1035-44 A.D.)-Vijayapala (*C*.1044-70)-Vikramasimha (1070-1100 A.D.).

The Narwar Branch (*Circa.* 1075-1125 A.D.)

Gaganasimha (*C*.1075-1090)-Saradasimha (*C*.1090-1105)-Virasimha *C*.1105-1125)

The King Vajradamana was recorded to have ruled from *C*.975-995 A.D. This epigraph has thus extended his rule to 1010 A.D., which is extremely important information for the history of the Kachchhapaghata (later Kachhwaha) dynasty of Gwalior and Amer (Jaipur).

CONCLUSION

Epigraphically, the excavation at Sikri has provided significant material to throw light on its archaeology, though it has been carried out in a restricted area. These inscriptions show that the tradition of temple architecture continued in this region for more than 800 years. Most interesting of these is an inscription on the pedestal of a Saraswati image. It mentions King Vajrama who can be identified as Vajradamana, son of Laksamana of the Kachchhapaghata dynasty rulling at Gwalior. It can now be established on the basis of this inscription that the sway of the Kachchhapaghata dynasty extended to the Sikri region, which was located on ancient trade route passing through Mathura (Surasena), Sikri (Saik), Kagarol, Muchukunda and Gwalior (Gopagiri), across the Chambal (Carmanvati).

It appears that subsequently the Kachchhapaghata King Dulha-Deva or Dhola-Rai married to the Marwari daughter of the Badgujar chief of Dausa, and the Kachchhapaghatas migrated to Amer (modern Jaipur) where they established a principality of their own and became famous as Kachhwahas. The Sikri region came under the possession of a branch of the Badgujars who, thereby, came to be known as *'Sikarwars'*. These Rajputs were holding Sikri during the Sultanate period. Owing to continuous onslaughts of the Turkish armies, they gradually dispersed to Karauli and the nearby regions. But they still trace their roots to Sikri and regularly visit it for such basic rituals as *'mundana'*. History of their period (*C*.13th to 15th century A.D.) is still buried underground.

It appears that there were Jaina, Vaisnava, Saiva and Sakta temples on the banks of the lake, at Sikri and the area around it in 10th -11th centuries A.D. Mahmud Gaznavi, the iconoclast, raided the area (Bulandshahr, Mahaban, Mathura, Bayana and Gwalior) in 1018-1019 A.D. and it is quite likely that he demolished these temples. But the sculptures, found here, bear dates around 1044 A.D. which shows that either he by-passed it without molesting its temples, or these were rebuilt after his return. It is more probable, however that these temples were destroyed by 'Alauddin Khilji (the Delhi Sultan who ruled from 1296 to 1316 A.D.) during his invasion of the Ranthambhor fort (1300-1301 A.D.). His mosque is still found in the adjoining village Sikri confirming his presence in the area. The fact stands out that whenever the Delhi Sultan (from 1194 to 1526) went on iconoclastic raids on Gwalior and Bayana, he passed through Sikri, on the way, and Sikri was thus a soft target of their depredations.

[3] The inscription was discovered in 1866 by Caption W.R. Melville who was in charge of Gwalior Survey at Dubkund in the Shivpuri district of Madhya Pradesh. The inscription has been described and reported in Journal of the Asiatic Society of Bengal, Volume XXV, p. 168; Archaeological Survey of India Reports, Vol. XX (1882-83), p.99; Epigraphia Indica Vol.II (1894), pp.232. A detailed study of this inscription with translation is recently published in Corps Inscriptionum Indicarum, Vol. VII, Part 3 on the Insctiptions of Chandelas, Kachchhapaghatas etc, by H.V. Trivedi in 1889, pp. 528-535.

[4]This inscription was reported by Alexander Cunningham in his Archaeological Survey of India Reports, Volumes II (1862-1865) pp. 357; edited by Rajendralal Mitra in the Journal of the Bengal Asiatic Society, Vol. XXXI (1862), pp. 400; re-edited by Kielhorn in Indian Antiquary, Vol. XV (1886), pp. 33 and edited recently by H.V.Trivedi in the Corpus Inscriptionum Indicarum, Vol. VII Part 3 on the Inscriptions of Chandelas, Kachchhapagatas, etc, 1989, pp. 535-548.

[5]This inscription was translated by Fitz Edward Hall in the Journal of the Americal Oriented Society, Vol. VI (1858-60), pp. 542 and recently edited and updated by H.V.Trivedi in the Corpus Inscriptionum Indicarum, Vol. VII Part 3 on the Inscriptions of Chandelas Kachchhapagatas etc., pp. 552-555.

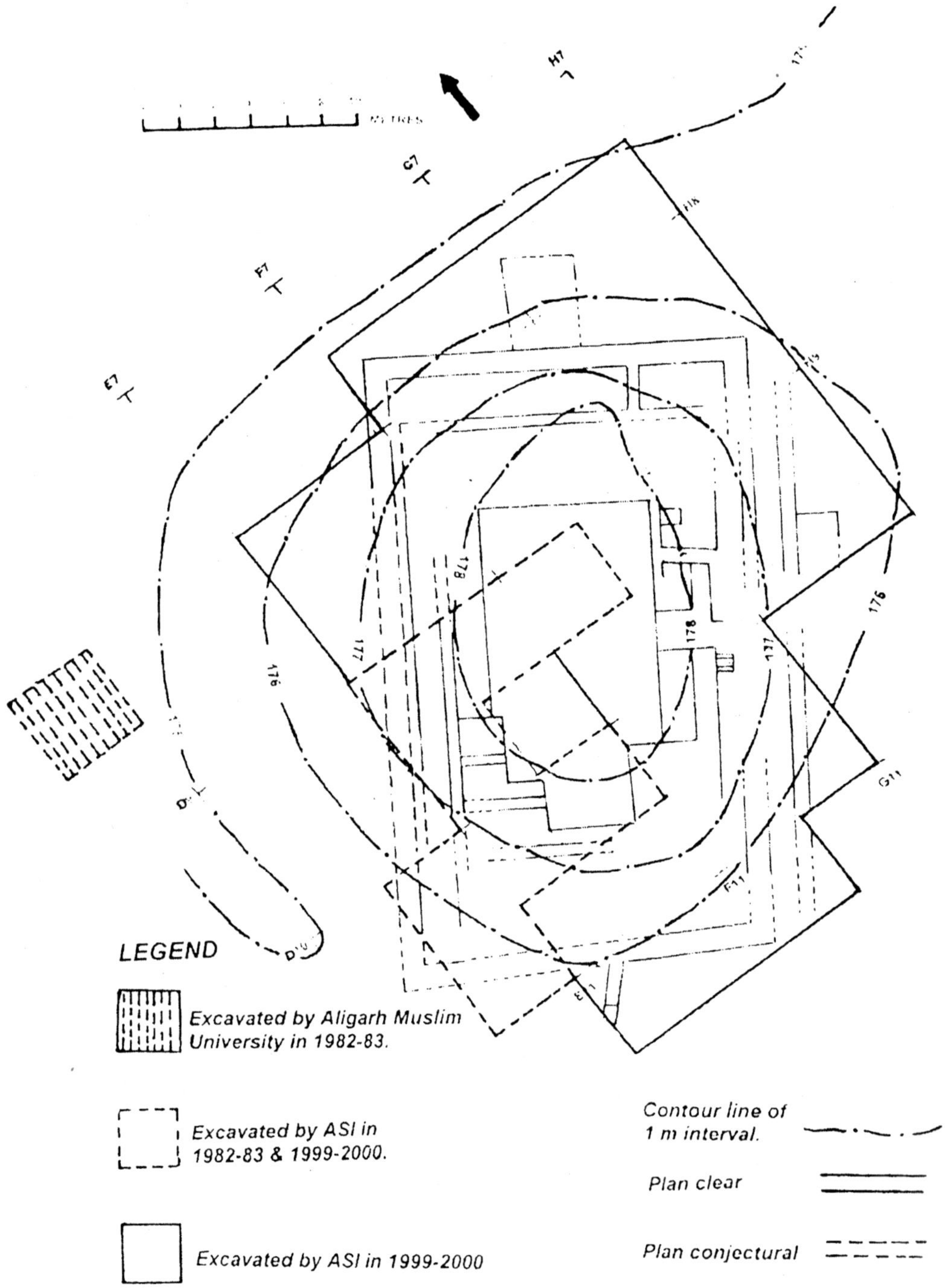

Fig. 1. Map showing the excavated trenches in the year 1982-83 and 1999-2000 at Birchhabili Tila, Sikri village, district Agra.

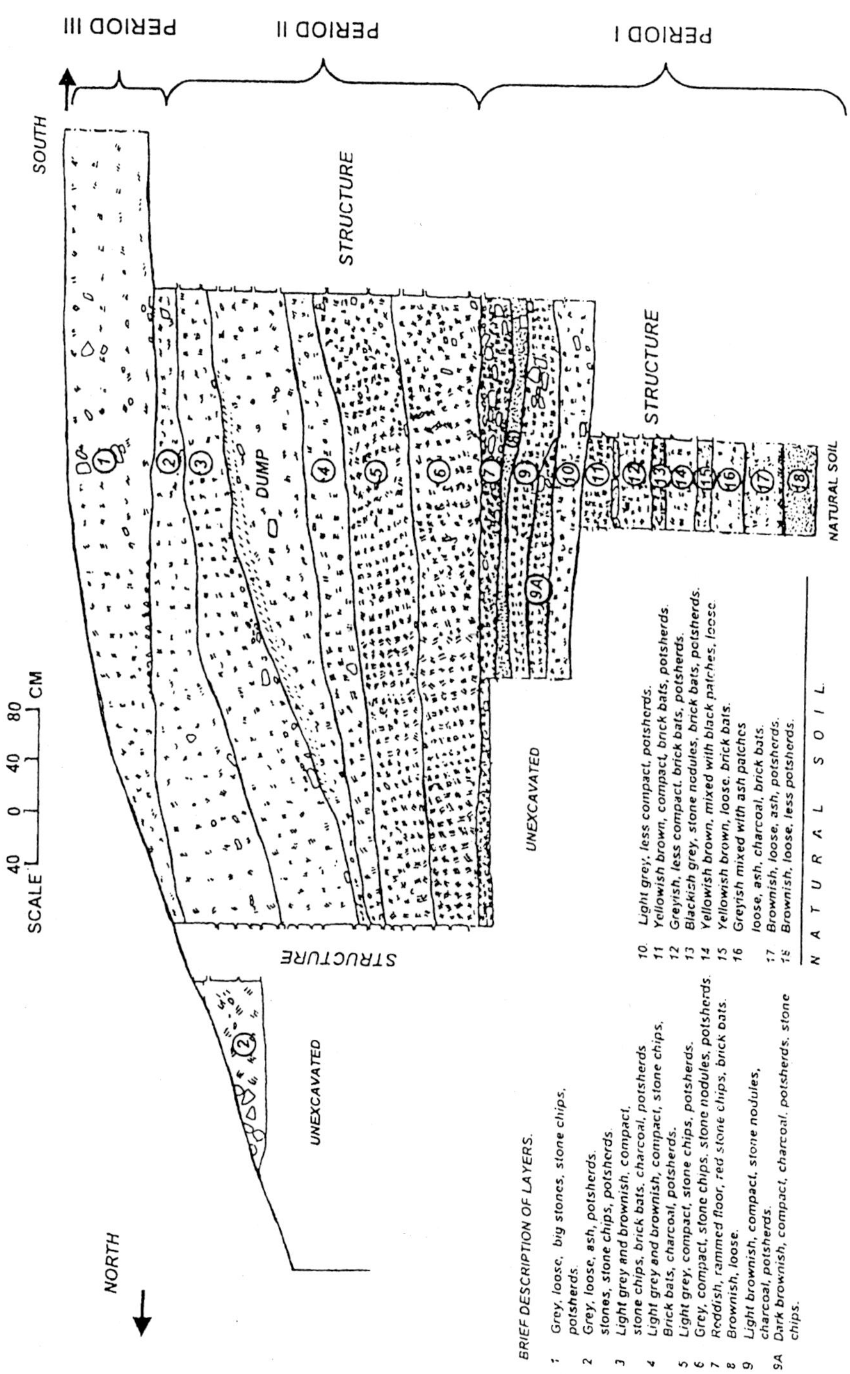

Fig. 2. Section of F-8, facing west, Birchhabili Tila, Sikri village, district Agra.

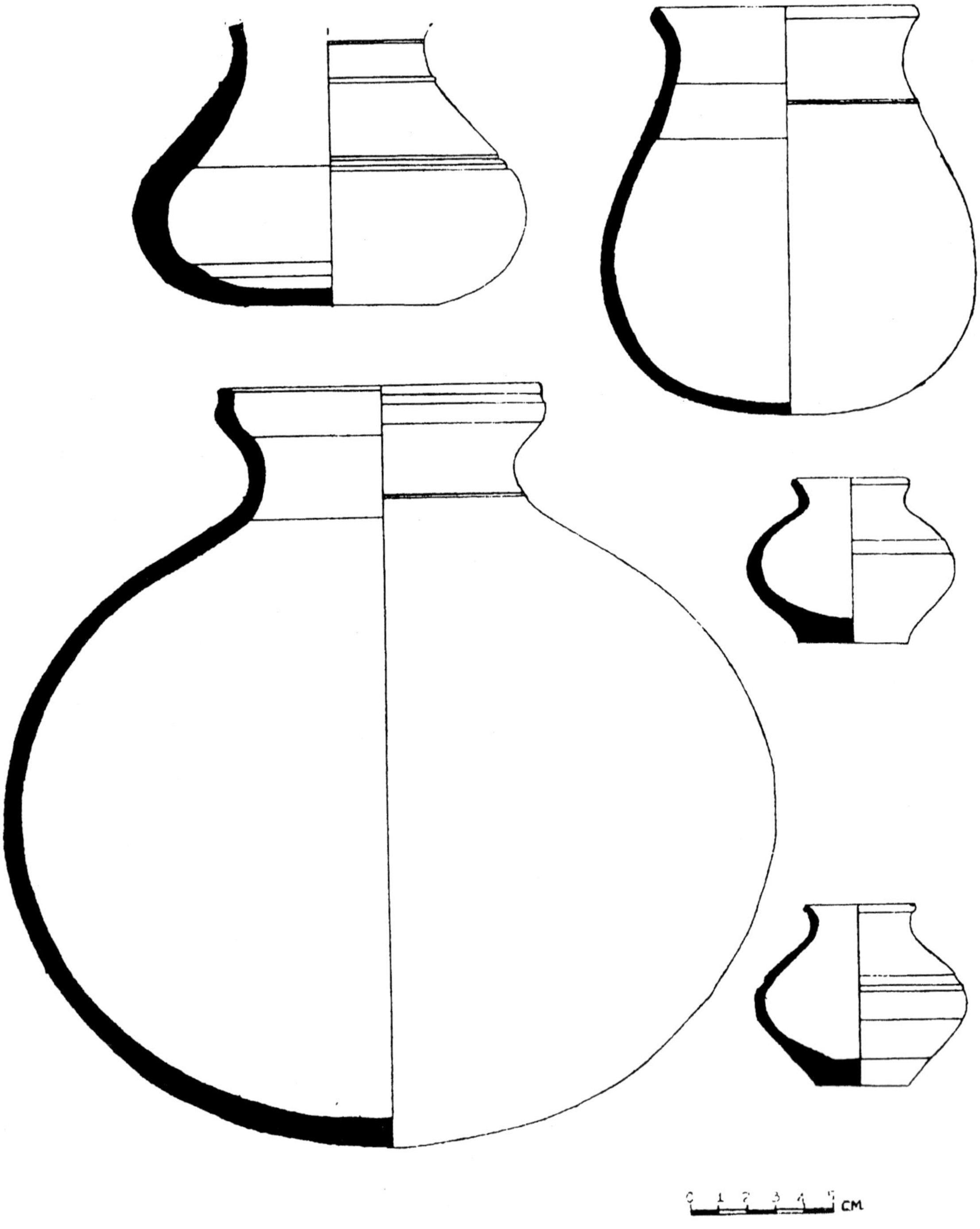

Fig. 3. Red ware, Period I, Birchhabili Tila, Sikri village, district Agra.

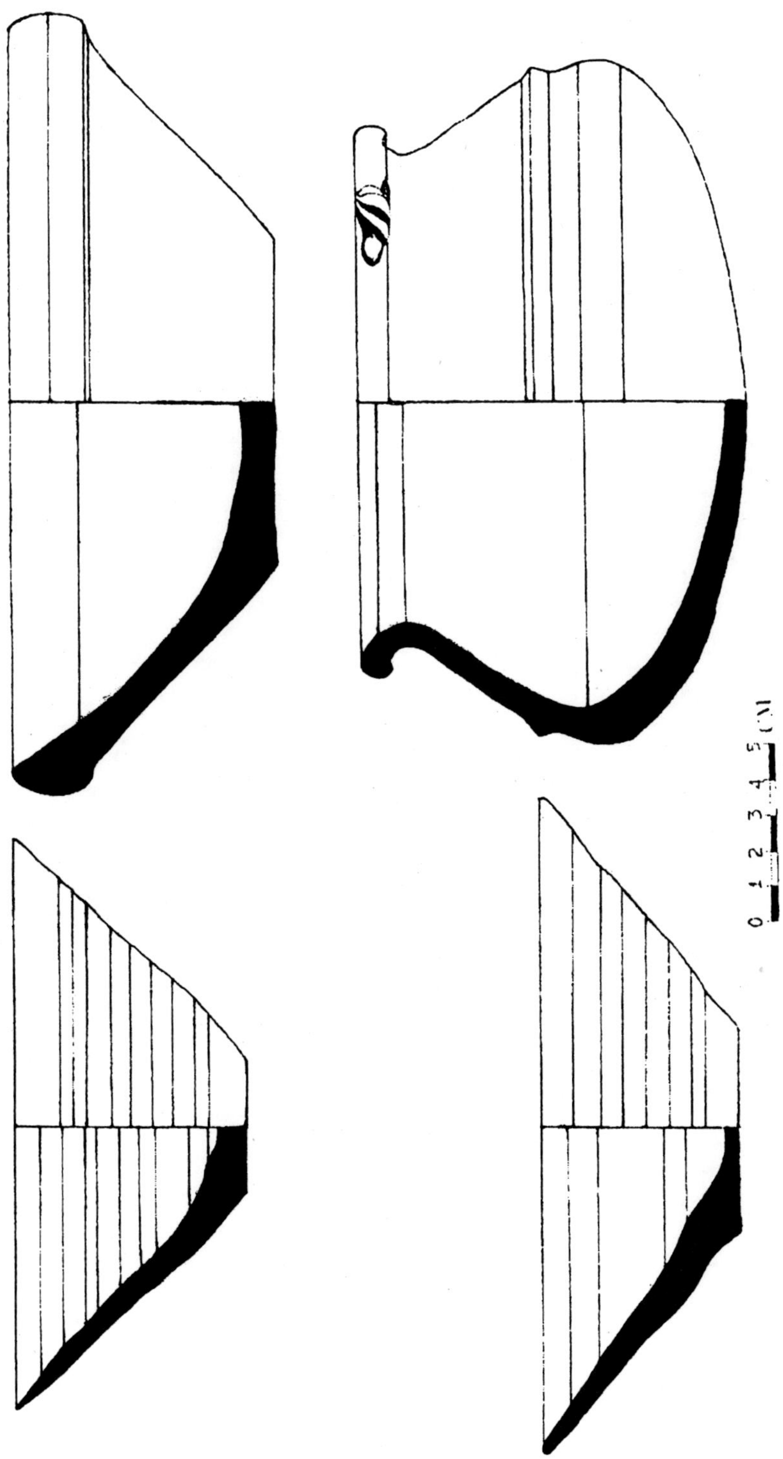

Fig. 4. Red ware, Period I, Birchhabili Tila, Sikri village, district Agra.

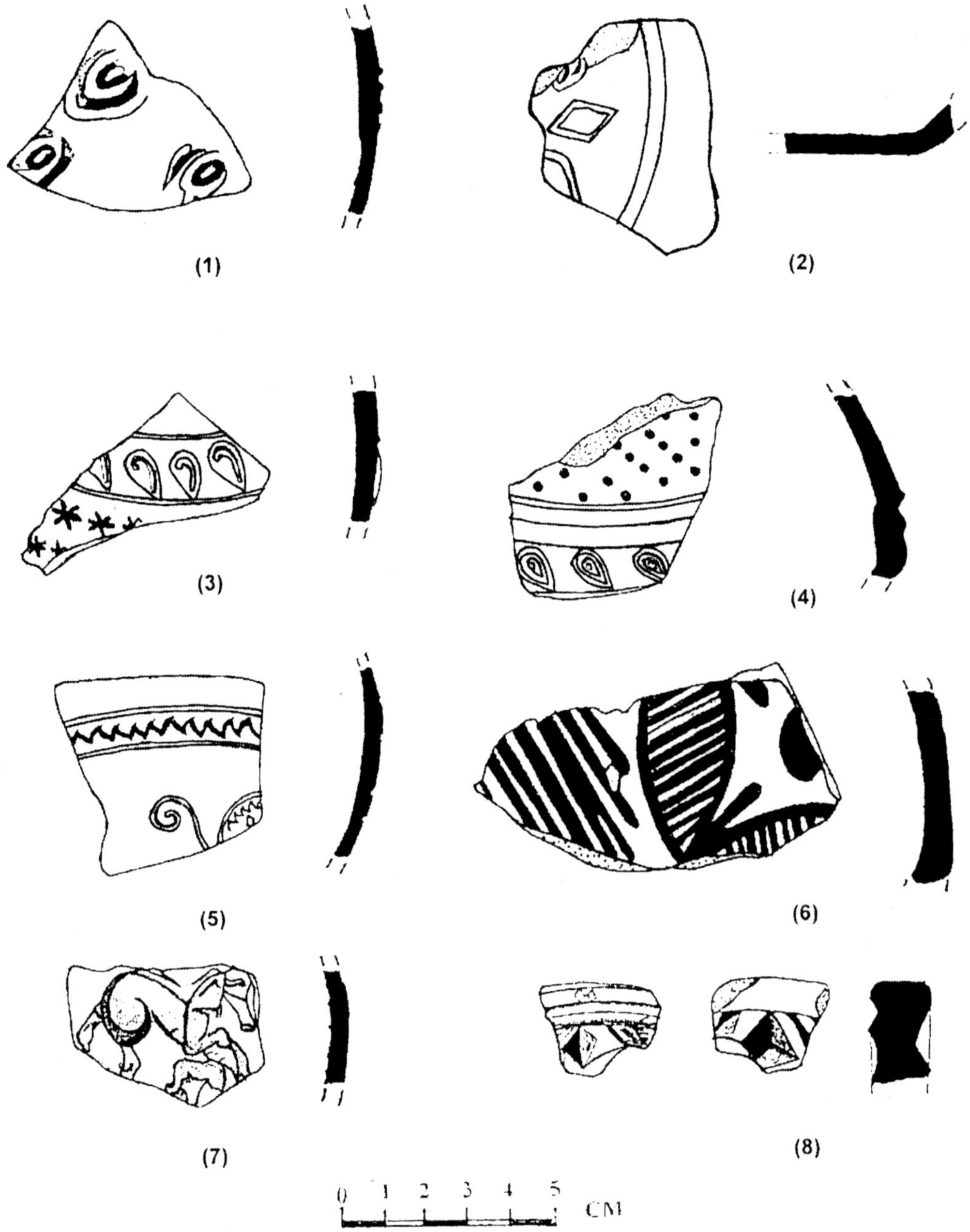

All are red ware sherds of Period I
(1) & (2)-Stamped decorations.
(5) & (8)-Incised decorations.
(6)-Decorated with black coloured paintings on red ware.
(7)-Depiction of horse figure in low relief.
Rest are decorated in appliqué.

Fig. 5. Decorative potsherds, Period I, Birchhabili Tila, Sikri village, district Agra.

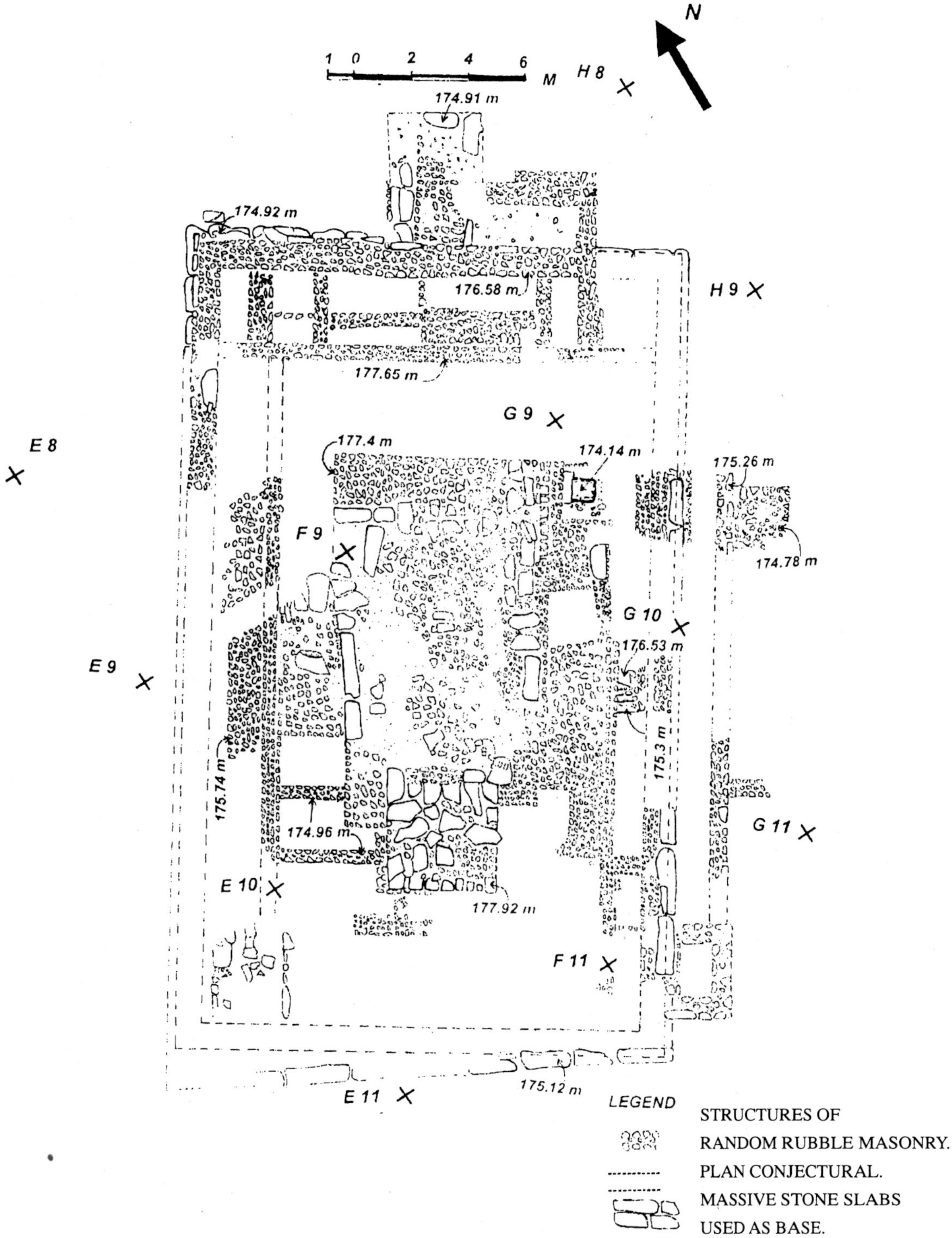

Fig. 6. Temple Plan, period II, Birchhabili Tila, Sikri village, district Agra.

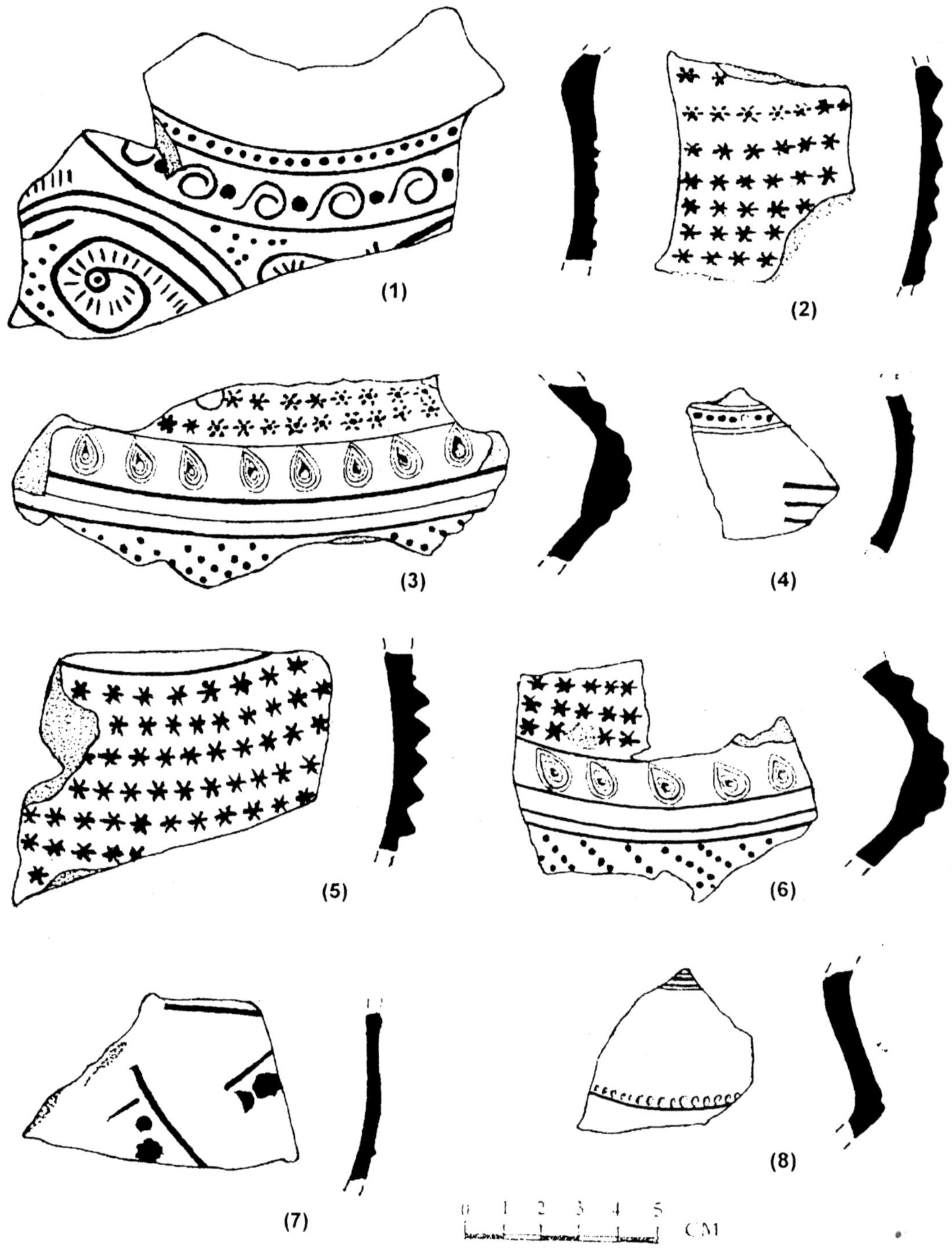

All are red ware sherds except (8) which is black ware sherd.
All the decorations are in appliqué except (8) which is an incised decoration.

Fig. 7. Decorative potsherds, Period II, Birchhabili Tila, Sikri village, district Agra.

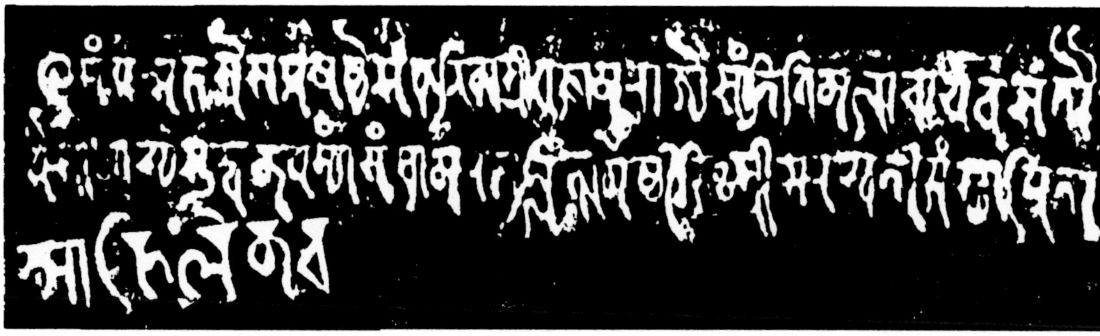

ओं (सिद्धम्) संवत्सहस्रे सप्तषष्ठे सैकरिक्यश्रीवज्रामराज्ये सांतिविमलाचार्यवसतौ वैसाखस्य सुद्धनवम्यां संचामरभल्लिक्यशेंष्ठीभिः स्रीसरस्वती संस्थापिता आहिलेन च

ओं (सिद्धम्) विक्रम संवत् १०६७ बैशाख शुक्लपक्ष की नवमी (१०१० ईसवीं) के दिन सीकरीका के निवासी श्री वज्राम के राज्य में शांतिविमलाचार्य की बस्ती में संचामर और भल्लिक्य गोत्र वाले सेठों के द्वारा श्री सरस्वती की प्रतिमा स्थापित करवाई गई । और आहिल ने भी

Om Siddham! The Sresthis of Sancamara and Bhallikya gotras installed the image of Sri (Srutidevi) Saraswati, in the habitat (locality) of (Muni) Santi-Vimalacarya, at Sekriyya (Sikri), in the reign of (the Kachchhapaghata King) Vajrama (Vajradamana) on the ninth of the bright fortnight v.s. 1067/1010 A.D. And Ahila also (contributed)—

• यहां ऐसा प्रतीत होता है कि आहिल उस शिल्पी का नाम है जिसने मूर्ति उत्कीर्ण की है। उसका भी योगदान इस मूर्ति की स्थापना में है । यह आहिल नाम मूर्तिकार ने बाद में जोड़ा है, शेष लेख की अपेक्षा आहिल नाम सुन्दर और बड़ा लिखा हुआ है ।

It appears that 'Ahila' was name of the sculptor who carved this wonderful image of Saraswati. He also contributed to the installation of this image, this way which is why he inscribed his name at the end of the epigraph. The word 'Ahila' is written in longer and more elegant letters than the rest of the inscriptions.

Fig. 8. Inscription found on pedestal (padapitha) of Sruti Devi Jaina Saraswati sculpture.

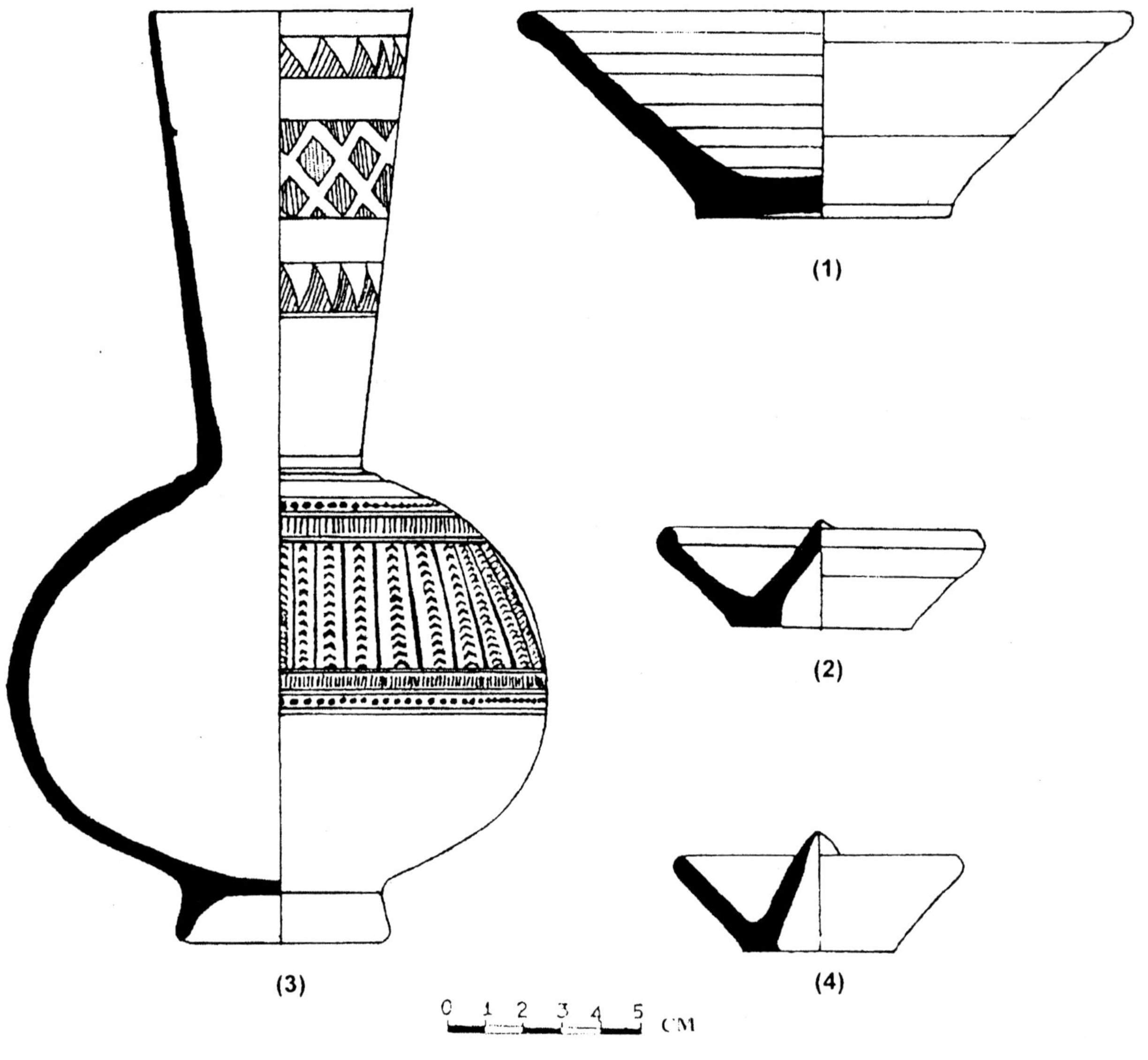

All are red ware except (3) which is a buff ware

Fig. 9. Pottery of Period III, Birchhabili Tila, Sikri village, district Agra.

Further Excavation at Ojiyana

B.R. MEENA AND ALOK TRIPATHI*

Excavation at Ojiyana (Lat. 25^0 53' N, Long. 74^0 21' E) has brought to light many new facts about Ahar culture (Meena and Tripathi, 2000a: 30-31; Tripathi, 2000: 6-14). Recent excavations have added greatly to our knowledge gathered from earlier excavations at Ahar (Sankalia *et al* 1969), Balathal (Mishra *et al* 1995: 57-79; 1997: 35-59; Mishra 1997: 251-273), and Gilund. Despite these excavations some of the riddles about the authors of this indigenous culture of southeastern Rajasthan and the origin of development and decline of this culture are yet to be solved.

The Jaipur Circle of the Archaeological Survey of India took up the excavation at Ojiyana in the year 1999 - 2000. A brief account of first season's work has already appeared in the *Puratattva* No. *30* (Meena and Tripathi, 2000b: 67 - 73). Encouraged by the outstanding results of the excavation it was decided to take up further horizontal excavation on this important site of Ahar culture next year.

Although the main concentration of the sites of Ahar culture have been found in southeastern Rajasthan, but this culture had spread far beyond the Banas valley. Like Ojiyana, which is unusually located in the hilly terrain of Aravalli, some sites have also been reported from Chambal and Narmada valleys in central India. With the discovery of more than one hundred sites of Ahar culture in Rajasthan and Madhya Pradesh, the extension of this culture can be traced from Ahar in the west to Eran in the east, and Ajmer in the north to Navdatoli in the south.

Earlier excavation had revealed 7.5 m thick single culture deposit on the slope of the hill. The entire deposit is divided into three phases based on the pottery and structural evidence. 2.07 m deposit of layer (26) to (21) is marked as phase I. 3.74 m deposit of layer (20) to (8) is assignable to phase II and remaining 1.67 m deposit of layer (7) to (1) is marked as phase III.

In phase I, white painted black-and-red ware user early settlers came and settled on the rock near fertile land. According to the requirement of the area, they made necessary changes and developed new style of construction to suit local environment. The succeeding phase was the phase of prosperity that continued for a long period. In this phase big houses were built of stones. Phase II is further sub-divided in two structural phases II-a and II-b. Due to the limited area of excavation no complete house plan of Phase II-a could be unearthed. In Phase II-b, a definite well-planned settlement pattern emerges with public and private structures. The houses in this phase had many rooms and chambers for different use. Structures of Phase III mark a sharp decline. A devastating fire destroyed the last settlement on the site.

*Archaeological Survey of India, Janpath, New Delhi

The excavation of second field season was conducted from January to June 2001. After ascertaining the cultural sequence and unearthing house complex and other structures last year, the main objective of this excavation was to know more about the habitation pattern and structural activities at the site. The excavated artefacts are still being studied for preparation of detailed technical report and this brief account is based on the study in the field.

In all about fifty trenches were laid at two different places. The excavation concentrated around the eight trenches, which were excavated on the northern slope of the hill in the first field season. The earlier trenches were reopened and renumbered in order to have systematic horizontal excavation. Excavation was also resumed in two earlier excavated trenches, down to slope, to ascertain the northward extension of the habitation.

One of the objectives for the excavation of this year was to study the settlement pattern of Phase II-b. In order to achieve the above objective nineteen more trenches, measuring 5 m x 5 m, were laid judiciously adjacent to the previous years trenches. The excavation resulted in unearthing important public and private structures.

The most important structure unearthed this year is a thick fortification wall around the site. The thickness of the wall varies from 1.80 m to 2.0 m. The lower portion of this wall was made of huge stones measuring up to 85 cm in length where as the upper portion was made of random rubbles set in mud mortar. The wall running to the north of the settlement was exposed to a length of 45 m. Surface features suggested that this wall encircled the entire settlement which spreads in about 4.5 hectares area on the northern, eastern and southern slopes of the hill.

Habitation inside this wall was well planned. Straight streets were laid running east to west parallel to the fortification wall (pl. 1). By the side of the street were house complexes with several rooms, chambers with mud brick partition walls and open courtyard. On the other side of the house complex also runs another street parallel to the earlier one. It clearly suggest a proper planning and systematic lay out of settlement in Phase II-b.

A complete house complex unearthed between two parallel running streets represents the developments in structural activities in this phase. In this house four chambers were built on a platform to the south of open courtyard. These four chambers divided by mud brick partition walls of single brick thickness were used for different purposes. Two of the chambers were empty and there is no evidence to suggest but third was meant for keeping kitchen goods, utensils and for preparation of food like grinding grains etc. and the fourth chamber was the kitchen. First two chambers were open towards courtyard whereas the third and fourth chambers were partially covered with mud brick wall and had a narrow opening with a small projected platform in front to provide passage from one chamber to other.

The walls of the house were made of stones and were plastered with mud. Roof of the entire complex was probably thatched. A boundary wall made of random rubble surrounded the courtyard. To the east of the open courtyard were built two living rooms. The partition wall between these rooms was badly damaged but a huge stone slab with one straight side clearly marks the position of the door leading from one room to the other. A small portion of the street to the south of this house was unearthed last year. But due to partial exposure it was misinterpreted as long narrow room. The horizontal excavation this year cleared the entire plan of the house flanked by two parallel running streets (pl. 2).

After a careful study of surface features and the behaviour of the fortification wall, twenty-four trenches were also laid on the western end of the site. Soon after the removal of upper layers the remains of a huge wall surrounding the habitation got exposed. Excavation in these trenches unearthed the fortification wall (pl. 3) to a length of about 70 m at the western end of the habitation.

Later phase mark a clear decline in structural activities and also degeneration in civic system. In this phase encroachments were made in the streets and houses were not so spacious and planned like the preceding phase. At one point the entire street was encroached by erecting a mud brick wall between the fortification wall and a house located to the south of the street. The houses were still built of stones but they were very poor in construction, smaller in size and did not follow the earlier plan of the settlement. The orientation of the houses also changed.

Perhaps with the collapse of civic system people

started collecting their crop in houses instead of granaries. Big circular pits were dug to store the grains. The walls and the floor of these storage pits were made carefully to protect stored grains. Several such circular structures for storage were noticed on the site and one complete circular structure of about 180 cm diameter was unearthed in the trench YA 3 and YA 4.

This circular structure was made in later phase after cutting the boundary wall of a house of phase II-b. It is interesting to note that the diameter of this circular structure is equal to the thick fortification wall and also the street that runs parallel to the fortification wall. It is also located very next to these structures. The filling inside this pit was homogenous with some stones fallen from its wall. The stones were more on the top and as we went down, the number of stones decreased.

In the last phase, the houses were made of wattle and daub. Thick layer of ash, burnt and baked pieces of mud plaster and postholes capped with charcoal tell the story of devastating fire, which destroyed the last settlement on the site.

The antiquities found this year include a large number of beads of steatite and beads of shell, bone, faience, terracotta, carnelian and agate; ornaments and pieces of copper; saddle querns, ring stones, hammer stones, sling balls, terracotta animal figurines, hopscotch, toy cart wheels, etc.

The excavation yielded exceptionally large number of terracotta bulls, both naturalistic and stylized. Based on their size, position and size of the hump and style of their faces, these figurines can be divided in several broad groups. A good number of bulls were also painted.

The paintings are mostly white and seldom black. Examples of black painted bulls are very few but over 50 bull figurines are painted in white. On the close study of these painted bulls, few patterns are found common. White paintings on these bulls make them unparalleled in contemporary cultures. These white painted bulls, being unique, may also be termed as "Ojiyana Bulls". These Bulls perhaps were the cult objects and the paintings were probably executed during the rituals.

Several cow figurines unearthed at Ojiyana are the most outstanding discovery. Modeling of cow here was not experimental but frequent as is evident not only by the number of cow figurine found but also by the different styles of modeling these figurines. Alike bulls they were also objects of rituals and some also bear the traces of white paintings.

It is surprising that the cow was not only known but also used by the people of earlier cultures but it was not depicted. In Harappan art, a variety of bulls have been found represented in various forms but cow was never depicted. The situation in other contemporary and later Chalcolithic cultures remained unchanged where good numbers of other animal figurines have been found but no cow figurine is reported so far. Unearthing of 12 terracotta cow figurines from the deposits of phase II imply that the people of Ojiyana were somehow different from all other contemporary cultures that could experiment in art. The cows figurines found here can be divided in two broad groups on the basis of the fashion of making their udder. In some of the cow figurines uro-genital organs are also shown by two pinches at the back. Depiction of genital organs of cow seems suggesting that they believed in fertility cult and perhaps the cow was also worshipped.

Good number of toy-cart wheels both of terracotta and pottery are found in all the phases. Some of the terracotta wheels also depict incised spokes. The sizes of wheels vary considerably.

Gamesman of different shapes and sizes are found in all the phases. All the gamesman found here is made of terracotta. The size and shape of these gamesmen vary from small conical to long tubular.

Spindle whorls made of terracotta are also unearthed in the excavation. Some of these are tastefully decorated with incision and pinching. The finding of spindle whorls evident that the people at Ojiyana were also familiar with spinning.

A large number of sling balls made of stone and terracotta are found in all the phases. Some of the terracotta balls are very small and might have been used as marble also. The stone used for sling balls is invariably quartz, which is locally available in abundance.

Hopscotches seem to be very popular, as large numbers of hopscotches made of pottery are found in all the phases. Size of these hopscotches varies considerably. Besides common circular hopscotches some rectangular hopscotches are also found.

Stone beads from Ojiyana include the beads of carnelian, agate and limestone. These materials are not available locally and might have been imported. It is interesting to note that no bead of quartz is found which is locally available in abundance. It suggests that these stone beads were not manufactured locally.

Steatite beads out number beads of all other materials. The common shapes among steatite beads are micro beads, globular, thin and thick disc beads. If the number is any indication of popularity or availability, the beads made of steatite were most popular perhaps because common man used them.

Saddle-querns, mullers, hammer stones of quartz, ring stones etc. are some of the objects of stone worth mentioning. Some of the saddle-querns and hammer stones must have been used for agricultural products and it constitute an important aspect.

A variety of floral remains, charcoal, charred grains, seeds etc. have been collected in the process of flotation. Main crops grown by settlers included the cereals, millets, pulses and oil seeds. Some of the crops identified during preliminary study of these floral remains are - barley *(Hordeum vulgare)*, dwarf-wheat *(Triticum sphaerococcum)*, bread-wheat *(Triticum aestivum)*, rice *(Oryza sativa)*, ragi-millet *(Eleusine coracana)*, Italian-millet *(Setaria italica)*, jowar-millet *(Sorghum bicolor)*, horsegram/ kulthi *(Dolichos biflorus)*, lentil *(Lens culinaris)*, field-pea *(Pisum arvense)*, moth bean *(Vigna aconitifolia)*, gram/ chick-pea *(Cicer arietinum)*, til *(Sesamum indicum)* and sanflower/ kusum *(Carthamus tinctorius)*. These crop remains are found in association with wide range of remains of weed and other wild taxa.

Large number of bones of cattle, wild and domesticated animals, birds etc. have also been found and carefully collected during the excavation. These faunal remains are in the process of scientific study by archaeozoologist.

Conclusion

7.5 m thick deposit of Copper Age at Ojiyana, is divided into three phases based on structural activities and changes in pottery. White painted black-and-red ware continues in all the phases although there are changes in shapes, designs, treatment and firing techniques. It remained important ceramic tradition throughout, along with red ware.

It was always a question that why this group of people of Ahar culture came and settled in this rough and hilly terrain. There is no clear evidence to answer this question conclusively but one may infer reasonably that the mineral wealth of this hilly region might have been the attraction for Copper Age people of Ahar culture to settle in this rough terrine. This region is rich in copper oreand the copper was extracted in this region since antiquity. Aravalli schist also contains crystals of garnet, which one time was much reputed as a gemstone.

Excavation has also yielded some antiquities, which are unique in Ahar culture. White painted terracotta bull and terracotta cow figurine are found for the first time. Some of the antiquities unearthed here provide definite evidence of its relations with Harappans and perhaps with other Chalcolithic cultures. A Harappan type faience bead (Vats, 1974: 404-405; pl. CXXXIII, fig. 9d, e) and circular terracotta cakes (pl. 4) suggest some distant relationship between Harappan and Ahar culture sites.

The habitational period could be bracketed between 3000 B.C. and 1500 B.C. as per the relative chronology offered by comparative study with excavated material from other sites of Ahar culture. Further detailed study, analysis of data and detailed scientific studies will throw more light on this less known Copper Age culture. C^{14} dates of the samples collected during the excavation will help in building a firm chronology.

The excavation at Ojiyana has contributed a lot to Protohistory of India in general and Ahar culture in particular by providing new information about this Copper Age culture of southeastern Rajasthan. The well planned big house complexes between parallel running streets and a fortification wall all around the settlement are the evidence of a planned settlement which is possible only in a strong civic society. The features and finds in various phases show a cultural continuity, a phenomenon of permanent settlement, besides the inherent growth, development and decline along with the assimilation of new ideas. The results of this excavation are very important and valuable in the broad assessment of entire Ahar complex.

Acknowledgements

We are thankful to Shri R.C. Agarwal, excavator of Ahar, for his guidance and encouragement through out. Thanks are also due to the Director General and Directors of Archaeological Survey of India for their valuable suggestions and encouragement. Thanks are also due to Dr. S.K. Saraswati of Birbal Sahni Institute of Palaeobotany, Lucknow, not only for devoting his valuable time for studying the floral remains on the site but also for providing his report in a very short period. Authors are also thankful to their colleagues namely S/Shri Brij Raj Singh, Rajendra Yadava, S.C. Gupta, S.K. Mathur, S.K. Apharya and Saini and M.S Rawat of Jaipur circle of Archaeological Survey of India for making this excavation a success.

REFERENCE

Meena, B.R. and Alok Tripathi, 2000 a, Rajasthan main ek adwitiya tamrayugeen sthal - Ojiyana, *Rajasthan Sujas*, Directorate of Information & Public Relations, Jaipur.

Meena, B.R. and Alok Tripathi, 2000 b, Excavation at Ojiyana, *Puratattva, No. 30*, New Delhi.

Mishra, V.N., Vasant Shinde, R.K. Mohanty, Kurush Dalal, Anup Mishra, Lalit Pandey, Jeevan Kharakwal, 1995, Excavation at Balathal: Their Contribution to the Chalcolithic and Iron Age Cultures of Mewar, Rajasthan, *Man and Environment XX.1*, Pune.

Mishra, V.N., Vasant Shinde, R.K. Mohanty, Lalit Pandey, Jeevan Kharakwal, 1997, Excavations at Balathal, Udaipur District, Rajasthan, (1995-97), with Special Reference to Chalcolithic Architecture, *Man and Environment XXII. 2*, Pune.

Mishra, V.N. 1997, Balathal: A Chalcolithic Settlement in Mewar, Rajasthan, India: Results of First Three Seasons' Excavation, *South Asian Studies. 13*.

Sankalia, H.D., Deo, S.B. and Ansari, Z.D., 1969, *Excavations at Ahar (Tambavati) 1961-62*, Pune.

Tripathi, Alok, 2000, *Recent Excavations in Rajasthan* (Ed.) B.R.Meena, Jaipur.

Vats, Madho Sarup, 1974, *Excavations at Harappa, Vol. I*, Varanasi.

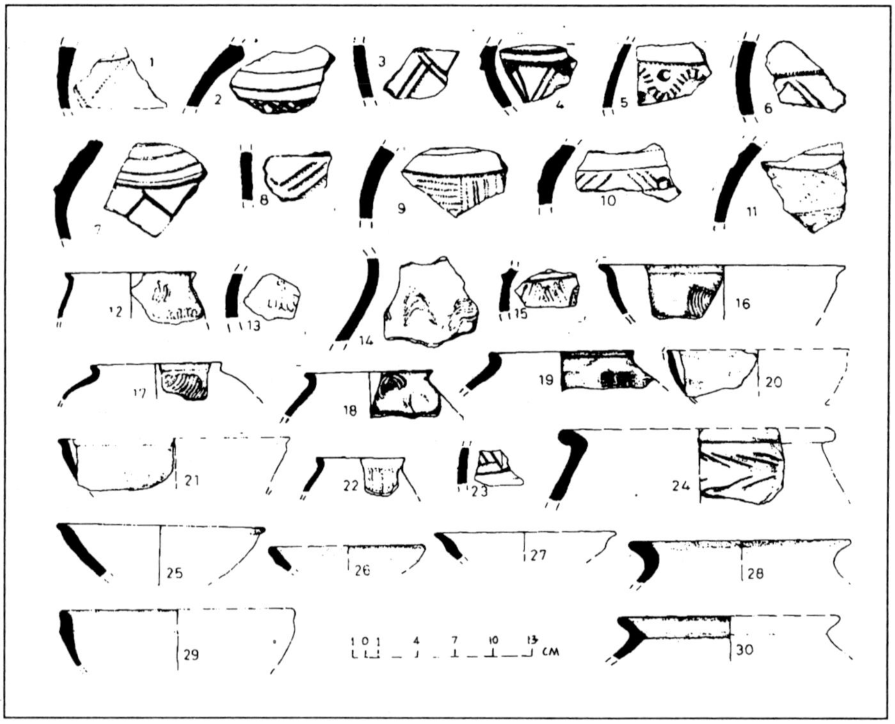

Fig. 1. Ceramic Assemblage.

Bhaitbari Excavations–
A Reappraisal

AJAY MITRA SHASTRI*

Vadagokugiri, better known as Bhaitbari, in Tura district of the west Garo Hills division of Meghalaya was subjected to a small-scale archaeological excavation by the Prehistory Branch of the Archaeological Survey of India under Shri A.K. Sharma in January-March 1992 which attempted to probe the archaeological potential of the region. The result was immensely rewarding, as it revealed in spectacular discoveries proving *inter alia*, that it was a flourishing township dating from pre-Christian centuries and had close link with the rest of India culturally. It has yielded positive evidence of people practicing Vedic-Puranic religion involving temple ritual and worship of Puranic divinities including Siva, Ganesha, Kali, Ugra-Tara and Saraswati and demi-gods like Vidyadharas and prevalence of religious practices like asceticism and other rituals. The excavation has also yielded some secular figures including dancers and instrumentalists.

Sharma has published a report of the work very promptly with beautiful illustrations. While the work and its prompt publication elicit great admiration, it is not possible to agree with some of his deductions and identifications of which he himself appears to have been aware. The present paper aims at reviewing some of the findings and iconographic identifications and underscores the urgent need of sustained archaeological work in North-Eastern India.

Introduction

Not much attention has been devoted to the archaeological potential of the north-east viz. Assam, Meghalaya, Mizoram, Nagaland and Arunachal Pradesh as well as some other regions. What little work has been done till recently was confined to its Prehistory. Till recently the history from archaeological remains of the region was almost non-existent. And the notion that its major part remained isolated from the mainstream of the socio-religious life of the rest of India was exaggerated. From this view point the work done by A.K. Sharma deserves high accolade. He carried out small-scale diggings in Manipur (Sharma nd.) and Meghalaya (Sharma 1993) with astonishing results demonstrating the region's close cultural links with the rest of India and underscoring the urgent need for considerable future work.

The site in Meghalaya excavated by him is the small village of Vadagokugiri or Bhaitbari (25° 5' N, 90° 2' E), about 8 km west of the well-known town of Phulbari on Phulbari-Tura road in the Tura district of the West Garo Hills. The work extending over a very small area during just two months (January-March 1992) proved highly rewarding with unexpectedly rich evidence of the prevalence and popularity of indigenous Indian religions and establishing cultural unity with the rest of India. What is noteworthy is that within this period of about two months

*'Pranchi', 23, Vidya Vihar, Rana Pratap Nagar, Nagpur-440022.

work at a number of sites was undertaken, and the excavated mounds were situated nearly one to two kilometres apart from one another. However, it is difficult to agree with some of his conclusions and iconographic identifications of some of the terracotta figurines. In fact, he was himself conscious of the shortcoming as indicated by some of his observations (Sharma, 1993: p. VII). We take this opportunity in these pages to make a few observations on the findings, especially iconic.

Besides the fortification with moat, he has identified a huge *stupa* dating from around first century A.D. on the north-western fringe of the fortified township. The mound in question was 5.75 m high from the ground level and had a maximum diameter of 30 m at the bottom. According to him, in order to understand its structural composition, the entire structure was divided into grids and 'a quadrant was opened on the top, keeping in view, the exact centre of the *stupa*, apart from other grids around'. He has visualized all usual components of the *stupa* including *harmika, vedika, anda, bhumis* and *medhi* approached by stairways on the four cardinal points and *pradakshina-patha* and has concluded that the whole structure was built on a pyramidical (sic) fashion with three receding tiers of brick platforms. It appears that nearly 34.5 m long *vedika* was raised for laying a brick platform around the dumped earth for the dome or *anda*. Above it was the 31.5 m long *medhi* followed by three receding terraces *(bhumi)*. Constructing box-chambers, which are enclosed by brick walls, has formed the terraces. The boxes have been filled with brickbats and compact clay. It was approached by a flight of steps in the centre of these chambers, and as other sides have been denuded of bricks, its continuous remains are visible on the southern side only. He has also visualized the possibility of there being miniature votive *stupas* all around the main structure (Sharma 1993: 31-35).

But he doesn't appear to be sure in the matter. He observes; "in the absence of any relics in the excavations carried out so far, and any other top structural remains like *harmika*, etc. may doubt about the available structure being a *stupa*". Next he proceeds to counter this. But his answers don't carry conviction. He says, for example, that "the quadrant opened on the top was not laid exactly in the centre of the complex" and that "the centre is yet to be exposed" (Sharma 1993: 33-34), which is at variance with his earlier statement that has just been cited. Moreover, there is nothing specifically Buddhist like footprints *(padukas)*, etc. yet exposed. In view of these facts the presence of the *stupa* can't be confirmed, its possibility can't be denied though. All that is permissible in the present state of our knowledge is that the mound represented the side of some imposing structure, its exact nature remaining unascertainable at present, as all its sides couldn't be exposed in the short span of time available.

Temple-Complexes

Temples of Puranic deities are well documented. At least two groups of these temples have been unearthed: one almost in the centre of the fortified township and the other on the north-western side adjoining the riverbank. Each group has at least ten to twelve mounds which, basing on the surface indications and their location, may be designated as temple-mounds. The first group has five tanks, the largest one being 400 x 180 m on the south; rests are close to each other, side by side and close to the riverside. Most of the temples of the second group are located around a rectangular tank that still has plenty of water with blooming lotuses and lilies. It is important to note that the architectural texts *(Silpasastra or Prasada-lakshana)* prescribe location of the temples in the proximity of water and vegetation (Shastri 1996 LV, p: 495). All around the tanks were spotted numerous architectural fragments of temples such as *amalakas*, miniature *sikharas*, decorative pieces with floral designs, lintels and door jambs *(dvara-sakhas)*, as well as cult objects like Siva *lingas* and *yonis*. Some of these have been collected and kept inside a makeshift bamboo structure under an imposing banyan tree on the eastern embankment and are still worshipped by the local Koch people as their ancestral deities. And on the top of the opposite eastern bank inside a bamboo grove are collected several structural stone fragments of large temples worshipped by the local Garos as their village deities. Numerous architectural remains of different dimension and brickbats as well as fragments of divine figures were found lying in the adjacent area.

The extant evidence seems to indicate that almost all the temples were built of bricks, and probably only a few were of stones. Local reports show that all mounds yielded a large number of decorated and sculptured terracotta plaques, from time to time in the course of collecting wood, digging and ploughing. Two big boulders show in bas-relief elevation of principal shrine and these were found lying in a stream on the eastern fringe of the fortified township. These models show a combination of the elements of the *Pidha deul* and the *Rekha deul* forms of temples. These as well as other numerous architectural fragments revealed that at least some of the temples were built in the Orissan style with visible impact of the Pratiharas and may be dated to the period roughly between the seventh and eleventh centuries A.D. One of these is an octagonal Siva temple (Sharma 1993:36-42).

The last one is certainly one of the unique finds not only in this part but also in the whole of India. But it is difficult to agree with Shri Sharma in his description of this octagonal Siva temple as an *ashtamurti* shrine containing eight Siva-*lingas* (Sharma 1993:38 and 42). Since the word *ashta-murti* has absolutely nothing to do with the number of *lingas,* but refers just to the eight elements combined symbolically in god Siva as described by the celebrated poet-dramatist Kalidasa in the invocatory stanza of *Abhijnana-Sakuntalam*[3]. In art, eight faces of god Siva represent this combination. Such an exquisite stone figure dating from early Vakataka period has been found at the well-known site of Mandhal (Nagpur district, Maharashtra)[4] and also at Mandasor (Madhya Pradesh) dating from around sixth century A.D.

Terracotta Plaques

One of the most startling finds of Sharma's work is the rich yield of terracotta plaques, often exquisite, representing Puranic deities in various postures and depictions of other socio-religious themes connected therewith. These differ in fabricating quality depending on the skill of the sculptor artist. These include also *Sivalingas* and *yoni-pithas* to which reference has already been made. Also figures of the elephant-headed god Ganesa in various poses, including dancing (Nritya-Ganesa) have been reported and, what is most interesting, they are the largest numerically (Sharma 1993:44-49). This perhaps reveals the great popularity of his worship which was supposed to remove obstacles. Other figures are those of three-eyed Siva, Uma-Mahesvara, goddesses Kali (dancing as well as seated), Ugra-Tara, Vaishnavi and Sarasvati, the semi-divine Vidyadhara, Tantrik ascetics and females and males dancing and playing musical instruments like *mridanga.* These plaques have been described in great detail and illustrated (Sharma 1993 43-73) While these descriptions and illustrations form the main basis of our discussion, it is not possible to agree with some of his identifications. The following captions reflect our views.

Siva Trinetra

No. 31 (Pl. XXXII) is a fragmentary seated figure with four hands, third and fourth one separating from the elbows of the two normal hands. The god is seated in *padmasana.* He wears a necklace with pendants and a close-fitting decorated necklet *(graveyaka)* and in the two ears elongated ear-rings *(kundalas)*, and his head is adorned with a five-tiered *jata-mukuta* and the outer ends of his headband are depicted as flying on the two sides. In his upper right hand, he holds an *aksha-mala,* the right lower hand is kept on the right knee. While the objects held or postures of the hands on the left cannot be determined as their end-parts are broken away. On his right is depicted a flying Vidyadhara (Sharma 1993: 50) holding a garland in his two hands as a mark of reverence. The left portion of the plaque must have depicted the same scene, but it is now broken. Sharma has identified the god as Brahma whereas the presence of the third vertical eye *(Tritiya netra)* in the centre of the forehead (Sharma 1996:140) leaves no doubt about his identify with god Siva, one of whose cognizances is the vertically disposed third eye (Shastri 1996:140). This is also sometimes a characteristic mark of Indra, but he is out of question in the present context due to the absence of other features like his elephant mount. This is one of the most beautiful figures of the god from the north-east.

Sarasvati

Two figures holding *vina* are illustrated (pls. XXXIII-XXXIV) and described as Vinadhara (Sharma 1993:508:52). Their general make-up is somewhat different, the only connecting link being provided by their holding *vina.* Both figures are well preserved, the second one being comparatively of a cruder execution artistically. The figures are placed within a conical trifoil arched niche resting over two pillars with a somewhat different composition. Sharma recognizes the figures as female but calls them Vinadhara. The figures are two-armed, standing in *tri-bhanga* posture, holding a *vina* with the fingers of the two hands. She wears a headgear with three vertical tapering prongs projecting from top with its butt and bands flying on either side and *kundalas*, three short necklaces coming just below the neck, a long garland running from her shoulders to the knees resembling *Vanamala* or *Vaijayanti* adorning generally god Vishnu. Her arms are adorned with a series of armlets and bracelets and the ends of her waistband and folds of garment are clearly visible.

She is not a secular figure and has to be identified as Sarasvati, the Indian goddess of learning. The posture of holding the *vina* goes well with this equation. It would show that along with gods Ganesa and Siva, the goddess Sarasvati was also popularly worshipped by the ancestors of the present inhabitants of North-Eastern India.

Ascetic

There are numerous terracotta plaques depicting ascetics, either observing penance or just seated. One such well-preserved plaque found in the debris of the southern side of the collapsed wall of Temple No. 1(Sharma 1993:62-63) is an ascetic figure of some interest. It is seated with folded knees and fingers of both the hands, which are folded, are shown resting on the thighs with the palm inwards and touching or pointing towards, protruding (or pot-belly) abdomen. The legs are disposed sideways, which is rather an unnatural posture. The hair tied in a single knot above the head, wears a floral *kundala* in each ear, bracelets and armlets in the upper and lower arms, stranded necklace touching the ornamented band above the protruding belly. The folds of lower garments are visible and an end of the waistband is seen between the legs; its lower end is shaped like a brush or chowrie. The execution is quite crude.

Sharma describes it as a female figure whereas there is no sign of femininity and facial features are also not feminine. He further calls it 'An Ascetic Pregnant Woman' (Sharma, 1993: 62-63, Pl.XLIII) which is indeed and anathema and a contradiction in terms, for asceticism and pregnancy are simply contradictory and consequently, a totally unimaginable concept. Perhaps he was led into the trap by the protruding and the hanging end of the waistband. The plaque is simply a representation of a male ascetic performing some *Tantrik* rite. Of course, the adornments don't go well with the *sannyasa* or asceticism and hence the figure ought to be taken as observing austerities only.

Another scene is captioned 'Arjuna in penance' (pp.60-61). It is only the upper part of the plaque with the entire lower portion and the right portion of the upper half missing. In its undamaged condition it must have been one of the most exquisitely modelled forceful panels as would follow from even a casual glance at the portion now available. It depicts in high relief an emanated male figure with thirteen rows of ribs and their ends joining the sternum in the middle of the chest in the shape of beads being clearly visible. His hands are raised up and folded with palms clasped together over his head. The face is damaged and its looks can't be made out. But the disheveled hair is visible behind the raised hands and clasped palms. He wears *kundalas* in ears and a bracelet each in his two hands. On both sides bearded male figures are seen. The one on his right is wearing a necklace and ear-rings and holding some non-descript object in his folded hands, while the figure on his left is depicted as holding a rosary (?) in his extended right hand and above it a bowl-like object, whereas the left hand is not seen. He also wears a necklace and ear-rings. In the present fragmentary state it is not possible to say anything except that the plaque represents a scene of great penance. Sharma is inclined to identify it as Arjuna's penance for securing the *Pasupatastra* from god Siva. But there is nothing distinctive to sustain this. There is no fight of Kirata-Siva that is necessary for such identification. Such scenes known *as Kiratarjuniya* are in South Indian art and there are fundamental differences between the present depiction and others.

Vidyadharas

There is a plaque found from the northern side debris of Temple No. 1 which is captioned as *Gandharva* by Sharma (66-67, Pl XLV). It depicts a flying male figure holding with his two hands a flower-garland, represented to his right like a bow, by its two ends. The left hand is stretched across his stomach. He is decked with earrings, necklaces, armlets, bracelets and waistband. On his head tilted to left, he wears a crown with a tapering end. It may be a kind of *karanda-mukuta*. The forward movement is indicated by the posture of his legs and body.

As stated above, Sharma identifies the plaque as a Gandharva. But Gandharvas are described as musicians in Indian literature and are generally shown as carrying some or other musical instrument, which is altogether missing here. On the other hand he is shown flying and holding a garland with its two ends which is a typical characteristic of Vidyadhara figures in literature and art. As such the figure ought to be labeled as Vidyadhara.

Dancer

The excavator labels 'Dancing girl' as one of the plaques from Temple No.1. But, though breast-like protuberances give the impression of its femininity, it has moustaches, which are suffice to indicate its male character. It is a dancing male figure with his left hand stretched downwards and the right raise upwards holding a bowl-like object. His legs are bent, and feet shown sideways. He wears an upper scarf *(uttariya)* with its ends flowing on sides and a lower garment *(kati-vastra)* whose folds are visible on the thigh and between the legs. He is decked with a row of three rings on each foot, wristlets, armlets, necklaces and earrings of the *sisa-patra* design. The head has a band-like covering. The execution is quite rough.

The above will show that the ancestors of the present-day Garos were steeped deep into Puranic tradition and had similar spiritual experiences and religious practices.

The excavation was conducted on a very small scale but has yielded spectacular results, and it only underscores the urgent need for concerted archaeological work on a large scale at this place.

NOTES

1. The excavated site was Sekta near Imphal, which revealed the evidence of urn-burial and linked the region with the Gangetic plains and pushing back, at one stroke, its history to 3rd—2nd centuries B.C. For details, see A.K. Sharma, *Manipur: The Glorious Past*, Aryan Books International, New Delhi.

2. He observes, 'As so far there is not a single site systematically excavated in Meghalaya, in spite of all the shortcomings and handicaps in not being a student of Art and Architecture, I had presented (sic) the facts as an excavator in record time so that the area and people, so far deprived of their glorious past, could point out to the world and say that they are the proud descendants of one of the advanced civilizations and culture of India.' See his *Emergence of Early Culture in Northeast India (A Study based on Excavation at Bhaitbari, Meghalaya)*, Preface, p. vii. (Sharma 1993: 25-30).

3. (Compose Sanskrit verse)

या सृष्टिः स्रष्टुराद्या, वहति विधिहुतं या हविर्, या च होत्री,
ये द्वे कालं विधत्तः, श्रुतिविषयगुणा या स्थिता व्याप्य विश्वम्।
यामाहुः सर्वबीजप्रकृतिरिति, यया प्राणिनः प्राणवन्तः,
प्रत्यक्षाभिः प्रपन्नस्तनुभिरवतु वस्ताभिरष्टाभिरीशः ॥

4. Now in the Central Museum, Nagpur.

REFERENCES

Sharma, A.K., 1994. *Manipur the glorious past*. Aryan Boks Internation New Delhi.

————1993. *Emergence of Early Culture in North-East India (A Study based on Excavation at Bhaitbari, Meghalaya).*

Shastri, Ajay Mitra, 1996. *Varahamihira's India*, II, Aryan Books International, New Delhi, p. 495.

Cultural Ecology of Mauryan India

M.K. Dhavalikar*

The Mauryan era is undoubtedly one of the most glorious epochs of Indian history when the Indian genius flowered as never before and there was a marked development in every field of human activity. Indian history can truly be said to have begun with the Mauryan rule as the earliest and most reliable historical documents-the Asokan inscriptions began to occur from this period. In a short span of a century-and-half, so much progress was made that India found its rightful place on the world map. Our knowledge of Indian history of the pre-Mauryan times is far too sketchy, and whatever precious little we know is mostly based, not on reliable historical evidence, but on myths and legends occurring in literature-the Puranas and Buddhist stories-which, unless corroborated by convincing documentary proof, cannot be accepted as history.

The present paper attempts to seek the factors responsible for the sudden exuberance, which made Mauryan India prosperous. Let it be made absolutely clear at the outset that a favourable environment is always a very important factor in the development of human societies; more so, in a country like India where the entire life cycle is heavily dependent on the monsoon rainfall. It is rightly observed that agriculture in India is a gamble with nature, for every third year is a bad year and every fourth, a famine.

Mauryan India could not have been prosperous without a strong agricultural base, and for this a favourable environment was the basic minimum. The role of environment in human life is now being recognized as never before. The entire world is presently worried about the deteriorating environment, and, if, remedial measures are not taken on a war footing, the very existence of all life - human, plant, animal will be endangered in the 21st century. If this is the situation at the beginning of the third millennium when technology has immensely advanced, one can imagine what must have happened twenty three hundred years ago when man had to cope with nature with his primitive technology. Man has to adapt to his environment. This study of human adaptation with nature has given birth to the sub-discipline of cultural ecology. Julian Steward, its proponent, describes it as a methodological tool for understanding the adaptation of man to his environment. The uniqueness of man is that he can survive in any environment because of his tremendous capacity for adaptation. Plant and animal do not possess this quality; certain species can survive only in certain environments. But man can live in tropical forests or Arctic cold. This he can do only because of culture, which according to the new definition of New 'or' Processual archaeology is "an extra-somatic means of adaptative system that is employed in the integration of a society with his environment and with other socio-cultural systems". (Binford 1972:20).

*'Srivatsa', 33, Nav Ketan Society, Kothrud, Pune-411029.

"Man enters the ecological scene, however, not merely as organism which is related to other organisms in terms of his physical characteristics. He introduces the super-organic factor of culture which also affects, and is affected by the total web of life" (Julian Steward 1955:36).

He Further Adds "Cultural ecology seeks to explain the origin of particular features and patterns which characterize different areas rather than to derive general principles applicable to any cultural-environmental situation".

Historians have also recognized the importance of the role of environment in history and in this respect the Annales school of France has made pioneering contribution. It was founded in the forties by Lucian Febvre and Marc Block and flourished under its most ardent advocate, Fernand Braudel. The goals of the Annales School are almost identical with those of "New or Processural Archaeology". The explanation of culture change is the prime concern of New Archaeology and the annalists place equal emphasis on the study of continuity and change. In culture-process, environment plays a dominant role, which Braudel too stressed. To him, history of man is nothing but the history of his relationship with environment, which is a great constraint in the development of human cultures. He wrote: "The environment is a hindrance beyond which a man and his experience cannot go. For centuries man has been a prisoner of climate, of the animal population, of a particular agriculture, of a whole slowly established balance from which he cannot escape without the risk of everything being upset." (Braudel 1980:30). Braudel's verdict certainly amount to ecological determinism-or Green Imperialism in modern parlance-but is valid for India where our entire life cycle depends on the monsoonal rainfall.

If we examine the cultural process in India during the last five thousand years, it becomes clear that there were only two phases of prosperity; first during the Harappan times (*C*.3000-2000 B.C.), and secondly in the Early Historical period (*C*.5th century B.C. to 5th century A.D.) whereas all the remaining centuries are marked by degeneration and decay. The most important factor responsible for these ups and downs was environment. When it was favourable, tremendous progress was achieved and when it was adverse, decline set it. There is adequate evidence to suggest a favourable environment during the Mauryan period. Megasthenes, the ambassador of the Greek ruler Seleucus Nictor to the court of Chandragupta Maurya, was stationed in the capital city of Pataliputra for a few years. He was a keen observer of the happenings in the Mauryan Empire and has recorded what he saw in his *Indica*. He writes at one place "Famine has never visited India". (*Indica* I: 35). This is certainly a bold statement, especially when we know that the country is prone to frequent droughts and floods, both of which cause untold sufferings to the populace. We can take it that there was no famine during the years of Megasthenes' brief stay in India and convincing evidence is furnished by a contemporary authority. Kautilya in his *Arthasastra* (II: 24; 116) has given the amount of rainfall in different parts of the country.

The quantity of rain that falls in the country of *Jangala* (forests) is 16 *dronas* half as much more in moist countries; as to the countries which are fit for agriculture-$13^{1/2}$ *drones* in the country of Asmakas (Maharashtra); 23 *dronas* in Avanti; and in immense quantity in western countries, the borders of the Himalayas, and the countries where water channels are made use in agriculture. When one-third of the requistic of rain fails both during the commencement and closing months of the rainy season and two-thirds in the middle, then the rainfall is (considered) very even. (II, 24, 116). Kautilya appears to have believed in the predictions about rainfall in different parts of the country on the basis of astrology, particularly the positions of Jupiter, Venus and Sun. What is more, he also gives a classification of clouds (Shamasastry 1960: 127-28).

"There are the clouds that continuously rain for seven days, eighteen are they pour minute drops; and sixty are they that appear with the sunshine. This is termed rainfall. Where rain, free from wind and unmingled with sunshine, falls so as to render three turns of ploughing possible, there the reaping of good harvest is certain".

It is noteworthy that the earliest reference to rain gauge is to be found in Kautilya's Arthasastra (II, 5, 58). He states "in (front of) the store house, a bowl with its mouth as wide as an *Artni* shall be set up as a rain gauge". Although Kautilya does not say anything about its shape, it is clearly a length measure of 18 inches, which was the same as *hasta* (hand) and is still in vogue in rural India where it is known as *hath* (cubit) (Shamasastry 1960: 56). Accoding to Kangle (1963: II, 84, f.n. 7), the gauge is square in form, each side being one cubit, and further adds that the capacity of the vessel should be one *drona*.

It will thus be clear that central Maharashtra (Asmaka) received 27 in. (680 mm) of rainfall, Malwa in Madhya Pradesh (Avanti) 46 in. (1150 mm), 32 in. (800 mm) in dry lands and 48 in. (1200 mm) in wet lands. Dry lands probably indicate the regions where rainfed agriculture was practiced, whereas wetlands denote areas with irrigation. Central Maharashtra (Asmaka) at present receives about 18-20 in. (450-500 mm) of rainfall and hence 27 in. in the Mauryan period was much higher. Similarly in other areas too, it was higher. This is corroborated by Arrian's remarks. Alexander invaded India in 326 B.C; he was accompanied by Nearchus, a historian, whose account now partly survives in Arrian's *Indica* which belongs to the 1st cent A.D. It seems that while crossing the Indus, Alexander had to face the southwest monsoon in September 326 B.C. He states that these winds blow in summer from the sea to the land and make navigation difficult (*Indica,* ch. 21-22). Similarly while returning in autumn Alexander came, the Indus was in flood. It has been averred that "Arrian's remarks suggest increased rainfall during Alexander's time (perhaps connected with known heavier rains over western Europe and north-eastern Africa in the middle of the first millennium B.C.)" (Warren 1987: 141). But much more important is Arrian's observation which suggests the connection between Indian monsoon and Nile floods:

"India is visited by rain in summer, especially the mountains... and from these the rivers flow swollen and muddy. In the summer also the plains of India are visited by rain, so that pools cover a great part of them, and Alexander's army had to avoid the river Acesines (Chenab, a tributary of the Indus) in the middle of the summer because the water overflowed the plains. Therefore from this it is possible to conjecture the cause of the similar condition of the Nile, because it is probable that mountains in Ethiopia are visited by rain in the summer, and the Nile being filled by them overflows its banks into the Egyptian country." (*Indica,* ch. 6)

It may be questioned what Nile floods have got to do with Indian monsoon. Actually there is a very close connection between the two, which has been clearly established by Gilbert Walker, a former Director General of the Meteorology Department of Government of India. He studied the rainfall pattern of India and northeast Africa, particularly Ethiopia, from 1840 to 1910 and showed that there is a very close correspondence between the two for the simple reason that northeast Africa gets the same monsoon rainfall that we receive in India. The years of drought and of flood in India and northwest Africa are the same (Walker 1986: 16-22). It should further be noted that Egypt is almost a desert, but is fertile because of the Nile. There are two Niles, White and Blue, and the floods are caused only because of floods of the Blue Nile, which comes from Ethiopean highlands. Nile flood data is available for centuries, the earliest one going back to 2900 B.C. (Bell 1970). The records are sporadic in the earlier period, but from 621 to 1520 A.D. they are available for almost every year (Dhavalikar 1999). This data is of immense help to us in reconstructing the past environment in India.

In Europe too the period from 400 B.C. to 400 A.D. was marked by a warm phase for which there is convincing palynological, archaeological and literary evidence. Glaciers in the Alps had begun to retreat and the passes became free for traffic (Lamb 1977:II, 424). It is exactly during this period that unusually high flood were recorded in the Nile (Butzer 1976:29) indicating a vigorous monsoon in the upper reaches of Ethiopia. This is evident from large Roman towns as at Lepics Magna as also villas and farmsteads, which have been discovered in the deserted countryside in North-Africa (Shaw 1976). The sea level is supposed to have risen by at least one metre during Roman times because of the warmer climate (Lamb 1982:155). Scientists tell us that when the temperate lands enjoy a warm climate tropical countries like India receive a good rainfall (Currie and Fairbridge 1985:111).

Higher rainfall in India in the Early Historical period, more particularly in the earliest phase I the 5th -3rd century B.C. is also suggested by archaeological evidence. At many of the capital townships of the great republics *(Mahajanapadas)* excavations have brought to light ramparts which were originally mud embankments, built along riverbanks, as a measure of flood protection. This is clear from the study of early fortifications at Ujjain, Kausambi, Rajghat, Sravasti and many other early cities. At Ujjain, on the Sipra, there is evidence of frequent damage to the embankment, which was therefore buttressed with fired bricks and reinforced with wooden logs; the moat was also lined with burnt bricks. From the plan of the fortification, which is polygonal, it appears that the moat was originally a channel for diverting the flood water of the river. This can be surmised from the fact that the moat does not completely run around the mound. M.S. Mate, who has studied the early fortifications observes:

"The massive mud walls reinforced by timber and externally riverted with burnt bricks could not interpreted as embankments meant to resist floods... Their substantial sizes involve tremendous labour and utilization of men and material on a truly vast scale. Such an effort would be undertaken by any society only if it is faced with a problem of such immense magnitude. An invading army need not have a rampart of 75 m basal width or a succession of subsidiary ramparts as wide when put together. The same is true of the so-called moats with widths of 30 m and above and reaching to 300 m in the case of Kausambi at one place. These would be more appropriately called diversion channel" (Mate 1969-70:68).

Increased rainfall caused floods, which led to the problem of water management. There are some excellent examples of this period. One is that of the dam which was built at Girnar during the time of Chandragupta Maurya (*Ca.* 323-300 B.C.) on the confluence of the rivers Suvarnasikata (Sonrekha at present) and Palasini on the outskirts of the present town of Junagadh in Gujarat, not far from the western coast. The dam was built in order to protect the provincial Mauryan capital at Junagadh, and later under Ashoka, canals were constructed by one Tushapha who, as his very name suggests, was a Parthian but was appointed governor of the western province of the Mauryan empire. There was a devastating flood, perhaps a cyclone in November A,D. 150 when the dam burst and the lake, which was named Sudarshana, became 'Durdarsana'. This happened when Rudradaman, a Mahakshatrapa of the Western Kshatrapa family, was ruling. He got the dam properly repaired but the same calamity befell again where repairs were carried out. Similar dams were there in other parts of the country as the *Kunal Jataka* (No. 356) suggests. According to the story, two communities the Sakyas and the Koliyas, were fighting over distribution of water from the dam across the river Rohini. When Buddha came to know of the impending conflict, he came there, preached them, and prevented the two communities from fighting among them.

A number of canals were dug in different parts of the country in this period. A large ancient canal originally excavated by a Nanda king sometimes in the 5th century B.C. has been referred to in the Hathigumpha (Orissa) epigraph of king Kharavela, who ruled in the first century B.C. One of the Nanda kings of Magadh had conquered Kalinga (Orissa) but Kharavela invaded Magadha in the course of his conquests. The king performed many deeds to acquire religious merit; he constructed several bunds, repaired old ones, restored gardens and built tanks and lakes at a cost of 3500 coins. He also extended the canal from Magadh (central Bihar), which was originally dug by a Nanda king three hundred years ago upto his capital city Tosali. The term used in *Panadi* (Sk. Pranali) and hence it is suggested that it may not be a large canal, but a narrow water course (Sircar 1966:26). There is no doubt that the term *Pranali* connotes a small water channel, but considering the distance between Tosali, which was close by Bhubaneshwar, the present capital of Orissa, to Rajagriha in Bihar, it is doubtful, if a small water course from an adjoining state would have been adequate to carry water over such a long distance; it was in all probability a large canal. It may perhaps be the same as that which has been noticed at Kumrahar, which represents ancient Pataliputra, the imperial capital of the Mauryans. It ran almost parallel and close to the wooden palisade; it was some 14 m wide and 3 m deep and was ultimately connected with the Ganga (Altekar and Misra 1959:25 ff).

Another canal of the Mauryan period was unearthed at Vidisha in Central India, which was a provincial capital of the Mauryas. It was probably an inundation canal dug with a view to divert the floodwater of river Bes which flows close by about a kilometre from the site. The canal was traced to a length of about 60 m and must have been longer, still it was 3.5 m wide and about 1.5 m deep. Its sides were plastered with lime mortar, which, according to D.R. Bhandarkar, who excavated it, was of very high quality, far superior than Roman examples. The walls had a downward slope for reducing the force of water; they were built of fired bricks set in lime mortar. There was a flight of steps in the middle of the south wall, which suggests that water was also used for domestic consumption. (*Arasi* 1914-15: 69-71)

Water Management

Kautilya has devoted considerable attention to water harvesting and management systems. In the *Arthasastra* (II: 24, 18), we come across some of the water lifting devices such those operated by hand *(hasta-pravartinam)* by shoulder *(skandha-pravartinam)*, the mechanism for carrying water in channels *(srota-yantra)* and for lifting water from rivers, tanks, lakes and wells *(nadi-saras-tatakas-kupodghatam)*. But it is not clear what exactly was the nature of the *srota-yandra*. Could this be the Persian wheel, which involves the use of gear? Since this was a complex mechanism, a trained personnel was required for its maintenance that was probably the same as *odayantrikas* of inscriptions (Luders' List No. 1137) and the *jalasutradas* of South India where there were also water diviners *(kupa-darsakas)*. (SII.XII:2)

There is considerable controversy about the Persian wheel. The Harappans drew water from their wells probably by means of a pulley, which is perhaps the same as the *asma-chakra* of the Rv. (X.101.7). But in the Early Historical period we come across references to water lifting machines *(ghati-yantra)* and it is therefore, necessary to examine what exactly they were. According to some, they were not much different from the 'Persian wheel', which is said to have been introduced into India during the medieval times (Habib 1980). It is supposed to be of two types: the *noria* which consists of a wheel with pots or buckets attached to its rim; and the *saqia* which is a pully having a chain or jars suspended from a bar over a well. The former *noria* can be used in the open, on a reservoir, whereas the other *saqia* is useful for wells. The Persian wheel consists of a vertical wheel carrying pots to be rotated by gearing it to a horizontal wheel, which is turned by man or animal. However, it has been shown that the so-called 'Persian wheel' was in use in India much earlier, on the basis of epigraphical (Joshi 1971) and literary evidences (Nath 1970) and even supportive art forms are available (Agrawal 1966). It is pertinent to point out in this context that there were two types of water-lifting devices in ancient India viz. the *rahata-ghadiya* and *udghatam (Arthasastra* II, 24, 18) or *odayantra*. The former was a simple device consisting of a ring with pots attached along its margin, whereas the other was a complex mechanism for the maintenance of which water engineers *(odayantrikas)* were required. The *rahatta* could be manually operated, but for the latter bullocks were yoked. The former *(kupa-chakra)* may have been used for drawing water for domestic consumption, and the latter was fitted on rivers and lakes for irrigating fields, and hence animal power was required to operate it. It is the same as *srota-yantra* of Kautilya (II, 24, 18) and the *rahatta-ghata-yantra* of Buddhist literature (Gopal 1980: 121 ff). It is probably illustrated in a tenth century carving from Mandor (Rajasthan), which depicts a number of soldiers and horsemen on sides, and in the centre is the *ghati-yantra* at work (Agrawala 1966).

It has been suggested that the 'Persian wheel' in some form was known to ancient Greeks and Egyptians even in the 3rd century B.C., and was possibly introduced in India in the 1st-2nd cent A.D. as a result of contact with the Roman empire, where it was used widely (Joshi 1971:27). This is corroborated by the reference to *odayantrika* in a Nasik cave inscription (Luders List No. 1137). The contrivance seems to have existed in India much earlier in the 6th - 5th century B.C. as the evidence from Panini's *Ashtadhyayi* would suggest. He uses the term *yugavarttra*, which has been taken to mean the yoke and the rope or strap by which the bullocks were driven for raising water (Agrawala 1953:204). This reference is of crucial importance because, this type of mechanism involves a gearing system. It is assumed that the invention of gears, which involves toothed wheels, is ascribed to Archimedes around 212 B.C. and it could not have appeared earlier. But if Panini's evidence is any indication, then this invention can be said to have taken place much earlier in India.

Wells

The well-digging technology is probably the contribution of the Harappans as they built the earliest wells for water. There is no evidence for wells in the post-Harappan times, but they came to be built on a large scale in the Early Historical period. Ring wells begin to occur from the 6th century B.C. and although they have been used for draining sullage water, the possibility of some of them being wells cannot be ruled out (Pande 1966). Wells were dug and instead of leaving them with bricks, terracotta rings were fitted into the sides in order to prevent them from caving. Later, however, ring-wells go out of vogue and instead we have wells which were lined with burnt bricks.

Widespread use of wells for water is indicated by references in *rahatta-ghadiya* or the water wheel, whereby water could be drawn from the well. It was a wheel with water pots, the like of which can be seen even today in north Indian villages. It is noteworthy that the particular type of pot which is attached to the water wheel at present is almost identical with that found at Early Historical sites in North India which is known as Ahichchhatra 10 a type. (Ghosh and Panigrahi: 1946: Type 10 a), which begins to occur from the earliest levels of the NBP phase (600-200 B.C.).

Socio-Economic Life

With adequate rainfall and efficient water harvesting systems, agriculture was no doubt in a flourishing state. A variety of iron tools and implements came into use. The use of iron plough helped in bringing large tracts of land under cultivation. The hard compact black soil of Central India, Western India and the Deccan, which could not be effectively tilled by the Chalcolithic farmers in the absence of iron tools, could now be brought under cultivation. Its fertility and the moisture retaining capacity led to increase in agricultural productivity. The growth of agricultural yield because of congenial environment and improved techniques such as the transplantation of paddy in the middle and lower Ganga basins (Sharma 1983:96-97) finally brought many new areas under colonization. The population too increased fast and several new towns came into being Pataliputra, (present Patna in Bihar), the ancient capital of Magadha, became the largest city in South Asia; its population is estimated as 2,70,000 and the city was spread over an area of 2200 ha. (Allchin 1995:69). There were several large towns in the Mauryan empire some of which had even suburbs as for instance Vaisali, which was the capital of the Lichchavis. It frequently figures in ancient literature. It was an extensive settlement, which was divided into three parts, one each for *Brahmins*, *Kshatriyas* and *Vaishyas* of which, two have been traced in the course of excavations. Those three localities mentioned in the literature have been identified. Vaishali-Raja-Vishal-ka-gadh; Vanijya-*grama* (*bania*), Kundagrama-Brasokund and Kollaga-Koluha (*Arasi* 1913-1914: 98; Deva and Mishra 1962). It is not unlikely that some other cities too had a similar arrangement. Incidentally, it may not be out of place to mention that the Harappan metropolis of Dholavira in Kutch (Gujarat) was also divided into such four watertight localities.

Demographic growth led to new settlements in areas where habitation had not taken place earlier. In Deccan, the Neolithic-Chalcolithic farming communities had not occupied coastal areas where rainfall is very high, but in the Early Historical period, many new towns and villages came into being in that area. Sopara (ancient Suparaka), which is now a suburb of Mumbai, became the largest port, as important as Mumbai is at present. Banavasi (ancient Vaijayanti) in Karnataka became a flourishing trade centre and so also Kondapur in Andhra Pradesh. In the north and Central India too habitation spread very fast. In the PGW period (*Ca.* 1000-600 B.C.) there were hardly 400 settlements, but the number increases in the NBP (Northern Black Polished ware) period (*Ca.* 600-200 B.C.) to over two thousand.

Although a favourable environment marked the Mauryan epoch, there is little doubt that droughts and famines were not totally absent. There may have been a few, though of less intensity and of short duration. There is a very strong Jaina tradition of a twelve-year-old famine caused by severe drought during the reign of Chandragupta Maurya who, then is supposed to have travelled to South India with a large number of people. Chandragupta is said to have been converted to Jainism towards the end of his reign, when probably a severe drought lasting for twelve years occurred. He went with Bhadrabahu, the Jaina saint, to Sravanabelgola (Karnataka) where he died in the orthodox Jaina way, by slow starvation (Thapar 1997:17). There is probably an allusion to it in the Srvanabelgola inscription. It is quite likely that the dreadful drought may have occurred probably at the end of Chandragupta's reign as the epigraphical evidence indicates. The Mahasthan (Dt. Bogra, Bangladesh) stone plaque inscription and the Sohagaura (Dt. Gorakhpur, U.P.) copper plate inscription, both of which are written in Mauryan Brahmi, record relief measures the state should taken in times of famine. The grain stored in the state granaries was to be distributed to the famine stricken people, and even loans were to be advanced from the royal treasury. These records have been rightly assigned to the early Maurya period, and were probably issued during the reign of Chandragupta Maurya (Ibid: 7-8).

In this context, the recent discovery of an inscription at Vaddamana (Dt. Guntur, Andhra Pradesh) is significant. The epigraph, carved on a pillar, was recovered from the excavation at the site, which brought to light the remains of some Jaina stupas. This shows that Jainism had reached South Indian before Buddhism did. Interestingly, the pillar inscription contains the name of Godasa, a disciple of Bhadrabahu who is said to have accompanied Chandragupta Maurya to the South, when there was devastating famine in North India. *(IAR 1982-83: 2-3; 1983-84 : 2-3)*

Similar evidence is supplied by the Sohagaura cooper plate, which can be dated to the third century B.C. and may even be earlier. It clearly states that the grain stored in the three storied granary at Vamshagrama (modern Bansgaon) should be distributed to the people of four villages which are named in times of drought and famine. This order was issued by the *Mahamatra* of Sravasti who was equivalent of the present day Director of Civil Supplies. Emperor Asoka had appointed *Mahamatras* as heads of different departments of administration and the inscription may belong to the Mauryan times. In this context it must be stated that Kautilya too, in his *Arthasastra* (iv, 3, 208) has listed measures that authorities should take in times of drought and famines. He states that the government should build granaries in every village and town, and acquire grains from farmers, store them in granaries and distribute it among the famine stricken people. These measures are not different from the rationing system that was introduced for the first time by the British government in India during the Second World War. The term used by Kautilya is *bhakta-samvibhaga* which means equal distribution, and denotes rationing. He further suggests that if necessary, the famine stricken people should be shifted to areas where food is available. The most important measure that he suggests in building bridges and forts to provide employment to the affected people. These public works, according to him, would alleviate the sufferings of the poor to some extent. (Moti Chandra 1945)

The foregoing discussion amply demonstrates that the favourable environment was to a considerable extent responsible for the prosperity of Mauryan India. This, however, happened not only in India but also almost all over the Old World as is evident from the rise of empires, the Macedonian and Roman in Europe, Achemenid in West Asia, Han in China and from the Mauryan to the Guptas in India. The foundation of the Golden Age of the Gupta was firmly laid during the Mauryan era. When the environment became adverse from the fifth century A.D. the empires began to decline. It only goes to show that environment plays a dominant role in the evolution of human cultures, and hence the importance of the paradigm of cultural ecology in archaeology and history.

BIBLIOGRAPHY

Agrawal, R.C. 1966. Persian wheel in Rajasthani sculpture. *Man in India* 16:87-88.

Agrawal, V.S. 1953. *India as known to Panini* Lucknow: University of Lucknow.

Allchin, F.R. 1995. *Archaeology of Early Historic South Asia- The Emergence of Cities and States.* Cambridge University Press.

Altekar, A.S.and V. Misra 1959. *Report on Kumrahar Excavations* (1951-55), Patna: K.P. Jayaswal Research Institute.

ARASI *Annual Report of Archaeological Survey of India.*

Bell, Barbara 1970. The oldest records of Nile Floods. *Geogr. Jr.* 196:569-76.

Binford, Lewis R. 1972. *Archaeological Perspectice*, Chicago: Aldine.

Braudel, Fernand 1980. *On History,* Chicago: Chicago University Press.

Butzer, K.W. 1976. *Early Hydrolic Civilization of Egypt : A Study in Cultural Ecology.* Chicago: Chicago University Press.

Currie, G. and R.W. Fairbridge 1985. Periodic 18.6 year and cyclic 11 year induced drought in northern China and some global implications. *Quarterly Science Review* 4: 109-34.

Deva, K. and V. Mishra 1960. *Vaishali Excavation 1950.* Vaishali: Vaishali Sangh.

Dhavalikar, M.K. 1999. The Golden Age and After : Perspective in Historical Archaeology. *Presidential Address, Indian History Congress,*

Calicut 60th Session.

Ghosh, A. and K.C. Panigrahi 1946. Pottery of Ahichchhatra. *Ancient India* 4 : 37-59.

Gopal, Lallanji 1980. *Aspects of History of Agriculture in Ancient India.* Varanasi: Bharati Prakashan.

Habib, Irfan 1980. Change in Technology in Mediaeval India. *Studies in History II(I)* : 15-39.

IAR *Indian Archaeology : A Review.*

Joshi, M.C. 1971. *An early inscriptional reference to Persian wheel,* Prof. K.A. Nilakanta Sastri Vol. 214-17. Madras: Sastri Fel-Committee.

Kangle, R.P. 1963. *The Kautiliya Arthasastra* 3 pts. Bombay: University of Bombay.

Lamb, H.H. 1972 & 1977. *Climate-Past, Present and Future.* 2 Vols. London: Methuen.

Luders, H. 1909-10. Luders' *List of Prakrit Inscriptions, Epigraphia Indica* : Vol. 10.

Mate, M.S. 1969-70. Early historic fortifications in the Ganga Valley, *Putatattva* 3 : 58-59.

Moti Chandra 1945. Rationing and other famine relief measures in ancient India. *JUPHS* 18 (1-2): 18-30.

Nath, R. 1970. Renant vs. the Persian wheel. *JASB* 12: 81-84.

Pande, B.M. 1966. Ring wells in Ancient India. *BDCRI* 19:15.

Shamastry, R. 1960. *Kautilya's Arthasastra* Mysore: Mysore Printing & Pub. House. 6th edition.

Sharma, R.S. 1983. *Material Culture and Early Social Formations in Ancient India* Delhi: Macmillan India Ltd.

Shaw, B.D. 1976. Climate, environment and prehistory in the Sahara, *World Archaeology* 8:133-149, world.

Sircar, D.C. 1966. *Indian Epigraphical Glossary* Delhi: Motilal Banarsidas. SII, *South Indian Inscriptions.*

Steward, Julian H. 1955. *The Theory of Culture Change-The Methodology of Linear Evolution,* Urbana: University of Illinois Press.

Thapar, Romila 1997. *Asoka and the Decline of the Mauryas,* Delhi: Oxford University Press Revenue Edition.

Walker, Gilbert 1986. *Long Range Forecasting of Monsoon Rainfall-Collected papers of Sir Gilbert Walker,* New Delhi: Indian Metrological Society.

Warren, Bruce 1987. Ancient and Mediaeval records of the monsoon winds and currents of the Indian Ocean. In Fein & Stephens (ed), *Monsoon,* 137-158, New York: John Willey & sons.

Archaeological Importance of Doiyang-Dhansiri Valley of Assam

HEMENDRANATH DUTTA*

The Doiyang-Dhansiri valley (93° 08' - 94° 03'-N and 25° 08'-26° 08'- E) lies in the southern central part of Assam and is the southward extension of the alluvial Assam valley between Naga Hills in the east and Mikir Hills in the west. Some parts of southwestern region of the valley owe their origin to the erosion of the Dhansiri(Singh, 1987:308). The Barail ridge ranges in the southwestern part of the valley. As such geographically, the Doiyang-Dhansiri valley comprises more or less a compact region surrounded by hills on three sides. The valley is open only on north where it merges with the Assam valley. As a result, the region is often found with an undulated topography, criss-crossed by meanders, *nulla*, and *beel* swamp and dead streams. The Dhansiri is a southern tributary of the Brahmaputra. It rises from the northern flank of Thingtubam peak of the Barail range. The river is 352 km in length and joins the Brahmaputra at Dhansirimukh. It has a catchment area of 1220 sq km. The Doiyang is the principal feeder of the Dhansiri and rises from the mount Zapfo (9890 m) of Naga Hills. It is 200 km in length and has a catchment area of 7424 sq. km and the confluence is called the Dui-noi-mukh.

Archaeological Finds

Evidence of archaeological remains are found in the Doiyang-Dhansiri river system including their tributaries. In the year 1978, a number of Brahmi characters were found at a depth of 1.30 m at Dubarani (Sainia 1979-80:33) on the Dhansiri. A careful study reveled that these are individual Bramhi characters engraved upon small stone pieces. These have been identified as *a, a, I, I, JA, ma* and paleographically datable to C.A.D. 200-300[1]. These characters seem to have some numerical (Sircar 1965:234) value and perhaps used as seal impressions. Further investigation conducted by this author reveal that the region at Dubarani covering almost 4 sq km area yielded brick structures, brick reinforced ramparts, ditches, tanks, moats and a series of canals that lead to the Dhansiri flowing at a close proximity. Investigation lead to confirm that the site at Dubarani on the Dhansiri in reality was an ancient fortified settlement. The site was rectangular in plan, fortified by ramparts and ditches *(parikha)* and was planned taking into account the natural topography and was in the form of an *auduka* recalling the principles laid down in the *Arthasastra* of Kautilya and Manasara's *Silpasastra*. Enoromous brick remains found often with stone sculptures, system of canals connecting the site with the Dhansiri indicate that the site was in all probability a capital. It was fortified to provide security to the inhabitants as also facilitating navigation via Dhansiri and the Brahmaputra.

To the north of Dubarani, at a distance of 4 km at

*Exploration Officer, Directorate of Archaeology, ASSAM.

Alichiga-Tengani exists another site on the Dhansiri, duly connected with the latter with a system of canals. The site is fortified and found with embankments and *(setubandha)*, surrounded by ditches *(parikha)*, laid down on a squarish ground plan based on in the *Arthasastra* of Kautilya. Ground plan of a large (288 m x 288 m) and a smaller (60 m x 60 m) squarish embankments *(setubandha)* exit at Alichiga-Tengani. A ditch (135 m x 35 m) well connected to the Dhansiri seem to have been used as a dock for a fleet of boats. Remains of brick structure were also found in the central part of the fortified embankment. These lead us to believe that the site was a *pattana* or harbour and at the same time it was developed as an *arama* (pleasure garden) on the principles laid down in the *Arthasastra* (Bhattacharya, 1963: 74-77 and 212) and Manasara's *Silpasastra*. (Acharya, 1927:40)

This author recovered two epigraphical records from this *setubandha* at Alichiga-Tengani viz. (i) a terracotta clay seal and (ii) a stone inscription with impressions of two pairs of human footprints. Both are engraved in eastern variety of Brahmi datable to *C*.A.D. 400-500 and reads *Sri Vasundharavarmana* and *Sri Ratnavarmana* respectively. The Nagajori-Khanikargaon fragmentary stone inscription recovered from Sarupathar, an adjacent region of Dubarani and a stone slab inscription from Dubarani also records the name of Sri Vasundhara-Varmana. The antecedent of Sri Vasundharavarmana and Sri Ratnavarmana are not known, as their names don't occur in any of the existing genealogies of the royal houses of ancient Assam. It is possible to postulate that Sri Vasundharavarmana and Sri Ratnavarmana belonged to a collateral branch of the Varmanas of Kamarupa as their surname suggests. Sri Vasundharavarmana and Sri Ratnavarmana apperar to be a lineal descendent of Vajradatta (brother of Bhagadatta) who had obtained the lordship of Uparipattana as indicated by the Parvatiya copperplates of Vanamalavarmadeva (Sharma 1978:120-21). With its fortified *setubandha* or embankment and commercial harbour *(pattana)*, located on the Dhansiri, the region of Alichiga Tengani could be well identified with Uparipattana of ancient Assam. All earlier scholars like P.C. Choudhury (1987) M.M. Sharma (1978:3) opined that the region of Deopani in Doiyang-Dhansiri was included within the ancient Pragjyotisha-Kamarupa kingdom. But our investigation proves that the region was ruled by an independent line of Varman rules (different from the Pushyavarmana of Kamarupa kingdom of ancient Assam). In this context, the information offered by the Allahabad stone pillar inscription of Samudra Gupta referring to the existence of two kingdoms viz. Kamarupa and Davaka as the lands of the "frontier kings" or *"pratyanata nrpstis"* (Sharma 1978:311) is very important. This record makes it clear that a regional kingdom emerged in the northeastern region prior to the Guptas. The kingdom of Kamarupa with its capital at modern Guwahati and the kingdom of Davaka flourished in the Kapili valley of present Nagaon district. As such the region of Uparipattana with the prefix *uppari* to *pattana* covered the region of Upper Assam or Ujani Assam at least up to Tinisukia or Bengmara, where stone sculptures of Dubarani group have been found[2].

That the regional kingdom of Uparipattana was a development largely due to evolution of a regional society of native ethnic tribes dwelling the region since primordial times. The Doiyang-Dhansiri valley as discussed, being surrounded by hill ranges, is secluded, and this factor of geographical isolation contributed to the development of a strong regional society that promoted the state formation process in the valley since early Christian era. The rcference to Mahattara Brahmadatta and Vaji in the Nagajori Khanikargaon fragmentary stone inscription (Sharma 1978:310-11) indicates the development of village administration of the Gupta type in the valley during fifth century. The reference to *Agrahara Gourivataka* donated to some Brahmana found in this record indicates *Branamanical* expansion into new areas. The reference to *Mathapati* (Sharma 1978:305) indicates the existence of a class of priest in charge of temple. The reference of Gourivataka to some Brahmana found in this record (Chutia 1997:2) indicates Brahmanical expansion to fresh areas.

The concept of regional society is found reflected in the development of regional art. Sculptures belonging to a native idiom under the shadow of the Post-Gupta art-tradition were carved in the region. Stone, metal, terracotta and wood were the media used in the expression of art. The sculptures are in round, showing broad shoulders and chests, large or swollen belly with youthful physiognomy. In facial features, benign spiritual expression is found. Syncreatism is one of the characteristics of these sculptures and very often the sculptures are inscribed. Discovery of a figure of Vishnu in wood datable to *C*.A.D. 700-800 confirms that wooden art attained matured stage in this region during the Post-Gupta period (Gupta 1996:52-55). Even the characters of inscriptions engraved in the epigraph of the region were ornamental in character. Saivism was the predominant religion and numerous figures of principal and subordinate Saivite figures, Saptamatrikas and other deities such as Surya, Bhakta and such other divinities as kettle drum *(dava) sankha*, were carved. Several Harihara sculptures in stone as well as one in bronze were found. The Deopani Vishnu image has been found with an inscription, which proclaims Siva as the lord of the three worlds.

Two figures of Vishnu are found holding *akshamala* suggestive of syncretic forms. Of these Vishnu images, one is found at Borpathar and the other at Dergaon. Both these figures have been found with *akshamala,* one in each of the right palms of the figures.

Conclusion

The archaeological potentiality of the Doiyang-Dhansiri valley is very rich. But the Potential of the region remains virtually unexplored. On the basis of our surface finds and field work, it is found that the Doiyang-Dhansiri river system calls for a river based culture and contributed to the emergence of a regional society, development of a regional political kingdom in the upper Assam or Ujani Assam during the Gupta and Post-Gupta periods. This regional kingdom covering the entire upper Assam was ruled by a hitherto unknown line of rulers of ancient Assam, different from the Varman dynasty established by Pushyavarmana of Kamarupa. Sri Vasundharavarmana and Sri Ratnavarmana were the lineal descendants of this dynasty. The inhabitants of the region maintained contact with the cultural forums of central Indian settlements. It seems possible that local availability of iron and existence of a native iron smelting process have contributed to the development of agriculture that led to economic prosperity and material progress.

NOTES

1. Personal communication from Dr. Dharmeshwar Chutia, Principal (Retd.) Government Sanskrit College, Guwahati, Assam.

2. Stone sculptures belonging to the Dubarani group have also been found at Dergaon, Na-Kachari, Namti, Barhola covering the areas of Upper Assam or *Ujani Assam*.

REFERENCES

Acharya, P.K. 1972. *Indian Architecture according to Manasara Silpasastra*.

Bhattacharya, Tarapada, 1963. *The Canons of Indian art*, pp.74-77, p.212.

Choudhary, P.C. 1987. *History of civilization of the people of Assam from earliest times to the 12th century* A.D. (Introduction).

Chutia, Dharmeshwar, 1972. A Fragmentary Inscription from Sarupathar area, *Journal of the Epigraphical Society of India*, vol. XXIII, p.42.

Deo, S.B. 1981-83. Historical Archaeology: Review and perspective, *Archaeological Perspective of India since Independence*. No. 13 & 14, pp. 94-95.

Dhavalikar, M.K. 1971-72. Archaeology of Guwahati, *Bulletin of the Deecan College Research Institute* Vol. XXXI-XXXII, p. I, pt.II . p.146.

Dutta, Hemendranath 1996. A Rare wooden Visnu figure from Borpathar, *Journal of Assam Research Society*, vol. XXXIII No.2 pp.52-55.

Indian Archaeology 1968-69. A Review (IAR) p.2-4, Indian Archaeology 1970-71-A Review p.4.

Indian Archaeology 1974-75. p.7.

Roy, S.K. 1992 Religious Institution and pottery of Assam: An Ethno-archaeological study, *Bulletin of Department of Anthropology*, Gauhati University VI, 87-98, pp.87-98.

Saikia, P.C. 1979-80. A note on some archaeological relics in and around Borpathat (Golghat) Assam: An Apprisal, *Journal of Assam Research Society*, vol. XXV, p.33.

Sharma, M.M. 1978. *Inscriptions of Ancient Assam*, p.120-121.

Singh R.L. *et al* (ed) 1987. *India-A-Regional Geography*, p.308.

Sircar, D.C. 1965. *Indian epigraphy*, p.234

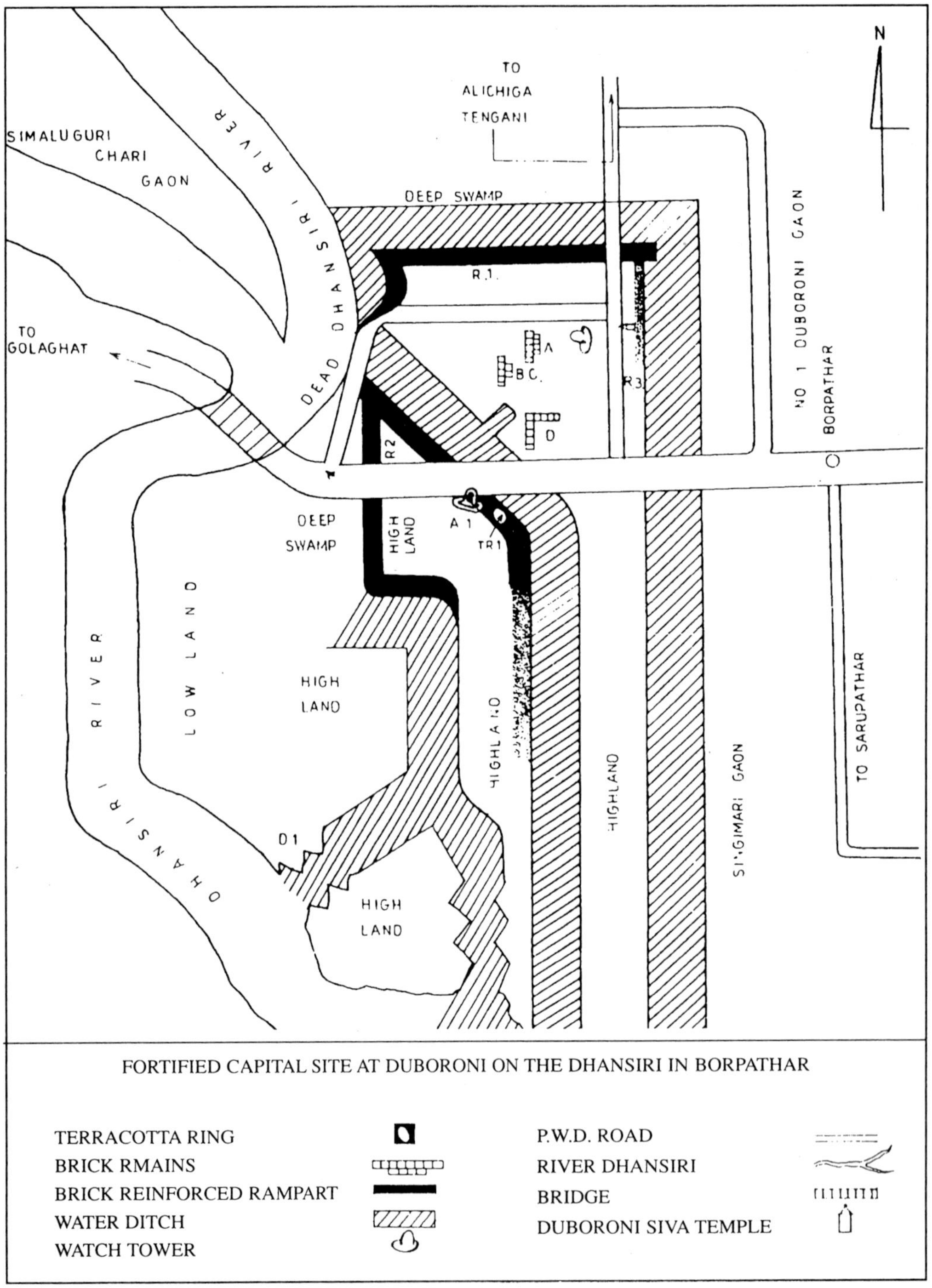
N
TO
ALICHIGA
TENGANI
SIMALUGURI
CHARI
GAON
DEEP SWAMP
TO
GOLAGHAT
DEAD DHANSIRI RIVER
R.1.
A
B C.
D
R3
R2
NO 1 DUBORONI GAON
BORPATHAR
DEEP
SWAMP
HIGH
LAND
A 1
TR1
LOW LAND
RIVER
HIGH
LAND
HIGHLAND
HIGHLAND
SINGIMARI GAON
TO SARUPATHAR
D1
DHANSIRI
HIGH
LAND
FORTIFIED CAPITAL SITE AT DUBORONI ON THE DHANSIRI IN BORPATHAR
TERRACOTTA RING
BRICK RMAINS
BRICK REINFORCED RAMPART
WATER DITCH
WATCH TOWER
P.W.D. ROAD
RIVER DHANSIRI
BRIDGE
DUBORONI SIVA TEMPLE

Fig. 1.

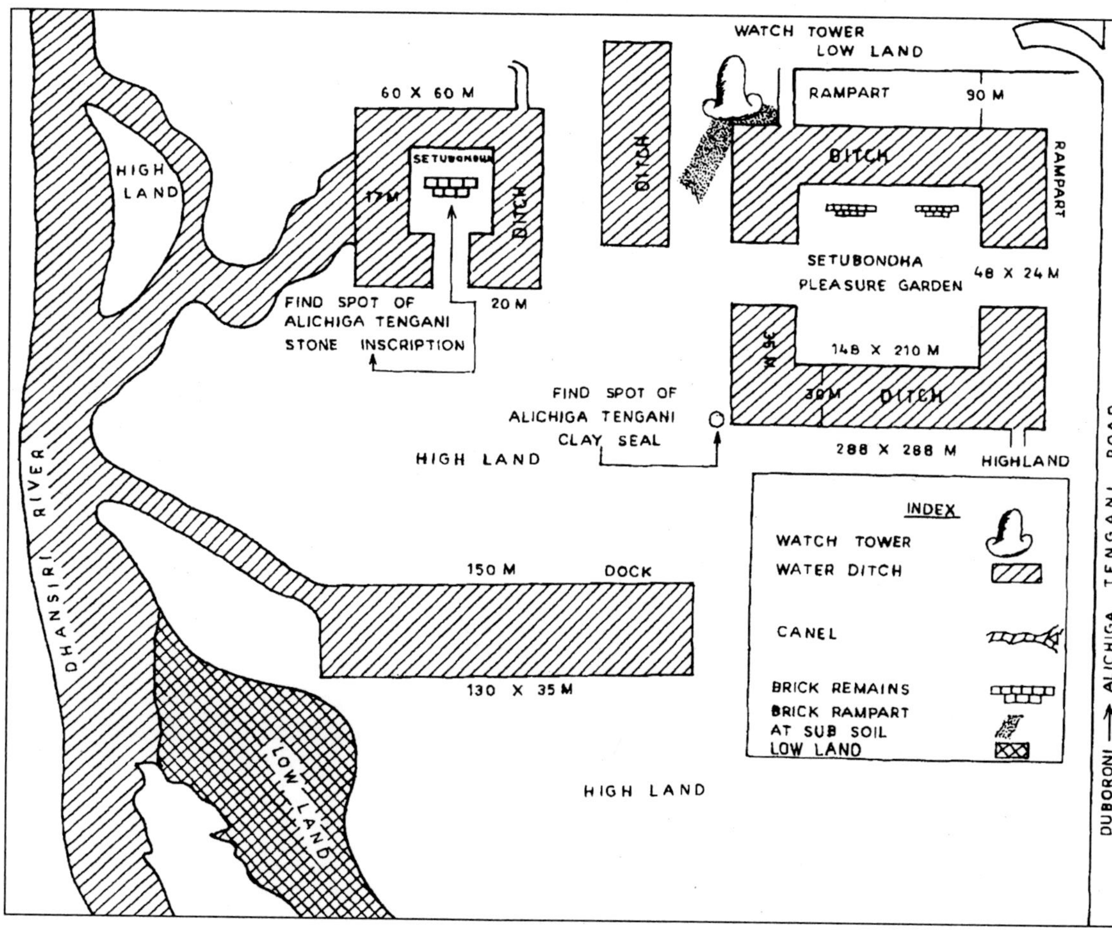

Fig. 2. *Setubandha* Port (Paṭṭana) cum Pleasure Garden (ĀRĀMA) on the Dhansiri at Alichiga–Tenani Borpather. Not to Scale.

The Traditional date of Asoka Maurya: Archaeological Evidences—A Consideration

A. SUNDARA*

Preliminary Remarks

In recent years, there is a trend rather striking, to revive studies (Sethna 1989, 1992; Deo *et al* 1993; Fawley 1996; Pradham 1996; Singh 1994; and Majumdar *et al* 1951), to re-examine the traditional history and it's dating as known from the Puranas and other similar literary works, more comprehensively. A dispassionate and systematic approach to and critical review of the subject may yield useful and factual information for better understanding of the least known history of the remote past of our country. I have been trying to examine over a few years about the regional tradition *vis-à-vis* its archaeological findings in north Karnataka and the results (Sundara 1991: 41-43, 1992; 1995; 1998) are quite encouraging. This has led me to re-examine the dating of Asoka's rule over Karnataka too, in relation to his ten minor; two major edicts and versions of Kalinga separate edicts located at eight places (Krishnan 1987) and the associated human settlements nearby in the region.

The Problem

William Jones (Teignmouth 1807) had placed ten kings of the Mauryan dynasty beginning with Chandragupta, between 1502-1365 B.C. and according to another calculation, it is 1535-1219 B.C. Thus Asoka Maurya's period would be 1448-1409 or 1496-1457 B.C.; the difference between the two calculations being too big to reconcile.

He found that Puranic accounts were so confusing, varyi and not supported by any other contemporary accou , therefore, gave them up as unreliable. He thereafter turned his attention to the Greek accounts and after their peru l he thought they were acceptable. And in the course of his studies, he was able to identify Sandrakottas and Palibotra referred to in Megasthenes' *Indica* respectively with Cl andragupta Maurya known then from the *Bhagavata Purana* and Pataliputra. These identifications, (Teign Mouth 1807) in 1783, were considered to be a "sheet anchor of Indian History". A little later, James Princep succeeded in the identification of Asoka with *Devanampiya Piyadasi* and of the five alien names of the II and XIII major edicts of the emperor with the contemporary West Asian kings (JASB: VII 156). All these strongly supported Jone's identifications and were more or less implicitly accepted and followed by most of the eminent Indian scholars till recently.

However, since then, some of the scholars here and there now and then such as Bhuler, Troyer (1859) did question the validity of these identifications; the latter on the basis of *Rajatarangini,* opined that Asoka ruled

*'Sundaryshri, Near Sri Hanuman Temple, Bharati Nagara,DHARWAD-580001 (Karnataka).

around 1260 B.C. Some scholars, especially in recent years, such as Narayana Sastri (1937), Krishnamachari (1985), Sri Rama Sathe (1985), S.D. Kulkarni (1988, 1993, 1995), David Frawley (1996) and others have seriously questioned these identifications and the relative chronology of early Indian history.

Further, some scholars have been pointing out the inadequacies and other possibilities, contrary to the theories of William Jones and others. For instance, Jones in the matter of the identification of Sandrokottas with Chandragupta Maurya considered the list of the kings from only one Purana i.e. the *Bhagavata* in which the traditional history is traced up to the end of the Mauryan rule. In some of the other Puranas, the history is narrated up to the end of the Gupta rule. In Gupta dynasty there were two Chandraguptas, I and II whom, Jones did not consider for alternate identification because of non-availability of relevent Puranas then. Moreover, unfortunately he died the very next year after his announcement of the identification. It has not been explained as to why Megasthenese is silent in his account about Chanakya and especially his remarkable efforts in making Chandragupta, the Maurya king secure in whose court the former is said to have been ambassador of Seleucus Nikator, the Greek Satrap. The absence of Palibotra as surname, or for that matter any surname to their personal names, as stated clearly by Megasthenese, in the names of the Mauryan kings, is totally ignored. Although Magadha of the eastern kingdom is too well known at least from the time of the Kuru-Pandavas of the *Mahabharata*, why Megasthesese in spite of his being present in the capital of the kingdom refer to it in a general manner as "*Prassi*" i.e. *Prachya* (= eastern)? While making efforts seriously to identify Sandrakottas with Chandragupta Maurya, why did not Jones try to identify the other Greek names of the kings who are said to have been preceded and succeeded Sandrokottas as known from the other classical Greek accounts? With regard to Princep's identification (JASB: VII) of the five names mentioned in Asoka's major edicts nos. II and XIII, with West Asian kings supposed to have been contemporaneous with Asoka. Madalasa Devi has argued that they are actually the names of the *Janarajyas,* not of the kings ruling them.

It is against this background, a critical examination of findings from archaeological excavations of sites with Asokan edicts in Karnataka bearing on the problems relating to the chronology of Asoka's rule over the region becomes a necessity.

Karnataka: Archaeological Evidence

The existence of ten minor edicts of Asoka, in as many as seven places besides Brahmagiri, fragments of XIII and XIV major edicts, versions of two separate Kalinga edicts also, were discovered in Sannati, the most remarkable and prolific Buddhist site. In fact, the personal name *"Devanainpiya Piyadasi"* mentioned in edicts, was Asoka, was for the first time known from the edict in Maski. It mentions *"Devanain Piya Piyadasi raja Asokasa"*. The two minor edicts in each of the two other places: Udegolam and Nitturu also contain the personal name of the emperor. In particular, the most noteworthy point in the Brahmagiri edict is the mention of the name of the place also as 'Isila', the administriative headquarters of the *mahamatras* in Suvarnagiri, the southernmost province of the empire. It was in search of Isila, Krishna in 1942 (1942:100-109), the then Director of the State Department of Archaeology, discovered an extensive habitation site with numerous megaliths nearby. He also laid 16 trenches in order to trace the Mauryan town site. Six cultural periods in sequence were recognized as follows:

The Microlithic (Roppa), the Neolithic, the Iron Age Megalithic, the Isila (Mauryan), the Satavahana, and the Early Kadamba-Chalukyas cultures.

Also, he could discern clear overlap between the last phase of the Neolithic and the beginning of the Iron Age-megalithic and the last phase of the latter with the early phase of the Early Historical period. Besides, the burial pottery and iron objects from megaliths excavated were found to be similar to those from the Iron Age culture of the habitation site. Unfortunately the findings of his excavations were never fully published because of his premature death in 1947. However, a brief report in the Annual Report of the Department containing all points is found. In the light of Krishna's excavations, realizing that the site is quite promising for tracing the salient cultural milieu of South Indian megalith-builders and for fixing the relative chronology of the culture, Wheeler got excavated stratigraphically the habitation site and ten megaliths. The cultural sequence of the site he found out from his excavations has been published in *Ancient India*

No. 4.

However, the objectives of the excavations and the studies that followed thereon by Wheeler, the Asokan edict and the Mauryan Isila phase were hardly recognized. Certainly, in addition to the South Indian Megalithic problems, the Mauryan cultural phase in the site highlighted previously by Krishna should also have been one of the major objectives of Wheeler's excavations. From his arguments and dating of particularly the Megalithic culture, it is implied that the edict is meant for the people of the Polished Stone-Axe culture, would indirectly indicate the people of this culture at least in small number were literate. But, other than the Sindhu-Sarasvati civilization, so far no evidence of literacy or use of script, has been found in any of the Protohistoric, Neolithic or Chalcolithic and even in the immediately succeeding southern Iron Age cultural milieu prior to the Mauryans. The general notion is that the people of these cultural stages were non-literate. It was in this context, later Haimendorf (Indo-Asian Culture) with regard to Wheeler's arguments regarding the probable period of the settlement of the Megalithic people, pointed out the anachronism: a Brahmi edict for the preliterate community. He observed that it was meant probably for megalith-builders.

South of Brahmagiri, Chandravalli, about 2 km from Chitradurga, was excavated by Krishna (1931) earlier in 1928 and a good report was published. Apart from neoliths on the surface, he could recognize two cultural stages that can be identified as the Megalithic and the Early historical, essentially the Satavahana. Also, remnants of some brick buildings of the latter were found. This sequence of cultures clearly confirmed in Wheeler's excavations in the site. But no brick structures were, and then discovered. In 1978, the site was again excavated by the Archaeological Survey *(IAR 1977-78)* and traces of Neolithic culture (in the Chalcolithic stage), preceding the Megalithic and remains of brick buildings of the Early Historical, immediately succeeding the Iron Age-Megalithic, were revealed. It appears that in Chandravalli, there was a continuous and regular human settlement right from the Neolithic Brahmagiri, and beyond probably the early phase of the Early Kadamba indicated by the Brahmi inscription of the period of Kadamba Mayurasarma.

In 1954 excavations at Maski (Thapar 1958) where there is an Asokan edict, the picture of the cultural sequence in character and behavior is virtually the same as that was obtained at Brahmagiri but varyied for one feature: there is no overlap between the Chalcolithic and the beginning of the Iron Age Megalithic. However, there is no distinct cultural break as such. Surface explorations by me (Sundara 1978) in Jatinga Ramesvara, about 5 km from Brahmagiri, near the edict, Koppala, Udegolam and Nitturu clearly disclosed three cultures.

Koppala, now a district headquarter, with two copies of the Asoka's minor edict, locally known as *"Palki gunda"* and *"Gavi matha"* inscriptions also is found to have an ancient site with three cultures (Sundara 1976) as in the other sites mentioned above. Besides, there is a separate site with megalithic porthole chambers in the proximity.

Sannati is exceedingly rich in Buddhist relics of the Satavahana period, succeeding the Mauryan. The latter is known from a few objects such as a highly polished ornate stone disc with figurine in *bas-relief* characteristic of the Mauryan period and a few pieces of Northern Black Polished pottery. The Mauryan phase is distinctly represented by major rock edicts nos. XIII and XIV of Asoka and the versions of the two separate Kalinga edicts (Sharma 1994). The phase here is of greater importance than that in Brahmigiri with the administrative headquarters of the *Mahamatras*. By far, the most important is the occurrence of a sculptural panel, displaying a king with an attendant holding a parasol over his head and accompanied by two queens. Below the bas-*relief* is a label inscription *"Rano Asoko"*. In this site were found a few polished stone axes implying the existence of the Neolithic-Chalcolithic stage as well. The site was continued to be prominent even during the Satavahana period as evident from inscriptions of kings of the dynasty, such as Gautami putra Satakarni, Vasisthi Putra Pulumavi, apart from the Buddhist *stupas* in the adjacent locality namely Kanaginahal, and sculptural remains in profusion overshadowing even Banavasi, another important Satavahana site in north Karnataka. Further, though not in Sannati, but not far away from the place in Shahabad area, were found Iron Age megalithic remains. All these appear to be quite significant for understanding the Mauryan period in Karnataka.

Such in brief is the cultural sequence, in all sites with Asokan edicts in Karnataka. In fact, this is more or less the picture revealed in the other sites nearby Mauryan edicts, such as Sanganakal, Piklihal, Tekkalakota and Hallur i.e. more or less the Krishna-Tungabhadra *doab* and the Tungabhadra valley region.

Analysis

From the above review of explorations and excavations in areas with Asoka's edicts under study the emerging noteworthy points are:

1. Generally, there is a clear overlap of cultural stages, the Neolithic-Chalcolithic phases and the immediately succeeding Iron Age Megalithic and the Megalithic and the 'Andhra' i.e. Early historical excepting at Maski where there is clear break between the earliest and the next.

2. The early and late phases of the Megalithic culture are respectively overlapping the late Neolithic in the Chalcolithic (the exception being Maski) and the Early Historical phases and consequently, there is no exclusively distinct Megalithic phase in Brahmagiri. At Maski only, the early phase (layers 5-9, about 1.35 m in thickness) of the Megalithic is typical of culture. The overlap, about 30 cm of the Early historical culture is small. Here was found a small lead coin apparently of the Satvahanas. The Early Historical excluding the overlap is about 60 cm in thickness.

3. The Early Historical period evidently comprises two phases: the Mauryan and the Satavahana. Though the Satvahana phase is vindicated from coins largely found at Sannati, Chandravalli as well as Banavasi and Vadgaon-Madhavapur, the Mauryan cultural phase immediately preceding the Satavahana, is not identified at sites and even at Brahmigiri by Wheeler, though Krishna did; (Maski and Sannati with Asokan edicts bear witness). However, the 1947 Chandravalli stratigraphic sequence appears to be quite clear in this respect and indicate the two major phases of the Early Historical: Satavahana (Layers 1-10) and pre-Satavahana without any coins and with Russet coated white painted pottery overlapping with the Iron Age Megalithic phase (Layers 13N-11). But no such phases have been distinguished so for. It may therefore, be noted that in particular in layers 7-9 are found many coins mostly of Maharathis, feudatory to the Satavahanas. Even layers 10 has yielded a coin of Maharathi. This fact would imply that the Satavahana rule over this region began a little earlier i.e. before the Maharathis became their feudatory. Layers 11 is likely to be of the beginning of the Satavahana power and layers 12 is relatively contemporaneous with the Sunga-Kanva rule over Magadha; while Layer 13 would signify Asoka's rule over this part i.e. sometimes after the beginning of the Megalithic culture from layers 13 NE.

The so-called 'Rouletted' Pottery occurred in layer 9. Recent researches on this pottery revealed that this pottery is not of Roman origin as stated by Wheeler, but was manufactured in Tamluk region sometime in the 3rd cent B.C. or a little earlier. One punch-marked coin characteristic of the Mauryan age, as a survival was found in layer 7, as also a silver Roman coin of Tiberius, minted during A.D. 26-37, in layer 5. Thus in general, there is reliable consistency in the stratigraphic position of the archaeological and numismatic evidences. This approximate sequential equation goes very well with Brahmagiri and Maski. The Mauryan rule in these areas, more or less, coincides with layer 7 at Br. 21 and layer 8 at MSK-10.

4. Both at Chandravalli (layer 13 NE-Megalithic) and Vadgaon-Madhavpur, there is pre-Satvahana i.e. contemporary Mauryan phase. And there are no edicts of Asoka at these sites.

^{14}C Dates

1. There are many ^{14}C dates[4], some are calibrated. There are eighteen for the Neolithic-Chalcolithic and two for the Iron Age Megalithic in North Karnataka. Especially the dates for the Periods II and III of the Neolithic-Chalcolithic from Watgal (Shaffer 1995) are significant in this context.

Besides, there are eight Thermoluminiscence dates for the pottery from the four excavated megaliths in Komaranshalli (Nagaraja Rao, 1990). The period dates on an average between *C.*1400-900. B.C. This chronological range is applicable to the early overlap phase of the Meglithic culture is North Karnataka. Relatively the latter overlap phase of the culture is datable to *C.*1000-300 B.C. On average, especially in consideration of the recent dates available for the Neolithic culture at Watgal (Lingsugur

Taluk.) the three phases of the Neolithic and the two overlapping phases of the Iron Age– Megalithic culture, may be dated as follow:

1. Neolithic; *C*.3000-2750 B.C.

2. Neolithic in the Chalcolithic stage

   Early phase: *C*.2500-1700 B.C.
   Late phase: *C*.1700-1000 B.C.

3. Iron Age Megalithic culture
   Early overlap: *C*.1400-900 B.C.

4. Iron Age Megalithic
   Later phase: *C*.1000-300 B.C.

The Megalithic culture in the middle Krishna-Tungbhadra region with Brahmigiri, Maski, Hire-Benkal and other sites, may be dated to *C*.1000-300 B.C. with a probability of an earlier beginning around 1200 B.C. in view of the 14*C* dates for the culture at Veerapuram and Ramapuram (Andhra Pradesh) on the one hand and on the other the intrusion of the Chalcolithic Jorwe culture from the upper reaches of the Bhima, along the Bhima river into the Krishna-Tungabhadra *doab* around 1000 B.C.

The Asoka-panel in Sannati with his personal name may be a reminiscent act of the people recalling from their memory of how the king appeared in person.

If this proposition is acceptable, why did he think of conquering this region? The plan of the conquest was certainly for some distinct and substantial gain. In all probability, the Megalith-builders of this region were widely very well known for the production of iron weapons of very high quality. In the *'Kiskindha kanda'* of Srimadramayana, Rama, who was to be declared as *Yuvaraja* of Ayodhya, while assuring Sugriva, the diffident and fearful *Vanara* chief in exile in the matter of conquering Vali his mighty brother, speaks of the highly superior weapons manufactured in "Kartikeyavana" in his possession. I have elsewhere identified this place with the Kumarasvamy hill near Sondur in Bellary district on the basis of the archaeological evidences of the region. (Sundara, 1995) The Brahmigiri megaliths excavated in 1947 were found to contain numerous iron objects of offence and defense. And the iron tools from the excavated Megaliths at Komaranahalli, Halingali, Rajur etc., as per scientific analysis, are found to be of steel of very high quality, probably made out of the local iron ore, by lamination technique. This is further evident from the popular Kannada word *'ukku'* for steel i.e. wootz in German. Hire-Benkal rock-painting no.1 is located in the vicinity of the Megalithic site, displays many horse riders as well as individuals carrying weapons apparently of iron. Mining of gold obviously in the Hatti region within a small distance from Hire-Benkal area, the richest in Megalithic sites in north Karnataka and bead production were the other industries of the megalith-builders, as evident from the occurrence of 33 gold beads from Br. Meg. No. IX besides numerous tiny steatite beads from other megaliths of the place. On account of the rich resources of these two and the production of these two metals by Megalith-builders the region was so prosperous that it attracted Asoka's attention.

A large section of the Megalith-builders of this region, are probably known as the Moriyas (Sundara, 1996) as at Hire-Benkal, Koppala, Brahmagiri, etc. in the past for, the megaliths in these and many other sites are even now known as *"Moriyarmmala"* (The site of the Moriyas.) *"Moriyara manegalu"* (= the dwelling of the Moriyas). Such names for megalithic site/port-hole chambers in particular respectively occur as early as 7th cent. In a copper plate record (A.D. 634) of a Ganga king Bhuvikrama (Gopal 1983) it was in vogue as late as 14th century as found in another copper plate record (A.D. 1219) of the time of Hoysala Vira Narasinhadeva. There are places having the name "Moriyavalli" village of the Moryan referred to in Kampli (Uttara Kannada) inscription of early 6th century of the Kadamba Ajavarma and 'Morigeri' in Huvina Hadagali Taluk of Bellary District. There was even a 'Moriya' family in Kurtakoti area referred to an inscription (SII) of A.D. 1087 belonging to the reign period of Vikramaditya VI, the most powerful Kalyana Chalukya king. In the inscription there are references clearly to the family as, *'Miriyavainsa'* five times, thrice to individuals as *'Moriyavainsaja'* and *'Moriyakulatilaka'*. That there was Moriya clan in the part of Karnataka and probably they were the megalith-builders are certain. Further, there was a Moriya folk community in the past in the eastern part of India having matrimonial alliance between the Moriya clan and with the royal Mauryan dynasty. Peacock was the totem of the Moriyas. In this context, it is interesting to note that in

Hire Benkal-Piklihal area with megaliths in rock paintings of the period of the overlap phase of the Neolithic-Chalcolithic and the Iron Age-Megalithic, are beautifully depicted peacocks in numbers (Sundara 1994). Whether these Moriyas are connected with the eastern Indian Moriyas on the one hand and with establishment of the Mauryan rule in this region are to be investigated.

Further there is one small but significant epigraphical reference to be considered. In particular, in Brahmagiri edict, the number of days of Asoka's *dhurma yatra* is indicated by number category (*varga* such as *eka varga, dasaka varga, sataka varga* etc.) numerals i.e. 200, 50, 6 (=256). This practice was the most ancient, prevalent since the time of the *Rigveda* up to the Early Historical when place value (*sthana such as eka, sthana, dasama sthana, sataka sthana* etc. system began in which case 200, 50, 6 would be written as 256.

Another important material evidence is thin flat, cut punch-marked coins of silver, base silver and copper, largely squarish which were in use in the Mauryan period as currency in commercial and other transactions. The technique, form, scheme and characteristic features of coins readily remind the Harappan copper tablets of somewhat bigger size, carrying a figure or design on one side and an inscription on the other. Coins of the kind were in use, but in a limited scale even in the post Mauryan period. In excavations at Chandravalli, Vadgaon-Madhavpur and Banavasi very few coins of this kind were found. But a big hoard of punch-marked coins in a copper pot carrying an inscription mentioning the name of the owner, 'Chantasa' in 2nd century Brahmi script was a chance find in Sindhogi, Koppal District. Such coins were cast in the early phase of the Satavahana rule. The tradition of producing coins of this type seems to have been developed in course of time from that of the Harappan copper tablets.

All these seem to indicate that the Mauryan period is nearer to the end of the Harappan and thus are corroborative to the chronological range of Asoka's rule suggested above. Hence there is need to re-examine thoroughly and comprehensively the traditional accounts of the history of our country in general as given in the Puranas and of the Mauryan history in space and time over a wider perspective such as the excavations in particular at Jaugada, Rajagriha, and Pataliputra etc. for which archaeological and epigraphical evidences are also available. Relatively the antiquity and development of the *Brahmi* script is required to be examined.

Appendix

^{14}C dates for:

1. The Neolithic culture in the Chalcoliothic stage:

(i) at Tekkalakota Period IA

3395+105
(3490+105)

3465+105
(3565+105)

at Tekkalakota Period IB

3625+105
(3730+105)

(ii) at Kodekal Earliest phase

2460+105 B.C.

(iii) at Terdal Earliest phase

3625+105
(3720+105)

(iv) at Hallur Tr. 1 Period IA

3560+105
(3660+105)

(*C*.1700 B.C. on average)

at Hallur Tr. 1 Period IB

3280+105
(3375+105)

2895+100
(2980+105)

Tr. 2. Period IB

3145+100
(c.1195 B.C.)

(v) at Budihal

Ash mound no. 1 Period IA

7950+210

Layer 6: 3750+30
Layer 9: 3805+35
Layer10: 3795+40
(i.e.c. 1800-1700 B.C. on average)

(vi) at Sanganakal Period IA

1590+110
1585+105
1550+105

(The beginning of the culture in this site was around 1600 B.C.)

(vii) Watgal Period IIA

4150+50
(On average 2563, 2524 and 2500 B.C.)

Period IIB

3910+60
(c.2313[2199], 2136 B.C.)

3510+100
(c.1871[1730, 1729 and 1685] 1530 B.C.)

The average date is 2300-2000 B.C.

2. Iron Age Megalithic Culture:

(i) at Hallur : C 14 dates

Overlap Phase

2820+100
(2905+100)

2970+105
(3055+105)

The average date is 1105+105 B.C.

905+100.B.C.

B. Thermoluminiscence dates

2. For the Iron Age Megalithic culture

(ii) at Komaranahalli.

Meg. II : Black-and-red ware pottery

3300+290
c.1440 B.C.

3080+260
c.1100 B.C.

Meg. III : Black-and-red ware pottery

3110+500
c.1130 B.C.

2910+470
c.930 B.C.

Meg. IV : Red ware pottery

3360+300
c.1380 B.C.

3180+280
c.1200 B.C.

Meg. IV : All Black-ware-pottery

3300+400
c.1320 B.C.

NOTES

Based on the paper presented with colour slides by Dr. Jitendra Das, Superintendent Archaeologist, Archaeological Survey of India, Bangalore circle, Bangalore in the last Congress of South Indian Numismatic Society held in Karnataka University, Dharwad in Feb.`2000.

BIBLIOGRAPHY

Agarwal, Madalasa Devi Age of Bharata war, *Age of Bharata War*, Agrawal, G.C., Delhi.

AI, No. 13, ASI, 1958. (04-141), Report on the 1954 Excavations at Maski, Thapar, B.K.

Ancient India, No. 4, Archaeological Survey of India, Govt. India, New Delhi, 1947. 181-310. Report on the Excavations at Brahmagiri and Chandravalli in 1947 by wheeler, R.E.M.

Annual Report of Deptt. of Archaeology, Mysore 1942. 100-09.

David Frawley *The Myth of the Aryan Invasion*, The Voice of India, Delhi 1996.

Deo, S.B. and Kamat, S.U.; *The Aryan Problem*, Bharatiya Itihasa Samkalana Samiti, Maharashtra, 1993.

Gopal, B.R. 1983. *Corpus of The Inscriptions of the Kadambas* vol. I, Institute of Kadamba Studies, Sirsi.

Indian Archaeology, A Review, 1977-78. ASI, (IAR). 27-29; fig. 5.

Indo-Asian Culture, Vol. II, No. 3. 238-47.

Journal of Asiatic Society of Bengal, Vol. VII.:156.

Krishnamachariyar, M. 1937. *History of Classical Sanskrit Literature*.

Krishna, M.H. 1931. *Excavations at Chandravalli*, DAM.

Krishnan, K.G. 1987. *Uttankita Sanskrit Vidya Aranya Epigraphs*, The Uttankita Vidya Aranya Trust, Vol. II Mysore. Inscriptions nos. 1-24.

Kulkarni, S.D. 1998. *Beginning of Life, Culture and History*, Vol. I.

————1993a. *The Puranas*, Vol. II.

————1993b. *Dharma and Vedic Foundation*, Vol. IV.

————1995a. *Glorious Epoch*, Vol. IV.

————1995b. *India Abroad*, Vol. XVI.

Moorthy, U.S. 1994. *Megalithic Culture of South India, Socio-Economic perspectives*, Ganga-Kaveri Publications, Varanasi. List of dates at the end.

Mujumdar, R.C. et al. 1951. *The Vedic Age*, Bharatiya Vidya Bhawan, Mumbai, Chapter XXIV.

Nagaraja Rao, M.S. 1990. Graves of The Early Iron Using People at Komaranahalli-Recent Evidence, *Archaeology of Karnataka*, DAM.

Pradhan, S.N. 1996. *Chronology of Ancient India*, Cosmo Publications, Delhi.

Rao Kapatral Krishna, 1970. Sri Chandralamba Parameshvari, *Karnataka Samskriti (Samshodhane)*, Usha Sahitya Male, Mysore.

Rice, B.L. 1903. *Epigraphia Carnatica*, Vol. XI, Mk. 2. Directorate of Archaeology & Museums, Govt. of Karnataka, Mysore.

Sathe, Sriram 1985. *Is Sandrokottas Chandragupta Maurya?* Sahitya Niketan, Hyderabad.

————1991. *Aryans : Who are they?* Bhartiya Itihasa Samkalan Samiti, Hyderabad.

Sethna, K.D. 1989. *Ancient India in a new light*, Aditya Prakashan, New Delhi.

————1992. *The Problems of Aryan Origins*, Aditya Prakashan, Delhi.

Shaffer Jim, et.al.; 1995. The Watgal Excavations : An Interim

Report, *Man And Environment*, Vol. 20, Part 2. Indian Society For Prehistoric And Quaternary Studies, Pune.

Sharma, Kartikeya, 1994. *Early Brahmi Inscriptions From Sannati*, Harman Publishing House, Delhi.

Singh, G.P. 1994. *Early Historical Tradition and Archaeology*, D.K. Print World (p) Ltd. Delhi.

Sundara A. *South India inscriptions*, Vol. XI, pt. 1. Ins. No.

————1976. Koppala: Itihasa Purvakala, *Gavideepti, Gavisiddheshvara Kripaposhita Vidyarthi Balaga*, Koppala. (97-103). (Prehistoric Koppala).

————1978. Chitradurga Parisara: Ittichina Puratattva Shodhanegalu", *Manavia Bharati* Vol. 2. Part.1. Karnataka University, Dharwad.

————1989. *Kings and Kingdoms*, Sri Babasaheb Apte Smarak Samiti, Nagpur.

————1992. Hidimba Pattana: Ondu Vimarshatmaka Tippani *Itihasa Darshana*, vol. 7. Karnataka Itihasa Academy, Banglore.

————1994. *Karnataka : Pragitihasa Kalada Kale*, Karnataka Lalita Kala Academy, Bangalore.

————1995. *Hampi* : The Ancient Kishkindha *"Visvambhara"* (Probings In Orientology) : Dr. V.S. Pathak Felicitation Vol. Harman Publishing House, Delhi.

————1995. *Srimadramayanada* 'Kartikeya vama' 'u' Sondurina Kumaraswami Bettave? *Itihasa Darshana*, vol. 10; 165-175.

————1996. On The Traditional Names of The South Indian Megaliths : *The Moriyara Mane*" Presented in the Annual Conference of the Indian Archaeological Society held in Delhi.

————1998. The Krishna-Tungabhadra valley : The Protohistoric Kishkindha of the Vanaras, Paper submitted in the seminar on River Valley Cultures organized by Indiragandhi Manava Samgrahalaya, Bhopal.

Teignmouth, 1979. *The Works of Sir William Jones*, (in vols.), Vol. IV 1807.

Thapar, B.K. 1958. Report on the 1954 Excavations at Maski, AI, No. 13, ASI, (04-141)

Troyer, M. (Tr.) 1859. Kalhana's *Rajatarangini*.

Kushan Rock Art along the Indus from Leh to Batalik

B.R. MANI*

Ethnic studies in the inner Asian interfluvial area give an interesting glimpse of the marvelous world of the Kushans in as much as they offer explanations for the interlinking of many specified and unspecified tribes in these regions. A new dimension was added to the research on Kushan penetration in Ladakh when A. H. Francke, during his survey in 1909, noticed the inscription of Vima Kadphises at Khalatse in Ladakh. He had noticed other Brahmi and Kharoshthi records in the region. Later, German and Pakistani scholars noticed a large number of such records and engravings down the Indus, around Chilas, Hunza and other sites on Karakorum highway.

In recent times many of such vestiges have disappeared due to unplanned blasting of boulders along the Indus for constructional purposes. But a greater threat has been imposed due to unmindful and fanatic destruction of Buddhist statues and other artefacts by the Taliban militia in the neighbourhood in Afghanistan, around March 2001. The pathetic news reports and articles in the volumes of newsletter of the Circle of Inner Asian Art, SOAS, London had disturbed everyone concerned with art, history, archaeology and overall the heritage. Alarming reports were that an unexplored rocket-propelled grenade was said to be embedded in the chest of the fifty-five metre Buddha at Bamiyan where the monastic cells had been used as barracks for the Mujahideen and the surrounding region had been heavily mined. Over 70% of the antiquities and art objects of Kabul museum including the entire famed coin collection have disappeared through looting and the majority of the remaining pieces becoming fragmentary. The whereabouts of the golden hoard of Tillya Tepe is not known and the site has been destroyed. The famous ivory objects of Begram are reported to be available for sale in Pakistan and in London market, the wall paintings in caves at Bamiyan were blackened by campfires. The collection of coins from Mir Zakah is still offered in Hadda along with monasteries and caves has been destroyed and the movable contents have re-surfaced on the International antiquity market. The excavated artefacts preserved in Jalalabad were raided by looters and from there a Bodhisattva head has found its way to the Metropolitan Museum of Art in New York and the famous sites having portraits of Kushan emperors at Surkh Kotal and Ai destroyed and bulldozed to facilitate the illegal operations of individual diggers.

It is quite disturbing to note that inspite of appeals made by world community, the large-scale devastation occurred there and humanity suffered great loss. Huge relief of a Maitreya Buddha in Mulbekh, Aapati and Kartse Khar in Ladakh were built later in the same tradition following the late Kushan Buddhas of Bamiyan, which require full protection today.

Ladakh has gathered within its small highly cultured

*Archaeological Survey of India, New Delhi-110001.

area a remarkable collection of different art styles. Widespread traces of cultural impacts of Tibetan Buddhism and art forms of the tenth and eleventh centuries A.D. have been found throughout ladakh as it had deeply penetrated into the socio-religious scenario and lifestyle of the people of the area. Except rock carvings and engravings of human and animal forms, a few smaller sites with Stone Age tools and Buddhist effigies in rock-relief, which are prior to the introduction of Tibetan Buddhism, far too little remains of the early culture of Ladakh.

The cultural heritage of Ladakh has always attracted attention of various scholars, researchers, archaeologists and explorers in the past. Apart from the accounts of European travellers Diogo D' Almeria, Fathers Francesco De Azevedo and Giovanni De Oliveiro of Seventeenth century and the account of Ipolito Desderi of the early eighteenth century, the regular detailed accounts of physical, statistical and historical nature were produced by Sir Alexander Cunningham in 1854 who travelled in the area in 1846 and 1847 by different routes in Ladakh. The first cultural mission of a high scholarly character was sponsored by the Director General of Archaeology in India in 1909 under A.H. Francke whose *Antiquities of Indian Tibet* still remains the most useful handbook for a scholarly traveller. Numerous articles and books have been published since then, including the works of David L. Snellgrove and Tdeusz Sorupski about religion, culture, monuments and other archaeological remains of the region besides certain spasmodic endeavours made by scholarly travellers.

Archaeologists from Germany and Pakistan under Karl Jettmar[1] and A. H. Dani[2] have explored a large number of sites in and around the Karakorum highway and have located numerous inscriptions in Brahmi and Kharoshthi datable to the early centuries of Christian Era and having names of Saka and Kushan rulers, Kshatrapas, high officials and local rulers besides human and animal figures and motifs engraved on boulders and rocks, many of which like ibex and other animal figures, hunting and dancing scenes and palm, sun, *stupa* and such other motifs are quite akin to those found in Ladakh. Geo-culturally the area comes under the same region, as also most of these sites are located on the banks of the Indus from Alam Bridge in the north to Kohistan area in the south having important sites at Chilas, Thalpan, Ziyarat, Hodar, Oshibat, Thor and Shatial. Towards north of Alam Bridge where river Hunza meets the Indus such sites with rock engravings have been located on the banks of Hunza up to the place of the same name identified as Hanosara (or Hanesara), Vishaya (district) by N. P. Chakravarti[3].

An archaeological investigation (fig. 1) in Ladakh was undertaken by the author in September 1998 for the study of rock engravings along the banks of Indus, Suru, Doda and Zanskar rivers and many new sites with engraved boulders and rock shelters were discovered[4]. The main emphasis was given to locate such sites on Kargil-Padum road (approximately 243 km) and beyond Padum upto Thongde (about 15 km) and along the banks of Indus from Leh to Batalik (approximately 175 km). The last mentioned track is very important to study the Prehistoric and Early Historic movements of nomads, traders, armed forces and cultural entrepreneurs as the route along with the Indus connected Ladakh with Tibet and Himalayan states on one side and Karakorum and Pamir on the other side through Hunza and Gilgit on one way and through Nubra valley on the other connecting Ladakh with the Central Asia and silk route the Ab-I-Wakhan which seems to be the ancient Wakan mentioned in the Kushan inscription of Huvishka dated in the year 28 from Mathura[5]. Lord of Wakan and Kharasalera *(wakanapatina kharasalera patina)* mentioned in the inscription as donors of a perpetual endowment *(akshayanivi)* of 550 *puranas* (gold coins), seems to be the ruler of Wakan and Kharasalera under the Kushans which can be identified with Wakhan and Kharchanal Dawan in the Khunjerab valley near Hindukush mountains.

The rock engravings, particularly those on boulders in river valleys, mostly embedded into the ground at varied depths, are the earliest remains of the cultural heritage of Ladakh as they depict scenes of Prehistoric, Early Historic and Later Historic life of man and culture of the region. The earliest ones are represented by animal figures of ibex, cattle, yak, goat, deer, dog, wolf, horse and human figures including those in hunting with bow-and-arrow or with spear and in dancing positions in groups, horse riders, fighting scenes and symbols of sun, palm, *swastika* and others. They were sometimes copied in later periods also as are evident from overlapping and scratching without patina and looking fresh on granite boulders. The latest engravings are represented by *stupas* or chortens with or without Tibetan calendar. During his expedition in 1909, A. H. Francke had mentioned about occurrence of Brahmi and Kharoshthi inscriptions in the region, which are hardly to be traced now. One such inscription mentioning Uvima Kavthisa and year 184 or 187 of some unspecified era was found near the old bridge at Khalatse which is supposed to belong to the Kushan ruler Vima Kadphises (fig. 2).

Unfortunately, there is no trace of this important inscription. While surveying this area recently it was noticed that a large number of boulders along the Indus have been destroyed in the recent past for construction of roads. A number of records and figures must have got vanished along with the Kharoshthi inscription and ibex figures have similarities with those found on the Karakorum highway and can be compared with the human figures with ibexes noticed at Tilichang, Rugdus and Nyurla which all may belong to the kushan period (figs. 3-5).

Francke had also noticed an early Brahmi and a Gupta inscription besides a number of Tibetan royal inscriptions around the Dard castle and chortens at Khalatse[7]. At Lamayuru also three inscriptions were discovered by him[8] datable to a period between 600 A.D. and 800 A.D. as also suggested by J. PH. Vogel on paleoecological grounds. Francke had noticed rock carvings with primitive figures (engravings) in between the stretch from Shargola to Kargil and Kargin to Drass at several places at Chanigund and Donngga-all in the Dard area[9] besides the sculptures and inscriptions at Drass, the last ones being now declared as protected monuments.

Regarding engravings of ibex figures on boulders and rocks, it is well known that it represents the local tradition of the area connected with the ceremony of ibex hunting, known as thuma saling, a term perhaps of Balti language, as also observed by A. H. Dani according to whom "the story refers to a ritual conception of a male ibex, which, if drawn on this rock, would lead to human pregnancy"[10]. This is in the context of Hunza rock, which is also applicable to other places of the region. The male organs of ibexes are also drawn at a number of places.

It has been a custom in Ladakh, as observed by Francke during his tours[11], that on the occasion of the birth of a child presents of 'flour-ibex', i.e., the figures of ibex made of flour and butter, were offered as thanks-giving and people also used to go to the pre-Buddhist places of worship, in particular, to pray to be blessed with children.

Fertility cult was very popular during the Early Historical period in India, especially during the Kushan period when terracotta figurines of Naigamesa and Naigamesi were modelled on a large scale and offered in cult worship. They had the face of goat over human body. On the basis of the epic mythology and ancient texts like *Kalasutra, Nieminathacharita* and *Antagada-dasao,* it has been suggested that the deity was worshipped to attain progeny and to take care of the evil influences occurring in the form of sickness[12].

The ibex figures found on boulders and rocks which are also related to such ritualistic offering may suggest their dating along with other associated engravings to the period around the beginning of the Christian Era when the nomads of the region entered into social order with the impact of Kushans who besides bringing about Buddhist missionaries also encouraged trade and commerce along this region with the trading centres on the silk route.

While moving 25 km from Mulbekh towards Bodkharbu one can take a bypass at Khangral just before Bodkharbu, which connects it with Shakar and further to Sanjak on the Indus. The turtle peak and Chigthan-Khar are the landmarks on the way. About 29 km from Khangral a number of boulders with engravings along with their later copies were noticed on the bank of the stream at a place called Skinbrisa. The stream joins the Indus 2 km ahead at Sanjak. At Skinbrisa no less than 47 ibex figures were noticed on a single boulder. Apart from the usual ibexes, a man hunting ibex with bow-and-arrow, ibex made with the help of two triangles and chasing buffalo scenes were found. The most striking depiction is that of a battle scene with horse riders, at least six on one side and four on the other holding long spears and two foot soldiers holding bow and arrows.

A thorough survey was made from Sanjak to Batalik along the banks of Indus in a stretch of 25 km, a little before up to the line of actual control between India and Pakistan. This area is famous for the people of a different racial stock called the Drokpas having Dard features, which are fond of wearing flowers and beaded ornaments and occupied Ladakh before its Tibetanisation. On this, about 2 km northwest of Sanjak at Tillichang, a rock-shelter was noticed in front of which there is a shallow rock-bowl which is the natural container of water and large boulders with primitive engravings, including several group dance scenes, man with triangular body, deer and ibexes; 2 km further ahead near Bema two rocks have similar scenes, including a man hunting with bow-and-arrow two animals which look like wolves, group dance scene, ibexes composed lines or two triangles making their body, some of which depicted with their organs and a sun circle. There is a rock-shelter also. About 2 km still ahead at Rugdus some boulders have been broken for road repairs. In one of the existing ones there are figures of ibexes, man with raised hands showing prominent palms, a man with bow-and-arrow and crown on his head, made with beaded impression, group-dance scene, four triangles making a human head, body and two palms, ibex with very long curved horns, cattle (yak) and several hunters of ibexes a little over 1 km ahead, at Dah, and 3 km from Dah, near Darkun, there are rock-shelters and ibex figures on boulders. Ibex figures were also found on boulders near village Darchick (16 km from Sanjak) and at Benny point (22 km from Sanjak and 5 km before Batalik).

Nearly 175 km stretch from Batalik to Alam Bridge in Baltistan along the Indus requires investigation as the area beyond it has been surveyed by German and Pakistani archaeologists and the area from Batalik towards east in the upper Indus basin has been surveyed by us. In the 150 km stretch from Sanjak to Leh further thorough investgation is required to record and protect the rock-engravings and there is a possibility of relocating and finding new Brahmi and Kharoshthi inscriptions in this area along the banks of Indus. A cursory survey by the author and previous explorers have revealed the occurrence of rock engravings of primitive type at Khalatse, Nyurla, Phyang and at a place about 18 km before Leh on the national highway. At Nyurla four boulders with engravings of goat, ibexes, horse riders hunting deer with bow-and-arrows, group dancers, men with different hand postures, a man riding a deer like animal, an animal with round face over a vertical neck were discovered. At a place 18 km before Leh, boulders with ibex figures, goats with long horns and body composed of two triangles and filled up elongated bodies and hunter aiming at an ibex with bow-an-arrow were noticed. There are late engravings on boulders near the two bridges on the Indus, one in between Saspol and Alchi and the other on both sides of river at Khaltse. Besides primitive ones, these engravings to a period around 9th century A.D. as also believed by Philip Denwood on the basis of orthography and onomastics and similarity of terms with those found in the records from Khotan and Tun-Haung and also in a Tibetan pillar inscription to 9th century A.D.[12]

Leh, the capital of Ladakh, seems to have developed into a city during this period as it was the meeting place of various traders and cultural missionaries trecking along divergent trade routes coming from south of the Himalayas[14] connecting the main land of the country and also from Tibet via Kailas-Mansarovar and Nyoma on one side and extending towards north via Nubra valley to Khotan, Yarkand, Kyzil and Kashgar in the Chinese Turkistan (Xinjiang province) where at Koutcha around Kyzil at the end of the 7th century A.D. there were 100 monasteries with about 5000 monks as informed by the Chinese pilgrims Huen-Tsang and I-Tsing and towards west via Khalatse, Batalik, Gilgit and Chitral to the area of Wakan under the Kushan empire. Such Prehistoric and Early Historic engravings on boulders can be traced upto mountain passes of Ras-Koh towards southwest of the Oxus across Indus basin in Baluchistan area[14].

The Kushan establishments of cities founded by Hushka, Jushka and Kanishka, as mentioned in the Rajatarangini of Kalhana which can be located between Baramulla and Srinagar, were also connected with the above mentioned route via Drass and Khalatse from where ancient remains, sculptures and inscriptions have been found. The so-called 'Kanika Chorten' (*stupa* of Kanishka) at Sani monastery in Zanskar which has the hemi-spherical dome (*anda*) which is not the usual feature of chortens in Ladakh, also suggests through the tradition about Kushan evidence in the area which on one with the route along the Indus through the difficult route along Zanskar, the river which joins the Indus near Nimoo between Leh and Khalatse at a distance of about 34 km from Leh.

Francke, during his observations and study of skulls recovered from the Dard graves near Leh, had suggested that they belong to the early centuries of the Christian era, between first to fifth centuries A.D.[15] Apparently, the Dard nomads must have helped in the trade of the area which got impetus during the Kushan rule and much of the engravings on the boulders seemingly date back to the period.

REFERENCES

1. *Zwischen gandhara und den seidenstrassen, felsbilder am Karakorum highway,* Entdeckungen Deutsch-Pakistanischer expeditionen 1979-1984, Mainz am Rhein, 1985.

2. A. H. Dani, *Human records on Karakorum highway,* Islambad, 1983; *Chilas the city of nanga parvat,* Islambad, 1983; *The sacred rock of Hunza, Journal of Central Asia,* vol. viii, no. 2, December, 1985.

3. 'Hatun rock inscription of Patoladeva', *Epigraphia Indica,* vol. xxx, 1953-54, pp. 227 and 230.

4. B. R. Mani, 'Rock carvings and engravings in Ladakh: new discoveries', *Pragdhara,* Journal of the U. P. State Archaeology Department, no. 9, Lukhnow, 1999, pp. 65-74, pls. 15-45.

5. *Epigraphia Indica,* vol. xxi, p. 55 ff, no. 10.

6. A. H. Francke, *Zeitschrift der deutschen morgenlandischen gesellschaft* (zdmg), 61, 1907, pp. 592 f; A.S.I., annual report, 1909-10, p. 104, *Antiquities of Indian Tibet,* part I, 1914, p. 94.

7. A.H. Francke, *Antiquities of Indian Tibet,* part I, Archaeological Survey of India, New Imperial Series. Vol. xxxviii, Calcutta, 1914, pp. 94-95.

8. *Ibid,* p. 96.

9. *Ibid,* pp. 105.

10. A. H. Dani, *op. cit.,* pp. 95-96.

11. Vidula Jayaswal, *Kushana clay art of Ganga plains,* Delhi, 1991, pp. 44-45.

12. Philip Denwood, 'On the inscriptions at Alchi', part IV in David L. Snellgrove and Tadeusz Skorupski, *The cultural heritage of Ladakh,* vol. 2, New Delhi, 1980, pp. 155-163.

13. Rock engravings of similar type as found in Ladakh have also been noticed at Tabo in Spiti valley (A. K. Sinha, 'Rock-engravings at Tabo, distt. Lahul and Spiti, Himachal Pradesh', *Puratattva* no. 21, New Delhi 1991, pp. 90-92.)

14. Mohammad Usman Hassan, 'Ras-koh: a crossroads of ancient civilization', *South Asian archaeology* 1985, op. cit., 189-95.

15. A. H. Francke, op. cit., p.

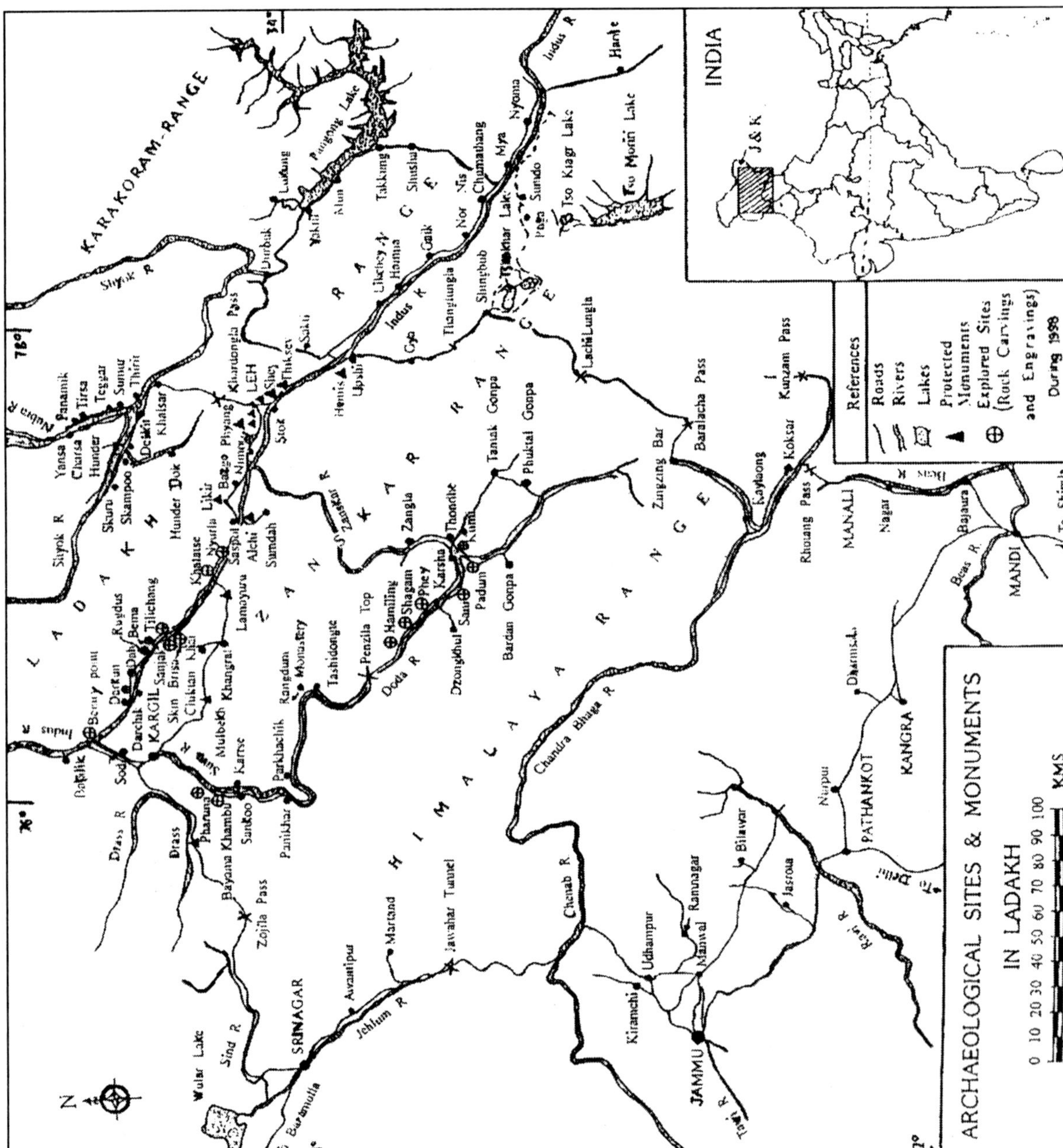
ARCHAEOLOGICAL SITES & MONUMENTS
IN LADAKH
0 10 20 30 40 50 60 70 80 90 100
KMS
References
Roads
Rivers
Lakes
Protected Monuments
Explored Sites (Rock Carvings and Engravings) During 1998
INDIA
J & K
KARAKORAM RANGE
LADAKH
ZANSKAR
HIMALAYA RANGE
LEH
KARGIL
SRINAGAR
JAMMU
PATHANKOT
KANGRA
MANALI
MANDI
Pangong Lake
Indus R
Shyok R
Chenab R
Jehlum R
Zojila Pass
Wular Lake

Fig. 1.

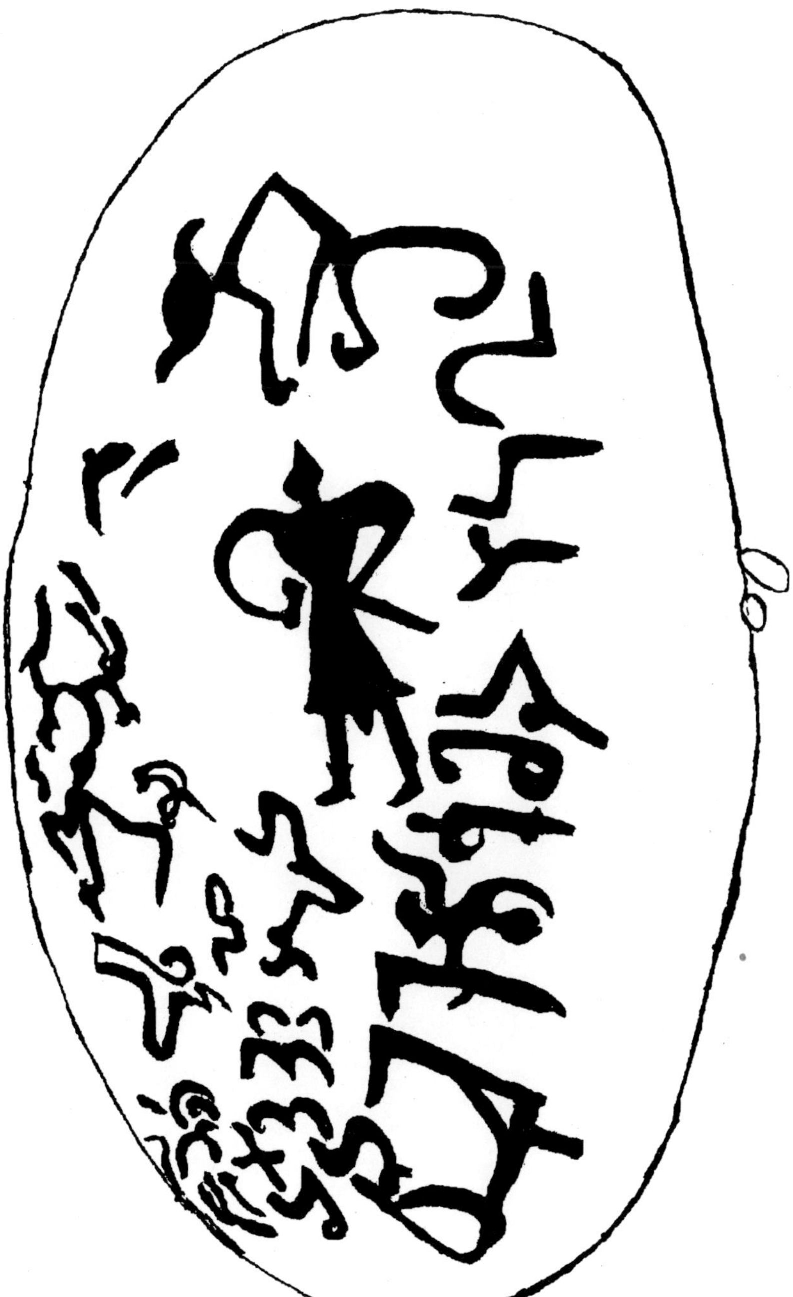

Fig. 2. Kharoshthi Inscription and engravings, Khalatse

Fig. 3. Rock engravings, Tilichang

Fig. 4. Rock Engravings, Rugdus.

Fig. 5. Rock Engravings, Nyurla.

A Rare Type of Ganesha in the National Museum of Ethnology in Leiden

M. KRISHAN KUMARI*

An image of Ganesa, which is unique and rare, is found in the National Museum of Ethnology at Leiden and bears the inventory number 1403-1681. The provenance of this image is Candi Singhasari.

In the early 19th century, ruins of several buildings were found near the village of Singhasari, near the town Malang in East Java. Candi Singhasari like other Indo-Javanese temples has a cella for the image of the main deity and on the outside or several niches for images of Dugra, Mahishasura Mardini (north), Ganesa (east) and Agastya (south). The entrance is on the west. The Durga Mahishasuramardini, Ganesa and Nandi images were transported to the Netherland in the early 19th century. The temple and its sculptures are generally assigned to the late 13th century A.D.

The height of the image is 154 cm and it is chiselled in high relief out of andesite or volcanic rock. Since the iconographic features of the image under study are not met with in any of the Ganesa images known so far in India and found to be very peculiar and interesting, an attempt has been made here to throw some light on its iconography as well as its religious significance with the help of texts and available Ganesa images from the Andhra region.

The stone image of Ganesa under consideration is in a seated position in the *Maharajalila asana* upon a throne of human skulls with the left leg folded and the right one raised. He is four-armed; the front left hand holds a bowl of sweetmeat and the front right holds a *kapala*. The back left hand holds an *akshamala* shown in upright position while the back right hand holds a *parasu*. On either side of his elephant head is shown a round disk surrounded by an irregular nimbus. The belly is not customary and is rotund belly of Ganesa. He wears a *naga yajnopavita*, anklets, armlets, *udara bandha* and rings on the first fingers on both feet. Interestingly, he wears skull earrings, which dangle on either side of his fan-like ears. The elephant-headed god turns towards the left side touching the sweetmeat held in his left hand. The image is adorned with an unusual headgear consisting of *kapalas* (skulls) carved in full form decorated with some ornamental designs both on the side and at the top. Three such skulls are carved in a row with little space in between, with one more skull above the central skull. In front of his hairdo is shown a crescent. He wears the lower garment that runs up to his feet with some beautiful conventional designs as well as figures of skull in stylized form. The vehicle of the god, the mouse is conspicuous by its absence. It may be mentioned here that in Indo-Javanese sculptures in general, the mounts of the deities are rarely represented. Here in its place is shown a row of seven skull arranged in a semi-circular fashion around the base of the seated

*Department of History, Andhra University,Waltair-530003 (A.P.)

image of the god. The anatomical features of the skulls and the image are proportionate. Another interesting iconographical detail observed is the presence of lines on the trunk of the god like the *brahma sutras* or lines drawn on the *rudra bhaga* or *puja bhaga* of the *linga* form of Siva. In this image under study seven lines are drawn horizontally one below another, while two curved lines are drawn in an inverted fashion a little above them.

Ganesa images from Java very closely follow the Indian tradition as observed by J.N. Banerjea (1956:360). One seated image from Java has been published which shows the god with four arms and the usual attributes (Banerjea 1956). Interestingly, the image is shown with the lower garment with designs on it like that of the image under study.

In Hindu pantheons, Ganesa images wearing skull in the headgear and skulls below him are unknown. However, it has been observed that some of the Hindu Gods and their iconographical forms crept into *Vajrayana* Buddhist art. This could be due to assimilation of Hindu gods into the Buddhist faith. Since the Buddhists have borrowed several Hindu gods and goddesses such as Siva, Surya, Ganapati and Sarasvati, the iconography of these gods has been changed considerably resulting in the emergence of separate *sadhanas* as well as independent shrines for housing them (Bhattacharya 1956: 344). This can be seen from the Ganesa images that appear not only in India and Indonesia but also in China and Tibet on painted banners (Clark 1937: 153). Among the Hindu gods that were borrowed by the Buddhists, Ganesa is a prominent deity. It is observed that in the later phase of Buddhism, Ganesa was worshipped under the name of Vinayaka (Bhattacharya 1956). There are several evidences to suggest that Ganesa occupied a consolidated position among Buddhists as the bestower of success and protector against evils (Das). Elaborate descriptions of Ganesa can be found in the Buddhists texts like the *Sadhanamala* and *Nishpannayogavali*, which are considered as the veritable mines of information on Buddhist gods and goddesses. Ganesa is described as having twelve hands with a single face and riding his *vahana*, the mouse. It further refers to *trisula*, sword and *kapala* as the attributes of the god in one of the *Sadhanas* of the *Sadhanamala* (Bhattacharya 1956). In the *Dharmadhatuvagisvara Mandala* of the *Nishpannayogavli*, Ganesa is described as standing on a mouse, with four-arms and an elephant face and a serpent *yajnopavita*. Further it is mentioned that he carries *trisula* and *ladduka* in a bowl and in the left hands the *parasu* and *mulaka*. However, a different description of Ganesa is given in another *Mandala* known as the *Bhutadamana Mandala*. According to it, Ganesa is to be carved as standing on a mouse, with three eyes, wearing the crescent moon, four-handed, carrying *mulaka* and *parasu* in the two right hands and *trisula* and *kapala* in the two left hands (*Nishpa*: 72). What is important to note here is the reference to the association of *kapala* with Ganesa that can be taken to mean either *munda*, the severed head of a human, been the cup or bowl made of skull or the full form of a skull (Bhattacharya 1956).

At Sankaram, popularly known as Lingalakonda or Bojjannakonda, Visakhapatnam district (Andhra Pradesh), a standing, nude and ithyphallic image of Ganesa is noticed on one side of the entrance to a rock-cut trough. The image carved in a very low relief shows the god with four arms. He holds a long sword pointing downwards in his right hand and a *damaru* in his back right hand. The front left hand holds a severed head held by the hair while the back left hand holds a long *trisula*. The end forks of the *trisula* are curved inwards with a long staff *(danda)* resting on the ground. The characteristic pot belly of the god is not prominent. The proboscis is shown as turned towards the left. He wears a *mundamala (kapala mala)* on his body. The mouse is absent below the figure of the image. Art historians feel that it has *Tantric* affinity. (Rao 1993:347/50). It is also suggested that this standing Ganesa image may belong to the Buddhist pantheon as this image is unique in having certain peculiar features like the absence of the vehicle of the god standing in *sampada*, nude ithyphallic with *mundamala* instead of a *yajnopavita* (Rao 1993:347-50). From the same site, Alexander Rea reported an image of Hariti (ARASI 1907-08). The presence of Hariti and the naming of the place as Bojjannakonda after Ganesa which is an important Buddhist site with *Chayagrihas*, monastic establishments, rock-cut caves, votive and monolithic *stupas* will undoubtedly reveal the Buddhist affinities of Ganesa. The *urdhvalinga* is generally shown in the image of Siva. In Andhra, the Nataraja image of Bikkavolu, now in the Madras Museum, and the images of Pala period, as well as a few images of dancing Siva of Bengal, Orissa and elsewhere display prominently the *urdhvalinga* although dressed adequately (Sivaramamurti 1974:191). This iconographical feature may show the *yogic* nature and the self-restraint of Siva in such forms. An early Gupta relief of a seated Ganesa has depicted the two-armed god with *urdhvalinga*, which is reported from a cave at Udyagiri (Bhilsa—Banerjea: 351). Here, the mount of the god is absent. The Ganesa image from Sankaram too is ithyphallic which is a unique feature.

While studying the Indian art forms with a socio-biological approach, it has been stated that Siva, who is a fierce god and for whom the battlefield is the playground, is adorned with skulls and bones in his terrific manifestation of Bhairava. In the case of Bhairava forms wherein the god is shown as *urdhvalingin,* it is explained that the erect phallus can be considered as a sign of terrifying power and victory (Bedaunx 1995:197 200). It may be mentioned here that an image of Bhairava with exposed genitals comes from Singhasari and is dateble to the 13th century A.D., which is now displayed in the Rijksmuseum of Ethnology in Leiden. It represents the god in terrifying form and in dance pose with skull ornamentation above a base encircled with skull. He has a decorated skull-headgear. Skull ear ornaments and armlets besides a long *hara* of skulls (*mundamala*—Scheurleer 1998:9). From the iconographical descriptions of the images of Siva and Ganesa who are shown as ithyphallic in certain cases, it may be assumed that the Ganesa image of Sankaram is shown in the *vira* aspect with the severed head in one hand and with an *upavita* of severed heads in the other.

As regards to the Ganesa from the Leiden Museum the absence of the mount and the row of skulls in its place below the seated image reveal the *Tantric* affinity of the diety. Further the representation of the skulls on the head and body of the image indicate the association of Ganesa with demons, as the portrayal of *kapalamala* are generally found in connection with the images of Siva. Alice Getty has observed the use of skull ornaments on the representations of Ganesa as a purely Javanese conception that is practically never met with outside of the Malay Archipelago (Getty 1971: 57). Citing a few more examples of Ganesa from this region may substantiate her observation. In her survey of the images of Ganesa and others from Singhsari and the exhibits of the Leiden Museum, Pauline L. Scheurleer has referred to two standing Ganesa images with skull ornamentation and the arrangement of the skulls in semi-circular fashion at the base of the icons (Scheurleer 1998: 37). It has been argued by Theodore Pigeaud that it has some connections with the esoteric practices and rites, and it is speculated that the *ganachakra* i.e., *gana*-circle is in some way associated with the *prayogakriya*, for elsewhere in this poem *Prayoga* seemingly is another name for Ganesa because he is described as "the remover of obstacles" (Pigeaud 1960: 49). With regard to the origin of such esoteric practices it may be suggested that the Indian religious practices were adopted and then transformed to strengthen the indigenous need and beliefs of the Malay Archipelago. In support of this hypothesis the image of Ganesa at Sankaram (India) can be cited with its iconographical peculiarities, which has Buddhist affinities. On the other hand, it has been argued by Nancy Dowling that the overlapping symbolism of the birth story of Ganesa and ritual head-hunting practices prevalent in parts of Southeast Asia are responsible for the demonic forms of Ganesa with skull decorations on his body (Dowling 1992: 130, Downs 1977: 123).

In Hindu mythology, in many respects, Ganesa has close connection with the *ganas*. According to a myth, Ganesa's ancestry is connected the elephant- headed demon Malini who drinks Parvati's bath water mixed with her seed/dirt and produces a son with five elephant heads (Jacobi 2: 807-808, Getty: 6-7, Agarwala 1978: 139-55). Hence Ganesa has one divine mother Parvati, who androgynously provides the creative substance and one demon mother who brings forth the five-headed child. By cutting off the four heads, Siva has cut away Ganesa's demon portion to render him fully divine, thus making Ganesa recognizable and acceptable to the gods (Courtright 1985: 129). In this context, it may be mentioned that the demons play an indispensable role in Hindu mythology of suffering and sacrifice sometimes crossing over the boundary from one mythological category to another, from gods to demons and vice versa. Since the myths about the demons are told from the god's point of view, the demons tend to lock bad, which is not true in all cases (O'Flaherty 1976: 94-138), (Shulman 1980: 317-46). Siva rewarded the elephant-headed Ganesa by placing him incharge of his entourage of semi-divine, semi-demonic followers, the *ganas*. The iconography of the Siva *ganas* or motley looking crew which strange faces alternately horrible and humorous and like their master, denizens of wild forest (Courtright 1985: 131). In Amaravati and Mathura schools of art Vinayakas are generally portrayed as elephant-headed demons or Yakshas as they were originally a team of *ganas* of evil disposition (Agarwal 1978: 139-55).

The four skulls prominently seen on the head of the seated Ganesa and those, which adorn his body, are suggestive of his demenic-ancestry. It is curious to note that Ganesa is shown here as seated on the seven skull-seat thus demonstrating that he is the head of the demons. Otherwise the iconography of the image generally tallies with the descriptions given in the texts like the *Vishnudharmottara purana* (Sircar, 1942-43: 121-25).

To understand the religious significance of the worship of Ganesa in the iconographic form it is essential to consider the Hindu mythological stories about Ganesa, wherein he is referred to as Vighnesvara, Vighnaraja and Vinayaka. His task is divine, his *dharma* is to place and remove obstacles. The destructive tendencies of Vinayaka and the connection of Ganesa with the Vinayaka demons, the groups of malevolent creatures, who lead people astray and place obstacles in their paths, are referred to in *Manava grhyasutras, (Vinayaka Kalpa)* as well as in *Agnipurana, Brihatsamhita*, and *Ishnudharmottara-purana*. (Courtright 132; Dresden 2: 14-21, *Agnipurana*: 264, *Brihat samhit* 58.9, *Vishnudharnottarapurana*, 2.105). All these references clearly point out the connection of Ganesa with the demons.

Earlier some studies have been made on the Ganesa image under discussion by P.H. Pott, Edi Sedyawati, Nancy Dowling and Pauline Scheuleer (Pott 1962: 23-31; Sedyawati 1994; Dowling: 1992, Scheuleer 1998: 2-1). They have tried to analyse the inclusion of skulls in the iconography of Ganesa on the basis of the mythological stories contained in the Javanese literature (Sedyawati 1994). The Javanese stories are very different from that current in the classical Indian texts. In a 12th century old Javanese *Kakawin smaradahana*, Ganesa's life-story is mentioned. According to it, Ganesa is born as the son of Siva and Uma, with the head of an elephant and he was made by Siva as the head of a *gana* and it was declared by Siva that he would by nature be a remover of obstacles and will destroy the enemies of the gods (Zoetmulder 1974: 294). Ganesa is described as very powerful, fierce and even cruel and he ultimately achieved success over the demons. Based on this story it has been explained by Edi Sedyawati that the image of Ganesa is shown as a cruel fighter and victor over the demons in his terrific appearance.

Another explanation offered on the religious and ritual significance of the images of Ganesa, Agastya and Mahishasuramardini at the temple of Singansari is related to the ancestor worship. It is argued that the royal family in the guise of Hindu deities affirm the primacy of ancestor worship as it is generally believed that the deceased members of the royal family are inseparably bound to the deified Hindu image in the central sanctuary who facilitates the flow of the intangible and mysterious powers of the ancestors to the ruling king (Dowling 1992). Further, while surveying the Indo-Javanese stone sculptures of 13th-15th centuries A.D., Pauline Scheurleer observed that other deities and supernatural creatures such as Bhairava and guardians flanking the pair of flights of stairs of the main temple of Candi Panataran A.D. 1347 have similar bases (Scheuleer 1998). Since the other images have jewelery or sacred threads comprising skulls, it is viewed by her that the skulls are part of a change in the iconography, in which the deities and supernatural creatures are depicted with demonic traits such as bulging eyes, fangs, *naga* for sacred threads a huge amount of hair, curls etc.

In the light of the observations and the study of the image under discussion, it is apparent that such iconographical forms of Ganesa are exclusive to Malay Archipelago. The critical analysis of the iconographical features of Ganesa image from Leiden Museum attempted here throws a welcome light on the rare and unusual figure of seated Ganesa with skull ornamentation, particularly in seeking its origins from India. It endeavours to draw the attention of the art historians on the unique sculpture of standing nude Ganapati decorated with *mundamala* reported from Sankaram of Andhra region with clear tracks and influence of *Vajrayana* Buddhism, which has some similarities from the point of view of both iconography and the religious symbolism with the image under discussion. Ganesa with the lines like the *brahma sutras* drawn on the trunk of the image is suggestive of some esoteric and tantric practices followed by the devotees. Further it can be seen from the Hindu religious traditions and mythological stories that are contained in the Sanskrit texts of different period, that Ganesa had demon- ancestry besides projecting the idea from the Javanese stories that Ganesa as the head of the *ganas* had engaged in a war with the demons in which he was successful. It is also evident from the Indian and Javanese mythological stories that he was made as the head of the *pramatha ganas* as well as the god of great respectability by Siva. It can safely be inferred that the Indian *Tantric* and religious rituals were responsible for the creation of such type of Ganesa in East Java image; perhaps influenced by Hinduism or *Vajrayana* Buddhism. It is difficult to explain their absence in the Indian territories.

Acknowledgements

*Photograph is by the courtesy of the Rijksmuseum, Amsterdam.

**I am profusely thankful to Pauline Lunsingh Scheurleer, Guest Curator, Rijksmuseum, National Museum of Ethnology, Leiden for drawing my attention to this image of Ganesa during my visit to the Rijksmuseum, Amsterdam and to Prof. Karel R. Van Koij, Chair of History of South Asian Art, Leiden University, Leiden, for offering their remarks and suggestions on my paper.

REFERENCES

Aggarwal, Prithvi K. 1978. "Some Varanasi Images of Ganapati and their Iconographic Problem", *Artibus Asiae*, Vol.XL 1, p.139-155.

Agnipurana, p.264.

Annual Report of Archaeological Survey of India, 1907-1908. p.164, Fig.8.

Banerjea, J.N. 1956. *The Development of Hindu Iconography*, Calcutta.

Bedaux, Jan Baptist 1995. "Comparative Iconology: A Sociobiological Approach" in K.R.van Kooij & H. Van der Veere (ed). *Functions and Meaning in Buddhist Art*, Groningen, The Netherlands, p.197-204.

Bhattacharya, B. 1958. *The Indian Buddhist Iconography*, Calcutta, p. 344.

Brihatsamhita, p.58.9.

Clark, W.E. 1937. Two Lamaistic Paintings, II, Cambridge, p.153.

Courtright Paul B., 1985. *Ganesa Lord of Obstacles, Lord of Beginnings*, Delhi, p.129.

C. Sivamamurti, 1974. *Nataraja, in Art, Thought and Literature*, Delhi, p. 191, Fig. 36. *Nishpanayovali*, p. 72.

Das, S.R. *Archaeoligical Discoveries From Murshidabad*, I ch, IX, p.47.

Dowling Nancy, 1992. *The Javanization of Indian Art* Indonesia,

Downs, R.E. 1977. Headhunting in Indonesia, in P.E. De Josselin de Jong (ed). *Structural Anthropology in the Netherlands*, The Hauge: Nijhoff,, p.123.

Getty Alice, 1971. *Ganesha; A Monographon the Elephant - Faced God*, : Munshiram Manoharlal, p.57.

Jacobi H.,Brahmanism *Encyclopedia of Religion* and *Ethics*, 2: pp.807-808.

Manavagrihasutras, 2.14-21, Dresden's Translation.

O' Flaherty Wendy D., 1976. *The Origins of Evil in Hindu Mythology*, Berkeley, pp.94-138.

Pigeaud Theodore, Java in the 14th century, Vol.3, The Hague, 1960. p.49.

Pott, P.H. Four Demonic Ganeshas from East Java *Medelingen van het Rijksmuseum voor Volkendunde* 15 (1962) pp.123-131.

Rao, D. Hanumanta A Unique Sculpture of Ganapati from Sankaramin A.V.N. Murty & I.K. Sharma, (ed.) Sri Ramachandrika (Prof. Oruganti Ramachandraiya Festschrift) Essays on Indian Archaeology, History, Epigraphy, Numismatics, Art and Religion, Vol.II, Delhi, 1993, p.347-350.

Scheurleer Pauline Lunsingh, Ganesha van Singosari op bezoek, in *Aziatische Kunst Jaargang* 28, Nr.2, juni 1998, p.9 Afbeelding 7 (inv.1403-1680).

Sedyawati Edi, 1994, *Ganesa Statues of the Kadiri and Singhosari Periods* (Jakarta, 1985) translated into English and published by the Royal Institute of Linguistics and Anthropology in Leiden.

Shulman, David D. 1980 *Tamil Temple Myths: Sacrifice and Marriage in South India Tradition*, Princeton, 1980, p.317-346.

Sircar, D.C. *Indian Culture*, IX 1942-43. p.121-125.

Vishnudharmottarapurana, 2.105.

Zoetmulder, P.J. 1974. *Kalangwan*, The Hague, p.294.

The Ancient and Medieval Roof-tiles from Karnataka

Rajaram Hegde*

The earlier type of roof-tiles found in archaeological sites of Karnataka are rectangular in shape with grooves marked by fingers on their outer face with two holes at the bottom, most probably to fasten them to rafters. Such tiles are abundantly found at Sannati (Howell J.R. 1995: Pl VII) and they are also commonly seen in the Early Historic sites of North India (Hartel H. 1976: fig. 6 and 1993: Pl 23). These tiles seem to have gone out of fashion by 3rd cent. A.D. in Karnataka and perhaps, completely in the later period. These were totally replaced by another type of tiles, which is the subject matter of this article. These are of different shapes and sizes and were in use from the Early Historic period to the Late Medieval period, i.e. for more than a thousand years. They are flat and one of the edges (obviously the bottom one) is bent a right or oblique angle. The other edge is treated variedly into a curve, triangle and two or three petal like designs. Their colour is usually dull red and sometimes they are of bright red or brown in colour. The size varies from 5 cm to 17 cm in width and 1 to 1.7 cm in thickness. The length of most of the tiles is not available, since a very few are recovered fully. The available specimens show a range of 26 to 18 cm in their length. Fabric ranges from course to medium. Few tiles have a considerably wide bend at the top and their surface is decorated with rosette designs and beaded borders.

*Deptt. of History and Archaeology, Kuvempu University, Shimoga, Karanataka-577451

Find Spots and Chronological Framework

These tiles are found in a considerably wide geographical area. These are available at Banavasi and Talakadu (Narasimhamurthy, 1997:106-110:Pl. 51, 52, 53, 54; Devaraj 1996:202; Illust. 2003-9 and 2354, 2356). Surface collections by the present author are from more than 25 sites. Sonda in North Kanara district in the north, Haigunda in west coast of the same district, Talakadu in south and Chandravalli in the east are the present geographical limits of this type of tiles. Such tiles were also noticed at Gangaikondakholapuram the capital of Rajendra Chola I. It is likely that these may be found in more extensive area than the above-mentioned limit. This article is based on the more intensively surveyed district of Shimoga, Karnataka.

The above sites yielding such tiles are of different period and nature. Banavasi is a settlement of the Early Historic period, which prospered during the Kadamba period; tiles found are of the Satavahana period. A few Satavahana coins are found along with them (Narasimhamurthy 1997:Pp 106). Gudnapur, excavated a few years back was the capital city of Kadamba king Ravivarman (Gopal 1985). Haigunda, datable from early Christian era, prospered as the capital of the Kekayas in the 8th or 9th century A.D. (Hegde Rajaram and Sarvmangala 1997: 75-77). Talakad is again an excavated site and is important for relative dating of these tiles. Here these tiles are recovered from Talakad IV-5 and 3; the earlier layer is assigned to the Ganga period and the later to a few centuries after the earlier ones (Devaraj 1996: 53-56). Unfortunately, we are not in a position to ascertain chronology of the site. Asandi is another site in southern Karnataka connected with a local line of the Gangas which ruled during 10th and 11th century A.D. Anagadi, was the earliest capital of the Hoysalas during the late 10th and early and 11th century. A majority of the sites explored for this purpose belongs to Early Medieval or Medieval temple sites in the Shimoga district. Though some of them being a part of settlements cannot be ruled out; the findspots were basically parts of the temple complexes: thus these tiles might have been used for the adjacent structures of these temples. In many cases, we have also brick remains of walls of these temples, which might have had such tiled roofs. That these tiled roofs were common and provided decorative motifs to the sculptors of this period can be seen in Santinatha temple of Bandalike. Here the *antarala* ceiling has sloping roofs for the aisles which bear patterns of these tiles treated as lotus petals, but arranged in straight rows like roof tiles. There can be hardly any doubt that this pattern indicates a tiled roof. Though the *antarala* of the above temple is dated to the later half of the 12th century A.D., the ceiling seems to have belonged to an older structure, may be of 10th cent A.D. This temple existed partially in stone from the 9th century A.D. and as per the present evidence the older parts were generously used when it was rebuilt in the 12th century. Thus the tiles found in the temple premises seem to be contemporary. Another interesting point is that the tiles depicted in the *antarala* ceiling of the above temple bear decorative designs.

The above-mentioned temples range from 8th to 13th century A.D. The Billesvara temple complex at Hamcha, the capital of the Santara rulers, has structures dating from the early Chalukya to the Rastrakutta periods. (Dhakey: 1986). The village Alase has remains which date back to the $8^{th}/9^{th}$ century A.D. Both these sites are situated in the interior forested region of the Western Ghat. A few more sites have yielded these tiles in this region. Coming to the medieval Banavasi region we have sites like Balligave, Talgunda, Bandalike, Udri, Kuppatur, Naralige, Kuppagadde, Barangi, Kodkani (fig. 1), Chikkamagadi, Bhairapur, Tagarti. etc. all of which were the temple centers of the 11th and 12th century A.D. Tile pieces were found around the premises of these temples. At Kodkani and Chikkamagadi heaps of tiles are found buried within the temple premises. Such piles might have been formed during the renovation of temples, in a later period.

Evidences are not clear about the probable time of commencement and disappearance of this type of tiles. As per the Banavasi evidence, the earliest use might have been 3rd century A.D. (Narasimhamurthy 1997:106-107). But their duration is not clear. So far as the terminal date is concerned, there are certain find spots like Keladi, Ikkeri, Bilagi and Sonda which emerged as capitals of the Late Medieval local powers where tiles are found associated with temple or residential remains. We do have positive evidence to assign them to the Late Medieval period in Ikkeri, which was developed as a capital by Keladi Nayakas in the 16th century (Chitnis K.N. 1974: 11). Here these tiles are found in ruins of structures in the palace enclosure. The present Ratnatrays Basadi at Bilagi where tile pieces are found was constructed in the 17th century A.D. The inscriptions speak of an old shrine at that spot, which might have been usually built of brick. But the old shrine might not be earlier than 16th century A.D.

Quite interestingly, sometimes in the Late Medieval period, an entirely different type of tiles had replaced these old ones. The new ones had curved lateral sides having a more or less flat surface or sometimes were semi-cylindrical. Their bottom was narrower and top splayed. These tiles had already come into existence in the 16th century as seen in the ruins of the entrance gate at Ikkeri where these are found along with the earlier flat types. We have pictorial representations of similar curved tiles as early as 2nd cent B.C. at Sanchi (Marshall J 1983; railing pillar of NW quadrant as also from excavations pl.23). However, there is no trace of them in Karnataka till Late Medieval period. This type was produced on a potter's wheel in the early modern period and continued till the end of last century, only to be replaced gradually by the modern types.

Tile Shapes and Sizes-A Possible Typological Evolution

As already pointed out, these tiles exhibit a variety of shapes and sizes. Tiles of the early Kadamba period are larger in size as witnessed in Banavasi and Gudnapur. The excavator of Banavasi has described these as "moderately rough clay and of a medium fabric, not neatly shaped, top (outer surface) is more polished and lower side is crudely made" (Narasimhamurthy 1997:106-107). They are 13 to 17 cm broad and wider at the bottom where the edge is usually bent vertically. The tile tapers slightly so that top is lesser in width by 1 to 1.5 cm. The edges are not exactly straight and surface is also not exactly flat. Three shapes are prominently represented in these tiles: first one has a curved or lotus petal shaped or triangular end; second rectangular and in third the end is shaped like two or three curved petal designs. Sometimes one or two straight groves are found on the outer surface. These tiles are usually around 1 to 1.3 cm thick. Such tiles are found in Haigunda also.

Tiles of the Early Medieval temple complexes are different. These show a great variety of sizes. Majority of them have a standard width ranging between 8 to 10 cm and the length varies between 18 to 22 cm. Their thickness ranges from 1.5 to 2 cm. A few sites like Asandi, Talgunda and Kuppagadde have yielded extremely smaller ones along with the above types. Such tiles are as small as to have a breadth of 4.5 to 5 cm and might not be more than 12 cm in length. All these varieties are neatly shaped with straight edges and are of an even plane. The surface is smoothened and the angles are more accurately treated. They also have a finer fabric. All these features hint about the high workmanship and skill of the tile makers of the Early Medieval Karnataka and give an impression that they had a better devise to mechanically produce them. The profuse use of these tiles during this period seems to have created a greater demand, which lead to innovations. This is exemplified in the decorated tiles. The tops of the decorated tiles are bent at wide angle and project up to 2 to 3 cm. The outer side of this bend was decorated in special cases with beaded borders and rosette medallions at the center. These designs seem to have been produced from moulds.

The shape of these Early Medieval tiles is basically a continuation of the earlier specimens. However, the typological evolution is also obvious. One end (bottom) of the invariably, an angular bend while the other end (tip) is either straight or triangular, or two or three pronged. Those with semi-circular ends are noticed in Asandi and similar ones are reported from Talakadu also.

The specimens found at Ikkeri are 8.5 to 7.5 cm in width, 22 cm in length and 1.1 to 1.5 cm in thickness and these tiles represent the 16th century developments of this type. These have relatively a superior fabric than any of the previous types and have polished surface. The age-old shapes and designs continued to be produced.

The above review of the shapes and sizes of these tiles reveals certain trends like diminishing size, increasing workmanship and accuracy of measurement as time advanced and this trend continued till the Late Medieval period as witnessed in the Ikkeri specimens. The gradual decrease in size during the post Kadamba-Ganga period is also revealed in the Talakad excavations. Here, those found in the later levels are smaller in dimension than those of the earlier layers (Devaraj 1996:56). The former ones are of the smallest variety to be found in this region. The tiles found in Gangaikondacholapuram are also of such smallest dimension and they are found in the palace-complex, probably belonging to the 11th -12th century A.D. Thus the smaller varieties had come into vogue during the Early Medieval period itself at least in certain pockets. Though such a variation in dimension might have been a result of different functional requirements, to explain the exact function of these smaller varieties remains vague. At present we can clearly distinguish between the tiles of the Kadamba period and those of the Rastrakuta-later Chalukya periods. If the typological evolution of these tiles is worked out in detail, they can be one of the handiest yardsticks for relative chronology in the Karnataka region.

Use of these Tiles

No doubt, these tiles were arranged on the sloppy roofs as any other tiles, but there are several questions regarding the functional value of different shapes and sizes. The earliest specimens were as large as the Sattavahana tiles. They were also provided with holes at the bottom, most probably to fasten them to the roof like the Early Historic ones as demonstrated by Hartel (1993:Pl 23) and Howell (1995: Pl VII B). It is quite possible that the Early Historic tiles devolved into this type through gradual flattening of their surface. The tile makers of the Kadamba period gradually developed a better substitute for the holes i.e. bending the bottom backwards so that it can hold the rafter firmly. As mentioned earlier, the *antarala* ceiling of the Santinatha temple at Bandalike presents a conventional representation of such a roof. Here the tiles are arranged in a row and each row overlaps its lower course.

One would wonder whether the different shapes of tiles of a particular period were used at different places on a single roof since all such shapes are available in the context of a single complex. It seems that the tiles with curved, pronged, triangular and straight ends were not decorative but were functional. We cannot imagine where and how the decorative tiles were used since their tip is bent and decorated they could not have been used anywhere else than in the lowermost course. The fact that they are found in the temple premises would suggest that they were used for religious structures, but how the tiny tiles of 5 cm breadth were utilized for roofing is still a most intriguing point.

Conclusion

The foregoing review of the Ancient and Medieval tiles of Karnataka leads to several problems regarding them. We have yet to work out a better understanding of their chronological span, typological evolution, exact pattern of their use etc. However they seem to be quite significant, because at present we have a dearth of archaeological information from the Medieval settlements and residences. The tiles can provide us some information about these settlements and they also can be indicators of the relative chronology of such sites.

Acknowledgements

I gratefully acknowledge the help received by my students and friends during my fieldwork, especially Sri Sripad Rao.

REFERENCES

Chitnis, K.N. 1974. *Keladi Polity*. Dharwar, Karnataka University Publications.

Devaraj, D. *et al* 1996. *Excavations at Talakad*. Mysore, Directory Archaeology and Museums.

Dhakey, M.A. (ed) 1986. *An Encyclopaedia of Indian Temple Architecture, Upper Dravidadesa, Early and Middle Period,* New Delhi: American Institute of Indian Studies.

Gopal, B.R. 1985. *Corpus of Kadamba Inscriptions*, Sirsi.

Hartel, H, 1976. Some Results of the excavation at Sonkh, A Preliminary Report, *The excavations at Sonkh Exhibition*, New Delhi, National Museum (reprinted from German Scholars on India Vol.II).

————1993. *Excavation At Sonkh, 2500 years of a Town in Mathura district*. Berlin: Dietrich Reimer Verlag.

Hegde, Rajaram, 1997. "*Use of Bricks in Temple Architecture of Medieval Karnataka: 10th to 13th cent. A.D.*" Proceedings of the Fifth Session of the Indian Art History Congress, Bhubhanesvar. Guwahati: Directorate of Museums.

Sarvamangala G. 1997. "*Haigunda - an Ancient River Settlement of Karnataka*" Proceedings of the Fourth Indian Conference of Marine Archaeology. Goa, Deptt. of Marine Archaeology.

Hawell, J.R. 1995. *Excavations at Sannathi 1986-89*. New Delhi, Archaeological Survey of India.

Marshall, John. 1983. (Second Reprint) *Monuments of Sanchi*. Delhi: Swathi publications.

Narasimhamurthy, A.V. *et al*. 1997. *Excavations at Banavasi 1969-72*. Mysore, Directorate of Archaeology and Museums.

Sharma, I.K. 1992. *Temples of the Gangas of Karnataka*. New Delhi, Archaeological Survey of India.

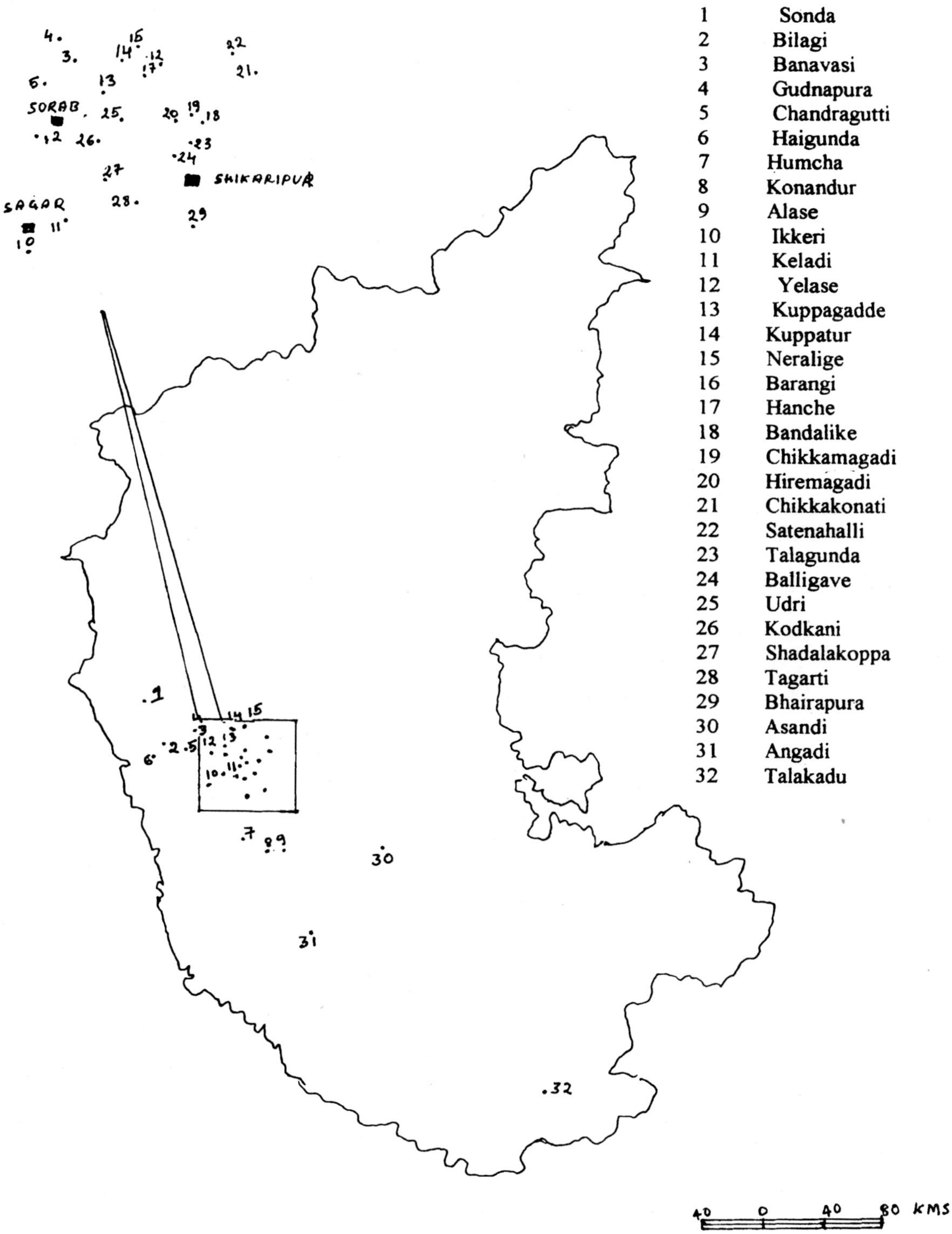
SORAB
SHIKARIPUR
SAGAR
1 Sonda
2 Bilagi
3 Banavasi
4 Gudnapura
5 Chandragutti
6 Haigunda
7 Humcha
8 Konandur
9 Alase
10 Ikkeri
11 Keladi
12 Yelase
13 Kuppagadde
14 Kuppatur
15 Neralige
16 Barangi
17 Hanche
18 Bandalike
19 Chikkamagadi
20 Hiremagadi
21 Chikkakonati
22 Satenahalli
23 Talagunda
24 Balligave
25 Udri
26 Kodkani
27 Shadalakoppa
28 Tagarti
29 Bhairapura
30 Asandi
31 Angadi
32 Talakadu
40 0 40 80 KMS

Fig. 1.

Tarati Copper Plate Grant of Kind Govindacandra of the Gahadavala Dynasty, Samvat 1173

D.P. DUBEY*

These copper plates, of which the contents are here published for the first time, were recently unearthed by a Brahmin cultivator in a mound at a place called Tarti, situated one km to the west of Holagarh Development Block headquarters in the Soraon tehsil of the Allahabad district, U.P., when he was leveling the south-west corner of the mound for appropriating land to his adjoining field. They were handed over to Mr. B.P. Verma of Allahabad, who lent them to me for examination and decipherment. On my visit to this village on 28th July, 2001, I did not notice any ancient antiquities of special interest. The village has, however, a small mound strewn with medieval bricks and pottery pieces. I am editing the inscription from the original plates as well as from the photographs supplied to me by Mr. Verma.

The plates were found carefully packed in a stone box, 55x51x12 cm externally, closed with a lid of the small material[1]. The plates are two in number, with their edges turned up, so as to serve as rims to protect the writting on the surface. One of them measures 37 cm broad by 28.5 cm high; the other is slightly smaller measuring 37 cm broad by 27.6 cm high, so as so fit into the larger one both the plates are shouldered on a circular ring passing through a hole in the centre of the lower part of the first plate and a corresponding hole in the centre of the upper part of the second plate. A bell-shaped massive seal, 8 cm high from top to bottom, fits on to the ring, about 1.3 cm thick and 7.2 cm in diameter, by a circular opening in the lower end of it. The surface of the seal is circular, about 6.2 cm in diameter. In relief on a slightly countersunk surface, it has, at the top, a representation of Guruda, with the body of a man and the head of a bird, kneeling half front and half to the proper right, but with the face turned quite round in profile to the proper right; across the centre, the legend *Srimad -Govindacandradevah*, in Nagari letters about 1.4 cm high; and below the legend, a conch-shell. The seal is of the usual Gahadavala type. Also the second plate itself has a barbed arrow below it, engraved at the proper right end of the inscription. The plates are 2 cm thick. The weight of the plates together with seal is 6.5 kg.

The plates are inscribed on one side only. The inscription covers a space of 32.5 cm by 25 cm on one plate and 32.5 by 24 cm on the other and consists of 39 lines of writing, of which 19 lines are engraved on the first plate and the remaining 20 lines on the second plate; each line contains letters ranging from 36 to 40 in number. The letters are well shaped; their height is about 1.2 cm. The letters do not show through on the reverse side of the plates at all. The inscription has suffered corrosion so that at some places the writing is quite illegible. But the reading of it may be restored from the other known records of the dynasty to which this grant belongs. Otherwise, the inscription is in a good condition.

*4A/2/1, Muirabad, Allahabad-211002 (U.P.)

The characters are in *Nagari*, the language is metrical Sanskrit in the first 13 and last 10 lines, which contain respectively the usual genealogy of the Gahadavala king Govindacandra of Kanauj and Varanasi and the imprecatory and benedictory verses. The remaining 16 lines are in Sanskrit prose and represent the formal historical portion of the record. As regards to Orthography, the letter *b* is denoted by the sign for *v* everywhere; the dental sibilant is frequently employed instead of the palatal and the palatal occasionally instead of the dental; a consonant following subscript *r* have often been doubled; combinations of consonants and nasals have been represented by both *anusvara* and a nasal of the same class. The letters *r, v, dh* and *c* in some places appear very much alike in form. Two forms of *bh* are noticed in line 23, the form of *bh* in *bhaume* being different from that of the regular form in *bhaumadine*. Regarding the vowal signs attention may be drawn to the different forms of medial *e* represented by *a* left-slanting top-stroke in *ararelavase* in line 24, though generally the left vertical form is employed, e.g. Instances of scribal errors of writing occur in *udadarah* (line 3) and in *ararela* (line 24), miswritten for *udarah* and *arela* respectively; besides some other irregularities due to the *apabhramsa* influence such as *Phaguna* for *Phaguna* (line 23). The record contains a few other mistakes, which have been corrected either in the text or in the footnotes accompanying it.

The date of the record is given in lines 22-23, both in words and in decimal figures, as *Tuesday, the 5th day of the the dark half of Phalguna in the (Vikrama) Samvat 1173*, when the Sun had entered the zodiac sign of aquarius (Kumbha-Sankranti). For V.S. 1173, *expired* the corresponding date, by the *purnimanta* reckoning, would be *January* 23, CE 1117; the said *tithi* having begun on that day at 16.20 hours and ended on the next at 14.10 hours.

The inscription begins, like all the other epigraphs (46 in number) of the Gahadavala king Govindacandra that have so far been published, with nine verses in different metres containing his genealogy, and ends with eleven benedictory and imprecatory verses. The formal portion is contained in the rest of the epigraph and is, as usual, in prose. I have given in full text of in inscription, but have ommited the translation, because it contains really nothing (excepting the date and the names of the localities and donee mentioned in it) that is not known to us from some of the other grants of the dynasty. The writer's name is not given[2].

The Gahadavala king Govindacandra is stated to have granted, on the date indicated above, the village called Tarambi situated in the *pattala* of Singaraura, after bathing in the Veni at his camp residence at a place called Arela, to the Brahmini Pandit Sri Sidhusarma who belonged to the Sankritya *gotra* and the Sankritya, Angirasa and Gaurivita *pravaras*. He was the son of Pandit Sri Yasakantha. The gift was permanent and the dones was entitled to enjoy all taxes including *bhaga* (share of crops), *bhoga* (periodical offerings), *kara* (taxes in general), and the special tax known as *pravanikara*[3], which has been variously explained.

In respect of the localities mentioned in the record, it is gratifying to note that all of them can be identified beyond all possibility of doubt. Vani is the famous confluence of the rivers Ganga, Yamuna and the invisible Sarasvati at Prayaga (Allahabad)[4]. It occurs also in another copperplate grant of Samvat 1184 of king Govindacandra[5].

We may without hesitation identify Tarambi *grama* with the village at which the plates were found and which is now called Tarti, a hamlet of the village of Hansarajpur, one km west of Holagarh, on the metalled road running from Soraon to Dahiyawan, in pargana and tehsil Soraon of the Allahabad district. It is about 9 km northwest of Soraon and 32 km north of Allahabad.

Arela is the the same as the modern village of Arail, the headquarters of the pargana of the same name, on the right side of the confluence of rivers Ganga and Yamuna, opposite to the Allahabad fort. It is of undoubted antiquity and also attracts large gathering of pilgrims during the *Maghamela*. It was the locality plundered by the orders of Sikandar Lodi in CE-1491, as stated by Ni'amatullah in his *Tarikh-Khan-i-Jahan*[6]. The *Virabhanudayakavya* of Madhava (composed in about CE-1555) says that Alarkanagar or Alarkapura stood on the bank of the Ganga near its confluence with the Yamuna[7].Vacaspati Misra (15th century) and Mitra Misra (17th century) mentions it as Alarkanagara[8], while Narayana Bhatta (16th century) mentioned it as Alarkapura[9]. But Vidyapati (CE 1368-1475), the famous poet of Mithila, states that a mud fort existed at the village of Arela, which was located to the south of Prayaga[10]. In fact, 'Alarka' is a sanskritised form, but neither of the two forms-Arela or Arail-would account for the term 'Alarka' linguistically. It was here that the Baghela chief Virasimha entered into a friendly alliance with the Mughal emperor Babur[11]. The Baghela rulers of Gahora-Rewa used to go to this place and live on the banks of the Ganga[12]. The accounts given in the *Humayun-nama*, written by the princess Gulbadan as well as by Jauhar, would make it clear that Raja Virabhanu (Pirbhan) Baghela, who happened to be at Arail, came to the rescue of the Mughal emperor Humayun against the pursuing Afghan army of Sher Shah Suri. He entertained him at Arail for a few days, supplied his retinue with provisions and escorted him to Kara-Manikpur[13]. The Mughal emperor Akbar granted Raja Ramacandra Baghela, the pargana of Arail and Piyag (Prayaga), together with its dependencies, as Jagir in CE 1569[14]. In his elaborate note on the 'Chaurasis', Elliot says that 'Raja Ram Baghela is said to have given 360 villages to the brahmanas of Arail[15]. Akbar changed the name of Arail to Handiabas[16], but the change was short lived. The Jangamas, a prominent Saiva sect, held some *bighas* of land in Madad- I -Mash, possessed one *gumbad* (bastion) and a *bagh* (garden) in the town *(Qasbah)* of Arail/Arayal in the time of Akbar[17]. Joseph Tieffenthaler (CE 1766-67) says that "Arel was a town, not far from the confluence, which formerly had a castle for defending the crossing of the Ganga"[18]. He further notes that the fortress of Arail was under the control of a Hindu Raja[19]. Remains of an old mud fort still exist there. There are several temples at Arail, of which those dedicated to Vani Madhava and Somesvaranath are old, the latter contains a defaced Sanskrit inscription. In CE 1600 Raja Man Singh of Jaipur is said to have visited the temple of Somesvaranath[20]. The temple of Veni Madhava contains a stone inscription fixed by the side of entrance to the *garbhagriha*. It mentions the names of Sivaji Vitthal Vincurkar and Girijabai Vincurkar who did some repair works in the temple in Saka 1707(=CE 1785) and in Saka 1866(=CE 1933), respectively. In CE 1735 Muhammad Khan Bangash laid seize of Arail but was defeated by the forces of Shah Nawaj Khan[21]. In CE 1751, Ahmad Khan Bangash, the Nawab Wazir of Farrukhabad, captured the town of Arail for attacking the fort of Allahabad from the south, but was compelled to raise the siege by the forces of Safdar Jung and the Marathas[22]. Firminger says that 'in 1764. The British arms'23 conquered Allahabad and Terhar or Areyl.

Singaraura, the headquarters of the *Pattala*, still exists under the same name on the left bank of the Ganga at a distance of 35 km northwest from Allahabad. A metalled road leading to the northeast for about 2 km from the place joins the Allahabad-Lucknow Highway at Mansurabad. The present name of Singraur is a distorted form of Sringaverapura, an ancient town mentioned in early literature, the site of which is marked by a great mound on the left bank of the Ganga. The name of Sringaverapura occurs on five occasions in the Ramayana[24], Guha, the chief of boatsmen, welcomed Rama, Sita and Laksmana there during their exile. The *Mahabharata*[25] describes it, where Rama crossed the Ganga, as a *tirtha*. Kalidasa refer to this place in his *Raghuvansa*[26], though the actual name is not found in the verse. Another reference to it is found in the *Uttararamacharita* of Bhavabhuti[27]. It is mentioned once in the *Bhusundi Ramayana*[28]. The *Adhyatma Ramayana* refers to this place thrice on different occasions[29]. During the Mughal period it was a town of considerable importance and was the headquarters of pargana Singraur which had a brick fort on the bank of the Ganga[30], but Safdar Jung (the Nawab Wazir of Avadh) shifted the headquarters of the pargana to Nawabganj because the Ganga had washed away the greater part of the town in the middle of the eighteenth century[31]. Joseph Tieffenthaler, who toured the district of Allahabad during 1766-67, refers to it as Sangror[32]. The ancient mound at Singraur was excavated during 1977-1980, which has yielded a four-fold sequence of cultures ranging in date from the 8th century BCE to the 13th century CE. An outstanding discovery was of a large-sized rectangular burnt brick tank of the Kusana period, which was fed by the waters of the Ganga while in spate[33]. This is held to be the largest tank ever unearthed in an excavation in the country and is described as the marvel of ancient Indian hydraulic engineering. A cache of thirteen Gahadavala silver coins, presumably of Govindacandra, with some sundry jewellery in a small pot, were found there during excavation from period IV[34].

TEXT35

[Metres: vv. 1,3,10,11,,13-18, Anustubh; vv. 2,19, Indravajra; vv. 4,7, Sardulavikridita; vv. 5,6,8,20, Vasantatilaka; v. 9, Drutavilambita; v. 12, Salini]

REFERENCES

Abul Halim, *History of the Lodi Sultans*, Idarah-I-Adabiyat, Delhi, 1974. Repr. pp. 68; K.L.Srivastava, *The Position of Hindus under the Delhi Sultanate*, 1206-1526, Munshiram Manoharlal, Delhi, 1980. Pp.85; *Virabhanudayakavyam* of Madhva, text and tr. by K.K. Lale and A. S. Upadhyaya, Rewa Darbar, Rewa, 1938. Introduction, pp. 23.

Adhyatma Ramayana, text and tr. by Swami Tapasyananda, Ramakrishan Math, Madras, n.d., II. 5.60, 8.14, VI. 14.40.

Ain-I-Akbari of Abul Fazl, tr. by H.S. Jarrett, Asiatic Society of Bengal, Calcutta, 1949, Vol. II, pp.172.

Another example is The Saheth-Maheth Plate of Govindracandra, Samvat 1186, edited by D.R. Sahni in the *Epigraphia Indica*, Vol. XI (1911-12), pp. 20-26, which was also found packed in an earthen box, 61 cm square and 7.5 cm high externally, closed with a lid of the same material.

Another copper-plate grant of Govindacandra, dated *Phalguna-vadi* 15, Tuseday, Samvat 1196 (=CE 1139), also refers to Samkritya, Angirasa and Gauricit as the names of three *pravaras* of the donee (D.C. Sircar, "Some Gahadavala Grants", *Epigraphia Indica*, Vol. XXXV, pp. 208, line 19). In the *Sanskrit* English *Dictionary* of Monier-Williams (Southern Publications, Madras, 1987, reprint, pp. 370) we come across Gauravita, Gaurivita and Gaurivita forms of the name of several Samans' mentioned in the Brahmana texts. The *Gotra-pravara-nibandha-kadambakam* of P.Chentsalrao (Government Branch Press, Mysore, 1900) refers to the name of a *pravara* as Gauruvita at one place (p. 245), but at another as Gaurivita (pp.168, appendix pp. 25). According to D.C. Sircar *(Epigraphia Indica*, Vol. XXXV, pp.206, fn. 5), the correct form of the name is Gaurivita.

Bhuparikramanam of *Vidyapati*, Ed. By Munishwar Jha, Mithila Sanskrit Parishad, Calcutta, 1976, III. 20-21.

Bhusundi Ramayana (Purvakhanda), Ed. By B.P. Singh, Vishwavidyalaya Prakashan, Varanasi, 1975. 103.142.

B.K. Thapar (ed.), *Indian Archaeology 1977-78-A Review*, ASI, Delhi, 1980, pp.56.

Debala Mitra (ed.), *Indian Archaeology 1979-80-A Review*, ASI, Delhi, 1983, pp.74.

Expressed by a symbol.

For a discussion on Veni see, D.P. Dubey, Prayaga: *The Site of Kumbha Mela*, Aryan Book International, and Delhi, 2001, pp.14-23.

For non-mention of the writer's name also see, "The Kamauli Plate of Govindacandra of Samvat 1171", Ed. By F. Kielhorn, Epigraphia *Indica*, Vol. IV (1896-97), pp.101-103.

From the photographs of seal and plates.

H.M. Elliot, *Supplemental Glossary of Terms used in the Northwestern Provinces, 1844*, Ed. By John Beames under the title History of Folklore and Distribution of the Races of the North-Western Provinces of India. Gian Publication, Delhi, 1980, repr. Vol. II, pp. 56.

Humayun-nama, tr. by A.S. Beveridge, Low Price Publications, Delhi, 1996, repr., pp. 135-136; R.P. Tripathi, *Rise and Fall of the Mughal Empire*, Central Book Depot, Allahabad, 1956, pp. 96.

Ibid, pp. 54; A.L.Srivastava, *First Two Nawabs of Avadh*, Shivalal Agrawal & Company, Agra, 1954, second edition, pp.163.

M.A. Ansari, *Administrative Documents of Mughal India*, B.R. Publishing Corporation, Delhi, 1984, pp. 2, 16-17; documents no. 2 and 3, dated CE 1574.

Mahabharata, ed. By V.S. Sukthankar et.al., BORI, Poona, 1933-59, III. 83.62.

Muntakhub-ut-Tawarikh of Abul Qadir Badauni, tr. by George S.A., Ranking, W.H. Lowe, Wolseley Haig, Asiatic Society of Bengal, Calcutta, 1898-1925, Vol. II, pp. 124.

Raghuvansa of Kalidasa, in *Kalidasa Granthavali*, ed. By R.P. Dwivedi, BHU, Varanasi, 1976, XII. 62.

Ramayana of Valmiki, Ed. By Vasudeva Luxman Shastri Pansikar, Indological Book House, Delhi, 1983, repr. II. 50.26. 83.19, VI. 111.28, 113.4, 20.

Read arelavase, ra is superfluous in *ararelavase*.

Read *kumbhasankrantavanke=api*.

Read *phalguna*^{0}.

Read *ityudarah*, one of the da is superfluous.

Read *vajinah*.

S.N. Sinha, *Subah of Allahabad under the Great Mughals*, Jamia Millia Islamia, Delhi, 1974, pp. 34, fn.7.

S.N. Sinha, *The Mid Gangetic Region in the Eighteenth Century*, Gitanjali Publishing House, Delhi, 1986, second impression, pp.53.

The Bhadavana Grant of Govindacandra of Kanauj, Samvat 1184, Ed. By N.C.Mehta, *Epigraphia Indica*, Vol. XIX (1927-28), pp.293, lines 13-14, reads.

The real nature of *pravanikara* cannot be determined. Roma Niyogi (*The History of the Gahadavala Dynasty*, Oriental Book Agency, Calcutta, 1959, pp.176) says that '*pravanikara* may have been some kind of road-cess'. According to D.C. Sircar, it was probably a tax on foreign merchants (Some Gahadavala Grants, *Epigraphia Indica*, Vol. XXXV, (1963-64), pp. 208, or "it was a tax levied from a class of merchants" (*Indian Epigraphical Glossary*, Motilal Banarsidass, Delhi, 1966, pp.262).

Tristhalisetu of Narayana Bhatt, ed. Ganesh Shastri Gokhale, Anandashram Press, Poona, 1915, pp.15.

Tirthacintamani of Vacaspati Misra, Ed. By Kamalakrishna Smrititirtha, Asiatic Society of Bengal, Calcutta, 1912, pp. 23; *Viramitrodaya* of Mitra Misra, Vol. X : *Tirthaprakasa*, ed. By Vishnu Prasad, Chowkhamba Sanskrit Series Office, Banaras, 1917, pp. 325.

Uttararamacaritam of Bhavabhuti, tr. by P.V. Kane and C.N. Joshi, Motilal Banarasidass, Delhi, 1971, fifth edition, I. 21.

Virabhanudayakavyam, II. 62, III.2 (Alarkanagara), XII. 29 (Alarkapura).

W.K. Firminger (ed), *The Fifth Report from the Select Committee of the House of Commous on the Affairs of the East India Company, July 1812*, Asiatic Society of Bengal, Calcutta, 1917, pp. 467.

Studies in Indo-Roman Trade to Indian Ocean Archaeology: Brief Review of Research

SUNIL GUPTA*

The historical discourse on early maritime contact between the Mediterranean World and India has its own long tradition. To trace the evolution of studies in long distance Mediterranean sea trade with the Orient we have to go back to the 15-16th century when the first editions of ancient Graeco-Roman works of geography were prepared from surviving manuscripts and published. This was the time when Europe was engaged in a major maritime quest to the east: to discover the long sea route to India by circumnavigating Africa. Columbus, seeking to discover a new western route to India, came upon America in 1492. Vasco Da Gama successfully rounded the Cape of Good Hope to reach Calicut in 1497. In this context, the resuscitation of ancient Hellenic knowledge of Oriental lands, especially India, was in keeping with the mood and spirit of the times.

The *Geographia* of Claudius Ptolemy was, a cartographic representation of the ancient world constructed in 2nd century A.D. Egypt was the first major work of Hellenic geography to be printed in 1477 (Gole 1983:25-30). The *Geographia* provides a detailed map of the Indian Subcontinent which includes the locations of coastal and inland settlements, names of rivers, river-mouths/deltas, mountains, coastal tracts and gulfs. Ptolemy set down the co-ordinates of all these places. Though Ptolemy's map of India is irrelevant for modern cartography (the shape of the subcontinent being highly distorted), it is still a goldmine of information for historical geographers (for review of Ptolemy's map see Gole 1983:25-30).

The first editions of the *Periplus Maris Erythraei* were printed in the 16th century in Italy. There were quick succeeding editions in the same century (Schoff 1912/74: 17). In 1507 was discovered a Medieval period copy of the Roman map of the world made in the 4th century A.D. The discovery was made public in 1511. The map was printed in 1598 by the Hapsburg Chancellor, Konrad Peutinger. The *Tabula Peutingeriana* or Peutinger Tables, as this ancient map is called, contains a section on India (again highly distorted) providing locations of towns, rivers and physical features.

The publication of these important redactions of ancient Roman geographical accounts of the East fuelled an emergent scholarship which carries on unabated. A number of translations of the *Periplus* and the *Geographia*, many of them appended with critical commentaries, were undertaken in the subsequent centuries. As many as twenty different editions of the *Periplus* have appeared since the first Italian editions. A few of the notable translations/commentaries are those by J.W. McCrindle (1879), W.H. Schoff (1912), G.B.W. Huntingford (1980) and L.Casson (1989). Editions of the *Geographia* of Ptolemy appeared in 1533, 1838, 1843 and 1883. The most critical redaction of the section of the

*Allahabad Museum.

Geographia relating to India has been done by J.W. McCrindle (1884:313-427).

Concommitant with the preparation of critical editions of the *Periplus* and *Geographia* was the emergence of a sub-stream of studies on the historical geography of India based on the data contained in these two books. Very simply the imperative here was to locate, by identifying place names on latest maps or through actual exploration, the settlements (especially ports) detailed in the *Periplus* and the *Geographia*. Of course, geographical references from other contemporaneous Roman and Indian texts were also taken into account. These parallel sources are the *Indika* of Megasthenes (4th c. B.C.), *Geographia* of Strabo (1st c. A.D.), the *Natural History* of Pliny (1st c.A.D.) and the *Jatakas*.

The first efforts towards identification of Indian settlements mentioned in the *Geographia* and other contemporary Roman and Indian works was made by F. Wilford in a series of articles published in the *Asiatick Researches* between 1794 to 1822. Christian Lassen in his monumental work *Indische Alterthumskunde* attempted a similar, and more comprehensive survey. This work was compiled between 1847-53. To illustrate Lassen's book, Henri Kiepert published the *Map of Ancient India with the Indian, classical and principal Modern Names* in 1853. The next major contribution was that of the French historian, M. Vivien de Saint-Martin, whose study *Etude sur la geographie Grecque et Latine d'Inde* published in 1860 with a special focus on the evidence of the *Geographia*, became a source-book for historical cartographers and explorers. Among the first fieldworkers to survey for sites of the *Periplus-Geographia* was Alexander Cunningham who published the *Ancient Geography of India* in 1871. In 1874, Henry Yule published his *Map of Ancient India*, mainly drawing from Saint-Martin's work. We may mention also the survey on the western coast of India carried out by Fergusson and Burgess in the 1870s who made claim to discovering a few settlements mentioned in Greco-Roman accounts. J.W. McCrindle published his translations of the *Periplus* and *Geographia* in the 1879 and 1884 editions of the *Indian Antiquary*. McCrindle's commentaries became the basic source on India for the later critical editions of the Periplus prepared by W.H. Schoff (1912), Huntingford (1980) and Casson (1989). In context of major works of historical geography focusing on Hellenic texts, we may also mention the detailed account of Nundolal Dey (1921) to precise the locations of the mouths of the Ganga mentioned in the *Geographia*. In the present study, a comprehensive review of the previous identifications of the coastal settlements named in the *Periplus-Geographia* has been attempted. The review integrates archaeological and geomorphological data emerging from prospections on the Indian coast during the last five decades.

By the beginning of the present century substantial primary records had accumulated for historical reconstruction of early Indo-Mediterranean contact to be possible. Besides the publication of old Greaco-Roman geographical and travel accounts and their informative corollaries, there were also now available material finds of long distance Roman maritime trade with India. The main artefactual indicators of trade were the Roman coins and coin hoards being regularly discovered across the peninsular India since 1787.

Among the first histories of Indo-Roman trade to be written was *Intercourse between India and the Western World* by H.G. Rawlinson (1916). A few years earlier Radhakumud Mookerji (1912) had published his seminal work *A History of Indian Shipping and Maritime Activity from the Earliest Times*. Mookerji's book records critical references to early contact with the Roman empire in Indian textual sources. The first reconstuction with main focus on Indo-Roman sea trade (as contrasted with overland trade) was undertaken by E.H. Warmington (1928) in *The Commerce between the Roman Empire and India*. Warmington's contemporary, P. Charlesworth was to make his contribution to studies of Indo-Roman trade in his book *Trade Routes and Commerce of the Roman Empire* (1951).

A seminal contribution to understanding Roman sea commerce with India was made with the publication of the report on excavations at the site of Arikamedu on the Coromandel coast in 1945 by Mortimer Wheeler and his associates (see Wheeler *et al* 1946:17-124). The Arikamedu diggings yielded a variety of Mediterranean artefacts (terra sigillata pottery, amphorae, Roman glassware, lamps and beads). The retrieval of a substantial quantum of original Mediterranean "indicators of trade" from stratified contexts opened the possibilities of reconstructing archaeological patterns of long distance Indo-Mediterranean sea trade. Wheeler drew from his experience of Arikamedu to author the first archaeological account of Indo-Roman trade in his book *Rome Beyond the Imperial Frontiers* (Wheeler 1954 , also see Wheeler 1976). Subsequent to Wheeler, Arikamedu was excavated by the French archaeologist J-M. Casal (1949). The third and latest expedition to Arikamedu (1989-1993) comprised an Indian-American team led by Vimala Begley (see Begley *et al.* 1996).

A large volume of research papers, seminar proceedings and monographs on early Mediterranean maritime trade with India have been released since Wheeler's historic excavation at Arikamedu. We may mention here some of the important publications such as *New Studies in Roman Commerce with the East* by M.G. Raschke (1978); *Roman Coins from India* by Paula Turner (1989); the latest translation of the *Periplus* by Casson refered above; *Rome and India, The Ancient Sea Trade* edited by V. Begley and R.D. de Puma (1992); *Ancient Rome and India,* edited by R.M. Cimino (1994); and *Archaeology and Tradition, Early Maritime Contacts in the Indian Ocean* edited by H.P. Ray and J-F. Salles (1996). The broader perspective is presented in *The Indian Ocean in Antiquity* edited by Reade (1996).

Review of Archaeological Sources

The early Indian Ocean as a historical idea has been in strong circulation in recent years. The archaeo-historical concept of the Indian Ocean is underpinned by the results of field work in the last 50 years. A brief review of archaeology on the Indian Ocean rim is presented.

In the Red Sea region, perhaps the most significant excavation from the point of view of the Indian trade has been at the site of Quseir al-Qadim (ancient *Myos Hormos*) on the Egyptian Red Sea coast. Quseir, a flourishing port of the 1st-2nd centuries A.D., was excavated by an American mission in 1979, 1980, 1982. Presently, a British team led by David Peacock of the University of Southampton is excavating Quseir. Excavations are presently going on at Berenice, another important Egyptian port active in the Indian trade. The Berenice excavations are being directed by Steven Sidebotham of the University of Delaware, USA. Earlier surface surveys of Berenice have been conducted by Meredith (1958: 56-70) and Riley (in Sidebotham *et al* 1989:127-166). Field surveys of the ancient desert roads connecting the Red Sea ports with emporia on the Nile have been conducted by Zitterkopf and Sidebotham (1989:155-193) and J.Y. Empereur of the French Mission in Egypt (personal communication). North of Quseir, close to the Gulf of Sinai, the late Roman fortified settlement of Abu Shah'r has been prospected by Sidebotham and his associates (Sidebotham *et al* 1989:127-166). In the neighbouring Gulf of Eilat Sinai, Flinder (1977:127-139; 1989:32-43) has explored the Island of Jezirat Fara'un which he identifies with the Biblical port of Ezion-Gebor from which King Solomon's ships set sail for the legendary Ophir (in India?). Explorations have been carried out in the eighties along the Jordanian coast of the Gulf of Eilat and Red Sea (for review of fieldwork see Sidebotham 1986; Bowersock 1983).

Along the southern Red Sea, prospections on the Saudi Arabian coast have been scarce. The reports of recent fieldwork on the Saudi coast can be found in the pages of *Atlal,* the official Saudi journal of archaeology. Excavation on the Ethiopian coast was undertaken by an Italian Mission in the thirties (Mordini 1967:19-25). Recently, Casson (1984) has discussed the location of the ancient Ethiopian harbour of Adulis mentioned in the *Periplus.* We may also mention here the ongoing excavations at Axum, the ancient Ethiopian capital in the early centuries A.D., by a British team. The excavations are being directed by David Phillipson of the University of Cambridge. Earlier, Axum was excavated by the British archaeologist Neville Chittick.

The Gulf of Aden littoral comprises the coastal tracts of the modern states of Yemen (including Socotra Island) and southern Oman to its north and Somalia to the south. This gulf was a great maritime "crossroad" in the period of Indo-Roman trade, supplying the Mediterranean world with large quantities of incense (frankinsense and myrrh) and providing berthing facilities for merchant vessels bound for India.

Since the fifties, fieldwork programmes in southern Yemen/Oman have brought to light the classical civilisation of south Arabia. Among the excavated sites are ancient ports mentioned in the *Periplus* and other Graeco-Roman accounts. The first important excavation in this region was at Timna, the capital of the Sabean kingdom at the turn of the Christian Era. Timna was excavated by the team of the American Foundation for the Study of Man (van Beek 1958:141-152; Cleveland 1965). The ancient harbour site at Khor Rori (identified with the port of *Moscha* in the *Periplus*) was also excavated by the American Foundation team in 1952 (Albright 1982) and again in 1960-62 (Cleveland 1960: 14-26). Recently, the ceramics from the American excavations at Khor Rori were studied afresh by Kervran and Yule (1993:69-106). Excavations at Shabwa, the ancient capital of the Hadhramauti kings, were undertaken by a French mission in the eighties. Since 1985, a joint Russian-Yemeni team has been excavating at the site of Qana (Bir Ali). This ancient port, flourishing between 1st-7th centuries A.D. as revealed stratigraphically, has been identified with *Kane Emporium* of the *Periplus* (preliminary reports on Qana by Sedov 1992:110-137; 1996:11-35). For a bibliographical review of the latest research on archaeology of southern Arabia see Avazini (1994:53-56). For the latest epigraphical evidence from southern Arabia for date of the *Periplus* see Robin (1991: 1-30).

On the Somali coast, a British team prospected the ancient port-site of Ras Hafun, identified with the harbour of *Opone* in the *Periplus* (Chittick 1976). Fieldwork at Ras Hafun and other sites on the Swahili coast has been reported in the pages of the Journal Azania of the British Institute in Eastern Africa (Nairobi, Kenya). Casson (1986:179-182) has critically studied the geography of Ras Hafun while associating it with *Opone* of the *Periplus*.

A number of Early Historic coastal settlements have been excavated in the Gulf region since the fifties. The numerous excavations have uncovered evidence of trade contact with India and the Mediterranean World during the Seleucid, Parthian and Sassanian periods (4th century BC to 7th century AD). The prospects of historical archaeology in this region commenced with the excavations of the Danish mission at Failaka (from 1953 to 1963) and Bahrain (between 1955 - 65). Subsequently excavations at both the islands were extended by the French mission which dug Parthian remains at Bahrain between 1979-81 and Hellenistic ruins at Failaka between 1983-89 (for complete review of Failaka - Bahrain excavations see Potts 1990: 103-96). In eastern Arabia, the important site of Thaj (ancient *Gerrha*) was excavated by a Danish team in 1982-83. Further south, at the mouth of the Gulf, the port-site of Ed Dur (ancient *Ommana*) was excavated by an Iraqi expedition in 1973. Thereafter a surface survey of the site resulted in publication of a comprehensive catalogue of pottery (Salles 1984: 241-270). In 1988-89, a multinational European expedition also excavated the site. Another important Early Historic port to be excavated in the lower Gulf is Suhar. Soundings at Suhar were first taken by an American team in 1958. In 1980, a French mission started excavations at the site (Kervran 1996: 37-58). Other excavated Iron Age sites along the Gulf rim are Mlieha, Bidya, Dhahran and Ayn Jawan.

In the Indian Subcontinent, the excavation of the Indo-Roman trading station of Arikamedu in 1945 by Wheeler *et al* (1946:17-124), initiated the archaeology of Indo-Roman trade. Wheeler's excavation of Arikamedu, which still remains the primary site for stratigraphic analysis of impact of Roman sea trade, inspired yet another excavation in 1947 by J.M. Casal (1949). The Arikamedu reports of Wheeler and Casal were reviewed in detail by Vimala Begley (1983:461-482). Begley and her associates went on to excavate Arikamedu for a third time between 1989-1993 (Begley *et al.* 1996).

Since Wheeler's excavation of Arikamedu, diggings at numerous Early Historic sites in the Indian Subcontinent have thrown up evidence of Mediterranean contact. In southern India the important excavated sites are Kaveripattinam, Kanchipuram, Vasavasamudram, Uraiyur, Alagankulam and Kodumanal in the state of Tamil Nadu; Chandravalli, Vadgaon-Madhavpur and Bhatkal in the state of Karnataka; and Amaravati-Dharanikota, Nagarjunakonda, Ghantasala, Yelleswaram, Kudavelli, Kondapur, Dhulikatta, Peddabankur and Salihundam in the state of Andhra Pradesh. In western India, Mediterranean artefacts have been recovered in excavations at Kolhapur, Nasik, Nevasa, Paunar, Paithan, Bhokardan, Soppara, Elephanta, Pauni and Adam in the state of Maharashtra; and at Dwarka, Amreli, Prabhas Patan, Nagara, Shamalaji, Dhatva, Bharuch and Padri in the state of Gujarat. In eastern India, recent reports indicate prolific deposition of Mediterranean material at Tamluk, Berachampa-Chandraketugarh and Kanthi in the state of Bengal. Mathura is the only excavated site in northern India (state of Uttar Pradesh) to yield Mediterranean material.

In Sri Lanka, the important excavation at the port-site of Mantai (Shinde 1987:327-336; Carswell 1992:197-203) brought to light rich evidence of Sri Lanka's Early Historic contacts with the Mediterranean and Indian Ocean lands. Recently, a project of comprehensive coastal exploration has been initiated on the southern coast of Sri Lanka (Bopearachchi 1996: 59-78). Also, another recent excavation was at Ruhuna has yielded evidence of links with India and Southeast Asia (Weisshaar, H-J., H. Roth and W. Wijeyapala 2001).

In Southeast Asia, the most significant excavations from our point of view have been conducted at the sites of Ban Don Ta Phet in Thailand (Glover 1990; 1996:129-158) and Sembiran in Indonesia (Ardika and Bellwood 1991:221-232; Ardika *et al.* 1993: 101-109). Both sites have yielded evidence of early maritime contacts with India.

This brief and sketchy review has been undertaken to point out the shifting pattern of research and the archaeo-historical idea of the early Indian Ocean which seems to be emerging. We need to consolidate this idea through theoritical and fieldwork initiatives.

REFERENCES

Albright, F.P. 1982. *The American Archaeological Expedition to Dhofar, Oman 1952-53*. Washington D.C.: Publication of the American Foundation for Study of Man.

Ardika, I.W. and P. Bellwood. 1991. Sembiran : the Beginnings of Indian contact with Bali, *Antiquity* 65 (247) : 221-232.

Ardika, I.W., P. Bellwood, R.A. Eggleton and D.J. Ellis. 1993. A Single Source for South Asian Export Quality Rouletted Ware, *ME*, XVIII (1) : 101- 109.

Avazini, A. 1994. The Red Sea and Arabia, in *Ancient Rome and India,* (R.M. Cimino Ed.), pp. 53-59. Delhi-Rome: Italian Embassy Cultural Centre and IsMEO.

Begley, V. 1983. Arikamedu Reconsidered, *American Journal of Archaeology,* 87 : 461-482.

Begley, V. and R.D. de Puma. 1992. *Rome and India - The Ancient Sea Trade.* Delhi: Oxford University Press.

Begley, V., P. Francis, Jr., I. Mahadevan, K.V. Raman, S.E. Sidebotham, K.W. Slane and E.L. Will. 1996. *The Ancient Port of Arikamedu - New Excavations and Researches 1989-92*. Pondicherry: Ecole Francaise D'Extreme-Orient.

Bopearachchi, O. 1996. Seafaring in the Indian Ocean : Archaeological Evidence from Sri Lanka, in *Tradition and Archaeology - Early Maritime Contacts in the Indian Ocean* (H.P. Ray and J.-F. Salles Eds.), pp.59-78. Delhi : Manohar.

Bowersock, G.W. 1983. *Roman Arabia*. Cambridge, Massachusetts and London, England: Harvard University Press.

Carswell, J. 1992. The Port of Mantai, in *Rome and India - The Ancient Sea Trade* (V. Begley and Richard Daniel De Puma Eds.), pp. 197-203. (Delhi : Oxford University Press).

Casal, J.M. 1949. *Fouilles de Virampatnam-Arikamedu*. Paris: C. Klincksieck.

Casson, L. 1986. The Location of Tabei (*Periplus Maris Erythraei* 12-13), Journal of Hellenic Studies,106 (1986): 179-182.

Casson, L. 1989. *Periplus Maris Erythraei*. Princeton: Princeton University Press.

Charlesworth, M.P. 1926. *Trade Routes and Commerce of the Roman Empire*. Cambridge.

Chittick, N. 1976. An Archaeological Reconnaissance in the Horn: The British-Somali Expedition, 1975, *Azania* XI: 117-134.

Cleveland, R.L. 1960. The 1960 American Expedition to Dhofar, *Bulletin of the American School of Oriental Research,* 159: 14-26.

1965. *An Ancient South Arabian Necropolis - Objects from the Second Campaign (1951) in the Timna Cemetry*. Baltimore: John Hopkins University.

Dey, N. 1921. The Early Course of the Ganges, *IA,* Vol. L, Jan-March 1921: 8-14, 33-43, 65-72.

Flinder, A. 1977. The Island of Jezirat Fara'un, It's Ancient Harbour, Anchorage and Marine Defence Installations, *The International Journal of Nautical Archaeology and Underwater Exploration* 6.2: 127-139.

Glover, I.C. 1990. *Early Trade between India and Southeast Asia.* Hull: Centre for Southeast Asian Studies.

1996. Recent Archaeological Evidence for Early Maritime Contacts between India and Southeast Asia, in *Tradition and Archaeology, Early Maritime Contacts in the Indian Ocean* (H.P. Ray and J-F. Salles Eds.), pp. 129-158. Delhi: Manohar.

Gole, S. 1983. *India Within the Ganges.* New Delhi: Jayaprints.

Huntingford, G.B.W. 1980. (Ed.) *The Periplus of the Erythraean Sea.* London: Hakluyt Society.

Kervran, M. 1996. Indian Ceramics in Southern Iran and Eastern Arabia, Repertory, Classification and Chronology, in *Tradition and Archaeology, Early Maritime Contacts in the Indian Ocean* (H.P. Ray and J-F. Salles Eds.), pp. 37-58. Delhi: Manohar.

McCrindle, J.W. 1879. Anonymi (Arrioni Ut Fertur) Periplus Maris Erythraei, *IA*, Vol. VIII : 107-151.

1884. Ptolemy's Geography of India and Southern Asia, *IA*, Vol.XIII, October : 313-411.

Meredith, D. 1957. Berenice Troglodytica, *Journal of Egyptian Archaeology,* 43: 56-70.

Mookerji, R. 1912. *A History of Indian Shipping and Maritime Activity from the Earliest Times.* Calcutta-Bombay: Longmans, Green and Co.

Mordini, A. 1967. Gold Kushana Coins in the Convent of Dabra Dammo, *Journal of the Numismatic Society of India,* Vol.XXIX, Pt.II: 19-25.

Potts, D.T. 1990. *The Arabian Gulf in Antiquity,* Vol.II. Oxford: Clarendon Press.

Raschke, M.G. 1978. New Studies in Roman Commerce with the East, *Aufstieg und Niedergang der Roemischen Welt,* II, 9.2, Berlin: 604-1076.

Rawlinson, H.G. 1916. *Intercourse between India and the Western World.* Cambridge.

Ray, H.P. and J-F. Salles (Eds.) 1996. *Tradition and Archaeology, Early Maritime Contacts in the Indian Ocean.* Delhi: Manohar.

Reade, J. 1996 (ed). *The Indian Ocean in Antiquity.* London: Keagan Paul International.

Robin, C. 1991. L'Arabie Du Sud et la Date du Periple De La Mer Erythree, *Journal Asiatique,* CCLXXIX, 1-2: 1-30.

Salles, J-F. 1984. Ceramiques de surface a ed-Dour, Emirats Arabes Unis, in *AOMIN.* Lyon: Reunion de Travail, 1982: 241-270.

Schoff, W.F. 1912/ reprint 1974. (tr.) *The Periplus of the Erythraean Sea.* New Delhi: Oriental Books Reprint Corporation.

Sedov. A.V. 1992. New Archaeological and Epigraphical material from Qana (South Arabia), *Arabian Archaeology and Epigraphy,* 3: 110-137.

1996. Qana' (Yemen) and the Indian Ocean: The Archaeological Evidence, in *Tradition and Archaeology, Early Maritime Contacts in the Indian Ocean* (H.P. Ray and J-F. Salles Eds.), pp. 11-35. Delhi: Manohar Publishers.

Shinde, V. 1987. Mantai: An Important Settlement in North-West Sri Lanka, *East and West,* Vol. 37, Nos.1-4, December 1987: 327-336.

Sidebotham, S.E. 1986. *Roman Economic Policy in the Erythra Thalassa (31 B.C. - 217 A.D.).* Leiden: E.J. Brill.

Sidebotham, S.E., J.A. Riley, H.A. Hamroush and H. Barakat. 1989. Fieldwork on the Red Sea Coast, The 1987 Season, *Journal of the American Research Centre in Egypt,* Vol.XXVI: 127-166.

Turner, P. 1989. *Roman Coins from India.* London: Institute of Archaeology Occasional Paper No.12 and Royal Numismatic Society Special Publication No.22.

van Beek, G.W. 1958. Frankincense and Myrrh in Ancient South Arabia, *JAOS,* Vol.78, No.3, July-Sept: 141-152.

Warmington, E.H. 1928/reprint 1995. *The Commerce between the Roman Empire and India.* Delhi: Munshiram Manoharlal.

Weisshaar, H-J., H. Roth and W. Wijeyapala. 2001. *Ancient Ruhuna.* Verlag Phillip von Zabern. Mainz am Rhein.

Wells, P.S. 1980. *Culture Contact and Culture Change, Early Iron Age*

Central Europe and the Mediterranean World. Cambridge: Cambridge University Press.

Wheeler, R.E.M. 1954. *Rome Beyond the Imperial Frontiers*. London: G.Bell and Sons.

Wheeler, R.E.M. 1976. *My Archaeological Mission to India and Pakistan*. London: Thames and Hudson.

Wheeler, R.E.M., A. Ghosh and Krishna Deva. 1946. Arikamedu: An Indo-Roman Trading Station on the East Coast of India, *Ancient India*, No.2: 17-124.

Yule, P. and M. Kervran. 1993. More than Samad in Oman: Iron Age Pottery from Suhar and Khor Rori, *Arabian Archaeology and Epigraphy*, 4: 69-106.

Zitterkopf, R. and S.E. Sidebotham. 1989. Stations and Towers on the Quseir-Nile Road, *Journal of Egyptian Archaeology*, Vol. 75: 155-189.

Balu: A Fortified Rural Settlement in Haryana

ARUN KESARWANI*

Haryana is a vast alluvial plain watered by the famous river Saraswatī and its tributaries. The high fertility of the land made the Early Harappans, the Harappans and the Late Harappans to settle here continuously for more than 500 years. Later on, the state was also occupied during the Painted Grey ware, the Northern Black Polished Ware, the Mauryas, the Kushanas, the Guptas, the Vardhanas, the Tomaras, the Gurjara-Pratihāras, the early Medieval, Medieval and late Medieval period. Large number of sites related to these cultures have been found in Haryana. So far as the Harappan period is concerned there are about 103 Early Harappan, 44 Harappan and 297 Late Harappan sites in Haryana (Joshi & Madhubala 1984). All the sites are found along the river Saraswatī, the Driṣadwatī and the Yamuna Palaeo-channels. This clearly shows that people settled over this land at large number of sites during the Early Harappan period. Only some of these villages could grow into the Mature Harappan stage. After the decline of this mature phase the large population migarated to other areas due to which even larger number of Late Harappan villages came into existence.

From the discovery of Harappa in 1921 and Mohenjo-dāro in 1922 much emphasis has been laid to explore and excavate urban centres only. Even after the indepedence in 1947 the first site extensively excavated by the Archaeological Survey of India was Kālibangān, District Ganganagar, Rajasthan on the confluence of the river Saraswatī and Drisadvatī. In Haryana too the Department of Archaeology and Museums, Haryana and Archaeological Survey of India, New Delhi excavated Banāwalī. The credit for excavating village sites goes to Suraj Bhan (1975) who not only extensively explored the Saraswatī and Satluj basins but also excavated Sīswāl and Mitāthal.

However, with this view in mind Suraj Bhan and Jim G. Shaffer (1977) explored Haryana and discovered Bālū (29^0 40' N-76^0 22' E), situated about 17 kilometer west of the present District Kaithal. It is located 4 kilometers north of the village Balu, where presently about 15000 people live. The site can be reached by bus from Delhi to Kaithal and from Kaithal to village Deban. Deban is situated on Kaithal to Jind road and from here the site, located at a distance of 4 kilometres, can be approached through a kachcha road running along the canal. It is presumed that daily life of the people depended on the river Āpagā, a tributary of the river Saraswatī, both referred to in the Rigveda. Presently Narwānā branch of the main Bhakhra canal flows through the north of the mound.

The Department of Ancient Indian History, Culture & Archaeology, Kurukshetra University, Kurukshetra excavated the site from 1978-79 to 1989-90, 1992-93 to 1994-95 and 1996-97, first under the direction of U.V.

*Chairman, Department of Ancient Indian History, Culture & Archaeology, Kurukshetra University, Kurukshetra.

Singh and Suraj Bhan and later under the direction of S.P. Shukla and assisted by B.K. Kathil, Arun Kesarwani and Mohinder Singh.

The site measures 250 metres east-west and 200 metres north-south. The total cultural deposit of the mound is 4.50 metres. A three-fold cultural sequence, marked on the basis of pottery tradition, termed as A (Pre-Harappan), B (Mature Harappan) and C (Late Harappan) was brought to light.

PERIOD A (PRE-HARAPPAN OR EARLY HARAPPAN)

Structures

The Pre-Harappans were the first settlers at Balu who occupied the natural soil of the mound. The total cultural deposit is not more than 1 metres and that too not throughtout the site. The complete house structure could not be noticed. The mud-bricks of size 30 x 20 x 10 cm were used throughout. A kankar- mixed clay bundh was constructed on the southern side of the settlement, possibly to protect the habitation from floods. This kankar-mixed clay was possibly obtained from the river Āpagā flowing nearby (Shukla 1977: 9). In trench M5 mud wall (40 cms in width) made of blackish clay, was exposed below the Harappan ashy material. It is found running from north-west to south-east direction. Below the Harappan mud-brick fortification wall another mud-brick wall, measuring 30 x 20 x 10 cm was traced and which rested on a 60 cm Pre-Harappan deposit. The wall had a receding face on its outer side with extremely hard brick (16 x 16 x 7 cm) and clay casing. Interestingly below this Pre-Harappan deposit another mud-brick (30 x 20 x 10 cm) structure was traced (IAR 94-95 : 27). The excavation carried out in trench N5 and N6 has revealed that the Harappans built their house over the Pre-Harappan deposit in this area. The remains of a double-oven have been noticed. A deep circular pit was dug out in one of the trench. This Pre-Harappan settlement spread over an area of 6700 square metres (Shukla 1977: 9).

Pottery

This period has yielded black-on red- ware, plain red ware, buff ware, grey ware and a few pieces of black-and-red ware. The red, buff and grey wares represented all the six fabrics (Singh & Bhan 1982 : 125). The main shapes in red ware are storage jars, water vessels, vases, basins, rusticated pots, bowls and cups. The vases are painted with broad black bands on the neck and shoulders. The painting is done in black and includes horizontal bands, groups of vertical, oblique and wavy lines, criss-cross and hatched triangles, arches, comb-marks, zig-zag lines, deep interior incised decorations, etc. (Singh & Bhan 1982 : 125).

Antiquities

The period has not revealed many antiquities except terracotta cakes, terracotta bangles and steatite beads.

Botanical Remains

The botanical remains found here were studied by Dr. K.S.Saraswat of the Birbal Sahni Institute of Palaeobotany, Lucknow. He identified rice (*Oryza sativa*), hulled barley (*Hordeum vulgare*), dwarf wheat (*Triticum sphaero-coccum*), bread wheat (*Triticum aestium*) green gram/munga (*Vigna radiata*), horse gram/kulthi (*Dolichos bioflorus*), Common vetch (*Vicia sativa*), musk-melon/kharbūjā (*Cucumis melo*), water-melon/tarbūja (*Citrallus lanatus*), wild jujube/jharberi (*Ziziphus nummularia*) and Harrā (*Terminalia chebula*). The evidence of water-melon provides the first definite evidence of its cultivation in the Pre-Harappan context. According to Shukla (1977: 9), Harrā is an important tanning material, it is laxative, tonic, has alterative properties and forms one of the constituent of Triphalā. The above evidence suggest that the Pre-Harappan people of Balu were great agriculturist and cultivated almost everything we grow today. They were also aware about the medicinal and aromatic qualities of certain plants and herbs.

PERIOD -B (MATURE HARAPPAN)

Structure

The total deposit of this Mature Harappan phase is 2.20 metres and its remains are found scattered all over the mound. According to Shukla (1997: 9), Harappan remains at Balu can be divided inot several stages - pre-fortification stage, fortification stage, late classical stage and post Harappan stage. The evidence of Pre-fortification stage can be noticed in the south-west and western part of the site. This portion of the mound was earlier occupied by the Pre-Harappans. Houses were constructed of mud-bricks measuring 40 x 20 x 10 cm Some betel-shaped *bhaṭṭis* have also been traced out. They were made above the natural soil.

In the second stage mud-brick (40 x 20 x 10 cm) fortification wall measuring 108 metres north-south and 96 metres east-west was constructed around the settlement. The general width of the fortification wall was 12 metres. At some place this rule was not adhered to and found to be more wider. It is interesting to point out that at other contemporary site the width of the fortification wall was not more than 5 to 7 metres (Shukla 1997: 10). A big bastion, measuring 15.10 metres and built of mud-bricks of various sizes (44 x 22 x 11, 40 x 20 x 10, 20 x 20 x ?, 26 x 22 x ? cm), have been exposed in the northern wall of the fortification. At the middle of the eastern fortification wall offset alongwith stairs were traced out. The settlement was duly planned with lanes and sub-lanes having a width of 1.45 to 1.90 cm. Houses were constructed at distance from the fortification wall. Entrance was in the southern corner of the eastern wall.

Three phases of building activity were noticed in trench C1. Mud-bricks (40 x 20 x 10 cm) walls of three houses were traced out. These are single brick-lined houses belonging to the late phase of the Harappan civilization. Carbonized wheat/barley were collected near the wall. A back side of mud-brick (36 x 18 x 9 cm) wall was found in trench D1. Another mud-brick (40 x 20 x 10 cm) wall diagonally running north-west to east-west was exposed in the south-east corner of the trench. The floor of this house was made of mud-lumps or broken mud-bricks. A broken S-shaped jar was found in the debris lying over it. Mud-brick (32 x 18 x 9 cm) floor, roughly triangular in shape, was unearthered in trench E1. A house with two walls and a stone quern in the floor was exposed in trench F1. The surface of the house is reddish in colour, indicating some sort of burning activity. The outside wall of another house was seen running diagonally, thus forming a lane between two houses.

Fire-places were found in trench H1 which were built time and again. These were successively plastered with lime. One fire-place was elliptical in shape. In its longer axis it is 169 cms and width 96 cm. Baked or unbaked clay were set to form the fire-place. Carbonized wheat/barley and charred bones were found scattered around this fire-place indicating some sort of ritual activity. In trench M1 to S1 houses were built time and again on earlier foundations using mud-bricks of 36 x 18 x 9 cm. In two houses burnt floors were traced which might have been used as places for keeping ovens. The partly preserved jar bottoms were found studded in lanes and may have served the purpose of soakage. An oval *bhatti* (150 x 130 cm) was found filled up with Harappan potsherds. Some Harappan mud-brick platforms with single courses of brick were found in trench P1.

A big house with several rooms planned diagonally was found. House walls were 80 cm wide and made of mud-bricks measuring 72 x 36 x 12 cm. The corner room measured 4.12 x 2.70 metres. It has five courses of mud-bricks with three courses of floor levels. At the depth of 50 cm an earlier mud-brick wall was traced out. The diagonally running wall indicates an open courtyard of the house (IAR 1995-96). It had an entrance in one of the room located in the north-west. In trench M3 a *gali* measuring 87 cm were found between two mud-brick houses. A house built by the Harappans had a *pucca* drain (Shukla 1977 : 10).

Pottery

The pottery of this period is a mixture of the Early Harappan, Bara, Cemetry-H alongwith the Harappan forms. Most of the pottery is black-on-red ware. Although some black-and-red ware, buff ware and some sherds with black and white parallel lines have also been recovered. The non-Harappan ceramics are characterized by black painted broad bands on the neck, use of white paintings, internally incised decorations and handmade cups. The typical Harappan shapes include large storage jars, vases, dish-on-stand, goblet, beaker, perforated jars, etc. The important designs painted in black on the pottery are animal and fish motifs, pipal leaf, hatched leaves, peacock designs, intersecting circles, horizontal bands, parallel lines and incised decorations, cord impressions, nail marks and pairing marks (Singh & Bhan 1982: 125).

Antiquities

The Mature Harappan phase at Balu has yielded large number of antiquities. Important antiquities are terracotta animal figurines, bangles, wheels, toy-cart frames, discs, sling balls, bird-shaped whistle, triangular and circular cakes and nodules; pestle, quern, beads, gamesman, weight and chert blades of stone; bangles or objects of shell; steatite beads; beads and bangles of faience and copper knife, point, pin, wire, arrow-head, hook, chisels, ring and bangles. A square steatite seal with *swāstik* symbol and a holed knob at the back withouut inscription is a notable find. One terracotta mould (35 cms in length) has also been recovered. It was possibly used for making metal bars. Such an evidence is not reported from any other sites. An interesting find is a discovery of three small steatite ear-stud having concentric desings. A piece of gold ornament has also been found. A terracotta bull figurine with conjoined legs is an interesting find, although it is related with the Pre-Harappan tradition.

Botanical Remains

During this period the Harappans continued to grow rice, hulled barley, dwarf and bread wheat, horse and green gram. The new evidence include naked barley (*Hordeum vulgare var*), lentil (*Lens culinaris*), Egyptian clover/barseem (*Trifoolium alexandrinum*), field pea (*Piscum arvense*), chick-pea/gram (*Cicer arietinum*), grass pea/khesari (*Lathyrus sativus*) and til (*Sesamum indicum*).

Moreover, the remains of date (*phoenix* sp.), grapes (*Vitis vinifera*) and kundaroo (*Coccinia cordifolia*) have also been found. The most interesting evidence is the presence of garlic at Balu. According to Saraswat (IAR 1996-97) garlic had its origin in Central Asia. Balu is the only site in South and South-east Asia which has yielded the sole evidence of garlic in archaeological context. It was used as a food, medicine or religious object by the First Egyptian dynasty (3200 B.C.). In an Egyptian document of 1550 B.C. 800 therapeutic formulae have been recorded out of which 22 were used in a variety of ailments. Garlic was included in the daily diet of the wealthy Egyptians and also in their funeral offerings (Shukla 1977 : 11).

PERIOD - C (LATE HARAPPANS)

Structures

The total cultural deposit of this Late Harappan phase is 1.30 metres. The classical phase of the Harappan culture began to decline. The surface of the mound was levelled. The fortification area was raised by spreading ashy soil. Mud-brick of 1:2:4 ratio were used for constructing houses. Different floor levels and mud-brick walls made of fragile bricks (30 x 20 x 10 cm) were traced in some trenches. In one trench a room measuring 2.5 x 1.45 metres were exposed. It might have served as a store (IAR 1994-95: 27). A diagonally running drain (width 13 cms) from north-west to south-east was traced in KX3 on the surface. Pots were found buried on both the side of the drain. It may have been used either for draining out rain water or for smelting. In trench L4 three *bhattis* were encountered. It appears that the area had been used for residential purpose after the earlier habitation shifted to other part of the mound. A number of circular and oblong *bhattis* and fire-places have been found. Some of it were built on the abandoned fortification wall and other areas. Remains of a kiln measuring 1.80 metres in length, 1.20 metre in width were also found. A house had a *pucca* drain built of wedge shaped bricks. Generally such bricks were used in the wells and it is probable that these were taken out from the wells and re-used in the drains.

Pottery

The pottery traditions of this phase show degenerate forms with oily surface, dull black painted designs with late Bara type incised decorations. It is comparable with Banāwali-III & Mitāthal-IIB, Bhagwānpura-IA and Daulatpur-I (Singh & Bhan 1982 : 125 and S.P. Shukla 1997). The important shapes are dishes-on-stand with drooping rim and undercut projected rim, storage jars, rusticated *handis* and high neck vases. Mostly these are painted in black and have incised decorations. Moreover, some Harappan and non-Harappan potsherds have graffiti marks (Singh & Bhan 1982: 126).

Antiquities

Antiquities of this period include terracotta nodules, triangular and circular cakes, bangles, ball, toy-cart frame, toy-bird, etc. Steatite beads and beads of semi-precious stones, copper arrow-heads, bone point and shell pieces have also been unearthed.

Discussion

On the basis of the above evidence it is presumed that the site is a perfect example of continuity and change as can be gleaned from pottery tradition and other material culture. Generally all Harappan fortified settlements are considered to be Urban centres but this does not hold true with Bālū. The fortified area is too small to be considered as a city. The typical, twin-mound system is not present except for one fortified mound. People at Bālū used only mud-bricks for constructing fortification and houses. Mud-bricks of various sizes were used although the ratio of 1:2:3 and 1:2:4, common to Pre-Harappan and mature Harappan phase, were followed. The grid planning, granary, system of writing, seals and sealings, monumental structures, all characteristic features of the Harappan cities, are absent here. This clearly indicates that Balu was not a city but a fortified rural centre. It can be presumed that the people of Balu were great agriculturists as is evident from the botanical remains recoverd at the site. Besides cereals like wheat, barley, gram and lentils, they also produced grapes, kundaroo, water melon, *Harrā, triphalā* and garlic. In south & south-east Asia, Balu is the only site which has yielded the remains of garlic in archaeological context. It can, therefore, be postulated that Balu was a major rural centre and served as an outpost of larger cities like Rākhīgarhī and Banāwalī, situated at a distance of about 55 and 70 Kilometres respectively. It is also possible that Balu might have supplied foodgrains, vegetables and other items of daily use to them. Even now-a-days nearby villages supply essential items of daily use to the cities and towns. Thus, undoubtedly Bālū occupies a proud place in the Harappan empire.

Acknowledgment

I am extremely thankful to Dr. Sukhdev Singh Saini, & Dr. S.K. Vashisht, Research Assistants in the Department for assisting me in the preparation of this report. I am also thankful to Sh. Karam Chand for neatly typing the manuscript.

REFERENCES

Bisht, R.S. 1978. Excavation at Banawali, 1974-77, *Seminar on Harappan Culture in the Indo-Pak Sub-continent*, Srinagar.

Joshi, J.P. 1993. *Excavation at Bhagwanpur 1975-76 and other explorations and excavations (1975-81) in Haryana Jammu & Kashmir and Punjab.*

Joshi, J.P., Madhu Bala & Jassu Ram 1984. The Indus Civilization : A re-consideration on the Basis of Distribution maps, *Frontiers of Indus Civilization*, Eds., B.B. Lal & S.P. Gupta, pp. 510-30.

Kesarwani, Arun 1992. Archaeological Activities of the Kurukshetra University, *Haryana Intach*, Jan. 1992.

Saraswat, K.S. Paleobotanical and pollen analytical Investigations (1996-97), *Indian Archaeology : A Review* (1996-97).

Singh, U.V. & Suraj Bhan 1982. A Note on the excavations at Balu, Distt. Jind (Haryana), *Indian Archaeology : New Prespectives*, edited by R.K. Sharma, New Delhi, pp. 124-26.

Shukla, S.P. 1997. Form of the Harappan Civilization as Revealed from the Excavations at Balu, Haryana, *Indian Museum Bulletin*, Vol. XXXII, Calcutta, pp. 8-1[illegible]

Suraj Bhan, 1972. Siswal-A Pre-Harappan Site in Haryana, *Puratattva*, No. 7, New Delhi.

Suraj Bhan 1975. *Excavations, at Mithathal (1968) and other explorations in the Sutlej-Yamuna Divide, Kurukshetra*, 1975.

Suraj Bhan and Shaffer, Jim G. 1978. New discoveries in Northern Haryana, *Man and Environment*, Vol. II, Ahmedabad, pp. 59-68.

Indian Archaeology : A Review, 1978-79.

Indian Archaeology : A Review, 1979-80.

Indian Archaeology : A Review, 1992-93.

Indian Archaeology : A Review, 1993-94.

Indian Archaeology : A Review, 1994-95.

Indian Archaeology : A Review, 1996-97.

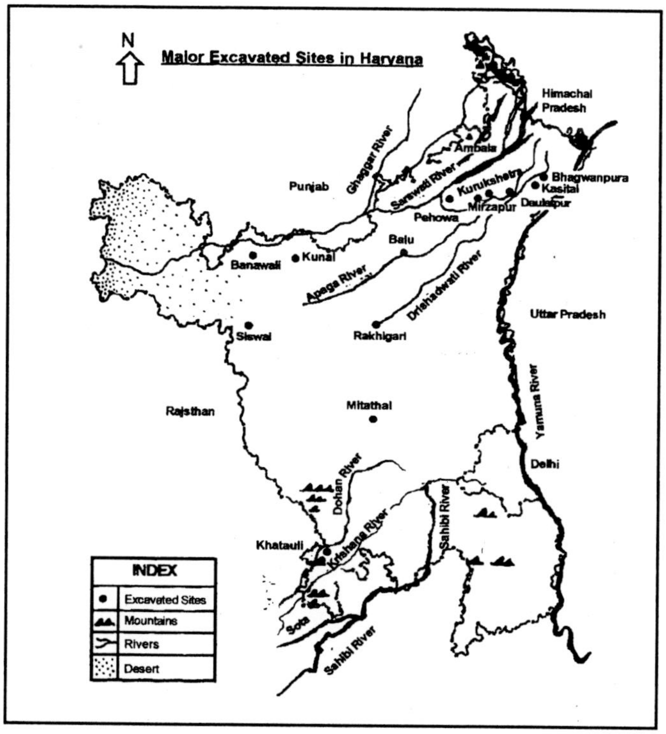
N
Major Excavated Sites in Haryana
Himachal Pradesh
Punjab
Ghaggar River
Saraswati River
Ambala
Kurukshetra
Bhagwanpura
Daulatpur
Mirzapur
Pehowa
Balu
Banawali
Kunal
Apaga River
Drishadwati River
Uttar Pradesh
Siswal
Rakhigari
Rajsthan
Mitathal
Yamuna River
Delhi
Dohan River
Khatauli
Krishana River
Sahibi River
Sota
INDEX
Excavated Sites
Mountains
Rivers
Desert

Fig. 1.

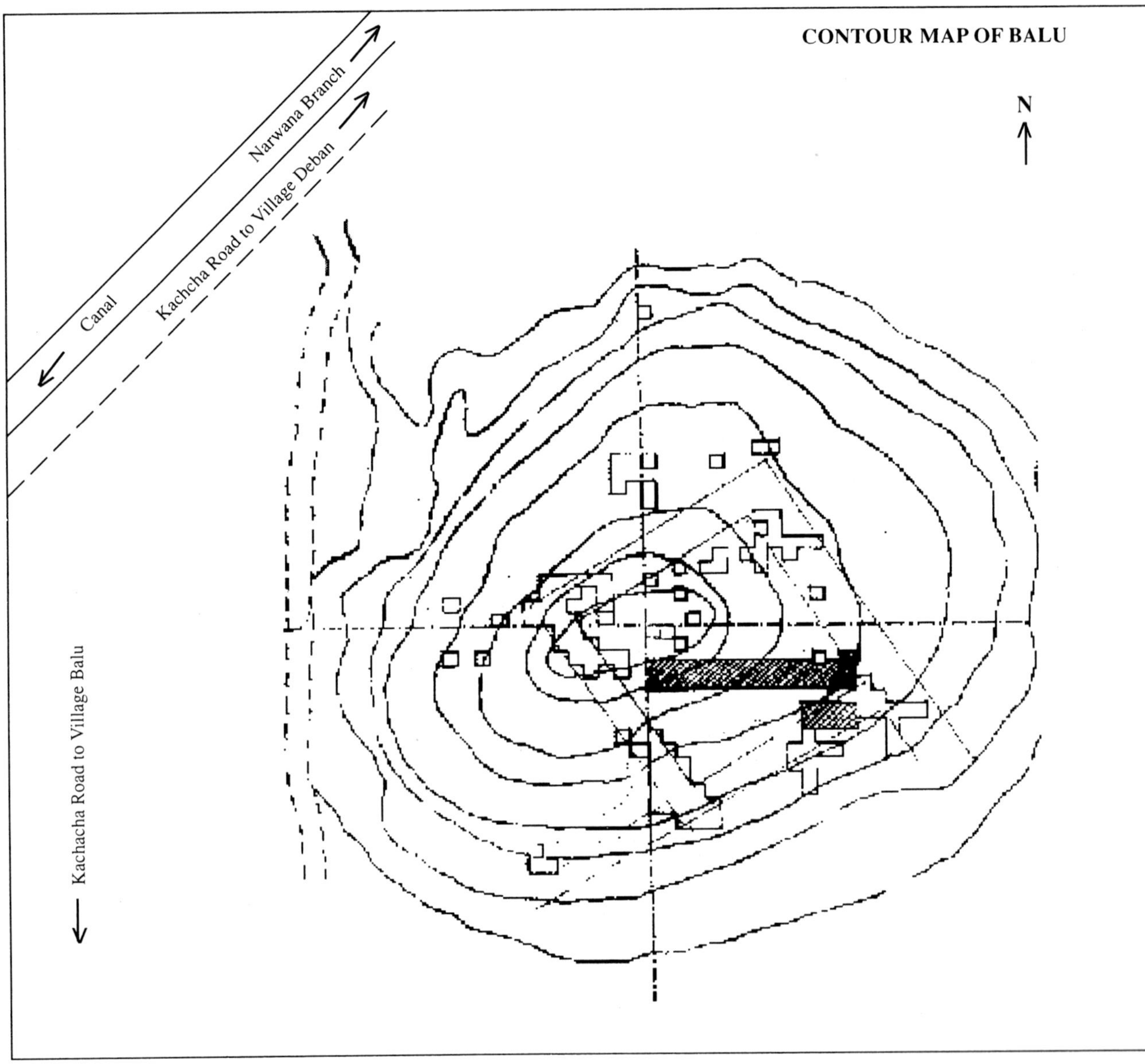
CONTOUR MAP OF BALU
N
Narwana Branch
Canal
Kachcha Road to Village Deban
Kachacha Road to Village Balu

Fig. 2.

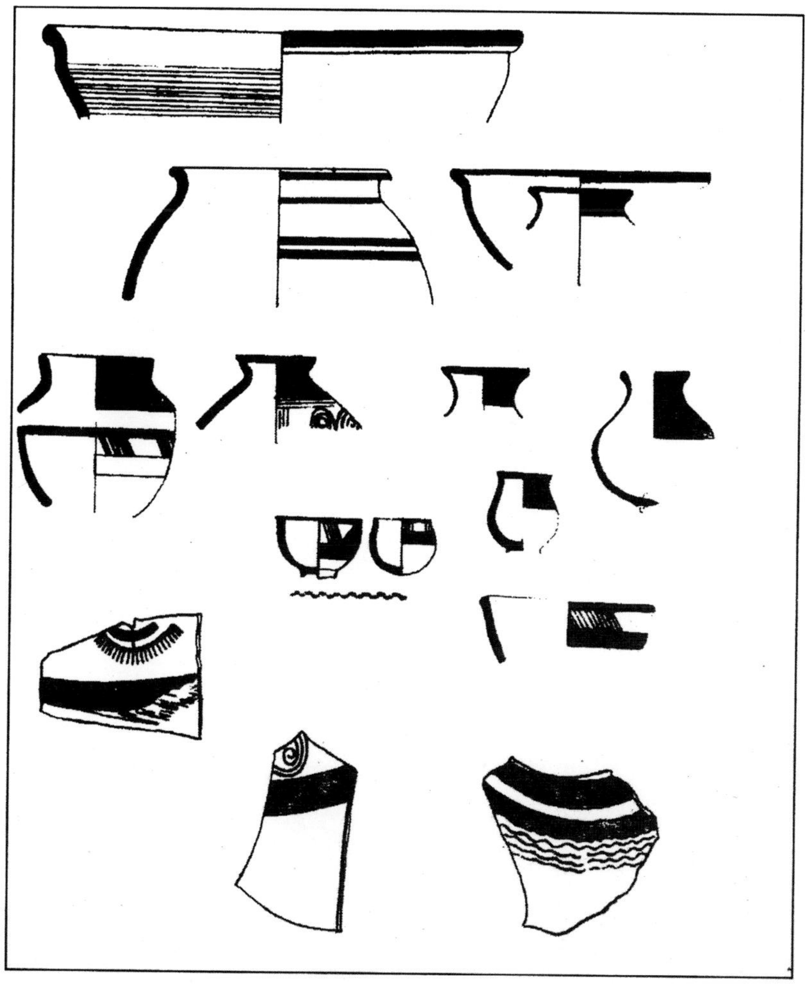

Fig. 3. Balu: Pre-Harappan Pottery.

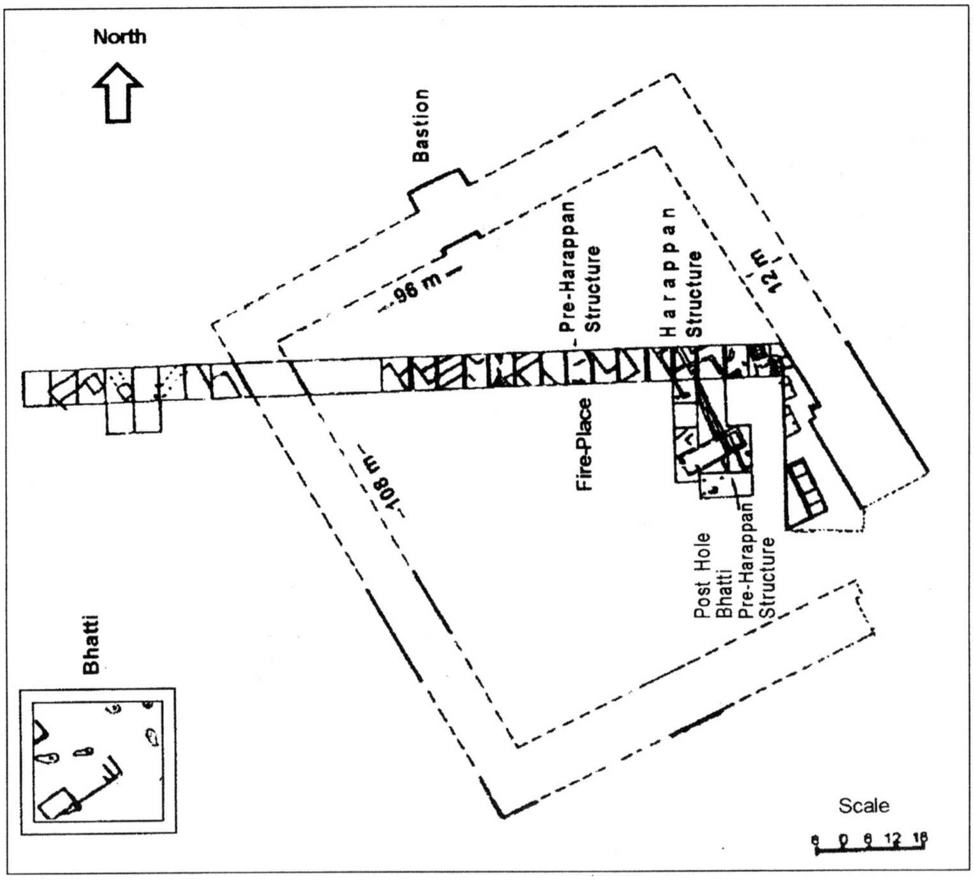

Fig. 4. Balu: Harappan Fortification & Structures.

Fig. 5. Bastion in theNorthern Fortification Wall.

Fig. 6. Layout of Harappan House.

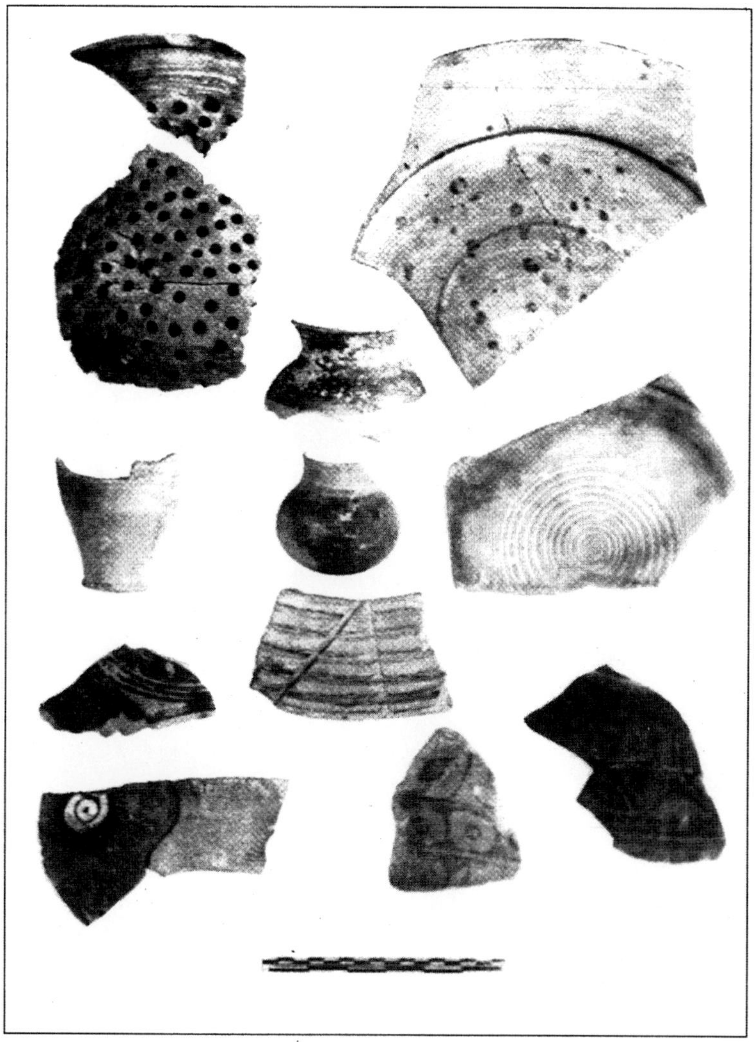

Fig. 7. Harappan Potery.

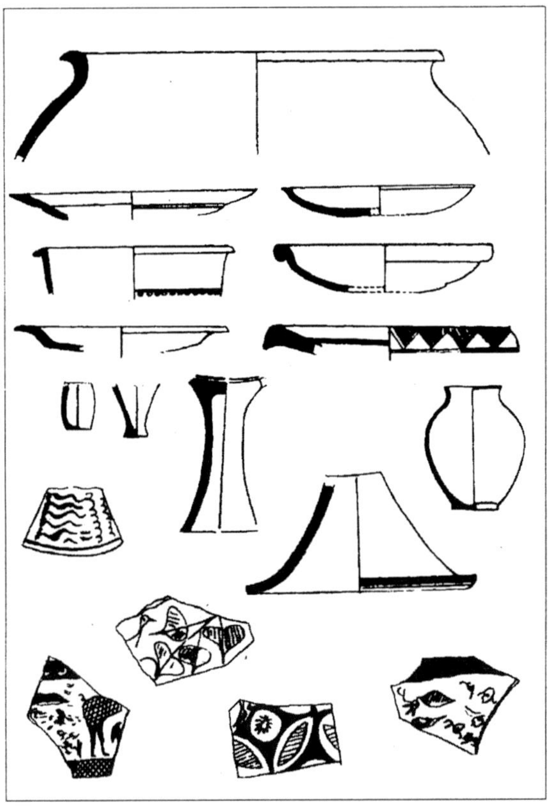

Fig. 8. Harappan Pottery.

Fig. 9. Terracota Toy-cart Frames.

Fig. 10. Terracotta Wheel, Ball & Animal Figurines.

Fig. 11. Terracotta Triangular & Circular Cakes Nodules.

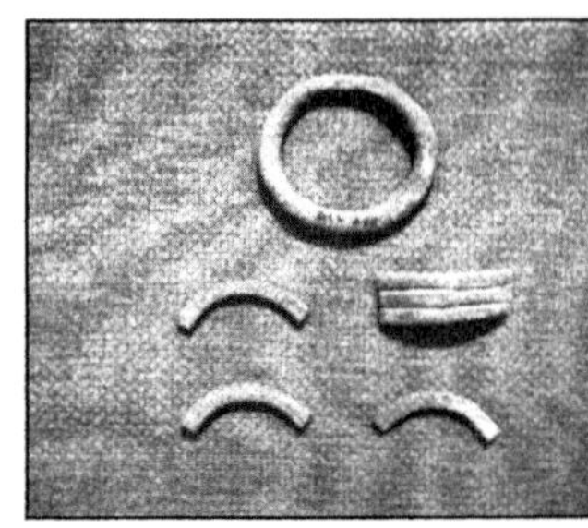

Fig. 12. Bone & Shell Objects.

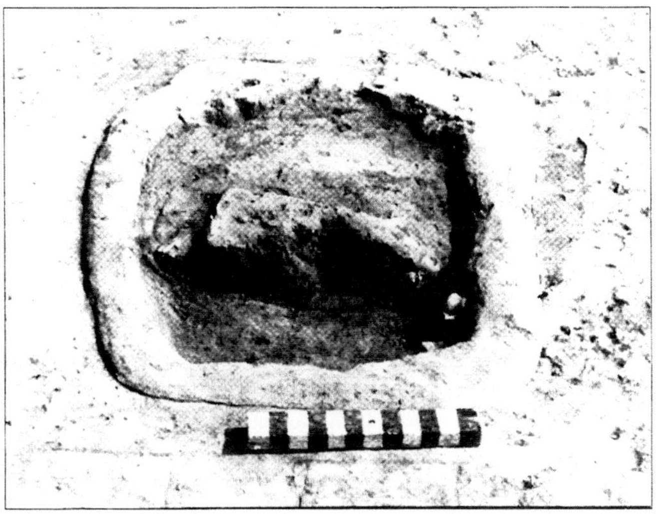

Fig. 13. Bhatti or Fire-place.

Fig. 14. Charred grains.

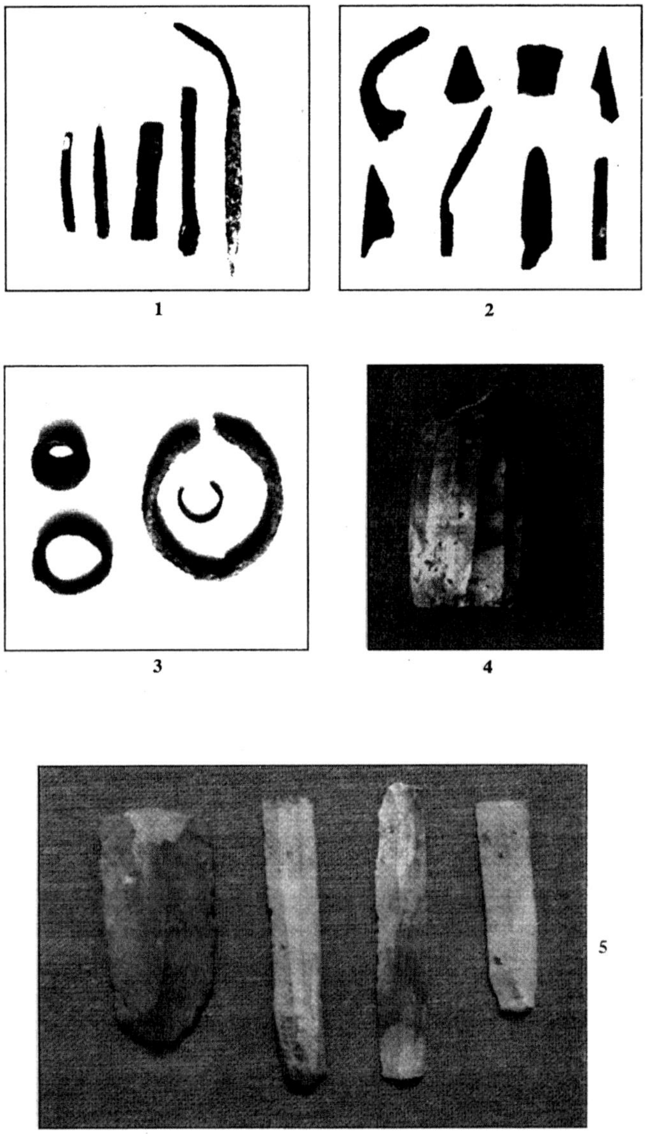

Fig. 15. Antiquities : 1, 2, 3 Coppertools, 4, 5 Chert core & Blades.

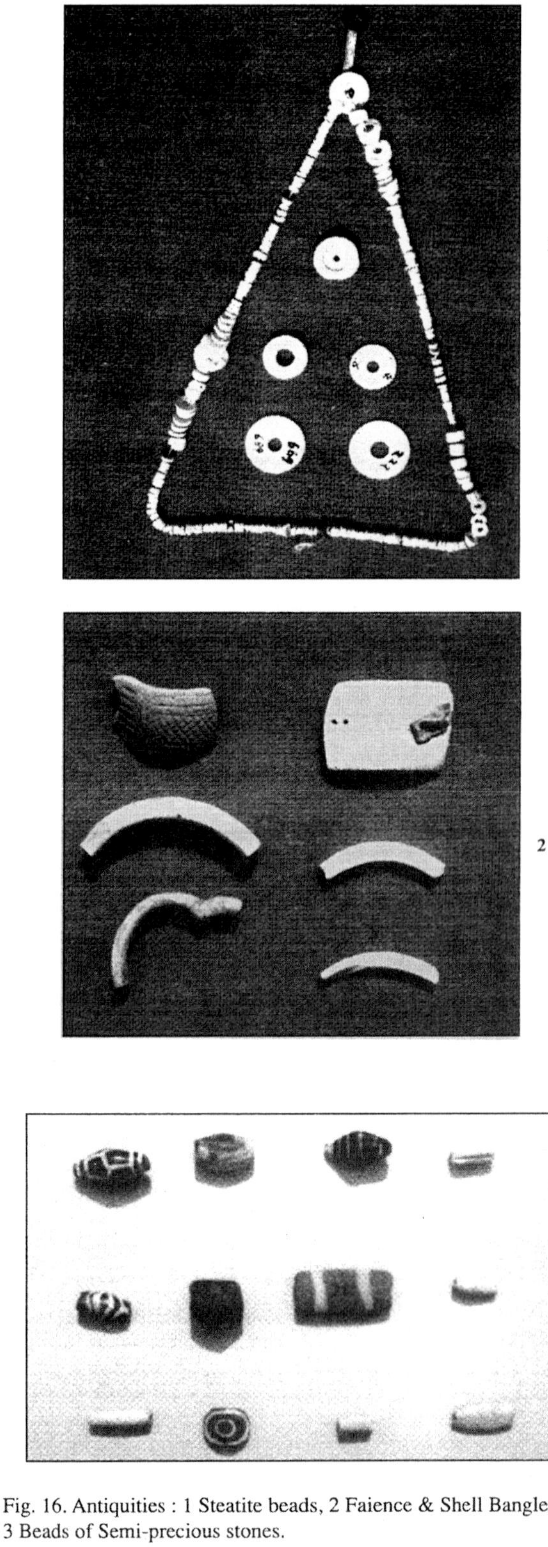

Fig. 16. Antiquities : 1 Steatite beads, 2 Faience & Shell Bangles, 3 Beads of Semi-precious stones.

NOTES AND NEWS

Neolithic Celt: Object of Charm for the Nishis of Arunachal Pradesh

Neolithic celts found in Arunachal Pradesh are considered as celestial objects by the local tribes. The present paper deals with the beliefs associated with the Neolithic celts prevalent among the *Nishi* tribe of Arunachal Pradesh.

Arunchal Pradesh, situated along the northeast frontier of the Indian Union lies between 26° 28`N to 29°39`N latitudes and 91° 30`E to 97° 30`N longitudes. It comprises an area of 83,578 square Kilometre in the mountainous region of the eastern Himalayas and is surrounded by Bhutan in the west, Tibet and China in the northeast, Myanmar in the east and southeast and vast plains of Assam in the south.

The ancient history and archaeology of Arunachal Pradesh is still obscure. Inspite of it being a potential area where many ethnic groups and cultural elements of different hues meet, not much has been recorded about its past. The studies regarding the past began in 1871 when John Anderson reported the first palaeolith from the region. Following this, several scholars have carried forth archaeological investigations in the area. A.H. Dani (1960)[1]. T.C. Sharma (1966)[2] and other have reported stray Neolithic tools in the recent years. The rich archaeological heritage of Arunachal Pradesh got an impetus with the excavation at Parsi Parlo[3] (28° `N and 93° `33 E) on the right bank of the Kamla river in the Lower Subansiri district which revealed a three-fold sequence of cultures, viz.

Phase I	-	Aceramic Neolithic;
Phase II	-	Ceramic Neolithic; and
Phase III	-	Ferrolithic

The Neolithic tools found in the excavation are mainly of two types viz. celts with lenticular cross section and quadrangular celts with rectangular cross sections. The other types, found in a lesser number are hog-backed type and slender chisels of jadeite. The tools in general are mostly made of sandstone, basalt, schist, quartzite, gneiss and jadeite, the last being available in North Myanmar and Eastern China. These celts show close affinity to their East Asian counterparts.

Apart from antiquarian values, neolithic celts have generated a lot of interest in the local populace, particularly the Nishi tribe, and many beliefs are associated with them.

The Nishis are among the twenty major tribal groups inhabiting Arunachal Pradesh. The Nishis (also called Nishings) belong to the Indo-Mongloid group of people and are autochthons of Papum, Pare and Lower Subansiri districts. Their western branches inhabit the East Kameng district and are also known as Bangni. The Nishis consider themselves as descendants of a common ancestor Abo-Tani and believe in a number of malevolent and benevolent spirits, the former exceeding the latter numerically. Hence we find a number of beliefs woven around many objects and beings. The celts, our present subject matter, are one amongst them, which have a good number of beliefs associated with them.

The Neolithic celts, variously called like *Doje-hunting* (Jungle God's Axe) and *'Talu-hey'* (Devil's Axe) are, as mentioned at the outset, considered to be heavenly objects and with the thunderstorms are strewn on to surface. These objects therefore generate reverence as well as fear among the people.

Sections among the Nishis consider the celts as a bad omen and term them as the Devil's axe or *Talu-hey*. Since these are believed to cause misfortune if kept within a house these are not kept inside but are either discarded or left untouched at the provenance.

Another section of the tribe considers them to posses magical charms and worships them as the Jungle God's Axe or the *Doje-hutung*. These celts are collected from the jungles or the agricultural fields and are hung at a special place, mostly the central pole of the bamboo hut so as to ward off evil spirits and save the hut from thunder or fire. Because of the strong beliefs, the celts are venerated and prayed upon when a family member falls ill. During illness, these are sometimes even kept at the ailing person's bedside. It is said that on listening to the invocations, the God would make the celt move on its own and then on further continuance of the prayers, the person would get well.

The Nishis are a honest lot, so there is by and large no risk of theft even when they move out having unlocked house. Perchance any theft occurs, the Nishis, with their strong beliefs about celts, sort out the case on their own. The people congregate at a place within the village where the village priest, called the Nyub is invited. He is supposed to hold a celt in his right hand and a bone of a tiger in the left hand. A person, out of the gathering, is then supposed to name the neighbouring villages. The belief of the people is that the celt would, on its own, starts shaking at the name of the thief's village. On identifying the village, the man is required to name the families residing therein. Since the Nishi villages are sparsely populated, the families can be easily named. The particular family to which the thief belongs is again identified in a similar way and finally the person is apprehended.

Another belief associated with the celts is that of its ability to help locate a missing person. The celt is first worshipped so that it shows the exact direction in which the lost person has strayed.

The above instances exemplify the various beliefs associated with celt that are of immense value to archaeologists as wonderful works of the Neolithic age. Since the tribes associate them with magico-cultural beliefs, these usually occur to archaeologists as stray finds retrieved from their huts or thrown away in fields.

The beliefs may be continuation of an age old or may be recently acquired sentiments resulting out of mere coincidences.

Acknowledgements

The article is primarily based on the conversations the author had with the local tribes during official-tour for explorations in Arunachal Pradesh. The author is highly thankful to S.K. Mitra, V.Shivananda and staff members of the Excavations Branch-I and Prehistory Branch, Nagpur of the Survey.

REFERENCES

1. Ashraf, A.A. 1990, *Prehistoric Arunachal study on Prehistory and Ethnoarchaeology of Kamla valley*, Itanagar.

2. Dani, A.H. 1960, *Prehistory and Protohistory of Eastern India.*

3. Sharma, T.C. 1966, *Prehistoric Archaeology of Assam-A study of Neolithic culture*, Ph.D. Thesis unpublished, London University.

Archaeological Survey of India,
Excavation Branch-I,
NAGPUR

Prabasu Sahu

Chandaukha - An OCP Site in Aligarh District

Ochre-coloured ware (OCP) was discovered by B.B. Lal in 1946 from the well-known copper-hoard site Bisauli in District Badaun and Rajpur Parsu in District Binjnor (Lal 1951). This new class of pottery is characterized by ill-fired, thick, ochre-washed and rolled in appearance, hence the specific term OCP was christened and presumably then, associated with copper hoard culture of Ganga-valley. Subsequently, the same class of pottery was found in excavations at Hastinapur from the lowest levels, i.e. period I (Lal 1954-55). But no copper implements or any structural remains were encountered during the excavation.

Since that time, so many OCP sites have come to light in subsequent explorations and excavations in the Ganga-Yamuna Doab. Of these, Baharia (Sharma 1971-72, pp. 42-43), Bahadrabad, Nasirpur etc. yielded copper-hoard and OCP. In the east, OCP has been recovered from Sringverapur period I which represents the eastern limit of OCP culture (Lal and Dikshit 1981). OCP as well as copper-hoard is reported from several sites in the middle Gangatic plain such as Pariyar, Tejpur, Mohan, Baugormaun, Dhaka Sarthauli, Indilapur, and Baharaia. Hardi, Deoti (Roy, T.N., 1983) and Saipai. Saipai is important one because a hooked sword and a harpoon were found *in situ* during the excavation in a stratigraphical context (Lal, 1971-72 and Wahal, L.M., 1969-70 and 1971-72, Purattatva No. 5, pp. 12-13).

In the upper Ganga-Yamuna Doab, frequency of OCP sites are more numerous than in middle Ganga plain. More than 250 sites have been reported from districts of Bulandshahar, Meerut, and Muzaffarnagar in western Uttar Pradesh. About two dozen OCP sites have been reported from District Saharanpur (Sankar Nath 1971-72, Purattatva No. 5, 16). Some of the sites of western Uttar Pradesh show predominance of late Harappan culture, the type sites are Alamgirpur, Hulas etc. while many other OCP sites in Bulandshahar, Meerut, Muzaffarnagar and Saharanpur district have revealed close affinities with each other, the important excavated type-sites are Bahadrabad (Sharma 1964, p. 11-13), Ambkheri (Despande 1965 and 1967), Nasipur, Bargaon, Alamgirpur, Hulas, Atranjkhera (Gaur 1993), Ahichchhatra (Banerjee 1969), Lal Quila (Gaur 1983) from where various kinds of OCP shapes and rich variety of painted and incised pottery have been reported. Apart from this, material remains is represented by stone pestles, querns, terracotta objects, pottery discs, human figurines and animal figurines, mudfloors and burnt bricks etc. have been reported from several sites which throw valuable light on their structural activities of OCP using people.

In the north, OCP continue to occur with pre-Harappan Pottery at Kotla Nihang Khan (IAR, 1954-55), Rupar, Bara (Sharma 1954-55) and Dher Majra (Olaf Pruefer 1952, Sharma 1954) fixing the northern limit of OCP culture on the Satlej. OCP has also been discovered at Katpalon near Jullundur (Dikshit 1967; 1969) on Drsadvati Valley. Suraj Bhan claims that 90 OCP sites have been discovered in the Ganga-Yamuna Doab from Noh near Bharatpur. OCP further extends in south upto the Mitathal District, Bhiwani in Haryana (Suraj Bhan 1969). Excavations at Jodhpura, Noh and Ganeshwar have thrown valuable light on OCP culture. Recently, the explorations of districts Jaipur, Sikar and Jhunjhunu in Rajasthan have revealed more than 200 OCP sites (Hooja and Kumar 1965). From Ganeshwar alone about 1000 objects of copper in association with OCP have been found (Agrawal and Vijai Kumar 1982). These include copper arrowheads, ring, bangle, spearhead, chisel, ball and celt etc. This indicates that OCP using people at Ganeshwar were well familiar with copper technology. Thus it is well attested that OCP covers a very wide geographical horizon from the confluence of Ganga-Yamuna Doab to Sutlej Valley including the Sarasvati and Drsadvati basin. In the west, it extends upto the Central Rajasthan.

Excavated sites like Atranjikhera and Lal Quila are located in the bordering districts of Etah and Bulandshahar respectively. The results obtained from both the sites were fruitful and encouraging and widened our knowledge about OCP using people. It also provided enough encentive to undertake exploration in Aligarh district, which was a cultural blank, so far OCP is concerned. Only three sites from the district Aligarh were reported namely Morthal (Gaur, and others, 1975), Jalali (Siddiqui, 1981), Kauriaganj (Sinha, 1965-66, unpublished). But we do not have the details of pottery or about the site. Thus our knowledge about the OCP sites in district Aligarh was scanty. In order to ascertain the distribution of OCP sites in Aligarh, the present author conducted an exploration in 1991-92 and 1992-92.

During course of exploration as many as one hundred fifty sites of Proto historical and Early Historical periods were explored. Of these, so many sites yielded OCP but in small quantity. Apart from this more than two dozen sites were also discovered from where good number OCP and variety of OCP shapes were found. Some of the important sites are: Khera, Tappal, Pipalgaon, Barood Khera, Pora, Gadrana, Jalali, Ogar, Chandoli, Sankara, Mudhakhera Chandaukha etc. However, Chandaukha appeared very interesting which we have explored thoroughly. The present paper is the result of our fieldwork.

The site of Chandaukha (27° 5'N. Lat. and 78° 6' E Long.) is located in Tehsil Koel of District Aligarh. It is 9 km towards north on Aligarh-Anupshahar road from district headquarters and the site is to the west of the village Chandaukha.

It is a single culture site and appears to be a largest settlement area measuring 570 x 570 m. Perhaps such an extensive mound (Fig. 1) has not been reported else where. The present author discovered the site in 1992, when the major portion of the mound was in an intact condition. Two mounds along the lake were noticed at that time. Now the entire site has been badly damaged by earth diggers. Unrestricted soil robbing is still continuing. It appears that with in very short time it will vanish altogether. This point has been indicated with dotted lines in the contour map of the site (Fig. 1). The rest of the mound looks flattish.

There appears to be clusters of settlement area but we could trace only three clusters of settlement area on southern, western and northern side of the lake. The southern part appears to have thickest habitational deposit of about 2:00-2:25 m. (Fig. 1-OD). In the toposheet of Survey map (SOI, Sheet No. 54I/I) two mounds along the huge lake have been indicated clearly. It was compared with remote sensing imagery data that clearify the lake. Satellite data of SPOT-HRV-1 (Scale 1:50,000) and LANDSOT-5 TM FCC (Scale 1:250,000) indicated depression upto long distance in the east-west axis and water bodies after long intervals. The depression has been shown with darkish tone along vegetational packages. It appears to be an extension of lake measuring 470x120 m. Now, it has been converted into the paddy fields. Dry channels of Sengar River has been shown in the eastern surrounding area along with vegetational packages and indicated with red band in the Satellite imagery. Probably, old Sengar originated from the lake. On the contour map, three clusters of habitational area have been shown as A, B, C. The remaining part of the original site is indicated as OD.

Area A: In this area, the habitational deposit varies from 2.00 m. to 2.25 m. The major part of the settlement has been converted in to the agricultural field. Only small part (OD A) having 2.00 m thick habitational deposit is still intact. It is very hard and compact in texture. OCP shapes and sherds as well as burnt mud clods with reed-marks and brick fragments were found lying over the floor.

An intact water-well, internally lined with wedge shaped finger-marked bricks measuring 30x24-19x6 cm is an important discovery of this site (PL-IB). The inner diameter is 1.32 cm while the outer diameter is 1.92 m. It is located in the middele of the habitational area of area A. Although, wedge shaped bricks are reported from late Harappan, as well OCP site such as Hardi, Lal Quila, Ambkheri, Bahadrabad, Mandi in Muzaffarnagar etc. but such evidence has not been reported from any other site. Thus it is a significant evidence. Another important evidence from this settlement area was a big pit full of ash. It could have been a kiln (information received by the owner of the land). Further excavation at this particular area could reveal the fact. A dish-on-stand (PL-IA) was also found from this area, which indicated Harappan influence. This specimen is of thick fabric; slipped as well as decorated with three parallel Zigzag incised lines. Besides this some other specimen of dish-on-stand were also recovered from the same area but were fragmentary.

Area B: It is an elevated part (OD-B) of the western peripheral area of lake and mound A. It may have been connected with habitational area A. Here OD is about 1.30 m in thickness. The major part of it has been converted into agricultural land, yet traces of structural activities such as mudfloor of solid, hard compact clay with pottery overlying it, was noticed in the disturbed area. Perhaps, habitational portion measuring 30x10 m was knowingly avoided by the earth diggers because of very hard and compact nature. Most probably, the clay brought from the lake was utilized for constructing smooth plateform as well as floors. Chunks of mud clods with reed-marks and brick fragments were also found from the same area (OD-B). In the northern exposed section, a layer-representing floor with pottery was clearly visible at the same level.

Area C: It is the western part of Chandaukha-2. Maximum disturbance has been done in this area. However, floor levels of compact clay could be traced in this area too, like area B. An interesting evidence of pot with bones (PL-2C) was recovered from the exposed section of mound-2.

Pottery Complex

Chandaukha assemblage (Fig. 2-6) shows a variety of shapes like that of Amkheri. It gives fairly good idea about the pottery recovered from the site. The bulk of the pottery was recovered from the exposed area of the mound 1 and 2. Apart from this, some important shapes and a pot with bones (PL-2C) were recovered from the exposed sections, from the upper deposit of mound 2 where as specimen of dish-on-stand (PL-IA) was found from lowest level of mound-1.

Chandaukha ware is generally of thick fabric and is made of well-levigated medium grained clay. The thickness varies from 2 mm to 2 cm. As a whole, pottery is wheel turned as well as hand made. The pottery which was recovered from the lowest level, bears thick slip, comparable to those recovered from upper deposit: ochrous, soft and rolled on in appearance, colour varies from pale-red to orange red. Perhaps, slip stuck with hard brown clay has been peeled off. Associated washed grey pottery continues to occur even at lower levels. Notworthy types included dropping vase, almost profile vase and other variety of this kind (Fig. 2), bowls, dishes, basins, lids, spouts, handles, ring base, disc base and dish-on-stands. Incised pottery was found in considerable number. Painted designs were found but in very rare cases. However, Bara compex are conspicouously absent at Chandaukha. Thus, Chandaukha were compares very well with those of other OCP sites like Bahadrabad, Ahchchhatra, Ambkheri, Saipai, Noh and Atranjikhera etc.

A typical vase having drooping rim (Fig. 2) is a new variety of this site, perhaps not reported from any other OCP sites. Recently, dish with drooping rim, ring base, disc base, lids with centeral knob and vessels with externally drooping rim etc. has been reported from Harappan levels along with hoards of golden jewellery from Mandi, District Muzaffarnagar (Puratattva No. 30, p.36).

Material Culture

Other associated finds include: a fluted core of chert, blade (granite?), stone ball, quern and pestles, T.C. bangle and pottery disc (PL-2A-D).

It is clear from the above findings that users of OCP were neither nomadic people nor it was a vagrant culture, but were living a settled life, near the natural source of water. Harappans affinity at this site may not be ruled out.

Acknowledgements

The authors' utmost gratitude is due to Shri B.B. Lal, the veteran archaeologist who patiently noticed the Chandaukha OCP and listened our related problems. We are also very greatful to Dr. K.N. Dikshit, Dr. S.P. Gupta, Chairman of Indian Archaeological Society and Prof. M.D.N. Sahi for their inspiration and encouragement.

The first-author is extremely thankful to Shri D.P. Rao, Director, NRSA, Hyderabad and the course Co-ordinators, Dr. A. Bhattacharya, Dr. S.K. Subramanian and other staff members for their immense help and co-operation. During my training programme on Remote Sensing for Archaeology, organized by N.N.R.M.S., Department of Space, Govt. of India, Hyderabad. We also pay our respectful thanks to Prof. Iqbaluddin and Dr. Mukhtar Ahmed of Remote Sensing Application Centre, A.M.U., Aligarh for providing Satellite imageries and for help in various ways.

REFERENCES

Agrawal, R.C., and Kumar Vijay, (1982): Ganeshwar-Jodhpura, Culture: New Traits in Indian Archaeology, In *Harappan Civilization Recent Perspective*, G.L. Possehl (ed.), New Delhi, pp. 125-134.

Bhan, Suraj, (1969): Excavation at Mitathal (Hissar), 1968, *Journal of Haryana Studies*, Vol. 4, No. 1, p.1-5.

Bhan, Suraj (1975): *Excavation at Mitathal and other explorations in Sutlej-Yamuna Divide*, Kurukshetra University, Kurukshetra.

Deshpande, M.N. (1967-2): Brief report of excavation at Ambkheri, *Indian Archaeology*, 1963-64, *A Review*, New Delhi, p. 56.

Dikshit, K.N. (1967-2): Exploration along the right bank of river Sutlej in Punjab, *Journal of Indian History*, vol. XLV, Part II.

Dikshit, K.N. (1969): Nature of the Harappan Wares in the Sutlej Velly, *Potteries in Ancient India*, Patna, pp. 55-56.

Gaur, R.C. and others, (1975): *Indian Archaeology*, 1966-67, A Review, New Delhi, and p.33.

Gaur, R.C. (1983): *Excavationsn at Atranjikhera*, Motilal Banarsidass, New Delhi.

Gaur, R.C. (1993): *Excavations at Lal Qila*, Jaipur.

Hooja, R. and Kumar, Vijay (1995). Aspects of Early Copper Age in Rajasthan, *South Asian Archaeology*, Helsinki, p. 323-339.

Indian Archaeology (IAR), 1972-73, A Review, New Delhi, pp. 29-30.

Indian Archaeology (IAR), 1973-74, A Review, New Delhi, pp. 23-24.

Lal, B.B. (1951): Further Copper-Hoards from the Gangetic Basin and a Review of the problem, *Ancient India;* No. 7, pp. 20-39.

Lal, B.B. (1954-55): Excavation at Hastinapur and other explorations in upper Ganga and Satlej Basin, *Ancient India*, No. 10-11, pp.10-11, 31-32.

Lal, B.B. (1971-72): A Note on the Excavation at Saipai, *Puratattva*, No. 5, pp. 46-49.

Lal, B.B. & Dikshit, K.N. (1981): Sringverapur: A Key site for the protohistory and early history of the central Ganga Valley, *Puratattva* No. 10. New Delhi, pp.1-7.

Pruefer, Olaf (1951): *Nalagarh: Interium Report on the Excavation carried out at Dher Majra*, Calcutta.

Roy, T.N., (1983): *The Ganges Civilization*, Ramanand Vidya Bhawan, New Delhi, and p.7.

Sharma, G.R. (1971-72): Excavation at Baharia, District Shahjahanpur, *Puratattva* No. 5, and pp. 42-43.

Sharma, Y.D., (1954-2): *Notice or reassessment of discoveries at Bikkun (Dher Majra), Bara, Kotli, Talapura, Chamkaur and Hawara, Indian Archaeology, 1953-54, A Review*, New Delhi, p. 48.

Sharma, Y.D., (1955-1): Brief report of continued excavations at Rupar, *Indian Archaeology*, 1954-55, A Review, New Delhi, pp. 9-11.

Sharma, Y.D. (1964): *Protohistoric Remains, Archaeological Remains Monuments and Museums*, Part I, New Delhi, pp.1-42.

Sinha, B.K., (1965-66): Notice of Discovery of Ochre Coloured Pottery *near Kauria Ganj, District Aligarh, Indian Archaeology, A Review*.

Siddiqi, J.M., (1981): *Aligarh District: A Historical Survey* (from Ancient to 1803 AD). Munshiram Manoharlal, New Delhi.

Wahal, L.M., (1969-70): Brief report of excavation at Saipai - Lichchawi, district Etawah, *Indian Archaeology, and A Review*. (1969-70).

Ranjit and Mohd. Abid

Department of History,
Aligarh Muslim University,Aligarh (U.P.)

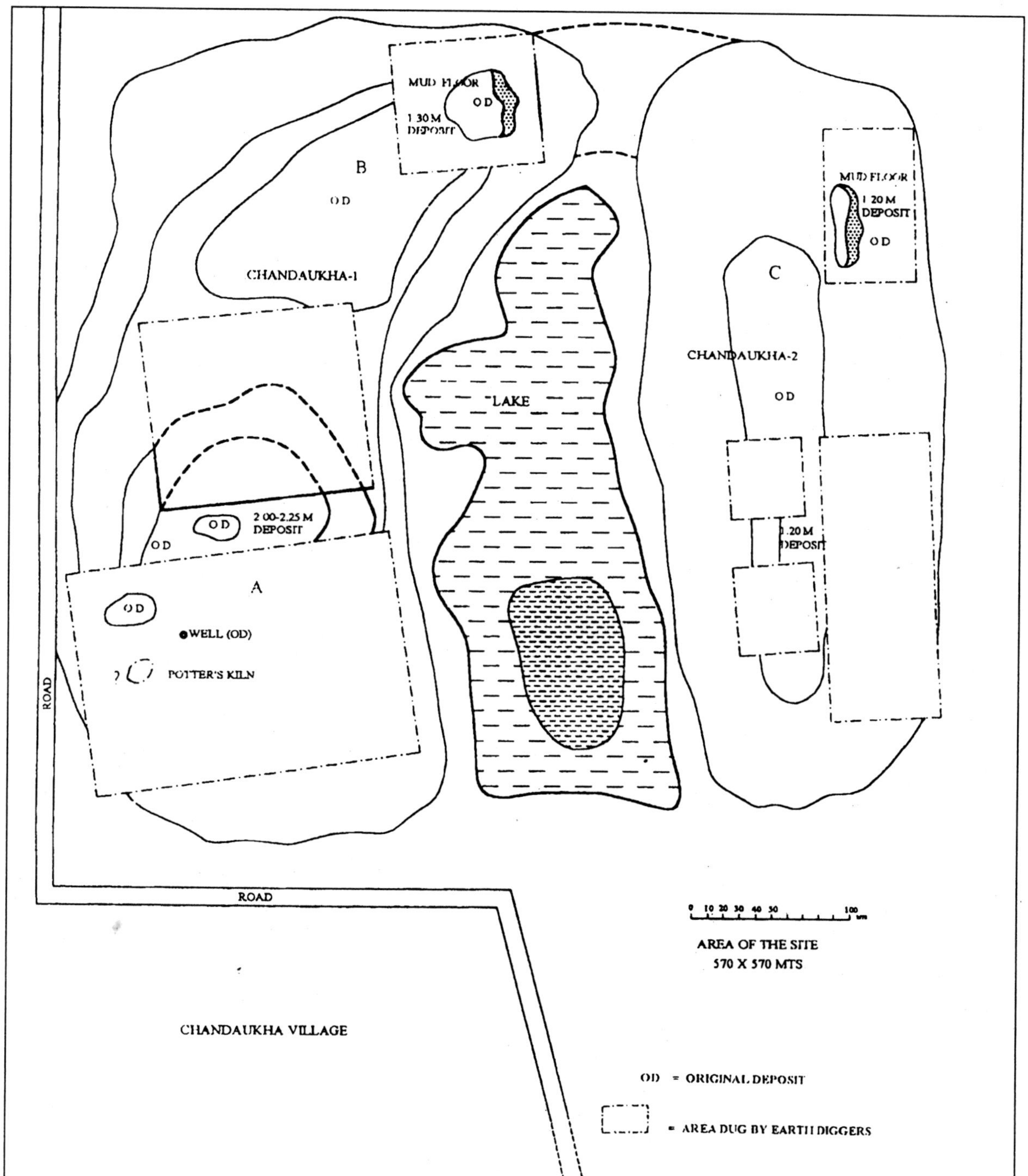

Fig. 1. A Site Plan of Chandaukha District Aligarh.

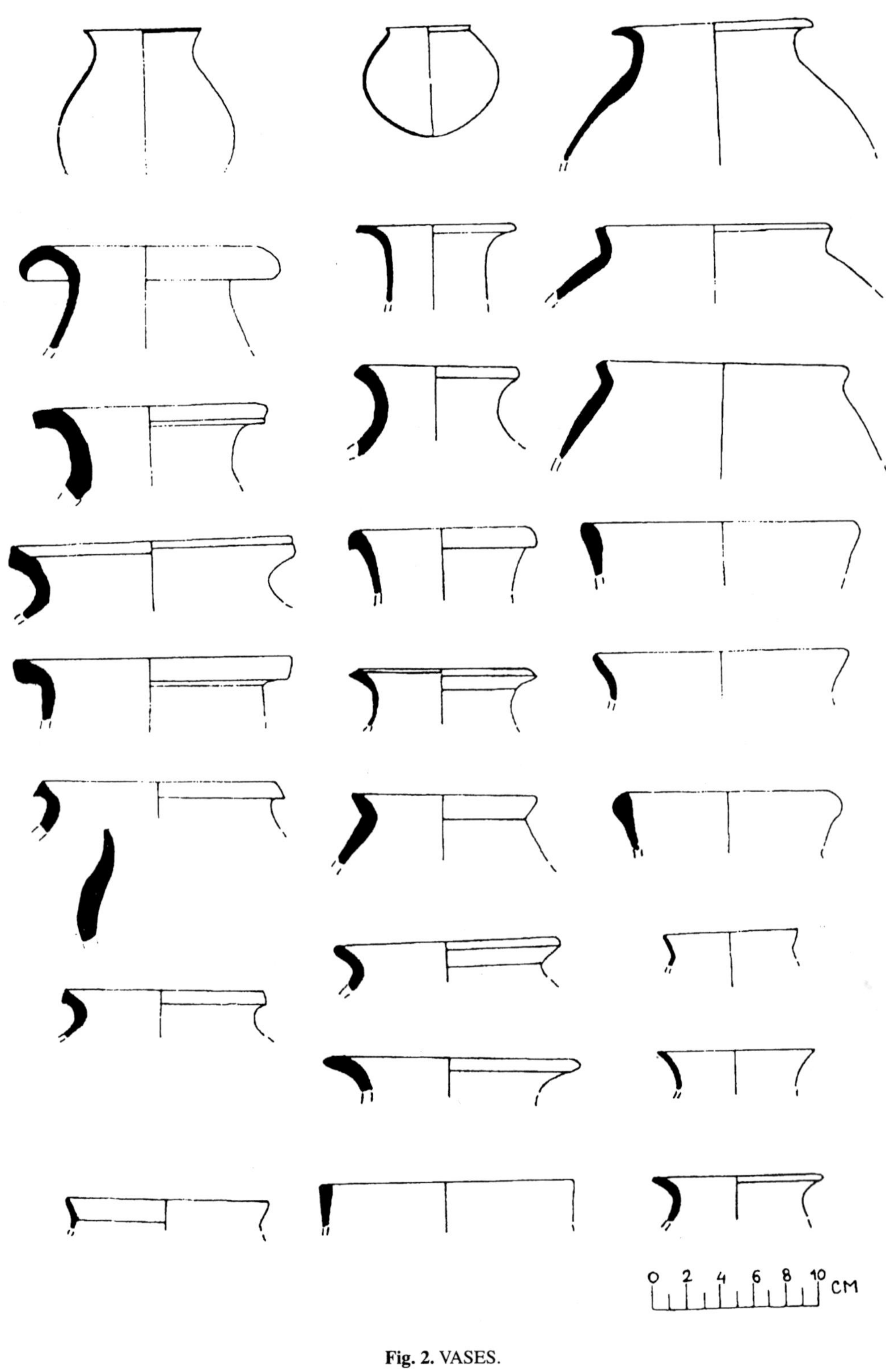

Fig. 2. VASES.

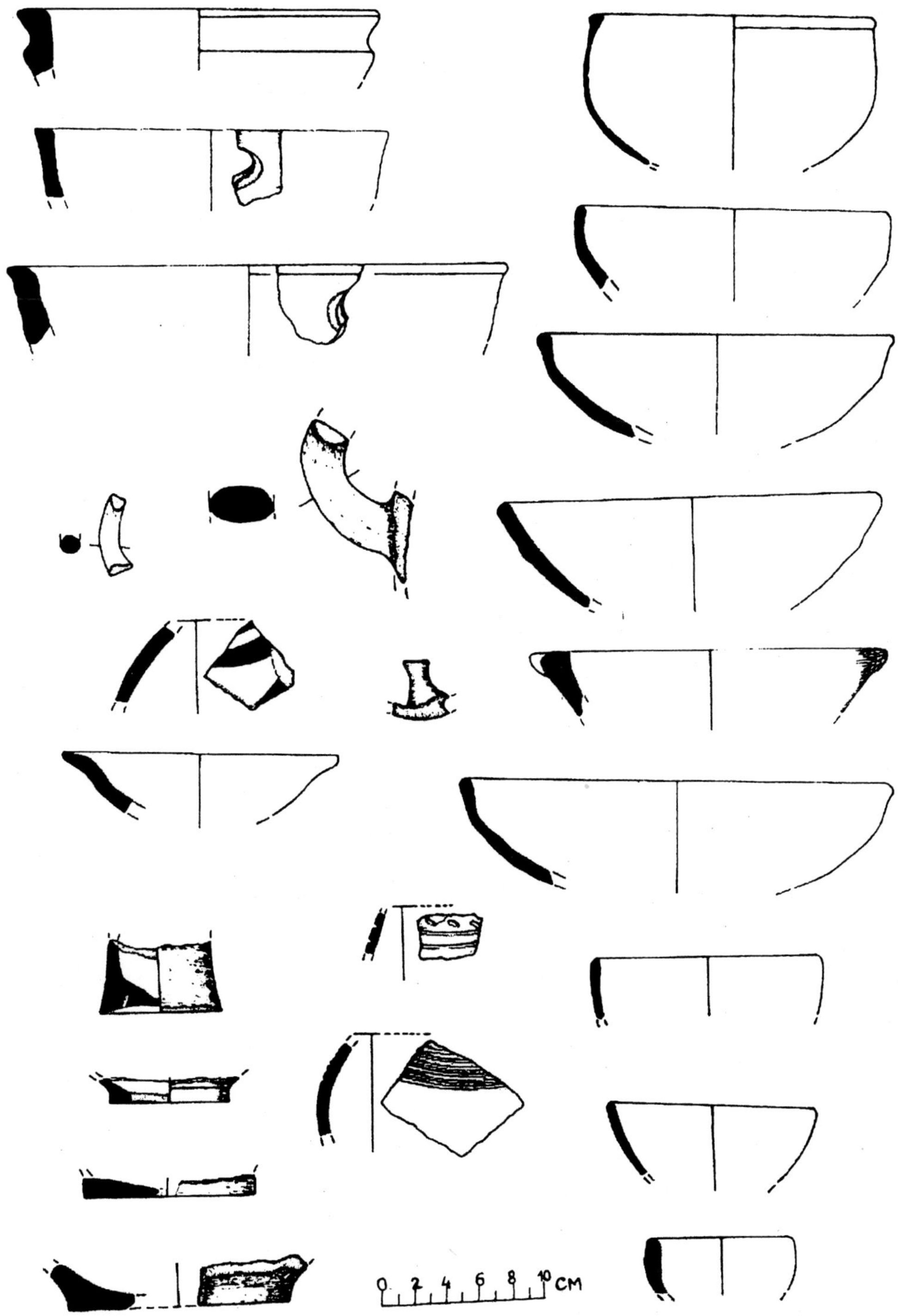

Fig. 3. Bowls, Bases, Lids, Handles, and Incised & Painted Sherds.

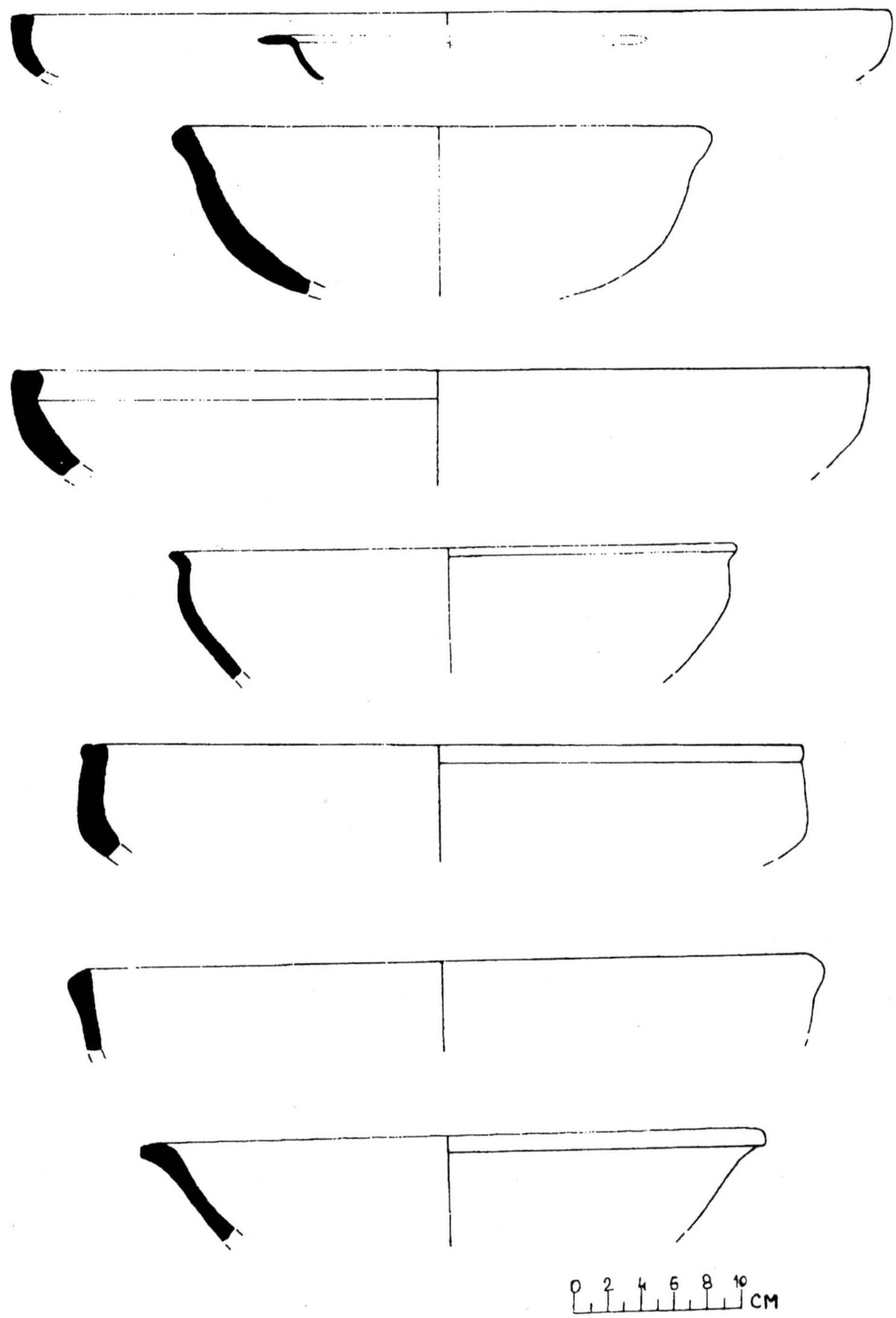

Fig. 4. Basins & Dishes.

Socio-economic and Religious Importance of Maluti Terracotta Plaques

Maluti, a small village of Dumka district, now in newly formed province of Jharkhand is famous for a cluster of beautiful brick built temples decorated with terracotta plaques of late Medieval period. It is situated only 16 kms west of Rampurhat (West Bengal) and 50 kms south of Dumka town. It is well connected by metalled road from both towns. Its nearest railway station is Mallarpur, which is only 10 kms from this village.

The temples of Maluti were brought to light in the year 1979 by A.K.Sinha, Director of Archaeology, Govt. of Bihar, Patna (Sinha 1979). Since then many archaeologists as well as art critics visited this village to know the importance of these temples. About 72 temples have been declared protected by the Directorate of Archaeology, Bihar, under the "Bihar Ancient Monuments, Archaeological sites and Remains Act, 1976" in the year 1981.

Historicity of this village is quite interesting. It is said that Nawab Alauddin Hussain Shah of Gauda (1493-1519 A.D.) awarded this region as a *Nankar-raj* or tax free state to a Brahmin boy Basant Ray for bringing back his queen's lost "Baj" (eagle). One of the rulers of this kingdom established his capital at Maluti and since then about 72 temples dedicated to Lord Shiva was constructed. Some of these are well decorated with terracotta plaques showing religious, social and economic themes of the prevailing society.

Architecturally, plan of these temples are very simple, having no regular shape. Generally, the architect combined *Nagara* and *Besara* temples plan to form a style of its own or constructed in typical "*Chala*" style of Bengal temple architecture, which consisted only one central sanctum or *garbhagriha* based on a square platform with a thatched roof shape.

The temple of Maluti are richly decorated with beautiful terracotta plaques made of well-levigated clay. Clay is the cheapest material, which satisfies the creativity of general people. That is why the artists use terracotta plaques, depicting different aspects of socio-religious life of the people, on the outer face of the temples not only to beautify them but also to satisfy the religious thrust of the people of this area.

The front walls of these temples are generally decorated with religious scenes taken from the wide range of legendary tales, the Epics and the Puranas. Among them, fight scene of Lord Ram and Ravana, figures of ten incarnations of Lord Vishnu, Mahisassuramardini and Kamala-Kamini are prominent one. Some small plaques depict Kartihaya Ganesh etc. In a singular specimen of Ram-Ravana fight scene, the monkeys are shown throwing stones over the demons. The story of *Kaliyadamana* of Lord Krishna reminds one of the supernatural powers of god. The *Vastra-haran* has been depicted in a natural way. Lord Krishna playing flute alongwith Radha is quite beautiful. The *Bakasurbadh* scene is also interesting. Apart from the Ramayana and Mahabharata scenes the artist depicts Lord Shiva on the bull, Goddess Lakshmi, Kali, Chhinnamastika, Manasa etc. in separate plaques systematically in the form of individual stories.

A number of terracotta plaques fixed in the temples of Maluti show different aspects of the society. One of the plaques shows farmer ploughing the field with the help of bull and furrow while in another plaque, we see four labourers carrying a palanquin of their master. Further, depiction of boat carrying the queen and sailing by the *mallahas* is elegant. This Naukavilas terracotta plaque is very popular in Bengali society. Cow's milk is treated as *amrit* since time immemorial. We see the milkman milking the cow and lady churning the butter in terracotta plaques fixed in the Maluti temples. One of the plaques is quite interesting in which we see women gossiping in a group. Most interesting point to note is the construction of two temples by washermen, which indicates that even the lower caste people of the society were pious and religious. These temples bear inscription also. Some of the plaques show security persons holding guns, which indicates that the rulers of Maluti were well acquainted with the use of arms and ammunition even during the early decades of 19th Century A.D. Hence we see that the master makers of Maluti terracotta plaques tried their best to depict each and every aspect of the society.

All these social scenes also throw light on the economic life of the people of Maluti. It shows that the society was divided into different groups and each group was engaged in different occupations to form a systematic economic infrastructure within the society. Their economy was based upon cultivation and domestication of animals. It seems that the milk industry was common. The relation between the king and his subjects was very cordial. The noble people of Maluti were interested in constructing temples instead of pucca houses.

The Maluti temples now in the newly formed Jharkhand state are one of the singular examples of Bengal's temple architecture and terracotta art. It may be called Vishnupur of Jharkhand state.

REFERENCES

Sinha, Ajoy Kumar 1979, Malutigram Ka Purattavika Mahattava.

Sinha, Ajoy Kumar, Santhal Paragana District through the Ages.

Rashmi Sinha

Technological Studies of Iron Implements from Nagara

Introduction

Material science methods and their applications in analyzing and interpreting artefacts from various aspects have come a long way. New archaeological concerns have led to new questions being asked and more exact methods are being adopted for the analysis of data. Various scholars have emphasized on technological studies of iron objects from various areas and varying periods right from the beginning of the 20th century. A great deal of research works in the field of metal technology and metallurgy has been published in the last four decades. Among them metallographic studies of iron objects from Prakash (Athavale 1967), Alamgirpur (Tandon 1968), Kausambi (Prakash & Singh 1968), Rajghat (Bharadawaj 1973) Dhatwa (Hegde 1973), Mahurjhahiri and Naikund (Gogte 1983), Padurajar Dhibi (Chattopadhyaya & De 1989), Khairadih (Agrawal et al, 1990) etc. are noteworthy.

Several Early Historic settlements have been excavated in Gujarat. Though a large number of iron objects have been recovered from these excavations, understanding of the nature and character of technology of this period still remains in embryonic stage. The objective of the present paper is to understand and assess the level of iron technology achieved by the Early Historical community at Nagara.

Nagara (22° 41' N; 73° 38' E) is situated in Cambay Taluka of Kheda district of Gujarat. The excavation of the site was carried out by Department of Archaeology and Ancient History, M.S. University of Baroda from 1963-1965 (Mehta 1968). The site revealed a cultural assemblage of four successive periods (period I-IV). Period I (700 B.C.-300 B.C.) represented by Black- and Red-Ware and an earthen embankment. Period II (300 B.C.-100 A.D.) is marked by the advent of NBPW. Terracotta seals and potsherds bearing Brahmi script (IAR 1963-64) were also recovered from this period. Period III (1st-9th century A.D.) was distinguished by iron knives, blades and arrowheads. The associated antiquities were Red polished Ware, Roman Amphore, Burnished Black Ware, semiprecious stones, copper coins, bells, gold foils, silver and lead coins, stone images, pestles, numerous fragments of conch, bangles and terracotta seals and sealing. The C-14 date for the Early Historical level of the site is 1945+90 and 2030+105 BP, i.e. 130 A.D.

In total 179 iron objects were obtained from Nagara. These objects were heavily corroded. The nails were showing some core without corrosion. The heavy calcareous and corrosion deposits on these were removed and the specimens were mechanically cleaned with metallic brushes. The chemical analysis and metallographic studies were conducted for six representative artefacts viz., one arrowhead, one spearhead and four nails. The objective of chemical analysis was to examine the constituents of the objects and trace elements present in them. The metallographic examination was done to understand internal structure of the metal, physical and mechanical arrangement of the component particles, kind of extraneous particulate matter, nature of mechnical and heat treatment applied on the object, etc.

Sample No. 1: Arrowhead

The arrowhead is broken from the tip and is heavily corroded. It has a tang and is weighing 14.86 gm.

Sample No. 2: Spearhead

The convex sided long blade of the spearhead is sharp on both the edges (Plate:1). It is tapering but end was broken. It has a clear prominent broken handle. It is of 68.57 mm length with a maximum width of 39.87 mm and weighing 58.34 mm.

Sample No. 3: Nail

The broken nail (Plate: 2) has featureless head and pointed working end. It is of 53.68 mm length and weighing 11.012 gm.

Sample No. 4: Nail

The nail is broken from both the ends. It has a featureless head, heavily siliceous surface and was corroded in deep. It weighed 13.75 gm.

Sample No. 5: Nail

The nail has featureless head, which is broken from both the ends. Heavily calcareous surface is corroded in deep. It is of 62.83 mm in length, 9.92 mm of thickness and weighing 16.55 gm.

Sample No. 6: Nail

This nail is of a peculier feature. It is having incurved coiled head and pointed end. It is 73.01 mm in length and is weighing about 18.8 gm.

Metods of Study

a) Chemical Analysis

The chemical analysis can provide information regarding the constituents of objects and determine the amount of components. The nature and proportions of the minor consitituents is a useful pointer to the source of ores, methods of extraction and their working in the case of an unalloyed metal. On analysis even the metal derived from a single source of ore will not give a proportion-by-proportion reflection of the elements present as minor constituents. This is due to the loss, which occurs during roasting, smelting, refining and casting. One must therefore expect the results of chemical analysis to reflect the vagaries of primitive working methods.

The analysis was done by Atomic Absorption Spectroscopic method (GBC 902 Double beam Atomic Absorption Spectrophotometer). Standard solutions of known concentrations are aspirated and the absorbance for a range of concentrations is noted. Once the instrument is calibrated the concentration of archaeological samples are measured. The concentration of elements is measured in parts per million levels and then the weight percentage is calculated. The concentration of elements present in the samples under study is indicated in table 1.

b) Metallographic Examination

Metallographic is the study of structural characteristics, that is the constitution of a metal or an alloy in relation to its physical and mechanical properties (Garside 1957). Microscopic studies facilitate an adequate understanding of various stages of manufacture of the object from the extraction of the metal, constitution of the metal, fabrication treatment, non-metallic inclusions, extent of corrosion etc. The microstructure reveals features such as grain size, grain shape, dendrites, inclusions and matrix constituents. Each of these characteristic features indicates the sort of treatment undergone by the object in the hands of the smiths.

Small sections were cut from each object by using electric saw. The specimen was mounted by using cold setting compound DPI-RR Cold Cure, Acrylic Repair material. The specimens were prepared by grinding and mechanical polishing. Final polishing was done on a polishing machine, in which velvet cloth applied with diamond paste was used as abrasive. During polishing kerosene was used as lubricant. Etching of the sections were done with 5% Nital (5 ml Nitric acid and 95 ml Methyl alcohol). The specimen was washed thoroughly in running water and then dried in absolute alcohol. In most cases an acid mixture, (92 ml HCL, 5 ml H_2SO_4, 3ml HNO_3) was also used for etching. To identify the metallographic features, the specimen was examined under Leitz Laborlux 12 Pol D and CarlZeiss, Neophot-2.

Results

Table 1: Chemical Composition of Iron Samples from Nagara.

Sp	Fe	C	S	P	Cu	Ca	Mg	Mn	Si	Ti	Al	Ni
1	60.02	0.04	0.08	0.14	0.03	0.38	0.01	0.02	1.7	Nil	0.12	Nil
2	62.15	0.06	0.10	0.14	0.01	0.43	0.02	0.02	1.6	Nil	0.11	Nil
3	64.12	0.12	0.09	0.04	0.02	0.31	0.11	0.01	2.02	Nil	0.10	Nil
4	63.97	0.05	0.08	0.04	0.02	0.41	0.16	0.01	3.05	Nil	0.1	Nil
5	64.15	0.22	0.07	0.06	0.04	0.20	0.15	0.01	2.01	Nil	Tr	0.06
6	63.97	0.21	0.08	0.04	0.02	0.30	0.17	0.03	2.05	Nil	Tr	Nil

Details of Microstructures

No. 1: Arrowhead

Pitting as well as fissures and furrows are noticed in the microstructure. Slag inclusions are uniformly arranged. Corrosion products surrounding ferrite matrix and oxide particles also could be seen in the microstructure. Relic carbide is clearly visible in the microstructure as curves and flows. Many banded features due to forging are also seen.

No. 2: Spearhead

The severe corrosion effect has left a brown thick layer of oxide on the surface. The section at low magnification indicated complete mineralisation and was having very few slag inclusions, which were not expelled during forging operations (Plate3).

No. 3: Nail

The structure is mostly ferrite. At some places 20-25% pearlite are seen. The pearlite is located in the grain boundaries (Magnification 500X). A cavity due to glassy evolution during solidification is observed in the structure. High carbon and low carbon strips are observed alternately. This layered pattern indicates that the object is made of two or more sheets. The welded boundaries are corroded.

No. 4: Nail

Microstructure showed layered pattern of the original tool at the central portion. The outer surface area was carburised and hardened. The area near the surface showed pearlite structure. Towards the inner portion pearlite decreases and ferrite matrix with pearlite colonies are seen. Preferential orientation of relic carbide structure in ferrite matrix with inclusions is also seen.

No. 5: Nail

The microstructure revealed few elongated slag inclusions and oxide particles. There are pearlite colonies at the edge with uniform equiaxed grains. There are grains of iron carbide at the grain boundaries.

No. 6: Nail

The microstructure showed different strips of high and low carbon. The welded portions of the strips are heavily corroded. High and low carbon areas are also observed.

Discussion

The amount of carbon present in the samples supports the fact that the specimen is of wrought iron and low carbon steel. The main impurities present are silica, aluminium, calcium, magnesium, sulphur and phosphorous. The relatively low amount of phosphorus and magnesium indicates that the ore used for the production of these tools are nearly pure. The substantial similarity of the impurities of these specimens suggests that they are made of similar ore.

The presence of slag in the metal imdicates that these objects must have been made out of iron extracted directly by the bloomery process and not from pig iron (Tylecote 1980). The uniform distribution of slag inclusions, which is the characteristic feature of wrought iron, is seen in the arrowhead. The structure of spearhead had been air-cooled after forging as indicated by the "normalized" structure. The studies indicated that the spearhead was fabricated from wrought iron on which some efforts were made to achieve carburisation. Carbon inhomogenity seen in the structures of the working edge of the spearhead is due to preferential decarburisation (Plate 4).

The rolled pattern is due to heat treatment. The presence of several layers in the microstructure indicates that the objects were prepared by forging together the layers of wrought iron sheets, which had been carburised (Lang and Williams 1975). The layering technique of manufacture of tools provided a way by which a tool could be made strong on its working surface (Muhley *et al.* 1977). The process of carburisation of larger block of iron consumes a lot of time compared to that of thin iron sheets. Number of thin iron sheets heated and joined together to get required object, saved the smith's time as well as imparted extra strength to the object.

Conclusion

It may be concluded from the present study that the metalsmiths of Nagara had great ability and workmanship. The chemical and metallographic studies indicated that smiths of this area were known for the extraction of wrought iron. Further, from the studies, it has been understood that the smiths from Nagara were skilled in preparing wrought iron, low carbon and medium steel. They were also aware of forging, welding and lamination techniques.

Acknowledgements

The author wish to acknowledge Dr. K. Krishnan, Reader, Department of Archaeology and Ancient History, M.S. University of Baroda for his invaluable guidance and constant encouragement. I also thank Dr. P.B. Joshi, Reader, Department of Metallurgy, M.S. University for his help in metallographic studies.

REFERENCES

Agrawal, O.P., Narain, H., Prakash, J. and Bhatia, S.K. 1990. Lamination Technique in Iron Artefacts in Ancient India. *Historical Metallurgy* 24(1):pp.12-26.

Athavale, V.T. 1967. Chemical Analysis and Metallographic Examination of Metal objects (Prakash 1955). *Ancient India* 20-21(1964-65);pp. 131-39.

Bharadwaj, H.C., 1973. Aspects of Early Iron Technology in India, *Radiocarbon and Indian Archaeology* (Eds.) Agrawal D.P. and Gosh, A.; pp. 391-400.

Chattopadhyaya, P.K. and De, S. 1989. Iron Objects from Pandurajar Dhibi *Archaeometallurgical Studies*, Steel India 12 (1): pp.33-41.

Gorside, E.J., 1957. *Process and Physical Metallurgy*, London, p.156.

Gogte, V.D., 1982. Megalithic iron smelting at Naikund: Discovery by Three-Probe Resistivity Survey and Efficiency of Iron Smelting by Chemical Analysis, *Naikund Excavations* 1979-80 (Eds) S.B. Deo and A.P. Jamkhedkar, pp.2-59, Bombay. Department of Archaeology and Museums.

Hegde, K.T.M. 1973. A Model for Understanding Ancient Iron Metallurgy. *Man* 8(3):pp.416-21.

Lang, J. and Williams, A.R. 1975. the Hardening of Iron Swords, *Journal of Archaeological Science*, Vol.2,pp. 201-202.

Mehta, R.N. and Shah, D.R. 1968. Excavation at Nagara, *The Maharaja Sayajirao University Archaeology Series No. 10*, Baroda.

Muhley, J.D., Wheeler, T.S. and Maddin, R. 1977. "An Iron Adze of the 5th-6th Centuries BC from Al Mina", *Levant*, Vol. 9, p.159.

Prakash, S. and Singh, R. 1968. *Coinage in Ancient India*. New Delhi: pp. 529-532.

Tandon, O.P. 1967-68. Alamgirpur and the Iron Age in India *Puratattva* (1), pp. 154-159.

Tylecote, R.F. 1980. Furnaces, Crucibles and Slags; *The Coming of the Age of Iron*, Yale University Press, London, p. 209.

Department of Archaeology and Ancient History,
M.S. University of Baroda,
Vadodara (Gujarat)

Ambika Patel

Conservation at Anup Talao, Fatehpur Sikri

Some misconceptions have been created about the recent conservation work executed by the Archaeological survey of India, Agra Circle, at Anup Talao in Fatehpur Sikri, and it is necessary to dispel them.

Anup Talao (lit. unparalleled Tank) is situated in front of Khwabgah Palace of Akbar at Fatehpur Sikri. Contemporary historian Badaoni says that it was completed in A.D. 1576, when the *Ibadat-khanah* (the house of worship) of Akbar was also finished presumably in its vicinity (Lowe 1973: 204:212). The profusely ornamented *Hujra* (chamber), situated on its northeastern corner (wrongly called Turkish Sultana's Palace) was most probably used by the emperor himself. It was here as Badaoni has recorded that Akbar used to receive visitors, including such honored guest like Mirza Sulaiman (Lowe 1973). Akbar's court historian Abu'l Fazl noted that an order was given in 1578 to fill the Anup Talao with copper, silver and gold coins, which were later distributed personally by the emperor (H.Beveridge, 1973:354-355, 374). Jehangir, Akbar's son, confirmed the event, though he named it 'Kapur-Talao' (Rogers & Beveridge, 1968:68-69). More confusing is the difference in their measurements: while Abu'l Fazl recorded that it measured 20 by 20 qaz. (53 by 53 feet, qaz measuring 32 inches) and twice at a man's height in depth (about 11 feet) (Beveridge 1973:354), Jehangir's measurements are 36 by 36 yards with a depth of 4.5 yards (96x96x12 feet, at 32 inches a *gaz*—Roger of Beveridge 1968:68-69), which exactly tallys with the existing tank.

Anup Talao (also called 'Char-Chamand' in popular parlance, owing to its four bridges) is a red sandstone masonry *pucca* tank, square on plan, measuring 96 square feet. In its middle are a platform *(mah-tab)*, 30 feet square, with *jalli* balustrade, and a *chabutarah* (raised seat) 12 feet square in its middle. The original *baradari* (pillared pavilion) built on this seat is no longer there. Four stone bridges, supported on stone piers, connect with it with four banks. Six broad stairs descended below the water level. The bed of the tank was paved with stone slabs, which were loosening and cracking. It was also observed, more alarmingly, that fine carvings of the adjoining buildings, mainly the profusely ornamented *Hujra* (chamber) of Akbar, were peeling off up to the dado-level, and it was apprehended that dampness was seeping into the adjoining palaces and damaging them through (salt) action. Its conservation was absolutely necessary.

When a few slabs of the bed were removed, it was discovered that this bed was not original and, at some point of time, the tank had been filled up with debris, rubble stones, mortar and mud. Another series of six stairs leading down to the original water-level, the original stone-paved bed of the tank about 3 feet (92 cm) below the last (i.e. the 12th) stair, and the original depth of 12 feet, as exactly recorded by Jahangir (Rogers & Beveridge 68-69) and approximately by Abu'l Fazl (Beveridge: 111:354), were exposed. Conservation of all was more necessary not only to prevent dampness penetrating into the foundations, and to make it watertight and damp-proof, but also to remove the debris and restore the tank to its original form.

It is significant to mention that, on investigation it was reported that there were frequent cases of drowning in the tank when it was in the original form. Young boys dived and were sometimes accidentally caught under the ceiling of the corridor (below the central island-platform) drowned. The last case of such a death occurred in early fifties (when son of one Master Moinuddin of Mantola, Agra died) and, on public outcry, the tank was filled up with debris, rubble stones, mortar and mud and thus burried the original floor level and the lower six stairs.

Here it may be pointed out that the tank was originally fed by a *nali* (water-channel) from the Hatipol (Elephant-Gate) water-works on the western side, and another *nali* from the eastern water-works (both drawing water from the perennial *baolis* (step wells). The water level in the tank was thus controlled and kept up to the brim of the bottom-reservoir and not above. That is why, 12 stairs were provided to reach to it. This is corroborated by the fact that the pillars of the tank, supporting the island-platform, have exquisite carved relief-capitals, which were intended to be seen above the water level. Originally, no rainwater was allowed into it. It was a Royal tank facing the King's personal palace and was meant primarily to bring down the temperature of the complex, and provide it with a beautiful environment. That is why several mini-tanks and canals were built on the eastern platform of the Khwabgah and the eastern edge of the tank (below the stone *saraparda*, now converted into a garden). Anup Talao was planned as the pivot of this water system for the exclusive use of the emperor. It may be reiterated that the original intention of builders was to keep the water level up to the bottom-reservoir but later rainwater was diverted into it, the drains were choked and excess water filled the tank up to the brim making drowning accidents a common factor. All these need to the restored to its original form.

The pillars supporting the island-platform (externally) make a corridor, which runs around a central chamber, which is closed. Nothing is known about it. More puzzling is the discovery of a stone masonry structure, which is plastered over in the northeastern quarter of the tank (in the direction of Hujra, or Akbar's personal chamber marked 'B' in the section, fig. 2). It is also closed on all sides, except a slanting ventilator in its roof.

Badaoni (Lowe: 11:272) has mentioned in 1579 about an attempt of a certain Hakim to build an under-water house at Fatehpur Sikri in a tank which measured 20x20 yards. He even described it. The attempt failed. But, he noted that Hakim 'Ali Gilani' certainly built such an under-water chamber at Lahore in 1594 and he recorded its chronogram: 'Hauz-I-Hakim Ali' (Lowe: 11:272), which gives the exact date: A.H. 1002 i.e. A.D. 1594, to confirm that it was actually finished. Abul Fazl corroborated that such an under-water room was built in 1594 by Hakim 'Ali Gilani' (Beveridge 111:1000). But it was built at Lahore, and not at Fatehpur Sikri.

What is this structure, which has now been discovered in Anup Talao for the first time? It is an enigma. Is it the same under-water chamber which certain Hakim tried to build at Fatehpur Sikri in 1579 and failed? Or, is it the one built subsequent to the successful execution of the Lahore experiment, which has not been recorded?

Whatever may be the case, this is a structure, which requires immediate conservation and research and it is imperative to investigate two of its problems viz.:

I. The balustraded island-platform stands on a room (marked 'A' in the section, fig.2), which is carefully closed by stone masonry on all sides, to make it water-proof, and hence inaccessible. This is against the medieval practice of construction. Either a system of open arches or beams should have been used to support it; but cannot be a solid mass of masonry. What is inside it? How was it accessible? And why and when was it closed?

II. The stone masonry structure, recently revealed in the northeastern quarter of the tank (marked 'B' in the section, fig. 2) is a total mystery. It is built, oddly and quite irregularly, partially on the original bed (bottom of reservoir) of the tank and partially on its stairs, and does not form part of original tank. That it has a ventilator in its roof suggesting the existence of some short of chamber. But this too is closed on all sides by stone masonry and therefore inaccessible. What is this structure? And when and why was it built?

It must be emphasized that no excavation, or digging of any sort, has been done at Anup Talao, and the Agra Circle of Arecheological Society of India has only removed the modern filing viz. debris, rubble stones, mortar and mud, which were used to fill the bottom/tank and its six lower stairs. The A.S.I. Agra Circle has not removed, or disturbed in any way, even a single original stone from its position (marked by red line in the accompanying drawing, fig. 2), and the question of any damage to the monument does not arise.

Those who have spread misinformations that Anup Talao has been excavated by Archaelogical Society of India had intention to find out Hindu sculptures and to scandalize the survey. It is absurd and one is amazed how the Indian History Congress in its last session at Kolkata could persuade to pass a resulation acccepting this wild allegation without visiting the site, without verifying the facts by any other means or by contacting the Archaelogical Society of India. It is a blatant lie which has been perpetrated with mala fide intention, just to prevent the nationally important archaeological excavation being carried out at the Bir-Chhabili Tila, just at the bank of the Fatehpur Sikri lake, about a kilometre away from Akbar's palaces, where a temple and Jaina sculptures of 10th and 11th centuries A.D. with inscription, including the unique image of 'Srutidevi Saraswati' dated A.D. 1010, have been unearthed.

REFERENCES

Beveridge, H, 1973, (Tr. in English) Akbarnamah of Abdul Fazl, Delhi.

Lowe, WH, 1973 (Tr. in English).

Muntakhabu't: Tawarikh by Mulla Abdul Qudir Badaoni, Vol.II Delhi.

Rogers, A. and Beveridge H. (Tr. in English), 1968 Jehangir Mafnah or Tuzuk-I-Jehangir, 2vm, Delhi.

D.V. Sharma

Superintending Archaeologist
Archaeological Survey of India
New Delhi

Gold Objects from Painted Grey Ware Levels at Jakhera

The Painted Grey Ware culture (1100-700 B.C.) represents an important period of early Iron Age phase of Northern India. Several excavated sites have provided evidence on industrial and agricultural productions and various aspects of the material culture. However, gold objects are not reported from any site except Jakhera. Jakhera (Sahi 1994) is the type-site where the excavations were undertaken on horizontal plan and covered the maximum area of PGW levels. Fourfold culture sequence has come to light at Jakhera; period IIIB represents the mature phase of PGW, which deserve a special mention. Besides many luxurious items in bone, glass, ivory, terracotta and S.P.S. etc. as many as 185 iron objects, 82 copper objects and 9 gold objects were also found from the PGW levels. Gold objects are quite interesting and suggestive of prosperous phase at this site.

The gold objects which were recovered from the stratified PGW layers comprise:

1. A leaf-shaped object slightly damaged and corrugated. It may be identified as the pendent of a necklace or part of it. It was manufactured from a thin sheet.

2. It is spiral of flat sheet with rounded terminals, intact and probably it could be identified as an ear ornament or a nose ring.

3. It is thick folded wire, hammer marks are quite clear and is squarish in cross section. It appears to be an electrum of silver, due to light yellowish in colour.

4. It is tubular in shape, made of very thin foil of gold and is in brittle condition. Perhaps it was used in covering any solid copper or any other metallic object or S.P.S. object.

5. It is coil of extremely thin wire; most probably it was used for embroidery work.

6. It is thin folded wire, round in cross section. Probably it was drawn through an instrument called *Janti* (a scale like instrument of thick metal plate having holes of various thicknesses, used for drawing fine wire of desired thickness. It is still used by local goldsmiths).

Out of nine objects, only six were identifiable and three tiny pieces of foils were of indeterminate nature. In the absence of metallurgical analysis, it would be very difficult to say about the alloying percentage of silver or copper. But it is certain that both copper and silver were employed in alloying. Alloying was done to harden the gold and to make it workable and to produce elegant lusture.

Among other important items found at this site mention may be made of goldsmith's Banknar (a typical instrument of goldsmith, commonly used by goldsmiths even now-a-days, for blowing hot flame on the metal). It was a noteworthy discovery of the site. The above-mentioned instrument *(Banknar)* is made of thin copper tube, hallow internally, cylindrical in shape and tapering towards one of the ends. It is most important tool of goldsmith which is used to control and concentrate the heat in smelting small bits of gold in the desired shape as well as soldering and fusing the joints of ornaments. Occurrence of unifinished objects more particularly a small crucible suggests that goldsmiths must have possessed adequate knowledge of its metallurgy. Many other tools of various types such as chisels, borers and awls used in smithy work were also found at the site from PGW levels. A unique specimen of pair of iron tongs from PGW levels at Atranjikhera (Gaur 1983) has also been reported (Plate XL.VIII).

Not only gold but to supplement it, copper was also used for making ornaments. Copper ornaments recovered from PGW levels included 6 beads, 9 bangles, a nose pin and an ear ornament while other objects were toothpick, antimony-rod-cum-nail-parers, and antimony rods. Beads of steatite, lapislazuli, amethyst and jasper were possibly used for decorating the golden jewellery. These beads were recovered from the corresponding mature PGW phase (Pd. IIIB).

An oval shaped furnace having light, whitish ash was found on the southwestern periphery of the mound JKH I. Its wall was plastered with husk mixed clay. It is interesting to note that a gold object mentioned above as item No. 4 was also found in the adjoining area. This indicates the working place of a goldsmith. Almost similar workshop of goldsmith is reported from the Harappan levels at Banawali (Bisht 1982) and Inamgaon (Dhavilkar 1997) from the Deccan chalcolithic levels. Gold objects have been reported from many Harappan sites but are found rarely in later levels.

Gold ear ornament reported from late Prabhas level (1700-1400 B.C.) bears striking similarity to those of decorated gold foil of Atranjikhera from Pd. IV. Both are impressed in floral motifs. But the foils encountered at Jakhera reveals no floral motif. A spiral earring akin to item No. 2 mentioned above, have been reported from Diamabad (IAR 1958-59). An impressed gold leaf showing human figure identified with fire god Angi, a circular gold pendent and small piece of chain was found from Purola, District Uttar Kashi (Nautiyal and Khanduri 1988-89). These were found from a pit chamber, which were placed in thick grey ware bowl. But this evidence comes from the historical level. According to excavator these objects were purposely placed. It has been suggested that gold as an auspicious and valuable metal was placed inside the chamber to propiciate Agnideva, who was the first diety to be worshipped in a sacrificial ritual.

In the *Rig Veda*, (II 5.6) Agni (Fire) is requested to accept *ahuti* from Juhu, the vessel that gives sacrifice. Gold and bricks are associated items of sacrificial Vedic alter (Kramarich 1976). The *Rig-Veda* also mentions the use of gold, during the sacrificial rites.

Almost similar evidence was noticed at Jakhera in PGW phase. A semicircular burnt-brick structure enclosing a shallow fire pit was exposed at KJH-I in trench C2 layer (8). Occurrence of gold objects and terracotta human figurines from the same area is probably an evidence of fire alter. Thus it can be concluded that gold was not only sign of prosperity and used in ornament but was also offered in sacrifices, because it was considered as a pure and sacred metal.

Gold also has medicinal proprieties. It is also considered to be a miracle cure for many ailments, which is alluded to in the *Atharva Veda*, (XI, I, 28). In ancient literary accounts throwing light on ancient chemistry, gold is regarded as a panacea for all ills. The gold *bhasma* is said to be a good tonic and is supposed to cure of various diseases. It is said to remove the ill effects of old age and thus used to restore the vigour of manhood, to sharpen the memory, improve the voice and colour of the body and to promote strength. Most probably the tiny pieces of gold foils found at Jakhera were a step in the preparation of gold *bhasm.*

Gold occurs as placer metal (alluvial or detrital) in the auriferous sands and gravels of a large number of rivers, which pass over auriferous rocks. This must have been a major source of gold in ancient India. The rivers of Punjab, Madhya Pradesh, Maharashtra, Bihar etc. yielded gold from the immemorable past until recent times. J. Abbott (1847) has described how gold was being extracted from the quartz hornblende bearing granite and gneiss rocks pounded by the boulders in the mountainous stream of Vipasa, where the rivulet Chukki meets the river. The attrition product, 'literally dust', was sieved and elutriated to obtain the 'black sand' containing gold. In half an hour, nine men were producing about two pounds of very fine and sparkling black sand. Then the material was amalgamated, and the amalgam put upon a piece of ignited cow dung, when 'mercury flew leaving the yellow gold'. This process might have been used in India for centuries (Biswas 1996). Gold is also noticed in Nijnor, Nainital and Garhwal in Uttar Pradesh (now Uttaranchal), where in usual methods of washing the auriferous sands found in the riverbeds such as the Ramganga, Sukhar Sot, Phike and Khoh in the Nagina Tehsil of the Bijnor district. In Early Historic times gold was obtained by washing alluvium from the Son River very near to Southeast border of Garhwal near Kalararh. In Madhya Pradesh alluvial gold is found in the sands and gravels of many rivers like Son a major tributary of the Ganges as well as in the Himalayan Rivers and Simla hills in the Bilaspur District. In North India, few ancient gold gold working are to be found in Cotanagpur and Bihar and in the District of Balaghat, Jaspur, Mandi, Raipur, Seoni, Bastar and Bilaspur in Madhya Pradesh. The goldsmith of Jakhera to obtain gold may have used the above-mentioned method.

Gold mines of South India have been the richest source for native gold right from the Pre-historic times. Most of the Neolithic sites like Piklihal, Kodekal, Maski, etc. are found around the Maski gold-field[21] near the Kolar (Allachin 1962). Some well-known ancient gold mining activities have been discovered here. At very early stages gold nuggets were collected from the surface and gold was mined by open cast method. Most of the gold obtained from these mines are mixed with silver. But it appeas to be most unlikely that the PGW people derived their gold from South India, particulary in view of the fact that gold bearing sand-dust was available in the river beds within their dispersal area. Trade contacts of the PGW people with the Southern India is yet to be properly established.

During the earlier Copper-Bronze age, gold has been reported from the Neolithic (Tekalkota), Harappan (Jalilpur, Kalibangan, Banawali, Kunal, etc.) and Chalcolithic (Diamabad, Inamgaon, Jorwe, etc). But during the early Iron Age, very few evidences have been reported hence the importance of Jakhera evidence is significant. The other site reporting gold pellets is Pandu Rajar Dhibi from Period III (Pre-NBP) (Desgupta 1964).

In Gangetic doab, during the early Iron Age, complete knowledge of metal technology and their sources is respect of copper, iron lead, arsenic and gold changed the life style of people. Crucibles have been reported only at Jakhera, which may have been used for processing gold.

In the absence of chemical analysis of the objects it is premature to make any guess regarding various aspects of gold-technology. But the evidence does suggest the presence of goldsmith at the site along with his craft.

To conclude it may be observed that Painted Grey Ware people at the site used to obtain metallic gold from gold dust found in neighbouring region as mentioned above. Local goldsmith smelted the metal and manufactured ornaments of various types, wires and foils. Thread like wire was used in embroidery work to cater to the taste of economically richer people, whereas foils were probably used to cover the copper ornaments for making it cheaply available. Most probably gold was also used for ritualistic rites as well as for producing medicines. Over all gold objects throw valuable light on the economic prosperity of the PGW people of Jakhera.

Acknowledgements

The author pays his respectful thanks to Prof. S.P. Gupta, Chairman Centre of Advance Study, Department of History, Aligarh Muslim University, Aligarh for encouraging me to make this maiden attempt and to Prof. M.D.N. Sahi for using the material from the excavated site of Jakhera and for helping and inspiring me in various ways.

REFERENCES

Allachin, F.R. (1962): Upon the antiquity and Methods of gold mining in Ancient India, *Journal of Economic and Social History of Orient*, Vol. V, pl. II, p. 209.

BANKAR, a typical instrument of goldsmith, commonly used by goldsmiths even now a day, for blowing hot flame on the metal

Biswas, A.K. (1996): *Minerals and Metals in Ancient India*, New Delhi. Vol. 2, pp. 327-28.

Bisht, R.S. (1982): *Excavations At Banawali* - 1974-77. In Harappan Civilization (ed.) G.L. Possehl, pp. 116-118.

Das Gupta, PC (1964): *Excavation at Pandu Rajar Dhibi*, Calcutta.

Dhavalikar, M.K. (1997): *Indian Protohistory*, New Delhi, p. 48.

Kramarisch, Stella (1976): *The Hindu Temple*, Vol. 1, p. 153.

Nautial, K.P. Khanduri, B.M. (1988-89): *Excavations of a Vedic Brick Alter* at Purola, District Uttar Kashi, and Central Himalaya. *Puratattva*, No. 19, pp.68-69.

Sahi, M.D.N. (1994): *Aspects of Indian Archaeology*, Jaipur, and p.39.

Department of History,
Aligarh Muslim University,
Aligarh (U.P.)

Ramjit

The Enigmatic Temple of Boudha Danda

Archaeological investigations carried out in and around the Sidhi district of Central India have yielded artefacts right from Prehistory to Historical and modern period. To suffice, interestingly the Vindhyan region has witnessed the rise and fall of various art schools, since the inception of erection of structural monuments in the Maurya-Sunga reign. The stupas, temples, monasteries, *vyakhyanasalas*, portals and ponds dotting the horizon, stand testimony to this fact. The Mauryas, the Sungas, the Guptas, the Kalchuris and the Pratiharas who had swayed here, were not only the great builders but gave patronage to art and artisans too.

Sidhi is not an exception. Our recent exploration here has brought to light some outlandish achievements which inturn may prove seminal in understanding the development of art traditions in the region in particular and in North India in general. Fossil bearing sites, Mara caves[1], monolithic temple[2], brick temple of Madfe Danda[3], are only a tip of iceberg. Future exploration, however, may reveal the repertory of archaeological remains of the region to help divulge the mystery of oblivion. Previously the region was considered a stronghold of the Kalchuris in Early Medieval period[4] and the monastery and a temple at Chandrehe was the only standing monument of paramount importance[5], which was highly eredulous to connoisseurs. Since then things are changing shape.

The present paper, however, discusses of Boudha Danda group of temples situated at Medhulia near Tenduha village of Singarauli Tehsil in Sidhi district. Abounding in lush green picturesque surrounding the temples stand poised in a dense forest near a perannial *Nalaha* named Suravan and is three kms away from Devara railway station of Central Rrailway on Katni-Chopan route. Near by are scattered tiny mounds of burnt bricks (4"x4"x4"), which are seven in number and a small mound of potsherds called Chaukiya. Broken pieces of *amalaka* (four or five) and other architectural members are conspicuous with their presence. Madfe Danda is not far away from here. One who wishes to visit Boudha Danda has to travel through undulated terrain and cross rivulets. Well-known Mara caves, as the crow flies, are twenty kms (approx.) from here.

Temple No. 1

Built in stone, both temples of Boudha Danda are of modest height (temple no. 1 is 4 m while temple no.2 is 3 m in height) and also facing to west. In horizontal plan, the temple no.1 comprises of a cubical *garbhagriha* (1.30x1.30x1.52 m) in ruins. Whose outer measurement is (2.70x2.50 m) and a *mandapa* (2.15x1.34 m.) in ruins. As only basal portion of the pillars of the *mandapa* are peeping from the ground, the existence of the same is merely conjectural. The hypothesis gains ground from the fact that frontal facade of the temple including the spire of the *sikhara* is badly in ruins, remains of the same could be located hither and thither. Door Jamb (1.15x80 m) seems rejuvenated is entirely plain. Left doorjamb is provided with an attendant. *Lalatabimba* at architrave *(uttaranga)* is adorned with an image of *Gajabhiseka-Lakshmi* or *Kamalatmika,* being popular connotation[6]. Two-armed goddess is seated cross leged on a full blossom lotus. Attribute in her right hand is a lotus stalk while left hand rests in her lap. Her enlarged ears are noticeable. Her headdress too is noteworthy. Devi is nicely rendered, attired and ornamented with *hara* and *mekhala*. Two elephants, one on each lateral side, are pouring water over the goddess with a vessel holding in their trunks. The sanctum sanctorum is devoid of the presiding deity; hence nothing concrete could be said about whom the temple was dedicated. Internally, the *garbhagriha* walls too are quite plain.

In elevation, the temple comprises of *adhisthana, jangha* and *sikhara*. *Trirathi* temple stands on a *padmapeetha* without a *jagati*. *Adhisthana* consists of its usual members *khura, kumbha, kalasa* and *kapotika*. *Kumbha* moulding is provided with human heads. While *kalasa* is adorned with *chaitya* dormer motif in low relief, a prominent feature of the Pratihara period temples in Central India[7]. The recess between the *kalasa* and *kapotika* moulding is relieved with *tula peetha* where as the same motif is occurring in the Central Indian Pratihara temples at the level of *kalasa* moulding[8].

Jangha is divided into three registers, the lowest being elongated while upper two are of the same length and width. The *bhadra rathika* is provided with a pilastered niche, divided into two. The upper niche on south facade contains an image of a seated female with an oval face, elongated ear and folded hands. The lower niche encases a dancing Ganesa. Four armed deity holds *parasu* in his right upper and *modaka* in right lower arm. Attribite in left upper arm is unidentifiable while left lower arm rests on his thigh. His trunk is directed upwards. Pilasters with capital are unpretanious. Each *bhumi* in *karna rathas* is carved with chaitya dormers containing two pilasters each, and a *lumas* hanging above in mid. The *bhadra rathika* on eastern façade, however, contains an image of the standing Sun God. His two hands are holding two full blossom lotuses. Northern *rathika* is with a famale deity, probably Parvati. *Jala pranali* too is seen in north. *Jangha* at its distant end is embellished with *lumas*, one chaitya dormer on each *karna rathas* and three chaitya dormers on *bhadra rathas*. Each chaitya motif contains a famale head with a unique headdress and earrings. *Varandika* separates *jangha* from *sikhara* and in between is a continuous row of *Tula peetha* in a sunken panel.

The *sikhara* of the temple is partially preserved and pinnacle being completely lost, nothing concrete could be said about its morphological configuration. Each *bhumi* invariably comprises of two compressed pilasters with stunted capitals. *Madhyalata*, however, is adorned with chaitya dormer motifs *lumas*. Two *amalakas* are resting on the *karna rathas*. The confines of the two *bhumis* are demarcated with a continuous row of *chaitya* dormers. *Salilanantara* too is noteworthy.

In the vicinity, to the north of the temple is placed a multilated Siva *linga* and a deity in sculptural manifestation beneath a tree -Siva. It seems as if they are still venerated by the local populace. Four-armed deity holds a spear in his right upper arm and a snake in left upper arm; rest of the hands is broken. *Jata mukuta* earrings, *har*, *mekhala*, armlet, sacred thread, anklets and shoes are prominently displayed. Eyes are half open as if in meditation. He has attired himself in *adhovastra*, fringes of which are hanging in front. An attendant is standing below right. In attenuated waist and elongated rendering of the body contour, the sculptor has achieved supremacy of skill. Where about of these specimens is still in desideratum and equally mysterous is the identification of the deity.

Temple No. 2

South to temple number 1 is erected a miniature temple number 2 (1.58x1.58 m) which also faces west. In horizontal plan it consists of only a *garbhagriha* (95x.95x1.10 m), devoid of presiding deity. Doorjamb (1.20x.85 m) too is quite plain. To whom was the temple dedicated, could not be ascertained. In elevation the temple has a low and simple *adhisthana* and *jangha* (1.00 m in height) is made up of slabs put vertically. Pyramidal *sikhara* with five tiers is *trirathi*. Each tier is carved with *chaitya* dormer motif but in low relief. Pinnacle is missing. The temple is cognate in style with that of the temple at Deour Kothar[9]. On stylistic considerations, probably both these temples are contemporary.

Discussion

To divulge the identity of the temple in question is still an esotericism before us. Though the region is well represented by the monuments and other art objects chiseled out by the Kalchuri artisans, the horizontal plan, elevation and motifs employed in the Boudha Danda temple suggests otherwise. In want of any inscription too, one has to rely on stylistic considerations and regional forces acting upon the temple building activity in the contemporary society. By the close of seventh cent. A.D., eastern central India experienced an upsurge and temples under-the influence of Pratihara idioms were started erecting with full vigour. The Pratihara art school seems to be a transitional phase between Post Gupta and Medieval art traditions.

The unpretentious plan, stunted *sikhara*, *chaitya* dormers carved on *kalasa* moulding in *adhisthana, tula* and *lumas* motifs are suggestive of Boudha Danda temple being a creation under the Pratihara traditions. Human head carved on the body of the temple is also indicative of the same. Pratihara temple at Sitamadhi has repeated the same idiom at *lalatabimba* and *sikhara*[10]. As Trivedi has suggested, the existence or non-existence of the *mandapa* may lead to ascertain the chronology of the temple some where in 8th-9th cent. A.D.

Since the temple is devoid of any presiding deity, to whom the temple was dedicated, could not be ascertained. *Gajabhiseka-Lakshmi* at *lalatabimba*, and continuous row of female heads in *chaitya* dormers speaks either of it being a Sakta or Vaisnavite temple. *Gajabhiseka-Lakshmi* from Nachna Kuthara of Gupta period[11] differs in iconographic features with that of the Boudha Danda. Also, one has to take into account the possibility of doorjamb being restored.

The *garbhagriha* is cubical, where as works like Aparajitaprccha and Mansar have divergent views regarding *Stri prasadas*[12]. Images of Ganesa and Parvati in *bhadra rathika* negate the possibility of the temple being dedicated to Vaisnava god or goddess. If the Siva *linga* placed under the tree is to be attributed to this temple then with the presence of Ganesa and Parvati it could be a Saivite temple.

Looking into the evidences available one would obviously be inclined to believe that Boudha Danda group of temples were erected under the shadow of the Pratihara art traditions, a reminiscent of the Central Indian style. The temple stands poised between the Kalchuri and Pratihara art motifs and thus acts as a harbinger of watershed. Here the artisans have successfully experimented with the new ideas in which they were competent enough and were inclined towards mysticism too[13], which casts expressions in the form of female human heads carved in Boudha Danda temple.

Boudha Danda temples are *Sakta*, Vaisnavite or *Saiva* temple, to answer the question is tedious, till more evidences are not coming into light. Neverthless, in all the likelihood it is discernible; it was either a *Sakta* or *Saiva* temple, preceptor to the generation yet to come.

Acknowledgements

My sincere thanks to Mr. M.K. Maheshwari of M.P. State Archaeology and Museums and Dr. Santosh Singh of Sidhi College, Sidhi for their help rendered during the exploration.

REFERENCES

Banerji, R.D. 1931, *Memoirs of the Archaeological Survey of India*, 23:32.

Conningham, A.1970, *Archaeological Survey of India Report*, XII: 20.

Mankad, Popatbhai Ambashankar (Ed.) 1950, Aparajitaprccha of Bhuvanadeva, Oriental Institute, Baroda, p.xcvii.

Singh, A.K. 1994, *A peep into architectural remains from the Vindhyas Symposia Papers*, Vol. II, World Archaeological Congress-3.

Singh, A.K. *Vindhya mein Pratihar shaili ke sthapatya (Hindi)*, Gaon Desh, Varsh Prathama, Ank 3-4: 14-16.

Singh, A.K. 1994, The Pratihara temple of Sitamadhi-some interesting features, *Krsna Smrti - Studies in Indian Art and Archaeology* (Eds. Agrawal & Mishra): 204-207.

Sullerry, S.K. 1998-99, a note of the Gaja-Lakshmi figure from Nachna Kuthara, *Kala* (Eds. M.N. Tiwari and Kamal Giri), V: 65-66.

Shukla, D.N., *Samarangana-Sutradhara (Bhaga Tritiya)*-Prasada Nivesa, p.146.

Stri prasadda belong to *ayata chhanda* and its length is invariably greater than the breadth (Aparajitprccha).

Strillinga buildings are rectangular and have female deities but the male deities can also be installed (Mansar).

Though dilapidated, ruins of a brick temple at Madfe Danda were a precious reward of the current exploration. Presence of a Siva *linga* with *argha* in the sanctum sanctorum suggests the temple was dedicated to Siva.

Vitana of the temple is lost and the *Jangha* is embellished with pilasters and floral pattern.

Trivedi, R.D. 1990, Temples of the Pratihara Period in Central India, p.16. Trivedi is of the view that *kapotika* is carved with chaitya window motif in the first phase Pratihara temples of central India. Where as, according to the present exploration, in eastern central India the *kalasa* is adorned with the same motif.

While making exploration in the region, we come across a monolithic temple perched on the hillock encasing the Ganesa Mara. Though of moderate dimension (3.80x2.90 mt.) whose ceiling is lost, perhaps it is the first monolithic temple reported from the region.

A.K. Singh

Department of Ancient Indian History,
Culture and Archaeology,
A.P.S. University,
Rewa (M.P.)

Faunal Remains from Apegaon, District Aurangabad, Maharashtra

Introduction

Apeagaon (Aurangabad District, Maharashtra) is situated about 16 km southeast of Paithan - an important trading centre of ancient India. The mound at Apeagaon (locally known as Ramatirtha) was excavated in 1976. At this site materials belonging to three Chalcolithic cultures (Ramatirtha, Malwa and Jorwe) dated to 16-10th century B.C. has been found (Deo *et al.* 1979). The faunal material from this excavation has been analysed (Badam 1979). However, in this report there is no mention of how many bones have been analysed as well as no measurements have been provided.

Traial Dig

In 1994, a trial dig of 1 x 1m was taken at the site of Apegaon, District Aurangabad, Maharashtra (Dr. Sheila Mishra: personal communication). Stratum, as 1-26 was divisible into two parts based on the pottery sequence. Stratum 15-26 (1.16-1.85 m) showed presence of "Ramtirth" pottery as has been defined by Deo *et al.* (1976), which was encountered in layer (6) in the 1976 excavation. The deposit above stratum 15 (0-1.16 m) showed presence of Black-and-Red Ware, Red-slipped Ware and Coarse Red Ware. However, the pottery assemblage did not reveal presence of Malwa-Jorwe culture (Sheila Mishra, personal communication). Based on radiocarbon date obtained from 2 m deposits, Deo *et al.* (1976) have identified the Ramtirtha culture belonging to the 18th century B.C.

Faunal Material

This report is based on bones collected from this trial dig in 1994. In 2000 the author visited the site and collected a few bones from a section cut during recent flood. The faunal collection comprises 221 bones (3149 g) of which 142 were identifiable (Table 1). It was not possible to identify 79 fragments, which weighed 219g only. Thus identification level was satisfactory as evidenced from both NISP (64.25%) as well as the total weight of the identified fragments (Fig.1).

Identification of bones was done using a comprehensive collection of skeletons of modern domestic as well as wild animals available in the Archaezoological laboratory, Deccan College. In addition, published species identification criteria such as Prummel and Frisch (1986), Joglekar *et al.* (1994) and Pawankar (1995) were used whenever necessary. A standard system of bone identification and faunal data recording developed by Joglekar (1991) was followed. As far as possible, the bones were identified to the species level and those could not be identified were grouped into broader classes-Cattle/Buffalo *(Bos/Bubalus)* and sheep/goat *(Ovis aries/Capra hircus).* The *Bos/Bubalus* group was partitioned according to the proportion of positively identified bones of these two animals. Thus it was possible to compare this group with that of the sheep/goat for its relative proportion at Apegaon 1994 collection.

Earlier Badam (1979) has identified a jaw of mongoose (*Herpestes* sp.), a few bones of *Cervus* sp. (Sambar/Barasingha), and shells of turtle species of *Trionyx.* All of these have not been found both in the 1994 and 2000 collection. The proportion of wild animals is small (only 13/142 bone: 9.15%), which is comprable to the other Chalcolithic sites in Deccan. However, the diversity of fauna is remarkable. Two large bovids (wild

The Species

The animal species represented in this collection are:

Domestic animals	Wild animals and molluscan species
Bos indicus (Cattle) (Plate I)	*Bubalus arnee*(Wild Buffalo) (Plate IIB)
Bubalus bubalis (Buffalo)(Plate IIA)	*Bos gaurus* (Gaur)
Capra hircus (Goat)	*Axis axis* (Chital)
Ovis aries (Sheep)	*Antilope cervicapra* (Blackbuck)
Gallus domesticus	Small Mammal of the size of here
	Varanus bengalensis (Monitor lizard) (fig.7)
	Lissemys punctata
	Lamellidence sp. (freshwater mussel
	Viviparus bengalensis

buffalo and gaur), chital, blackbuck and possibly hare were the mammals that were hunted at Apeagaon. Also two species of reptiles (monitor lizard and turtle) have been utilized for food. As it is a common practice even now, freshwater mussel has been used to supplement the diet. Among domestic animals, cattle seems to be have contributed a large share of meat (Fig.2).

Although this collection has no bifid spine of the thoracic vertebra of cattle, Badam (1979) has found such bifid spine at Apegaon, which showed that cattle at Apegaon was of humped type. Sheep/goat also had a sizable share (18/142 bones: 12.67%). At Apegaon domestic fowl was also consumed as evidenced from a solitary bone (coracoid). This shoulder bone of domestic fowl bears marks of chewing at both the ends.

It is interesting to note that Stratum 5 revealed 9 fragments of cattle pelvis, i.e. illium, ischium and pubis as well as the acetabular portion. These pelvic bones indicate presence of 4 individuals. Also in this collection, there are 7 fragments of the scapula (perhaps from 2 animals). Both scapula and pelvis contain good amount of edible meat. Such differential distribution of meat-bearing parts has been observed at other Chalcolithic sites in Deccan like Kaothe (Joglekar 1991), Walki (Joglekar and Thomas 1993) and Inamgaon (Pawankar 1995).

Bone Measurements

Bone measurements can be used to extract a variety of information about the animals in the past (Joglekar 1991, 1993-94). However, at Apegaon only a few bones were measurable (table 2-4). Bones were measured using an internationally standardized method given by A. Von den Driesch (1974). Some of the bone measurements are usefull to estimate the size of the animals. For example, the humerus and the astragalus measurements are useful to obtain size estimates.

The distal width (Bd) of the trochlea of a humerus (specimen no. APZ 12 has been used to obtain that fat-free carcass weight by applying the following formula given by Noddle (1973).

Formula: Fat-free Carcass Weight = 1.931(Bd) + 8.792 Kg.

Specimen no. APG12 gave an estimate 163.27 kg fat-free carcass weight of the cattle. Based on this point estimate it can be said that the cattle at Apegaon were of the similar type as seen at other Chalcolithic sites in the Deccan (Joglekar 1991). Similarly, it was possible to obtain a point estimate of the height at the withers of cattle based on an astragalus (APG 04) using the factor given by Zalkin (1970). The estimate of the height is 122.43 cm.

This shows that cattle at Apegaon were of large and tall variety that were comparable to other Chalcolithic sites like Nevasa, Daimabad and Kaothe (Joglekar 1991).

Concluding Rmarks

Since this collection is from a trial trench of small dimension at Apegaon, further quantitative estimate about economy and the mode of occurrence of various elements is not possible and would not be valid as well. However, a small trial dig has revealed a considerably sufficient evidence to throw light on the animal utilization at Apegaon. Inhabitants at Apegaon have used diverse wild fauna that included large bovids such as wild buffalo and the gaur. As it has been observed at other protohistoric sites in Peninsular India, hunting continued to be an important source of food even though at some sites incipient agriculture and pastoralism were the main occupations.

Acknowledgements

I am thankful to Dr. Sheila Mishra for giving me the faunal collection and Ms. Sonali Naik who assisted on the site. I thank Mr. Sunil Jadhav for photography.

REFERENCES

Badam, G.L. 1979. Faunal remains from Apegaon, in *Apegaon Excavations* 1976 (S.B. Deo, M.K. Dhavalikar and Z.D. Ansari), pp. 40-49. Pune: Deccan College.

Deo, S.B., M.K. Dhavalikar and Z.D. Ansari 1979. *Apegaon Excavations* 1976. Pune: Deccan College.

Joglekar, P.P. 1991. *A Biometric Approach to the Faunal Remains of Western India with special reference to Kaothe and Walki.* Unpublished Ph. D. Thesis, Pune: University of Poona.

Joglekar, P.P. 1993-94. Height at Withers: An Osteometric Approach to Faunal Remains, *Bharati* 20:31-38.

Joglekar, P.P. and P.K. Thomas 1993. Faunal Diversity at Walki: a Small Chalcolithic Settlement in Western Maharashtra, *Bulletin of the Deccan College Post-Graduate and Research Institute* 53:75-94.

Joglekar, P.P., P.K. Thomas, Y.Matsushima and S.J. Pawankar 1994. Osteological Differences between the Forelimb Bones of Ox (Bos indicus), Buffalo (Bubalus bubalis) and Nilgai (Boselaphus tragocamelus), *Journal of Bombay Veterinary College* 5(1-2): 17-20.

Joglekar, P.P. and P.K. Thomas 1993. Faunal Diversity at Walki: a small Chalcolithic Settlement in Western Maharashtra, *Bulletin of the Deccan College Post-Graduate and Research Institute* 53:75-94.

Noddle, B.A. 1973. Determination of the Body Weight of Cattle from Bone Measurements, in *Domestikationsforschung und Gerschichte des Haustiere* (J. Malolcsi Ed.), pp.248-260, Budapest: Akademiai Kiado.

Pawankar, S.J. 1995. *Man-Animal Relationship in the Early Farming Communities in Western India with special reference to Inamgaon.* Unpublished Ph.D. Thesis, Pune: University of Poona.

Prummel W. and H.J. Frisch 1986. A Guide for the Distinction of Species, Sex and Body Side in Bones of Sheep and Goat, *Journal of Archaeological Sciences* 13: 567-577.

Von den Driesch, A. *1976. A Guide to the Measurement of Animal Bones from Archaeological Sites*, Cambridge, Massachusetts: Harvard University Press.

Zalkin, V.I. 1970. *Drevniejsije domasnije zivotnije vostocnoj Europy*, Moskva.

Department ot Archaeology
Deccan College, Pune 410006.

P.P. Joglekar

Excavation at Sirpur

In Puratattva, Number 30 for 1999-2000 (110-16) Shri Jagatpati Joshi and Shri A.K. Sharma have given a brief summery of their on going excavations at the ancient site of Sirpur (Sripura) in the Mahasamund district of the recently formed state of Chhattisgarh. Earlier in the fifties of the last century this site was subjected to a large-scale excavation for three successive seasons by Dr. M.G. Dikshit (*IAR*, 1953-54, 12; 1954-55, 1955-56, 26-27). Both these operations resulted into highly important discoveries.

The site was already known to be a prominent centre of Vaishnanism, Saivism and Buddhism, all of which enjoyed the enlightened patronage of the Sarabhapuriyas and Panduvamsins who ruled over South Kosala comprising modern Chhattisgarh and adjoining parts of Western Orissa during 6th-8th centuries A.D. (Ajay Mitra Shastri, *Inscrriptions of the Sarabhapuriyas, Panduvamsins and Somavamsins*, I-II, New Delhi, 1995). Though all of the them were staunch adherents of Vedic-Puranic religious systems like Vaishnavism (the Sarabhapuriyas and some Panduvamsin rulers) and Saivism (more particularly the last known Panduvamsin king Maha-Sivagupta Balarjuna), it did not come in the way of their extending liberal patronage to Buddhism which is reflected in their fairly numerous inscriptions and in the account of the celebrated Chinese pilgrim Yuan Chwang, who visited it[1]. More so, Maha-Sivagupta, who prided himself in assuming the Saiva sectarian style *Parama-Mahesvara* as known from his fairly numerous epigraphs, is known to have made liberal donations to Buddhist establishments and others, must have followed his example. One of these from Mallar (Shastri, II, III: IX, 134-36) is a copper-plate charter and aims at registering his grant of a village in favour of the venerable order of monks of the four quarters *(chaturdis-arya-bhikshu-sangha)* resident at the small monastery *(veharika)* built by a layman at the village of Taradamsaka on the occasion of a Solar eclipse. The other is a lithic record (Shastri, 1995, II, III: XII, 148-49) of another layman belonging to his reign. According to the record a monk named Anandaprabha established a free feeding house for the monks living in a monastery at Sirpur by purchasing a hut from the *sangha* in the monastery *(vihara-kuti)*. He made some provision (which is specified in the record) for the feeding monks. Thus, we have strong epigraphic records of the patronage of Buddhism by king Maha-Sivagupta Balarjuna as well as laymen and for the existence of some monasteries for the residence of monks in his kingdom including Sirpur (Sripura), which was his ancestral capital.

Earlier excavations by Dikshit have confirmed it and brought to light, besides Saiva structures, quite a large number of large and small *viharas*, some of them quite extensive, of unique architectural pattern and prosperous as well as images of the Buddha and other Buddhist divinities and *stupas* (Dikshit, 1954-55, 24-26; 1955-56, 26-28). Curiously enough, he believed that 'one of the monasteries seemed to have been a nunnery as shown by occurrence of a large number of shell and glass bangles' (1954-55, 26).

The excavations were resumed after almost five decades, as stated above, by Sri Joshi and Sri Sharma, who also came across with the similar type of finds, viz. a Saiva temple and Buddhist establishments including temple and *vihara* which they call nunnery (Joshi-Sharma, 1999-2000, 113-16)[2]. Their conclusion is also based on the fact that 'almost all the rooms yielded a number of fragments of glass bangles in various colours with embossed designs. These indicate that the rooms were occupied by *Bhikshunies*' (Joshi and Sharma, 1999-2000, 115).

Both Dikshit, and Joshi and Sharma appear to have misled by conjecturing that some of the monasteries uncovered by them were nunneries because of the presence of glass-bangles in the rooms. As it is well known, the monks and nuns were not allowed to use any ornament and consequently there is no question of nuns decking with ornaments including bangles. Consequently this phenomenon ought to be explained in some other manner. Sirpur, being a highly important urban centre and Panduvamsin capital, must have attracted quite a large number of visitors, both male and female. In addition, it was also a great religious centre of Saivism[3] as well as Buddhism. These visitors must have included women. The Buddhist establiments catered to the spritual needs of lay worshippers including ladies. Infact, in a larger sense the Buddhist order (*Sangha*) was traditionally believed to have four components, viz. monks (*bhikshus*), nuns (*bhikshunies*), male (*upasakas*) and female (*upasikas*) lay worshippers. The remnants of bangles unearthed in these monasteries must be treated as representing the female lay worshippers who frequented these monastic establishments. It is especially noteworthy in this context that Sirpur in those days was a prominent industerial centre and the crafts practised there included making of bangles.

Even otherwise right from the beginning the number of nuns was far less than that of monks and the position of the nuns was far inferior as compared to that of their male counterparts. Consequently there are not so numerous allusions to nunneries as to the *viharas* meant for housing the monks. Even during the heyday of Buddhism (2nd century B.C.-early centuries A.D.) there are very few epigraphic references to nunnerie;[4] during subsequent period when Buddhism was comparatively on declining course, we can not expect many nunneries and unless we have specific references or other very strong evidences pointing in that direction it would be hazardous to dub any Buddhist monastery as nunneries.

However, Joshi and Sharma are still excavating and it is not impossible that a (or some) nunnery (or nunneries) may be spotted in future. That would, if found, be a highly important discovery of importance for the religious history of ancient India.

[1]Though he misconstructed the king's extending liberal patronage to his being an adherent of Buddhism.

[2]Infact, the caption of the 6th section of their contribution is 'Buddha Temple cum Nunnery'. See p. 113).

[3]Maha-Svagupta himself, as stated above, was a parama-Mahesvara and we have a large number of inscriptions indicating his lavish patronage to Saivism. In recent years a hoard of nine copper plate charters registering donations to a prominent Saiva establishment called Balesvara-bhattaraka at Sripura has been found and is being published by the present author. For a gist of these records, see our paper Balesvara-bhattaraka: A hitherto unknown Saiva establishment at Sripura, *Journal of the Epigraphical Society of India*, XVII, 1992, pp. 15-23.

[4]For some epigraphic references to nunneries in pre-Gupta inscriptions, see Ajay Mitra Shastri, An Outline of Early Buddhsim, Varanasi, 1965, pp. 143-44.

Ajay Mitra Shastri

'Prachi', 23 Vidya Vihar
Rana Pratap Nagar,
Nagpur-440 022

Archaeological Research Projects

Indian Archaeological Society
Report for the year 2000-2001

I ATLAS OF THE INDUS-SARASWATI CIVILIZATION

The Indian Council for Historical Research, New Delhi, sanctioned a three year project entitled 'Atlas of the Indus-Saraswati Civilization" to the Indian Archaeological Society. The atlas envisaged will be a cultural atlas which is to be prepared broadly as per the following synopsis:

Work -Profile

1. Geology and geography of the Indus-Saraswati Culture zone

1.1 Geological formation of Baluchistan, Sindh, Gujarat, Rajastan, Haryana and Western Uttar Pradesh

1.2 Neo-tectonic movements in the Himalayan, sub-Himalayan and Arid zones

1.3 Hills and Mountains

1.4 Rivers flowing as well as lost

1.5 Lakes

1.6 Shifting of rivers and Hydrological problems

1.7 Drying up of rivers and Climatic changes

1.8 Birth and growth of deserts and its effects on the history of Indus -Saraswati Civilization

1.9 Formation of new channels of old rivers

1.10 The history of Lost Saraswati, lost Drishadvati and present day Sutlej in particular, and many seasonal rivers in general

2. Architectural Remains

2.1 Residential buildings

2.2 Fortification and Gateways

2.3 Drains and Drainage System

2.4 Water Management Systems: Reservoirs, wells, Bunds etc.

2.5 Granaries and Warehouses

2.6 Other buildings

3. Cultural Assemblages

3.1 Pottery

3.2 Terracottas

3.3 Bronzes: [a] Figurines, [b] Tool and Weapons,[c] Utensils, [d] Other objects

3.4 Shell, Bone and Ivory

3.5 Steatite, Faience and Glazed items

3.6 Seals and Sealings

3.7 Weights and Measures

3.8 Stone objects: Stone tools, Blades, Pestles, etc.

3.9 Gold, Silver and Electrum Jewellery

3.10 Blades

3.11 Chart blades

4. Explorations and Excavations

4.1 Excavated remains at various sites

4.2 Environmental setting of the sites

4.3 Satellite photographs of the region

4.4 Geological studies of the regions

5 Literature and Archaeology

5.1 Early Vedic Literature and Harappan Archaeology

5.2 Later Vedic Literature and Harappan Archaeology

(I) The work done so far is as follows. Around 2000 sites have been noted along with their coordinates, i.e., Latitude and Longitude. These sites belong to the Early, Mature and Late phases of the Indus-Saraswati Civilization. Their break-up is as follows:

India Early-179, Mature-570, Late- 985 Total -1463

Pakistan Early-121[Hakra ware]+ 297 [EH] , Mature -317, Late-71 Total - 806

The sites have been further grouped according to districts as they exist this day, both in India and Pakistan

The sites have also been grouped according to river valleys.

Sites located outside India and Pakistan have been classified separately.

All these sites are now put on maps of different categories and different sizes. So far five maps have been generated.

Cultural notes on following subjects have been completed along with their bibliographical citations:

1. Water -management systems such as baths, drains, sanitary, sewerage, dams, reservoirs, wells, tanks, dockyard and moat

2. Archaeobotanical evidence on cereals like barley, wheat, oats, rice, millet, lentils, oil seeds, legumes, fruits, timber-fibrous, herbal and ornamental plants

3. Archaeozoological evidence on terrestrial, avian and aquatic species such as cattle, sheep, goat, elephant, camel, horse, pig, dog, cattle, rat, rhinoceros, chital, bear, wolf, hare, buffalo, nilgai, blackbuck, gazelle, spotted deer, sambhar, fowl, fish, oysters, crab, crocodile, turtle, and molluscus.

4. Storage system which includes granaries, warehouses, storage pits, corn bins, grain silos, pit silos, cubicles, oval, circular and cylindrical pits, storage jars, storage bins, chambers, grain pounding platforms, loading and working platforms.

5. Shell, ivory, bone and leather used to manufacture personal ornaments, professional tools, ritual objects, mathematical instruments, objects of domestic utility, combat, privy and decorative objects, toys, and agricultural tools.

Photographs, line drawings, conjectural views etc are also being prepared for the Atlas.

S. P. Gupta

II GROWTH OF CITIES IN ANCIENT INDIA

'Growth of Cities in Ancient India' is one of the three major research projects undertaken by the Indian Archaeological Society and funded by the Indian Council of Historical Research. The project was commenced on 1st January 2001. So far we have emphasized on the east coast of India, especially in Bengal and Orissa regions. Some of the ancient cities that are under investigations, are - Tamluk, Sisupalgarh, Khiching, Jajpur, Radhanagar, Langudi and Kaveripattinam.

For all these sites we have used both archaeological and literary data to access their socio-economic and religious aspects. This is an ongoing process. Our preliminary work on Tamluk has shown that a number of satellite centers had enclosed the ancient city. Similarly, the recently discovered ancient site at Radhanagar in Jajpur district of coastal Orissa is also surrounded by a number of Buddhist sites, the prominent one is Langudi, which is currently under excavation by the Orissa Institute of Maritime and Southeast Asian Studies, Bhubaneswar. The excavations here have revealed several rare discoveries for the first time in eastern India.

Sisupalgarh is one of the well-excavated sites in eastern India. The site was excavated by B. B. Lal in late 1940s. The subsequent works in and around the site have brought to light a number of important discoveries which are being incorporated in the present project.

Along with the documentation, we have prepared a comprehensive bibliography of articles and books. This is an ongoing process. We have also generated maps for a few sites.

The work so far done include:

1. Preparation of bibliography-50% work has been completed.

2. Source collection-Buddhist, Jaina and Brahmanical, 30% data have already been collected.

3. Data collection-literary and archaeological, 40% data have been collected.

4. Preparation of maps on river valleys and archaeological sites has been undertaken.

K. S. Ramachandran

III ARCHAEOLOGICAL RESEARCH METHODOLOGY

The project was sanctioned by the Indian Council of Historical Research from 1st September, 2000-the study takes into account of the scientific research methods used for archaeological purposes-archaeobotany, sedimentology, archaeological chemistry, biological methods, anthropology, computing archaeology, use of molecular archaeology, etc. for which and exhausitive bibliography has been made 8000 entries.

Again for better understanding for archaeological reconnaissance, Geographical Information Systems (GIS-Remote Sensing) has been very helpful. Notes on this method have also been prepared.

This project includes the study of palaeontology, biomolecular studies, dentalmocrowear studies, soil analysis, insect remains, microwear analysis, archaeological chemistry, and microvertebrate in archaeological excavations. Notes are being made on these subjects also.

As the project is mainly based on library work, journals and books published from 1980 onwards have been taken into account. One exception is the Journal of Archaeological Science. A summary of articles is being prepared as and when a journal is read and studied. Ultimately all these summaries will be evaluated and compiled for the use of archaeologists.

V.N. Misra

IV DOCUMENTATION AND CONSERVATION OF MANUSCRIPTS IN SATRAS OF ASSAM*

It was decided by the Indian Archaeological Society, New Delhi, to depute a team of three Conservators-S/Sri Ramesh Kumar, Anoop Kumar Srivastava and Sachin Kirkire under the technical guidance of the author to scientifically document the manuscripts, record their condition, carry out dust removal and to provide first aid to fragile documents.

*The financial assistance for this project has been extended by the Department of Culture, Govt. of India, New Delhi.

'Asom', the Sanskrit name of modern day Assam, is an important member of the north-east region of India. The seven States, which constitute the N-E Region, are popularly known as seven-sisters. Assam is a vast expanse of natural beauty with its majestic mountains, lovely woods, groves dense with trees, a variety of fruit-bearing trees and sounds of silence.

The inherent natural beauty and the healthy climate of the region attracted the great Vaishnavite saint, Srimanta Sankar Dev to establish 'Satra', religio-cultural institutions, in the early 15th century. His disciples, namely Madhab Dev, Hari Dev, Damodar Dev and their devoted followers carried on the mission of propagation of Vaishnavite faith in the initial stages but later on these 'Satras' developed into great social and cultural centers.

As in ancient India, such institutions were patronized by the kings and rulers who used to give grants-land, animals, money, etc., for the maintenance and proper upkeep of the 'Satras'. Today, various Satras in the North-East Region are in a difficult financial crisis because of the loss of patronage from the rulling, business and elite classes, and are finding themselves in a state of decadence.

Aim of the Project

All Satras possess a rich collection of manuscripts written and painted on 'Sanchipat'- handmade paper. For writing, ink was prepared from the urine of cows, and that was kept in iron containers for concentration. The ink is similar to the iron gall ink. Excess of moisture in the air for a number of year leads to high relative humidity (R.H.), resulting in biological degradation of manuscripts.

Methodology

The team established Guwahati as its base and first travelled to Majuli island where they went to Dakshinpath Satra, Auniati Satra, Samagurhi Satra, Bengena-Ati Satra, Garmur Satra, Uttar Kamlabari Satra. While documenting the manuscripts (mss.), the name of mss. (like, Ramayana, Bhagwat, Dasam, Guru Charitra, Kirtan etc.) the material on which the mass. was prepared (Sanchipat, Tulapat, paper, etc.), ink used, title and brief content, period, language, number of folios, size of mss., physical location, and its present condition, was properly recorded in a format.

After staying for one week at Majuli Island, which is the largest river island in the world, the team moved to Shual Kushi, which is 35 Kms from Guwahati. Here, Sri Sri Hati Satra was established in the 17th century. There were about 100 mss. in the collection of the Satra.

Barpeta is the district town and 3 Kms from the main town in Patbausi Satra, which is one of the oldest Vaishnavite monasteries in Assam. This was established by Saint Srimanta Sankar Dev himself sometimes in the year 1546 A.D. and he lived there for about 18 years. Saint Sankar Dev wrote 'barget' (devotional songs), drama, etc., in old Asamese and Sanskrit.

Other Satra visited at Barpeta are Patbausi Damodar Dev Satra, Madhav Deva Satra and Bahari Harideva Satra. From the above Satras, mss. were shifted to 'Uttar Purva Bharat Harideva Sangh', Guwahati.

The team visited Juniya Satra, which was established by the grandson of Shankar Deva.

The team then moved to district Nagaon, where they went to see Bali Satra which houses some of the earliest manuscripts (about 500 years old) in Assam. The mss. include titles like Bhagwat Purana, Gita Bhavartha Dipika, Sanskrit Grammar, Vishnu Sahastnam, Ratanmala, etc.

The other Satras visited by the team include Bardua Satra which has a collection of 14 mss. The mss. are kept in wooden almirah in a neat and tidy condition.

After a detailed documentation of the mss. conservation work will be taken up. More fragile mss. will be taken up first, which would be followed by others which may require minor repairs or restoration. The effort on the part of the Indian Archaeological Society, New Delhi is to prolong the life of these ancient mss. for posterity.

I. K. Bhatnagar

BOOK REVIEWS

B.B. Lal 2002 *The Sarasvati flows On -The Continuity of Indian Culture.* Aryan Books International New Delhi: pp. 148 Illustrations 114, Price Rs 1250

Never before a book of this kind was written - Prof B B. Lal in this book has convincingly proved that civilizations have come and gone in Indian history of 6000 years, but the culture of the Indus-Saraswati civilization now datable to 4th millennium B.C., continues to live in India even today. The so called 'modernity' in India which in effect means westernisation has as yet not been able to annihilate the sap of life which is ever flowing in the Hindu way of life and its belief system. The cities of Harappa, Mohenjo-Daro, Kalibangan, Lothal and Dholavira may have perished in the second millennium B.C. leaving behind no tradition of planned cities with impressive fortifications, roads and lanes, covered drainage system, complex systems of water management and long distance trade using the inscribed seals and sealings, but the culture of these cities of the yore nurtured and continued to be followed and practiced through the winding and dusty streets of Indian villages witnessing many a happy and sorrowful ups and down of history, sometimes getting turned into cities and towns and at other times once again deserted or reduced to the original village status.

Prof. Lal has picked up some of the charecteristic features of this continuing culture and compared them with the actual objects belonging to the Indus-Saraswati civilization and the actual objects as well as practices followed to this date, for example, the *Namashkar Mudra*, in which one holds both the palms together to greet a visitor is a marked feature of the terracotta figurines from the Indus -Saraswati cities of Harappan and Mohenjo-Daro is still followed by Hindus across the length and breadth of the country. Similarly putting Kumkum or vermillion in the central parted line of the hair -do was practiced both in the past and the present-terracotta emples from the past has been put juxtaposed with a picture of Smt. Rabri Devi, the Chief minister of Bihar, with her husband Shri. Laloo Prasad, with the same feature with the vermillion in the *Maang*, ie. Then parting line of the hairdo. Similarly, large and small bangles worn rightupto the upper arm were practiced then and even now. The kinds of cot used then and now have been shown by the author with actual archaeological remains and present day examples. An example of Siva Linga on *Yoni-Peetha* from Kalibangan has exact parallels in the Siva temples of India and everywhere in the country. Many toys and games also testify the same tradition. Fire-worship charecterized the Indus-Civilization then as now. Prof. Lal has given many more examples to support his thesis. Prof Lal thus provides a rich profile of Sarasvati, which nurtured the earliest civilization of South Asia for a long span, a glimbse of her course from adolescence to maturity, integrating the past with the present.

In the first two chapters, Prof. Lal surfaces a profile of the river not as a mere eulogy from literature, but also by precisely amalgamating literature, hydrology and archaeology, as well as focussing on seismic activity and also on receding glaciers. The comprehensive third chapter discuss the flourishing growth of Early Harappan settlements on the banks of Sarasvati, The author also traces the thread of continuity to the mature phase from abundant archaeological material such as settlement types, subsistence, technology and craft. Along with archaeological evidence, Prof. Lal surfaces the living tradition of the bygone civilization from ornaments, privies, games, recreation, town planning, kitchen utensils, agriculture, crafts, as well as religious and social metaphors in the fourth chapter. The fifth chapter is a retrospect.

Corroborated by 114 illustrations, this meticulous work is a retrospection of Harappan sites essentially in the Sarasvati Valley. It is a 'must' for everyone interested in Harappan studies.

S. P. Gupta

D.P. Singhal 2000 *(Second Edition) Buddhism in East Asia.* Books and Books, New Delhi, pp.235 Price not given.

Equally in past and present, Buddhism has found a strong traction in East Asia: China, Korea and Japan. It is an accepted view that India and East Asia (more particularly China) have shared diverse cultural ties with Buddhism as a backdrop since the dawn of the early Christian era. Thanks to the great Buddhist pilgrimage both India and China came together, navigating a rich wealth of culture and art that transshipped across far horizons of both the countries. Today Buddhism has been spearheaded as a way of life, as the religion has expanded many folds from its earlier viewpoint of personal enlightenment or salvation. Against this background late D. P. Singhal in his book *Buddhism in East Asia* attempts to understand the unique nature of Buddhism in East Asia from a historical perspective.

Singhal writes the fundamentals of Buddhism in his introductory chapter; besides a brief account on the history of the religion also appears in the same. Chapter II deals with central Asia, focusing on the history of discovery of Buddhist related antiquities in West Asia, more particularly in Afghanistan, western China and southern Russia. Taking into account the rich gamut of evidences, the author is of the opinion that West Asia, though also had witnessed spread of various religions like Zoroastrianism, Manichenism, and Nestorian Christianity, it was Buddhism, which dominated all others, bringing forth Indian religion, literature, arts and sciences into the realm of central Asian cultural life for about thousand years.

The evidences are primarily Kharosthi documents, a Sanskrit birch manuscript-dating back to 6th century B.C. (found in a castle called Zangtepe in Uzbekisthan), *stupas*, *caves* and *viharas* and a host of Hindu deities. According to the author, Afghanistan, especially its northern region around Balkh, was at the crossroads of central Asia, having a connection with Indian faiths: Buddhism and Brahmanism. Buddhism had also a strong footing in Tokharestan from the 2nd century B.C. to the beginning of 8th century A.D. Most of the Buddhist sites are located on ancient trade routes with Baniyan as the first important way station on the route that connected Kabul with Balkh. Singhal writes about the rich Buddhist treasures of Bamiyan, which is relevant, as the site has recently drawn attention worldwide on account of the mass scale destruction of its priceless relics by the Taliban extremists.

From Afghanistan, the author moves to eastward to Chinese Turkistan and Sogdiana, where he also finds similar evidence of contact alien with Indian ideology. He further discusses, how Buddhism made its way into Tibet from Udayana in India.

In the following chapter, the author has dealt extensively on Buddhism in China, tracing the Indo-Chinese relationship to as early as 4th century B.C., as during this period the Chinese annals depicted several geographic and mythological elements that seem to have been derived from India. There are also archaeological finds, indicating both land and sea connections with China from India. The relationship had been established mainly for the academic pursuit, as the Chinese monks travelled long distance to the famous centers of learning in India and its periphery. Following the Indian contact, the author turns into the classic Chinese philosophy, expounded by famous philosophers like Confucius and Tao Te Ching under the banners of Confucianism and Taoism. Yet Buddhism found more popularity than the formers, attracting both poor and rich together. The author discusses extensively about the penetration of the religion and its gradual spread in China.

From China, Singhal shifts over to Korea and Japan. Buddhism was introduced in Korea in the 4th century A.D., and reached to highest watermark under the patronage of Silla and Karyo dynasties. It became the faith of common people and the entire basis of Korea's religious life affecting the ideology, customs and morals of the people as well as the political and the economic life of the state. Buddhist temples and monasteries abound in Korea resembling closely those of China and Japan; tall and imposing trees, inspiring awe and devotion, wall them round. Even today, Buddhism in Korea holds a high esteem, and the Buddhists of the country are engaged in various public activities.

According to the author, Korea did not contribute a school of her own to Buddhism, yet acted as a cultural intermediary between China and Japan.

From Korea, Buddhism was spread to Japan, where at present the religion is practiced along with two others: Shinto and Confucianism. The spread of Buddhism in Japan inspired higher ideals and encouraged indigenous art and literature by providing a wealth of material for metaphysical speculation. With the establishment of a new impressive capital at Nara in 710 A.D., Buddhism further resulted in the development of elaborate methods of spiritual training, yet in coordination with a distinctive Japanese character. In the later period, Buddhism in Japan began to develop its own distinctive local schools of thought, and the most prominent being Zen (Chan or Dhyana) and Nichiren.

To sum up, Singhal's book indeed forms an ideal source for scholars of History, Religion, Philosophy and Anthropology, working on Indo-East Asia relationship both in past and present.

Jitu Mishra

M.K. Dhavalikar 1999 *Historical Archaeology of India.* Books and Books, New Delhi, pp.274, Price Rs 1050.

One of the neglected aspects of the archaeological research of India is the archaeology of the Historical period (6th century B.C. to 13th century A.D.). The book 'Historical Archaeology of India', a fill-up to the aspect, consists of seven chapters, followed by an exhaustive bibliography and an index. In each chapter, the author has dealt with a particular problem; all related to the second urbanization and its aftermath. While in chapter I, 'Prelude to History', he narrates the PGW culture and its various aspect, in the second Dhavalikar emphasizes on the cultural sequence of various regions, and a brief survey of archaeology from the time of Cunningham onwards.

Chapters III & IV form the core of the book, where the key issues like urban growth and urban decline have been described and discussed in great detail. On the urban growth, the author has recounted the ten criteria of Gordon Childe, necessary for the formation of a city. The norms have been the population growth, centralization of surplus, monumental architecture, ruling class, writing, art, trade, coinage, and exact and predictive sciences. He has examined these factors in relation to India of the historical period. As for population growth, the author has tried to show that there existed a hierarchy of settlements-*grama, nigama, nagara* and *janapada* in the earlier period-and villages *(grama)*, local centres *(sangrahana)*, sub divisional headquarters *(karvatika)*, divisional headquarters *(dronamukha)*, and the capital *(sthaniya)* during the later period (in the time of Kautiliya). The author finds elements present at archaeological sites are comparable with the tenets mentioned in the *Arthasastra.* According to Dhavalikar, growth of agriculture, and plough cultivation were the prime factors for the rise of population and cities. The period also witnessed a burgeoning of monumental architecture that evolved all over the country. An effective bureaucracy that was responsible for the smooth functioning of the cities was the hallmark of India's second urbanization. Besides, writing system and trade also played prime role towards the evolution of towns of Early Historic India. Coinage with specific weight standards too subscribed to the speeding up of urbanization.

The most important chapter of the book is the one on urban decline, where Dhavalikar lays special emphasis on environmental issues. In India, considerable prosperity and peace prevailed between the 5th century B.C. and 5th century A.D. This period also witnessed rise of several empires like that of the Mauryas, Sungas, Satavahanas and Kushanas under favourable environmental condition. Trade, both domestic and foreign, flourished under their patronage resulting far-reaching consequences. But the prosperity reached to an abrupt end, as there was instability in environmental pattern that began from the time of Kushanas on wards. The causes were several. Like, the mass deforestation, which was the result of extensive forest clearance for cultivation and overgrazing. According to him, deforestation perhaps was also the main factor for the downfall of the Indus civilization after 2000 B.C. Then the period of later Guptas (later historical period) also witnessed a prolonged dry phase. Dhavalikar postulates that the phenomenon was not peculiar to the Indian subcontinent but had occurred over a large part of the Old world. This can be inferred from various literary and archaeological evidences. Quoting the works of Sulman (1982) and Currie and Fair Bridge (1985), Dhavalikar argues that the climate in India was quite congenial from the 5th century B.C. to 4th century A.D., and during this period Europe enjoyed a warmer phase. From 4th to 10th century A.D., the river Nile in Egypt had a low rate of water discharge, affecting the monsoon pattern in both Africa and Asia. The less rainfall in the catchments of Nile River between 622 and 1000 A.D. also indicates the possibility of similar situation in Indian subcontinent, and that perhaps caused the decline of Early Historic cities in South Asia. The less rainfall in India is further evident in the contemporary literary classic, like the *Dasakumara-Charita*. To sum up, Dhavalikar postulates that when there was a warmer phase in Europe and Egypt similar conditions prevalent in India also and the fortunes of Europe and India are linked with climatic changes.

Dhavalikar is of the view that the Gupta period, which often referred to as the classical age in Indian history, also marked the beginning of decline of cities. This is also reflected in his presidential address at the Indian History Congress, where he has divided the Gupta period into early and late phases, the later indicating the decline. Besides environmental disorders the cities were also perished by the attacks of the Hunas. Coinage also declined in this phase, and showed the continuation of the Kushana motifs. Towards the end of the chapter, the author emphasizes the need of more researches on medieval archaeology.

Chapter V deals with pottery and chapter VI on cultural materials. In the latter, Dhavalikar emphasizes on cross-cultural traits of Early Historic period. According to him, *"The early historical period from Ca. 600 BC to 600 AD is teeming with knotty problems which are awaiting solution. This long span is generally lumped together either as pre-Mauryan to Kushan, as several sites were deserted by 300 AD, or in some cases Sunga-Kushan-Gupta from 200 BC-600 AD. This arbitrary periodization no doubt has some basis, but the question that then arises is weather the culture remained static all through these twelve centuries. And this was the formative period in Indian history when the very ethos of Indian civilization was being moulded. India was coming into contact with countries in the west, the north and east; foreigners were lured to invade because of our untold wealth, tribals were making inroads into our territories, finding employment at Indian courts, and others coming into contact by way of trade. In brief, many new influences were coming from different directions, and Indian influence was spreading to distant lands. Many foreign elements were assimilated into Indian culture in course of time"*.

In the concluding chapter VII, the author summarizes the results of important excavated sites, like Ropar, Hastinapura, Atranjikhera, Kausambi, Patna (Pataliputra), Sisupalgarh, Ujjain, Maheshwar, Nevasa, Prakash, Satanikota, Brahmagiri and Chandavalli, Maski, Arikamedu and Kaveripattinam.

Moreover only a few have written on this aspect; and the book by the author is significant and a welcome addition to the subject.

K. S. Ramachandran
Jitu Mishra

H.C. Bhardwaj 2000 ***Metallurgy in Indian Archaeology***, Tara Book Agency, Kamachcha, Varanasi. pp.217, 67 tables, 61 figures. Rs. 300/-

In recent years much emphasis is laid on the preservation and conservation of monuments of National importance but due attention was not given to the metal objects found in excavations and explorations. Due to change of shift in archaeology from mere classification and description to the interpretation and explanation now even small antiquities were studied in all its aspects. Stone, bone, shell, metal and terracotta objects have all of a sudden become important and attracted the attention of scholars and students alike.

The book 'Metallurgy in Indian Archaeology' is an extraordinary work by H.C. Bhardwaj, former Professor of History of Science and Technology in the Banaras Hindu University, Varanasi. This work by Prof. Bhardwaj is based on ancient metallurgical remains found during excavations and explorations all over India. It provides a detailed description of the techniques of metal smelting, alloying and casting in Ancient India. On the whole it covers the period from the Pre-Harappan times to the Northern Black Polished Ware/Megalithic Moreover, metallurgical remains upto the Gupta period have also been taken into consideration. Besides, the author also took adequate pains to study metal objects scattered in various museums of the country. The contents of the book have been divided into chapters.

All serious students of Indian Archaeology are aware of the rich metallurgical heritiage of the country. Copper, bronze, gold, silver, silver, lead and their alloys were extracted from ores and turned into objects from the Harappan times and still they are in use all over the world for one purpose or the other. During ancient period copper was used for making tools and weapons and silver and gold were used for making jewellery, coins, utensils and art objects. The Harappans and related cultures have a rich collection of copper and bronze objects which includes famous dancing girl from Mohenjo-daro, sixty kilogram of Daimabad bronzes and celts from Ganeshwar, Rajasthan but on the contrary Chalcolithic cultures of India could not follow the same tradition and show a decline in metallurgical techniques. According to Prof. Bhardwaj Painted Gray Ware and Megalithic people used iron tools and implements and by the 6th-4th century B.C. tools made of this metal was extensively produced. The famous Mehrauli Iron Pillar, bearing inscription of 'King Chandra' of the 4th century A.D. was also made of this metal. This Pillar was of pure iron (steel) and has not rusted uptil now. Only a few objects of silver was made during the Harappan period but after a long gap it resurfaced in the 6th century B.C. when large number of Punch-marked coins were made of this metal. The Indo-Greeks, the Western Kshatrapas, the Kushanas and the Guptas manufactured coins of gold; silver, copper and potin but the satavahanas used lead for this purpose.

The chapter-2 of the book deals with copper and bronze metallurgy in India, which provides necessary information about copper and its distribution and smelting in Prehistoric India. This includes Pre-Harappan, Harappan, Chalcolithic and Copper-Hoard metallurgy. It also reveals the source of tin and its impact on the arsenic-copper. Similarly, Chapter-3 discloses undiscovered facts pertaining to the archaeo-metallurgy of gold. In comparison to copper this metal appeared quite late and its earliest occurrence is dated to 4700 B.C. at Sialk-III but in Indian context it has been noticed in the Harappan, South Indian Neolithic, Chalcolithic & Megalithic cultures of Central India and Deccan, Painted Gray Ware, Northern Black Polished Ware, Buddhist Stupas and Early historical phases. The author has pointed out that gold in India is found in two forms (i) Placer-in alluvial sands and (ii) (Reef)-irregular masses in quartz veins or loads. Further, it also analyses the methods of extraction, purification and parting of gold and silver. Moreover, it also examines the chemical composition of gold objects. Chapter-4 accounts and explains the metallurgy of silver and lead in Ancient India. Silver objects are found at Mohenjo-daro, Harappa and Lothal. It has also been discovered at Gungeria, Junapani, Nagarjunakonda and Timargarh Gandhara Grave Culture. Punch-marked coins and Buddhist caskets were also made of this metal. Prof. Bhardwaj has very minutely discussed and critically analysed several other aspects also, like scarcity of silver after the Mauryan period and the sources of silver and lead.

In Chapter-5 the author explores and explains the contribution of Zinc and Brass in Indian History. Zinc is not found in archaeological context as a separate and independent metal except for its alloy. Brass appeared for the first time at Gezer (Palestine) and is dated to 1400-1200

B.C. and in Indian context it is reported from Atranjikhera and dated to 1150 B.C. It also enlightens us about the discovery, smelting and distillation of Zinc. In Chapter 6 & 7 Prof. Bhardwaj analyses and examines the metallurgy of Ancient Indian coins and, iron and steel in Indian Archaeology. In the last chapter he explains the socio-economic aspects of metallurgy.

On the whole the book is unique and full of valuable information and illustration on metallurgy in Indian Archaeology. It is hoped that the book will be very useful for students and scholors alike.

Arun Kesharwani

Kalyan Kumar Chakrabarti and Robert G. Bednarik 1997 *Indian Rock Art and its Global Context.* Motilal Banarasidass Private Ltd. pp.228 Price: Rs. 1700.00.

Rock art is one of the most significant legacies of Old world, depicting the artistic and cognitive expression of early men in a variety of forms and shapes. Rock art is found universally all around the world, and India is fortunate in having one of the three largest concentrations of this artistic heritage; the other two are South Africa and Australia. Kalyan Kumar Chakrabarti and Robert G. Bednarik in their book ***Indian Rock Art and its Global Context*** endeavour to place the uniqueness of Indian rock art against the background of such art depictions around the globe.

The book is divided into thirteen chapters, followed by a glossary of key words and an index.

Chapter **I,** deal with an introduction to rock art and the various issues that has been covered in the later chapters of the book.

In chapter **II,** the authors emphasize on the basic components of rock art: both technical and the artistic norms. Rock art in general has been divided into two basic types, such as petroglyphs and paintings. Petroglyphs are figures or motifs that were created by a reductive process, by removing some substance from the rock surface through hammering, chieslling, abrading, engraving or boring. Paintings have been typically added to the rock surface. The additive is either a paint, which is applied wet, or a pigment that was applied dry. The typology of rock art depended upon the local geology, ecology and the cultural conventions of the societies that produced these arts. The authors also write the relevance of rock arts towards understanding the cultural totality of ancient human communities.

In chapter **III,** 'Catalogue of Rock Art', the writers give emphasis on the limitations of present academic interpretations on ancient rock arts; in the later part they have discussed the need to reorganize the catalogue of Indian and world rock art along geographical divisions, rather than temporal, interpretational or any other.

In chapter **IV,** the authors explore the earliest antiquity of rock art in the world context. Refuting the traditional view of the origin of such art in Upper Paleolithic Europe (Europe has been considered as the first to witness a technological refinement in tool-making), the authors trace the beginning of artistic movement, though in a different form, to Asia and Africa. Substantial evidence of bone beads and pendants have been reported from these continents, and dated much earlier than the Upper Paleolithic phase in Europe. These seem to have been used to decorate human bodies. The findings also indicate the possibility of body painting and tattoos and many other forms of decorations that perhaps began about 300,000 years before in Africa and Southwest Asia among the Upper Paleolithic men. These certainly suggest a rather more developed cognitive sophistication than one would perceive on the basis of purely technological evidence from Europe. According to the authors, ***"some cultures are spiritually very rich and sophisticated, but have a simple technology, while others (such as Western civilization) combine the greatest technological sophistication with a distinct spiritual poverty"***. The authors are also of the view that the rock art probably appeared in the same time with the invention of red hematite that was used as raw material for the cave paintings. Further they argue that some petroglyphs (rock carvings) at a site in Madhya Pradesh in India are the earliest presently known rock art in the world.

Chapter **V,** provides an exhaustive account on Indian rock art along with a large number of colour plates, focusing on aspects like geology and conservation, materials, techniques and chronological tools, and the various cultural contexts. After making a brief review on history of discovery and researches of Indian rock art, the authors focus on various academic constraints and emphasize on cognitive aspects as a part of understanding the subject. Although rock arts are found all over the country, the largest concentration are within the region of Vindayas, stretching from Ganga-Yamuna in north and Narmada in south, in the present states of Madhya Pradesh, Uttar Pradesh and Rajasthan. In India, as there is a dearth of researchers, and lack of sophisticated technology and since thick forests and hills surround most of the sites, the authors feel that an ecological rather than a structural or chemical conservation would be more useful in protecting the heritage. They also plea for certain rock art regions of India to develop as world heritage parks in the same way as Tongariro National park in New Zealand or Kakadu National park or Uluru in Australia.

The authors trace the origin of artistic endeavour in India into the Upper Paleolithic period, on the basis of the evidence of beads made from Ostrich egg shells that have been found at Bhimbetka and Patne in central India. Ostrich is known to have extinct from India by the early Holocene period. Besides there are also other evidences of Paleolithic art that have been reported from various sites in the country. In the Mesolithic and Neolithic/Chalcolithic context, the concentration of rock art marked the highest. However, within the broad geological timescale, each cultural period had several distinctive features. The Megalithic associations are mostly concentrated in South India, depicting horse riders, graffito (compared with potters' marks on Megalithic Black-and-Red ware), script like alignment, and formation of human and geometric designs. In the later Historical period, we find costumes and trappings of war, chariots and boats, religious themes, and strokes look similar to Brahmi and other scripts. Towards the last part of the chapter the authors look at the parallels between the various elements of living traditions and that of ancient rock paintings. At the end, they conclude with a comparative study of Indian rock art with rock arts of the rest of the world.

The subsequent chapters deal with the rock art tradition of rest of Asia, Europe, Africa, Americas, and an overview of Australian rock art. Towards the end the authors propose the significance of rock art in the sphere of modern society.

The book is a welcome addition to the connoisseurs of rock-art studies in India and abroad.

Jitu Mishra

Muhammed Abdul Nayeem 2001 ***Origin of Ancient Writing in Arabia and New Scripts from Oman An Introduction of South Semitic Epigraphy and Paleography***, Hyderabad Publishers, Hyderabad, India. Price not given.

The text of the book is divided into two parts, namely, part one and part two. The part one is entitled as ' Ancient Arabian Scripts' and is covered into seven chapters. The part two is entitled 'New Scripts of Oman' and is covered into five chapters. All chapters are consecutively numbered from I to XII in Roman numerical. They are followed by an exhaustive bibliography and an index.

The part one is general in nature. It deals with the origin of writing, Semitic languages, forerunners of writings in Arabia, i.e., tribal marks or *Wasum*, origin of alphabets, Arabic Scripts and inscriptions, and, theories regarding the origin of writing in Arabia.

The chapter one discusses the general definition of writing, namely the dictionary meaning of writing, i.e., 'to write is to draw, and, to engrave.' The author has relied upon the definition of David Diringer that the writing is 'the graphic counterpart of speech.' All ancient rock-drawings, graffiti marks and engravings on various other materials in Arabia are a form of writing, which ancient man has left for posterity. Culture, which is defined as 'communicable intelligence', would not exist without writing.

The rock-drawings of Arabia, which date to the Epi-Palaeolithic period, i.e., 10,000 B.C.- 6,000 B.C. is the human record of man and animals in various forms, and walks of life. It is a pictographic stage, which is followed by signs symbols, lines and geometric forms, which are pictograms. These individual symbols, also called as ideograms, were used as tribal marks. The third stage is phonetic script. The writing in Arabia originated on the stone or rock, whether painted or engraved.

There are various systems of writing evolved at different places, and different times. However, with reference to Arabia the author has discussed only the Semitic languages, which are eventually allied with a group of languages, spoken in southwestern Asia. They originated in the same area, and there are a number of common elements in their phonology, morphology, vocabulary, and syntax. The Semitic languages are spoken in Mesopotamia, Syria, Palestine, Arabia and Ethiopia.

The second chapter deals with the four-runners of writing in Arabia. This does not represent writing in a real sense of the term, rather, this is the expression and communication of ideas, through various methods on different materials, namely face of the rock, stone, terracotta and clay, metal etc. The petroglyphs and petrograms were the means of communication of ideas and situations in ancient times. The other means were geometric symbols like lines and numbers. The tribal signs/ symbols (*wusom*) are also a form of embriyo-writing. Also, chapter three covers the origin of tribal signs, their types, their implication of symbols, and, signs of Neolithic period.

The origin of Arabian alphabets is derived from *bedouins* tribal signs (*wusum*). The tribal signs are of two types. Firstly they were primitive marks, which are body marks, carved on the body of animals to differentiate property rights of the body of an individual or tribe. They were in the form of various designs or irregular geometric forms. Secondly, they were form of signs or symbols, which ultimately resolved themselves into alphabets. The earliest tribal signs of both categories date from the Neolithic period, i.e., *Circa* 6000 B.C. There are various theories on the origin of writing in Arabia, which are discussed in the seventh chapter. Quoting the epigraphs and other archaeological evidence, the author has concluded that alphabets originated in Arabia itself, and, they did not borrow it from Pheoniciaus. Epigraphical and archaeological evidence cited by the author carries conviction that writing originated independently within Arabia and did not migrate from outside.

Chapters four and five discuss the Arabian scripts, their nomenclature and distribution. Linguistically the Arabian Peninsula may be divided into two regions namely- the Northern region and the Southern region. The various dialects and their inscriptions within these regions can be divided under two groups, i.e., North Arabian and the South Arabian. The author has baptised them as Sa' Kalhanic-A, Sa' Kalhanic-B. Chronologically the Arabs adopted two types of scripts, the cursive, and the monumental. The former is datable to the 2nd millennium B.C. the later to the 1st millennium B.C.

The part two is devoted to the two scripts of Oman. Archaeological excavation at Dhofar, during 1952 brought to light a stone inscriptions whose letters were similar to *Chaldaeakm* inscription recovered from Ur. Further epigraphical evidence from Dhofar was brought to light in 1989 by Ali Ahamed Mahhsh Al-Shan discovered the material and partially published it 1994. Prof. Geraldine M. H. King of Oxford launched upon the project of studying and investigating the material. She compiled a Magnum Opus in 1993 but it remained unpublished. She did not attribute etymological values to the letters of about 800 inscriptions. However, she clarified them into two scripts and labeled as script one and two. She also made available *Magnum Opus* to the author, who rectified and re-named a scripts as Sa' Kalhamic-A and Sa' Kalhamic-B, which is the ancient name of Dhofar. The work involved making provisional identification, and giving labels to the two letters, script and named by him. He also tried to correlate the two scripts. The study revealed that the two scripts belong to South Semitic alphabets. The form of the letter is cursive and cruder. The letters in the graffiti and inscriptions are either vertical or horizontal.

R.P. Sharma

Shashi Prabha Asthana, 1999 ***Mathura Kala-Catalogue of Mathura Sculptures in National Museumm,*** National Museum, New Delhi 1999, pp.120 Plates 144

A posthumously published work of Dr. Shashi Prabha Asthana on the entire collection of Mathura in the National Museum is a copious historical and physical documentation. Asthana discusses the literature and archaeology of the region in the introduction, to provide the cultural milieu of Mathura art. She traces the metamorphosis of the early township of Mathura, from a juncture of trade, ideas and religious denominations into the Kushana metropolis and the nucleus of early Indian art, and also evaluates its transition to the Gupta period.

Asthana has punctiliously documented 144 works of art with much scholarly insight. The sculptures of Vishnu, Siva and Devi and their other manifestations such as Balarama, Shashti, Vasudhara, Ekamsa and Hariti find place in this publication. Likewise, images of Ganesa, Skanda, Indra, Agni, Surya, Kubera, Nagas and Yakshas are also fully documented. The Buddhist art, in Mathura is a juxtaposition of symbolism and image such as *Torana* and, Buddha, Mahaparinirvana, and Bodhisattva, with a preponderance of Kushana style. The Jaina art includes sculptural and architectural remains such as *Tirthankaras*; Ayagapattas and Toranas .She has catalogued the dynastic art of Mathura incorporating royal portraits and Scythians, as well as the amorous Bachanallian scenes. The author has also scrupulously documented the architectural remains such as votive stupas, parasoles, rail posts, coping stones, *salabhanjikas, chandrasilas*, and lion capitals.

It has a fair and scholarly foreword by Dr S.P. Gupta, her teacher, and Dr. R. D. Chaudhary, her mentor has written the introductory note. The catalogue has 9 sections corroborated by 2 maps, 144 plates; a chronological table based on inscriptions, diacritical marks for transliteration and bibliography. This posthumously published work is well printed, a worthy tribute to the author. Muchmore, it is a valuable reference work for researchers and art historians alike.

B.S. Hari Shankar

Arun Kumar Biswas 2001 *Minerals and Metals in Pre-Modern India,* D K Printworld, New Delhi, pp. 228 Plates 39 Price Rs. 1200

Arun Kumar Biswas focusses on the history of indigenous technology which is fundamental in moulding our understanding of the past and restructuring the present. He analyses factors that led to the stagnation and eventual decay of technology and metal, mineral and gem industries in pre-modern India.

The work has seven chapters. After the introduction, Biswas discusses the travalogues and accounts on gem minerals, their distribution, various mines such as Kolar and Panna, and decline in diamond trade. The third chapter focusses on mining and processing of non-gem minerals documented from travalogues and geological reports. A critical review of processing, smelting techniques of producing iron and steel, types of furnaces and economic organisations and the decline of indigeneous industries are discussed in the fourth chapter. The fifth chapter documents India's primacy in brass and zinc making, the seventh on Bidri ware, tin coating, gold and silver wares, art of enamelling, as well as purification and recovery of precious metals, followed by conclusion. Biswas spotlights the isolation of the invading Turks and Afghans from the scientific tradition of Arabia and the Mughal extravagance in courts and their squander for zealous suppressions which detatched them from the maritime tradition of Persians and Arabs. Surfacing evidence, he highlights the retroversive effects that not only resulted in the loss of scientific vigour in India, but also sparked off communal tensions, which were ultimately exploited by European colonialists.

Well printed, 6 figures, 15 tables, 39 plates, an index and bibliography supplement the text. The work unfolds a curious area of study, which will benefit all research scholars of ancient history and archaeology.

B.S. Harishankar

D.P. Dubey [ed.] 2000 *Pilgrimage Studies 2000, The Power of Sacred Places.* Society of Pilgrimage Studies, Allahabad 2000 pp. 301 Price Rs. 500

Corresponding to trade, pilgrimages too transcend eccliastical and sociogeographic boundaries opening new spheres of interaction. The current book on pilgrimage studies, comprises a series of fourteen articles on sacred spots, spreading from western arid China, to the snow-capped Himalayas, as well as the hilly tracts of Vindhyas, Gandhamadanas and Sahyadris.

India as a geo-cultural entity is a product of pilgrimage. Therefore nothing is more important than the studies on this subject for all social and cultural histories of India.

As a matter of fact the institution of pilgrimage has charecterized all major religions of the world including Christianity and Islam. Hence the present study has much significance. The studies focuss on the *agamic* tradition of worship, the eulogies of Avanti, Nrsimhanatha, Sabari shrine and the Sakti pitha in Vindhyas, discusses the cultural interaction, formation of mythological strata, metamorphosis of ritual concepts, astrology, calendar as well as the sacred ecology. There are a few papers on pilgrimage-tourism, Buddhist cave sites in western China, and Sufi concept on pilgrimage.

The papers are corraborated by tables' figures and plates. As an emerging branch in anthropology, this well printed book on pilgrimage studies is useful for researchers.

B.S. Harishankar

K.D. Bajpai, R. Jamindar and P.K. Trivedi [eds.] 2000 ***Gleanings on Indian Archaeology, History and Culture***- 2 Vols. Publication Scheme, Jaipur. pp.261 Plates 60.

Felicitative and comemmorative volumes very often inform much on advances in historical and archaeological studies. Eighty-nine papers on various aspects of history and archaeology are presented here to comemmorate the late Prof R.N. Mehta.

Apart from a colourful profile of Prof. Mehta, there are six papers on Prehistory, four on Protohistory, sixteen each on historical archaeology, epigraphy and numismstics, twenty one on history, three on religion twenty five on art, architecture, murals, and heritage management and fourteen miscellaneous papers. The papers deal in general with rock art, Chalcolithic and Harappan phases, Mauryas, Kushanas, Rashtrakutas, trade and urbanisation, social dynamics under colonial rule, as well as female infanticide in Saurashtra. Each paper has contributed something new to the subjects of Indology.

There are 60 plates, as well as bibliographies corresponding to the papers. A good work extremely useful for historians and archaeologists alike.

Anuja Geetali

REPORT OF THE XXXIV ANNUAL CONFERENCE

Report of the XXXIV Annual Conference of Indian Archaeological Society held at National Museum, New Delhi from 1st-3rd December, 2000

The annual session of the Societies namely Indian Archaeological Society, Indian Society for Prehistoric and Quaternary Studies and Indian History and Culture Society for the year 2000, was held at New Delhi in collaboration with National Museum, New Delhi, and was inaugurated by the Hon' able Sri Ananth Kumar, Minister of Tourism and Culture, Govt. of India on the 1st December, 2000.

After the inaugural function, Sri M.C. Joshi delivered the Presidential Address of the Indian Archaeological Society, followed by Prof. K.R. Dikshit of the Indian Society for Prehistoric and Quaternary Studies and Prof. B.R. Grover of Indian History and Culture Society. The closing function was held on the 3rd December, 2000. In the National Museum and Dr. R.D. Chaudhary gave valedictory Address.

The Indian Archaeological Society conferred V.S. Wakankar Award with a citation, a shawl and a cheque of Rs. 21,000/- on Sri M.N. Deshpande, former Director General, Archaeological Survey of India, in recognition of his dedication to the growth of archaeology in India.

1st December, 2000: Afternoon Session

NATIONAL SEMINAR ON HARAPPAN CIVILIZATION

Participants: Prof. B.B. Lal, Prof. V.N. Misra, Prof. M.K. Dhavalikar, Dr. S.P. Gupta, Dr. Bhagwan Singh, Dr. R.S. Bisht, Dr. Amrendra Nath, Shri J.P. Joshi, Shri M.C. Joshi, Prof. D.P. Agarwal, Prof. V.H. Sonawane and Shri. K.N. Dikshit.

Speakers discussed the role of recent archaeological discoveries and their implications. Harappan Civilization vis-à-vis Vedic literature and how far they reflect each other was the other important issue. The issue of origin of Saraswati from the glaciers of the Himalayas or the present day Adi Badri was also dealt in detail.

2nd December, 2000: Forenoon Session

CONFERENCE PAPERS

Anoop Kumar Singh

Archaeological exploration in Salon and Unchahar Tehsil of Raibereilly District of Uttar Pradesh.

D.V. Sharma

Excavation at Birchabili Tila, Fatehpur Sikri, District Agra

R.P. Sharma

Kampliya-A Traditional History

A. M. Shastri

Bhaitbari Excavation-A Reappraisal

P. Singh and Ashok Kumar Singh

Further Excavations at Agiabir District-Mirzapur, Uttar Pradesh

2nd December, 2000: Afternoon Session

A.K Sinha and Kumar Anand

Further Excavation at Buxar

D.P. Tewari

Excavation at Charda, District Bahraich, Uttar Pradesh

B.D. Misra, Jain Pal and M.C. Gupta

Excavation at Tokwa-2000

B.R. Meena and Alok Tripathi

Excavation at Ojiyana-An Ahar Culture site

Ramjit and Mohd. Abid

Chanduka-An OCP site in Aligarh District

Sunil Gupta

South East Asia in the Indo Pacific Sphere: 3000 B.C.-300 A.D.

A.S. Gaur, Sundaresh, Sila Tripathi and K.H. Vohra

Marine Archaeological Investigation in Okhamandal Region

Inaugural of "Puratattva Bhawan"

B-17, Qutab Institutional Area, New Delhi-16

3rd December, 2000: Forenoon Session

CONFERENCE PAPERS (Open Session)

Sila Tripathi

Marine Archaeological Investigation in Indian and Portugal Waters

Punya Baruah

Maxims, Parables Imagery and Inscriptions- A Brief Appraisal

Vinod Seth

Inverse Heliodivertion of Written Scripts from 'Temso-Ma Jyotigamaya' Modes: Written Scripts Directions

Krishna Kumari

A Rare type of Ganesha Image in the National Museum of Ethnology in Leiden

Pradeep M.Saklani, B.M. Khanduri and Praveen Joshi

Cult of Nanda in the Central Himalayas- An Ethnographic Approach

Rashmi Sinha

Social Economic and Religious importance of Maluti terracotta plaques

Raghubir Singh Thakur

Meghalithic Menhirs of Western Rajasthan

D.P. Sharma

Prehistoric Cultures of India and South East Asia-A Comparative Study

Rajaram Hegde

Early Medieval Tiles from Karnataka

Anup Rajan Mishra

The first Farming Community of Mewar, Rajasthan: A Current Perspective

Mala Malla

Understanding the People, Culture and Society of Nepal

V. N. Prabhakar and D.V. Sharma

A Study of the Inscription discovered from Excavation at Birchhabili Tila, Fatehpur Sikri

Valedictory

K. N. Dikshit
General Secretary

THE INDIAN ARCHAEOLOGICAL SOCIETY

BALANCE SHEET AS ON 31.03.2001

LIABILITIES		AMOUNT	ASSETS		AMOUNT
CAPITAL FUND			FIXED ASSETS		
Op. Balance	1914016.10		(As per Schedule 'A' attached)		13,717,535.00
Add:L.M.Fees	40,500.00				
:Institutional Mem. Fees	5,000.00				
:Income over Expenditure	297,700.06	2,257216.16			
CORPUS FUND		1,500,000.00	Current Assets & Investments		
			Fixed Deposits	2410000.00	
BUILDING FUND		8,853,263.00	Accrued Interest	33111.00	2,443,111.00
Dr. A.K. Narain (Award) Fund		50,000.00	Advances		
			(As per Annexeure 'E' attached)		12,324.00
Donation for Cupboards		20,000.00			
Donation for Podium		25,000.00	Delhi Vidyut Board		86,886.00
Donation for Vehicle		200,000.00	Tax Deducted at Source	19388.00	
PROJECTS FUND				1863.00	21,251.00
(As per Annexure 'B' attached)		591,624.00			
Securities			Sundry Debtors		
(As per Annexure 'C' attached)		364,374.00	(As per Annexure 'F' attached)		161,134.50
ADVANCES					
Dr. S.P. Gupta		400,000.00	CASH & BANK BALANCES		
Bharat Sanskrit Parishad		1,500,000.00	Central Bank-14665		17,427.00
Akhil Bhartiya Itihas Sanklan Yojna	550000.00				
Less : Returned during the year	100000.00	450,000.00	S.B.I.-45062		78,313.97
Current Liabilities					
Sundry Creditors			S.B.I.-45082		47,715.65
(As per Annexure 'D' attached)		258,880.00			
Indian Bank-460017		129,392.35	Cash in Hand		14,049.39
		16,599,749,51			16,599,749.51

Sd/
Chairman

Sd/
Treasurer

Sd/
For Rajan Sharma & Co.,
Chartered Accountant

Place: New Delhi
Daed: 29.09.2000

(Rajan Kumar Sharma)
Prop.

THE INDIAN ARCHAEOLOGICAL SOCIETY

INCOME EXPENDITURE ACCOUNT FOR THE YEAR ENDED 31.03.2001

PARTICULARS	AMOUNT (RS.)	PARTICULARS	AMOUNT (RS.)
To Honorarium	90,125.00	By Grant from I.C.H.R.-Conference	45,000.00
To Municipal Taxes	300,000.00	By Grant from I.C.H.R.-Pura 30	13,500.00
To Publication Expenses	118,306.00	By Grant from I.C.H.R.-Pura 28, 29	30,750.00
To News Paper & Periodicals	661.00	By Donations	7,000.00
To Medical Expenses	66.00	By Sale of Literature	37,390.00
To Telephone Expenses	22,335.00	By Annual Membership Fees	2,910.00
To Conveyance & Travelling	58,740.00	By Delegation Fees	52,260.00
To Printing & Stationary	30,075.00	By Contribution for Conf-IHCS	50,792.00
To Electricity Charges	9,120.00	By Contribution for Conf-ISPQS	30,000.00
To Membership Fees	1,000.00	By Miscellaneous Charges Received	90.00
To Conference Expenses	82,563.00	By Bank Interest Received	263,382.06
To Conference Expenses-IHCS	50,792.00	By Rent Receied	1,057,500.00
To Establishment Expenses	19,212.50	By Grant-Majuli Project	25,000.00
To Repairs & Maintenance	145,438.00	By Grant-Forensic Lab Museum	100,000.00
To Staff Welfare	10,222.00	By Grant-Pilot Project	37,500.00
To Car Running & Maintenance	500.00		
To Car Insurance	12,900.00		
To Postage & Stamps	12,290.00		
To Internet Charges	199.00		
To Audit Fees	21,000.00		
To Bank Charges	1,204.50		
To Board Meeting Expenses	1,060.00		
To Diwali Expenses	100.00		
To Miscellaneous Expenses	230.00		
To Consultancy Charges	51,500.00		
To V.S.Wagankar Award	21,000.00		
To Website Development Charges	17,000.00		
To Professinal Charges	23,500.00		
To Majuli Project Expenses	25,380.00		
To Forensic Lab Museum-Exp.	93,600.00		
To Pilot Project	38,106.00		
To Depreciation	197,149.00		
To Excess of Income over Expenditure	297,700.06		
	1,753,074.06		1,753,074.06

Sd/
General Secretary

S/-
Treasure

Sd/
For Rajan Sharma & Co.,
Chartered Accountant

(Rajan Kumar Sharma)
Prop.

Place: New Delhi
Dated: 29.09.2000

OFFICE BEARERS OF THE INDIAN ARCHAEOLOGICAL SOCIETY

Patrons:
Prof. B.B. Lal
F-7, Hauz Khas Enclave
New Delhi

Prof. B.P. Sinha
68, Pataliputra Colony
Patna

Chiarman:
Dr. S.P. Gupta
B-17, Qutab Institutional Area
New Delhi 110016

Vice Chairman:
Dr. Y.D Sharma
B-16, Kailash Colony
New Delhi - 110048

Shri K.M. Srivastava
142, Venus Apartments
Inder Enclave, Rohtak Road
New Delhi - 110087

General Secretary
Shri K.N. Dikshit
B-322, Sarita Vihar
New Delhi 110044

Hon. Tresurer:
Shri K.S. Ramachandran
C-139, Sarita Vihar
New Delhi 110044

Secretaries:
Prof. V.N. Misra
Former Director
Deccan College, Pune

Shri R.S. Bisht
Director
Archaeological Survey of India
New Delhi

Dr. R.C. Aggrwal
Director
Archaeoloical Survey of India
New Delhi

Dr. R.D. Chaudhary
Director General
National Museum, New Delhi

Members of the Executive Committee:
Prof. Vibha Tripathi
Banaras Hindu University
Varanasi

Prof. V.D. Mishra,
Allahabad University
Allahabad

Prof. V.H. Sonawane
M.S. University Baroda
Vadodra

Prof. K.V. Raman
Madras University
Madras

Dr. V.S. Shinde
Deccan College
Pune

Shri J.P. Joshi
Fomer Director General
Archaeological Survey of India
New Delhi

Asst. Secretary:
Shri R.P. Sharma
New Dehi

Editor Manographs/Newsletter
Sh. K.S. Ramachandran
New Delhi

Headquarters:

INDIAN ARCHAEOLOGICAL SOCIETY
B-17, Qutab Institutional Area, South of IIT, New Delhi - 110 016
Tel.: 652-3728 Tele-Fax:011-696-0654
E-mail: ias_newdelhi@yahoo.co.uk
K.N. Dikshit: 694-8971
K.S. Ramachandran: 695-5209

Headquarters:

B-17, Qutab Institutional Area, South of IIT, New Delhi - 110016
(O) 6960654, 6523728 Fax:011-6960654
E-mail: ias_newdelhi@yahoo.co.uk
K.N. Dikshit: 694-8971
K.S. Ramachandran: 695-5209

Paddayya *et al.* Pl.1: Isampur: Excavated Trench

Paddayya *et al.* Pl.2: Isampur: Acheulian bearing Strata

Bhattacharya and Singh Pl.1: Adwariya : Location of the Site

Bhattacharya and Singh Pl.2: Adwariya : Stone Handaxes

Bhattacharya and Singh Pl. 3: Adwariya : Late Acheulian Tools

Bhattacharya and Singh Pl. 3: Adwariya : Late Acheulian Tools

Chakrabarti and Bhattacharya Pl.1: Chak Dhoyakure: General view

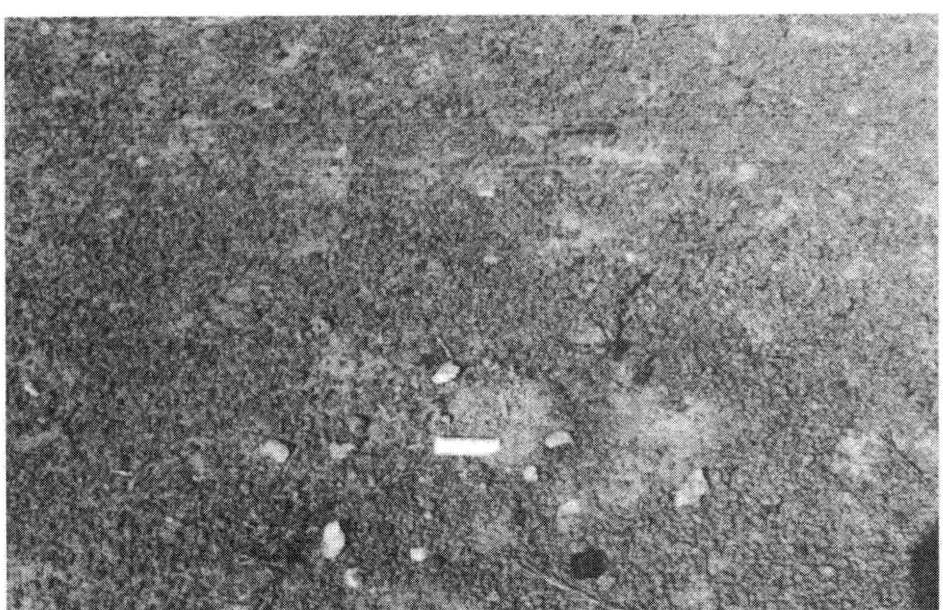

Chakrabarti and Bhattacharya Pl. 2: Manipur : An *in-situ* cluster of Microliths

Plate 1. S.P. Gupta: Image of the Yamuna Tear through the Siwaliks near Kalesar and Paonta Saheb (courtsey V. M. Puri)

A. Nath Pl. 1: Rakhigarhi : Structural Remains of Period 1(a)

A. Nath Pl. 2: Rakhigarhi : Structural Remains of Period I(b)

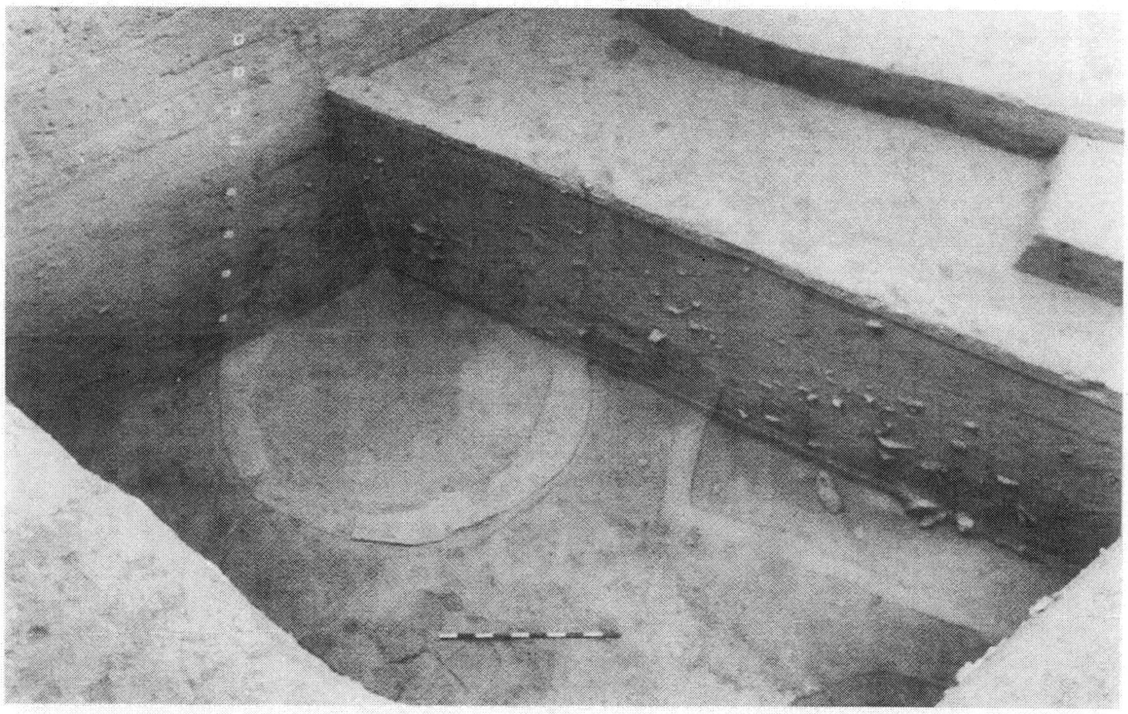

A. Nath Pl. 3: Rakhigarhi : Early Harappan RGR -1 Srtuctural Remains of Period I(a) and I(b)

A. Nath Pl. 4: Rakhigarhi : Human Burials. Period II

Sharma *et al.* Pl. 1: Bichhbili Tila : General View

Sharma *et al.* Pl. 2: Bichhbili Tila : Ambika Yakshini

Sharma *et al.* Pl. 2: Bichhbili Tila : Risbhanatha

Sharma *et al.* Pl. 4: Bichhbili Tila : Santinatha

Sharma *et al.* Pl. 6: Bichhbili Tila : Sruti Devi Jaina Saraswati

Sharma *et al.* Pl. 5: Bichhbili Tila : Parsvanatha

Sharma *et al.* Pl. 7: Bichhbili Tila :Yaksini Ambika with Consort and Son

Meena and Tripathi Pl. 1: Ojiyana: General view of Excavated Structures (View from the East).

Meena and Tripathi Pl. 2: Ojiyana: Excavated Trenches

Krishna Kumari Pl. 1: A Rare Image of Ganesa (Courtesy: National Museum of Ethnology, Leiden)

Hegde Pl.1: Bhairapur : Decorated Tile Pieces

Hegde Pl.2: Tagari: Decorated Roof Tiles

Dubey Pl. 1: Tarti : Copper Plate Grant of Govindacandra, V.S.1173

Dubey Pl. 2: Tarti : Copper Plate Grant of Govindacandra, V.S.1173

Dubey Pl. 3: Tarti : Seal of Govindacandra, V.S.1173

Ranjit and Abid Pl. 1: Chandaukha:Dish - on - Stand

Ranjit and Abid Pl. 2: Chandaukha: Intact Water Well, Brick Size: 30x24 – 19x6cm.

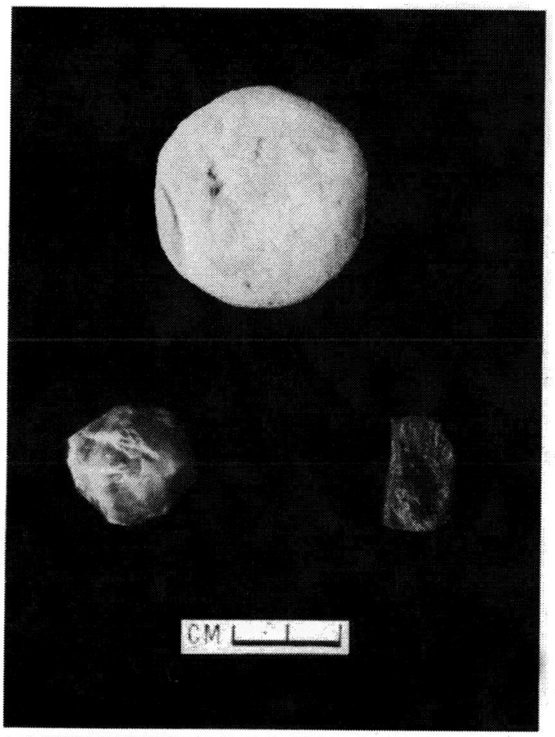

Ranjit and Abid Pl. 2A: Chandaukha: Pottery Disc, Fluted Core (chert) Blade (Granite).

Ranjit and Abid Pl. 2B: Chandaukha: Wattle & Daub (Burnt Mud Clods with Reed Marks).

Ranjit and Abid Pl. 2C: Chandaukha: Pot with Bones

Ranjit and Abid Pl. 2D: Chandaukha: Stone Objects.

Sinha Pl. 1: Maluti: Scene showing Ram-Ravana *Yuddha*.

Sinha Pl. 2: Maluti : Scene showing Mahisamardini Durga.

Sinha Pl. 3: Maluti : Scene showing *Nauka vilas*.

Sinha Pl. 4: Maluti :Scene showing Rama worshipping Shiva.

Patel Pl.1: Nagara: Spearhead

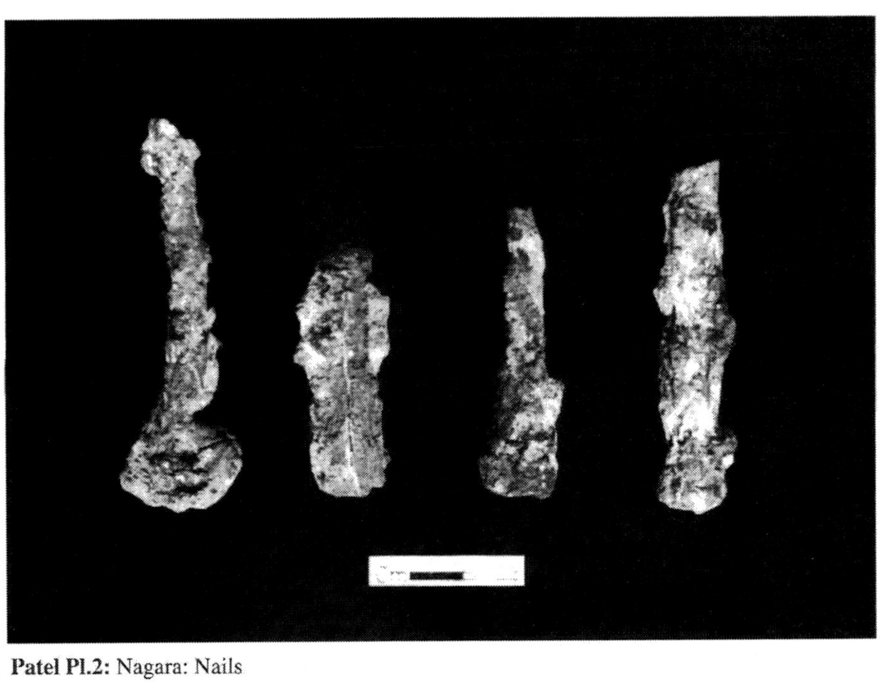

Patel Pl.2: Nagara: Nails

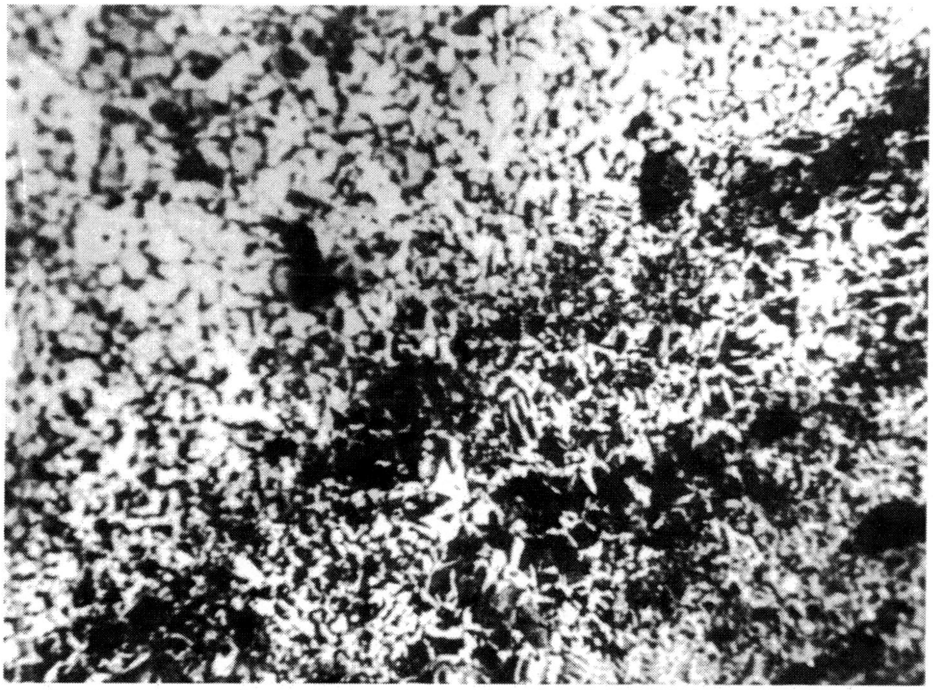

Patel Pl.3: Nagara: Photomicrograph Showing Carburised Working Edge of Spearhead (220X)

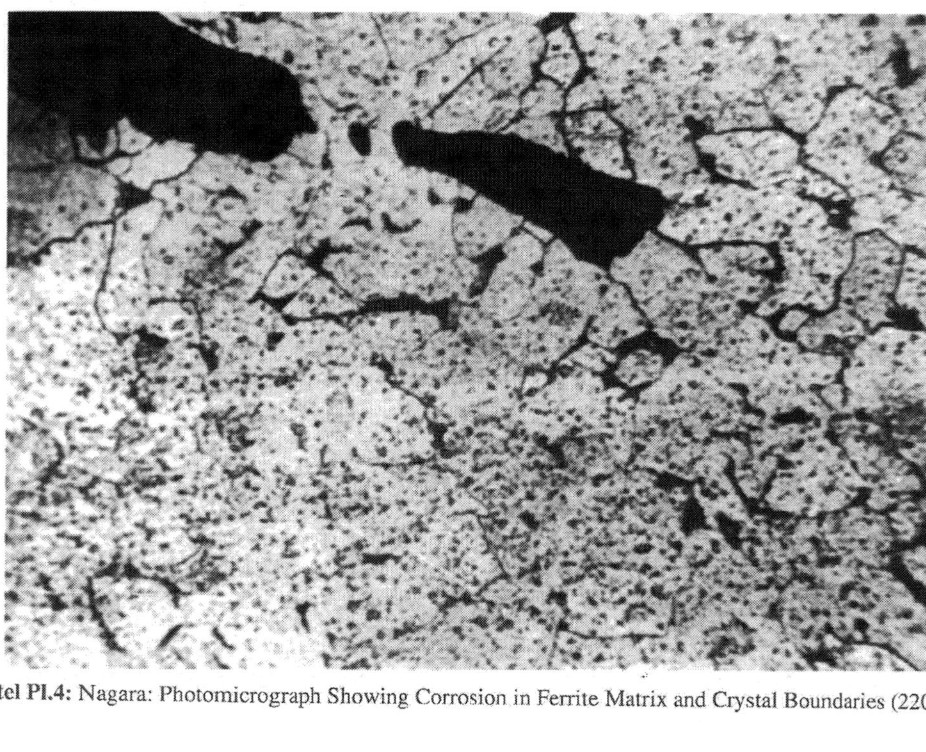

Patel Pl.4: Nagara: Photomicrograph Showing Corrosion in Ferrite Matrix and Crystal Boundaries (220X).

A. K. Singh Pl. 1: Boudha Danda: Temple no. 1(Southern Facade).

A. K. Singh Pl. 2: Boudha Danda: Temple no. 2.

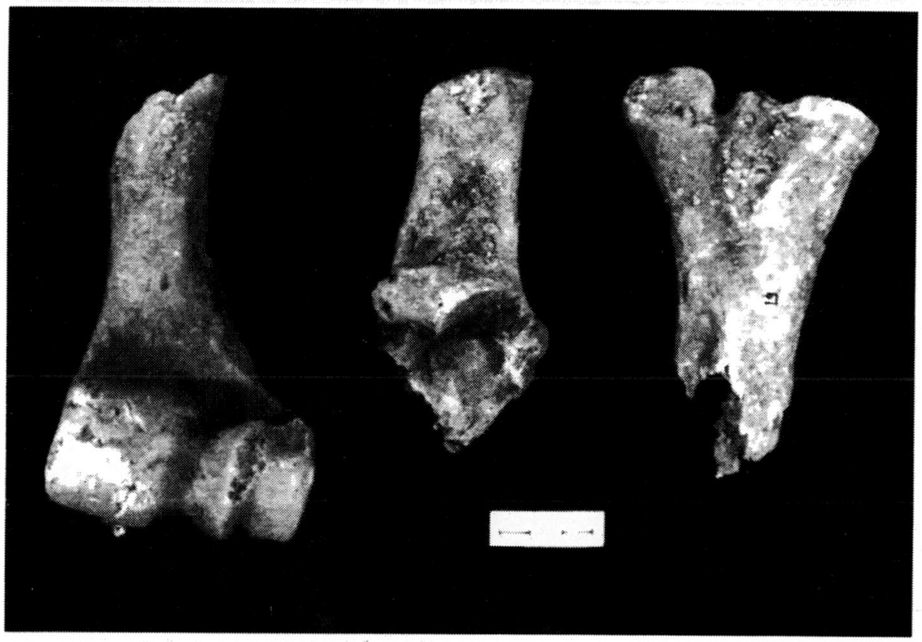

Joglekar Pl. 1: Apegaon 1994: Cattle bones.
1A Left – Humerus; Middle – Calcaneum; Right – Radius

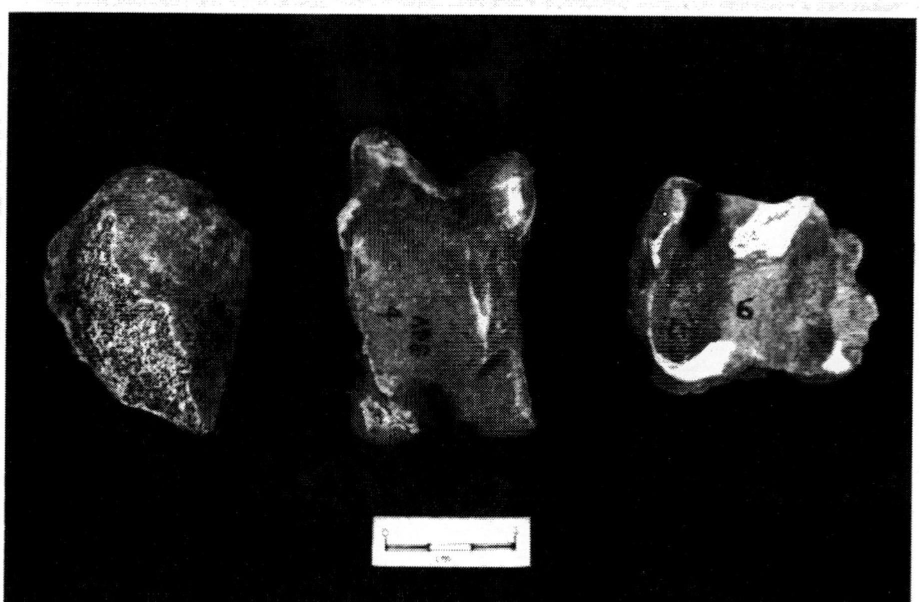

Joglekar Pl. 1: Apegaon 1994: Cattle bones.
1B Left – Patella; Middle – Astragalus; Right – Tibia

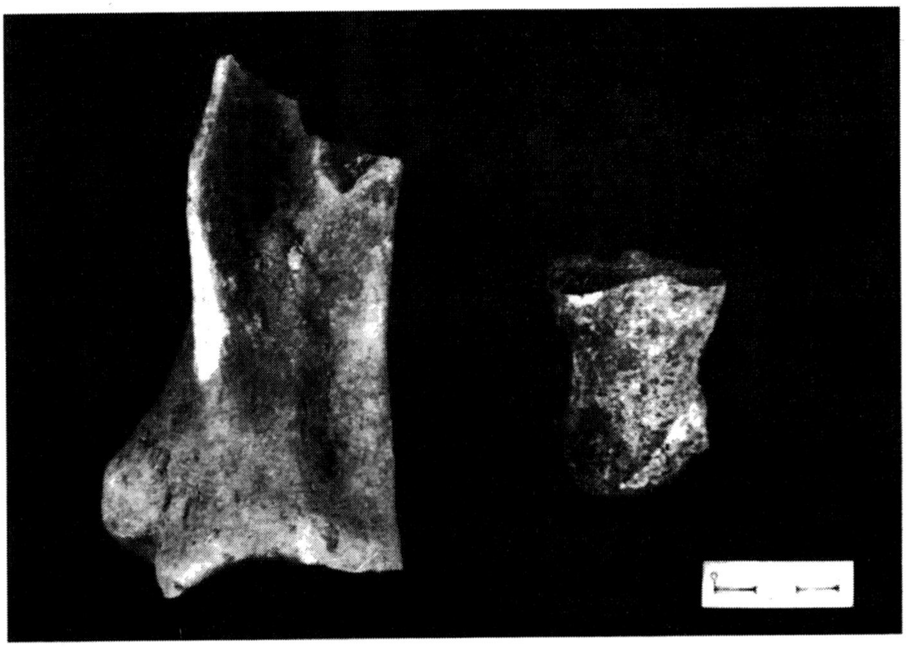

Joglekar Pl. IIA : Apegaon 1994: Buffalo Bones.
Left – Scapula of domestic buffalo; Right – Phalanx of wild buffalo

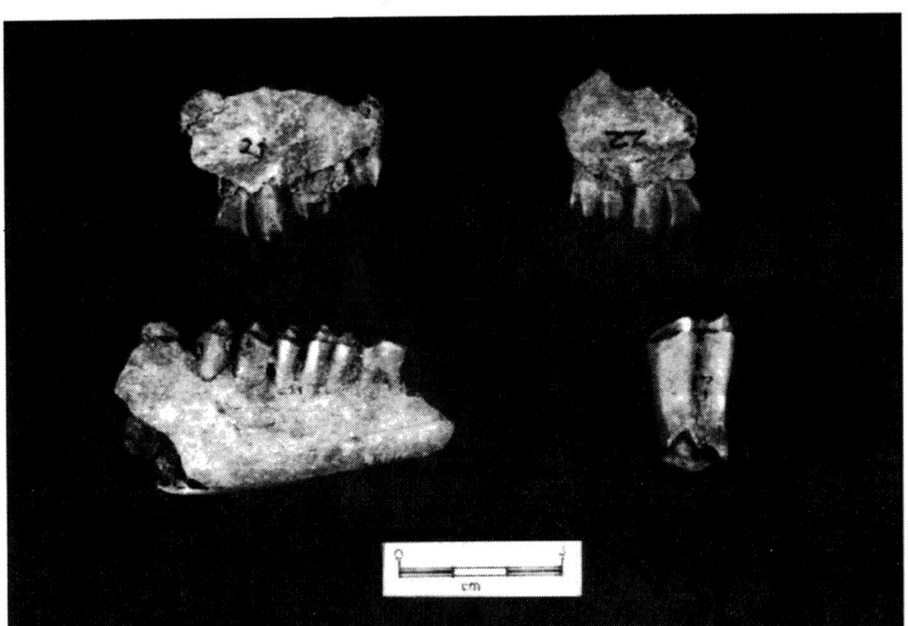

Joglekar Pl. IIB : Apegaon 1994: Sheep/Goat bones and Teeth.
Top – Maxilla; Bottom Left – Mandible; Bottom Right – Mandibular molar

January 26th 2001. Earthquake Disaster to Monuments in Gujarat

Pl. 1: Navlakha Temple, Ghumei in Jamnagar District, Gujarat. The temple is dated to the 12th century A.D.

Pl. 2: Siva Temple, Kera, Kachchh, Pre-Solanki Temple 10th century A.D.